The Oxford Book of Literary Anecdotes

The Oxford Book of
Literary
Anecdotes

edited by
JAMES SUTHERLAND

LONDON
OXFORD UNIVERSITY PRESS
NEW YORK TORONTO

Oxford University Press, Ely House, London W.1
LONDON OXFORD GLASGOW NEW YORK
TORONTO MELBOURNE WELLINGTON CAPE TOWN
IBADAN NAIROBI DAR ES SALAAM LUSAKA ADDIS ABABA
KUALA LUMPUR SINGAPORE JAKARTA HONG KONG TOKYO
DELHI BOMBAY CALCUTTA MADRAS KARACHI

ISBN 0 19 812139 3

First published 1975
Reprinted with corrections 1975 and 1976

Printed in Great Britain by
Richard Clay (The Chaucer Press), Ltd.,
Bungay, Suffolk

INTRODUCTION

WHEN Boswell was putting the finishing touches to his *Life of Johnson* he told a friend that it would be full of anecdotes; 'which word', he added, 'Johnson always condemned as used in the sense that the French, and we from them, use it, as signifying particulars'. In his *Dictionary* (1755) Johnson had defined the word anecdote as 'something yet unpublished; secret history'. By 1773, however, when he prepared the fourth edition, he realized that he must note a second meaning: 'It is now used, after the French, for a biographical incident; a minute passage of private life.' This second meaning, which Johnson had resisted but now felt he had to record, was only gradually establishing itself during his lifetime, and the older sense of 'something yet unpublished' was still current, and was to remain so for some time after his death. When John Nichols published his well-known *Literary Anecdotes of the Eighteenth Century* (1812–15) he was offering the public a voluminous collection of unpublished literary records. It is true that he occasionally included what would now be called an anecdote; but the bulk of his material consisted of lists of books, literary correspondence published for the first time, and biographical memoirs of authors, booksellers, and printers.

In this book the word anecdote is understood in its modern sense (defined in the *Oxford English Dictionary* as 'the narrative of a detached incident, or of a single event, told as being in itself interesting or striking'); and, so far from attempting to offer 'something yet unpublished', I have drawn almost all my material from published sources. I have not omitted any anecdote merely because it is likely to be generally known, but I hope that every reader will also find much that is new to him. The material available is so vast, and so much of it is buried in half-forgotten books, that I am well aware I must have overlooked or failed to discover many anecdotes that different readers will expect to find here. The only honest excuse for such omissions must be the one that Dr. Johnson gave to the lady who taxed him with a wrong definition in his Dictionary: 'Ignorance, madam, pure ignorance.' I can at least claim that in search of material for this book I have worked my way through innumerable biographies and memoirs, but I must emphasize that this is a personal selection: it was never my intention to emulate Sir John Lubbock, who produced a list of the Hundred Best Books, and to attempt to find the Hundred Best Literary Anecdotes—whatever they might be. So, too, I reluctantly decided at an early stage that I must restrict myself to the field of English literature, rather than try to include the literature of other countries with which I am less familiar.

I have had to make a number of difficult decisions. What can fairly be called a *literary* anecdote? Ideally, I suggest, this should relate to a writer in his capacity of author, as in Carlyle's account of how John Stuart Mill's maidservant accidentally burnt the manuscript of the first volume of *The French Revolution.* Most of my anecdotes meet this requirement, and others involve such ancillary activities as printing, publishing, librarianship, and even making a return for income tax. The single incident or event sometimes multiplies into several, without, I hope, preventing the whole from being regarded as an anecdote. But there remains a considerable residue of stories which, although more loosely connected with literature, I believe most readers would wish to see included, and which in any case I could not bring myself to omit. Such is the account of the famous dinner party at which Boswell contrived to bring Johnson and Wilkes together; or that nineteenth-century dinner party at which Carlyle watched the aged Wordsworth, completely indifferent to the babel of conversation around him, quietly eating raisins; or the story of the poet Campbell losing his temper with a London shopkeeper and being saved from arrest by the fortunate arrival of a Scottish-born policeman, who was moved not so much by the assurance that the man he had been called to deal with was 'Mr. Thomas Campbell, the distinguished poet', as by his dawning realization that he was 'Maister Cammel, the Lord Rector of Glasgow University'. Such anecdotes at least give us a characteristic glimpse of literary men, and so, by my standards, have the necessary qualifications for inclusion. On the other hand I have felt it right to exclude some stories which, however delightful, have no other link with literature than the fact that they were narrated by some man of letters. Of this kind is Coleridge's engaging account of the judicious-looking man he once sat next to at dinner:

Silence does not always mark wisdom. I was at dinner, some time ago, in company with a man who listened to me and said nothing for a long time; but he nodded his head, and I thought him intelligent. At length, towards the end of the dinner, some apple dumplings were placed on the table, and my man had no sooner seen them than he burst forth with—'Them's the jockies for me!'

If only Coleridge's silent companion had been one of Southey's uneducated poets, this would have been a very acceptable literary anecdote: the mere fact that it is told by Coleridge, even though he had been obviously indulging in some characteristic table-talking, hardly makes it so.

The natural milieu of the anecdote is conversation, and in the course of oral transmission it may be so much modified or improved as to differ considerably from the original version—always supposing that one can ever be sure of having traced any story to its source. If eventually it finds its way into print, one may have to choose between varying texts of the same story. On such occasions I have usually preferred what seems to be the standard version, which is normally the most finished, even although it may have no apparent authority.

To shape and polish an anecdote is one thing: to invent it altogether is another. Some of the best-known anecdotes are perhaps sheer invention. When John Wilson Croker was working on his edition of Boswell's *Life of Johnson*, Sir Walter Scott sent him several splendid anecdotes, including the one in which Boswell's father, Lord Auchinleck, said what he thought of his irresponsible son's hero-worship of Johnson:

> Jamie is clean gyte . . . Whose tail do you think he has pinned himself to now, mon? A *dominie*, mon, an auld dominie; he keeped a schule, and cau'd it an acaadamy.

If ever an anecdote sounded authentic this one does; but Professor Frederick Pottle has demonstrated, to the point of conviction, that it started from a crumb of fact that Scott found in the manuscripts of John Ramsay of Ochtertyre, and that what makes it so memorable (and so entirely convincing) is Scott's fertile imagination, working here in much the same way as it worked when he contrived a meeting between Jeanie Deans and the Duke of Argyle and gave us their subsequent conversation. It may well be that many well-known stories have this sort of equivocal generation.

Yet even if it may be hard to substantiate, an anecdote may have become so much a part of literary tradition that it must be given a place in a volume such as this, although any self-respecting biographer would feel compelled to reject it as untrue or only half-true. When Keats, writing to his brother and his sister-in-law in America, remarked that 'there are two distinct tempers of mind in which we judge of things—the worldly, theatrical and pantomimical, and the unearthly, spiritual and etherial', he placed in the second category 'Bishop Hooker rocking his child's cradle'. Keats is only one of innumerable readers of Izaak Walton in the past three hundred years who have been moved by that touching and visually pleasing circumstance. But is it true? Some thirty years ago Professor C. J. Sisson offered evidence to suggest that Walton's account of Hooker alternately tending his sheep and rocking his child's cradle could not be squared with the known facts of Hooker's life; and there can be little doubt that, so far as Mrs. Hooker was concerned, Walton was a prejudiced witness. But if he got some of his facts wrong, his story about the cradle is not necessarily false: if there is no evidence that Hooker ever resided at his living of Drayton Beauchamp (where the incident is said by Walton to have taken place), there is also no evidence that he did not; and if Mrs. Hooker with her growing family—for whose existence Hooker must surely bear some responsibility—expected her husband to give her some help occasionally in the house, she was doing no more than other wives have done before or since. On those and other grounds I have thought it right to give Walton's famous anecdote the benefit of the doubt. *Litera scripta manet.*

In arranging the anecdotes there were several possible alternatives. In a book designed primarily for desultory reading, they might conceivably have been presented in a haphazard fashion, or they might have been grouped under various subjects. It has seemed best to arrange them under authors following one another in chronological sequence (i.e. the authors who are the *subject* of an anecdote). Where a story involves a number of writers, I have entered it under the name of the one who seems to be most central to it: the other literary men or women involved will be found in the Index of Names.

I have tried to offer as wide a selection as possible from over a thousand years of English literature. For the earlier centuries good literary anecdotes are hard to come by; but for the eighteenth and nineteenth centuries my problem has been to make an acceptable choice from a plethora of material, biographical and autobiographical, in memoirs, reminiscences, letters, and elsewhere. In English, as in other literatures, certain authors will be found to have become in their own lifetime focal points for innumerable anecdotes, either because they were eccentrics and responded to social controls with a careless independence, or because they were unusually forthright personalities (who may also have liked to dramatize themselves), or because they happen to have had a Boswell, or for more than one of those reasons. It would have been only too easy to fill a large part of this book by concentrating on such writers as Johnson, Scott, Coleridge, Carlyle, Henry James, Wilde, and Shaw; but in the interest of variety I have thought it best to adopt a system of rationing.

If an anecdote is to live beyond its own day, it should not only be worth the telling, but it should be well told. Those two conditions are found together less often than may be supposed. I have included, for example, Izaak Walton's well-known anecdote (No. 20) of Sir Henry Wotton getting into trouble with James I for defining an ambassador as 'an honest man sent to lie abroad for the good of his country'; but my own feeling is that Walton has made a hash of his story. What actually occurred? Which version did Wotton write in the album—the Latin (as he says), or the English, or both? The ability to tell an anecdote well may not be the highest reach of literary achievement, but one develops a new respect for writers like Boswell, Lockhart, Carlyle, and, in our own day, Sir Osbert Sitwell, who can not only recall or envisage a total situation, but who have the creative ability and the verbal felicity to shape it into a memorable anecdote.

In setting forth my anecdotes I hope I have preserved the scholarly decencies. I have, however, modernized spelling and expanded contractions, and I have altered punctuation where it seemed likely to distract or impede the modern reader. In a book of this kind it seemed to me desirable to keep editorial interference at a minimum, and more especially to avoid a proliferation of square brackets and footnotes. On a few occasions, therefore, when an anecdote opens with a reference to 'he' or 'him' I have silently substituted a name, or where for some other reason it is not immediately intelligible I have supplied a few words. Any other information that may be required for the full understanding or appreciation of an anecdote is usually supplied, as economically as possible, in a headnote or footnote. I believe that on only one occasion have I sunk so low as to explain a joke. At the end of the volume the source of each anecdote is given, alternative versions are sometimes noted, and occasionally the question of authenticity is discussed.

I

CÆDMON (*fl.* 670)

IN the monastery of this abbess[1] there was a certain brother who was specially marked out by the grace of God, so that he used to compose godly and religious songs; thus, whatever he learned from the holy Scriptures by means of interpreters, he quickly turned into extremely delightful and moving poetry in English, which was his own tongue. . . . He had lived in the secular habit until he was well advanced in years and had never learned any songs. Hence sometimes at a feast, when for the sake of providing entertainment, it had been decided that they should all sing in turn, when he saw the harp approaching him, he would rise up in the middle of the feasting, go out, and return home.

On one such occasion when he did so, he left the place of feasting and went to the cattle byre, as it was his turn to take charge of them that night. In due time he stretched himself out and went to sleep, whereupon he dreamt that someone stood by him, saluted him, and called him by name: 'Cædmon,' he said, 'sing me something.' Cædmon answered, 'I cannot sing; that is why I left the feast and came here because I could not sing.' Once again the speaker said, 'Nevertheless you must sing to me.' 'What must I sing?' said Cædmon. 'Sing', he said, 'about the beginning of created things.' Thereupon Cædmon began to sing verses which he had never heard before in praise of God the Creator, of which this is the general sense:

Now we must praise the Maker of the heavenly kingdom, the power of the Creator and his counsel, the deeds of the Father of glory, and how He, since he is the eternal God, was the Author of all marvels and first created the heavens as a roof for the children of men, and then, the Almighty Guardian of the human race, created the earth.

This is the sense but not the order of the words which he sang as he slept. For it is not possible to translate verse, however well composed, literally from one language to another without some loss of beauty and dignity. When he awoke, he remembered all that he had sung while asleep and soon added more verses in the same manner, praising God in fitting style.

In the morning he went to the reeve who was his master, telling him of the gift he had received, and the reeve took him to the abbess. He was then bidden to describe his dream in the presence of a number of the more learned men, and also to recite his song so that they might all examine him and decide upon the nature and origin of the gift of which he spoke; and

[1] The Abbess Hilda of Whitby.

it seemed clear to all of them that the Lord had granted him heavenly grace. They then read to him a passage of sacred history or doctrine, bidding him make a song out of it, if he could, in metrical form. He undertook the task and went away; on returning next morning he repeated the passage he had been given, which he had put into excellent verse. The abbess, who recognized the grace of God which the man had received, instructed him to renounce his secular habit and to take monastic vows. She and all her people received him into the community of the brothers, and ordered that he should be instructed in the whole course of sacred history. He learned all he could by listening to them, and then, memorizing it and ruminating over it, like some clean animal chewing the cud, he turned it into the most melodious verse: and it sounded so sweet as he recited it that his teachers became in turn his audience.

2
BEDE (673–735)

[Cuthbert, later Abbot of Jarrow, writes to his friend Cuthwin to tell him of the last days of their revered teacher. The two men had been fellow students of Bede's at Jarrow.]

I ACCEPTED with much pleasure the little gift you sent me, and I have read with great satisfaction your pious and learned letter, in which I found what I so much wished for—that you are busily celebrating masses and holy prayers for Bede our father and teacher, beloved of God. And so, though out of love for him rather than from any confidence of skill in myself, it is pleasing to tell in a few words how he left this world, since this, as I understand, is what you want and ask for.

For about a fortnight before the day of our Lord's resurrection he was troubled with weakness, and particularly with shortness of breath, although he had no pain to amount to much. And so he lived on until our Lord's ascension, 26 May, cheerful and happy, giving thanks to Almighty God every day and night—indeed, every hour. He gave lessons every day to us his students, and whatever time was left he used in singing Psalms, as much as his strength would allow. He also cheerfully spent the whole night in prayer and thanksgiving to God, save only when a little sleep stopped him. But no sooner did he wake up than he would straightway muse in his usual way about the melodies of Scripture; nor did he forget to give thanks to God with uplifted hands. I tell it, and it is true, that never have I seen with my eyes, or heard with my ears, anyone so painstaking in giving thanks to the living God.

O truly happy man! He would sing the words of St. Paul the Apostle, 'It is a fearful thing to fall into the hands of the living God,' and much else out of Holy Writ, in which he would urge us to shake off the sleep of the soul and to think upon our last hour. And he also spoke in our own language about the terrifying departure of the soul from the body, for he was skilled in our songs:

Before the dread voyage none deems it fit
Wiser in spirit than the world's way
To ponder deeply ere parting hence
What sins or good deeds his soul has done
That after his death-day deemed shall be.

He would also sing antiphons to console us and himself, one of which is: 'O King of Glory, Lord of Hosts, who this day ascended triumphantly above all the heavens, we beseech you not to leave us as orphans but to send down upon us the spirit of truth, even the promise of the Father. Alleluia.' When he came to the words 'not to leave us as orphans', however, he burst into tears and wept a good deal. And after a time he began and repeated what he had started. He would do this all day long, and we who were listening wept and lamented with him. Sometimes we read, sometimes we mourned; no, rather we wept as we read. In such happiness we passed Quinquagesima until the aforesaid day; and he greatly rejoiced, giving thanks to God that he was deemed worthy to suffer such affliction. He would often repeat, 'God whips every son whom He receives,' and a saying of Ambrose's, 'I have not lived in such a way as to be ashamed of living among you; nor do I fear to die, for we have a gracious Lord.'

During those days, besides the lessons we had from him each day and his singing of the Psalms, he laboured on two little works that are worth remembering. He translated into our own tongue, for the use of God's Church, the gospel of St. John from the beginning to the point where it reads, 'But what are they among so many?' and certain passages from the works of Bishop Isidore, saying, 'I would not have my boys read a lie, and labour therein without benefit after my death.'

But when the Tuesday before our Lord's ascension came, his breathing began to grow much more difficult, and a small swelling showed in his feet. But he taught and dictated cheerfully all that day, and now and then he would say, among other things, 'Learn quickly, for I know not how long I shall hold out, or whether my Maker will take me before long.' It seemed to us, though, as if he knew very well the time of his going. And so he spent the night, awake, giving thanks. And when morning dawned—Wednesday, that is—he told us to write busily on the work we had begun, and we did so until nine. But at nine o'clock we walked in procession with the relics of the saints, as the practice of that day demanded. One of us who stayed with Bede said to him, 'There is still one chapter lacking in the book you have dictated; but it seems hard to ask you more questions.' But he answered, 'No, it is easy. Take your pen, calm yourself, and write quickly.' And he did so. At the ninth hour, Bede said to me, 'I have a few valuables in my casket—pepper, vestments, and incense. Run quickly and bring the priests of our monastery, so that I may share among them little gifts, such as God has granted me.' And I did so with trembling.

When they were all present, he addressed each and every one, urging them, imploring they should say prayers and masses for him—which they freely promised. But they all kept weeping and sorrowing, especially because he said they must not think to see his face much longer in this world. But they rejoiced because he said, 'It is time for me, if my Maker sees fit, to be freed from the flesh and go to him who made me out of nothing, at the time when I was nothing. I have lived a long time, and my merciful Judge has ordered my life well. The time of my going is at hand, for my soul wishes to see my King, even Christ in his glory.' This and much else he said for our instruction, and passed his last day happily until evening. And the boy called Wilbert, whom we spoke of before, said once more: 'Dear Teacher, there is still one statement that isn't done.' 'Very well,' he said, 'write!' And soon after the boy said, 'It is done now.' 'You speak very truly,' he said, 'it is brought to an end. Take my head in your hands, for it is very pleasing to me to sit facing my holy place where I have been used to pray, so that I may sit and call upon my Father.' And thus, upon the floor of his little cell, chanting '*Gloria Patri et Filio et Spiritu Sancto*' and the rest, his spirit passed from the body. . . .

3
ALFRED (849–901)

NOW on a certain day his mother was showing him and his brothers a book of Saxon poetry, which she held in her hand, and finally said: 'Whichever of you can soonest learn this volume, to him will I give it.' Stimulated by these words, or rather by divine inspiration, and allured by the beautifully illuminated letter at the beginning of the volume, Alfred spoke before all his brothers, who, though his seniors in age, were not so in grace, and answered his mother: 'Will you really give that book to that one of us who can first understand and repeat it to you?' At this his mother smiled with satisfaction, and confirmed what she had before said: 'Yes,' said she, 'that I will.' Upon this the boy took the book out of her hand, and went to his master and learned it by heart, whereupon he brought it back to his mother and recited it.

After this he learned the daily course, that is, the celebration of the hours, and afterwards certain Psalms, and many prayers contained in a book which he kept day and night in his bosom, as I myself have seen, and always carried about with him, for the sake of prayer, through all the bustle and business of this present life. But, sad to relate, he could not gratify his ardent wish to acquire liberal art, because, as he was wont to say, there were at that time no good teachers in all the kingdom of the West Saxons.

4
GEOFFREY OF MONMOUTH (1100?–54)

[We shall never know how much of Geoffrey of Monmouth's Latin *History of the Britons*, which was largely responsible for the creation of the Arthurian legend, was based on fact, how much was mythical, and how much was pure invention; but even in his own day it was looked upon with suspicion. The narrator of the following sardonic anecdote was Giraldus Cambrensis (1146?–1220?), a turbulent ecclesiastic and a man accustomed to speaking his mind.]

It is worthy of observation that there lived in the City of Legions in our time a Welshman called Melerius, who, under the following circumstances, acquired the knowledge of future and occult events. Having on a certain night, namely that of Palm Sunday, met a damsel whom he had long loved, in a pleasant and convenient place, while he was indulging in her embraces, suddenly, instead of a beautiful girl, he found in his arms a hairy, rough, and hideous creature, the sight of which deprived him of his senses, and he became mad. After remaining for many years in this condition, he was restored to health in the Church of St. David's through the merits of the saints. But having always an extraordinary familiarity with unclean spirits by seeing them, talking with them, and calling each by his proper name, he was enabled through their assistance to foretell future events. He was indeed often deceived (as they are) with respect to circumstances at a great distance of time and place, but was less mistaken in affairs which were likely to happen nearer, or within the space of a year. The spirits appeared to him usually on foot, equipped as hunters, with horns suspended from their necks, and truly as hunters not of animals, but of souls. He particularly met them near monasteries and monastic cells; for where rebellion exists, there is the greatest need of armies and strength. He knew when anyone spoke falsely in his presence, for he saw the Devil, as it were, leaping and exulting upon the tongue of the liar. If he looked on a book faultily or falsely written, or containing a false passage, although wholly illiterate he would point out the place with his finger. Being questioned how he could gain such knowledge, he said he was directed by the demon's finger at the place. In the same manner, entering into the dormitory of a monastery, he indicated the bed of any monk not sincerely devoted to religion. He said that the spirit of gluttony and surfeit was in every respect sordid; but that the spirit of luxury and lust was more beautiful than others in appearance, though in fact most foul. If the evil spirits oppressed him too much, the Gospel of St. John was placed on his bosom, when, like birds, they immediately vanished; but when the book was removed, and the *History of the Britons* by Geoffrey Arthur[1] was substituted in its place, they instantly reappeared in greater numbers, and remained a longer time than usual on his body and on the book.

5
WILLIAM TYNDALE (d. 1536)

AT this present time William Tyndale had newly translated and imprinted the New Testament in English, and the Bishop of London, not pleased with the translation thereof,[2] debated with himself how he might compass and devise to destroy that false and erroneous translation (as he said). And so it happened that one Augustine Packington, a mercer and merchant of London, and of a great honesty, the same time was in Antwerp, where the Bishop then was, and this Packington was a man that highly favoured William Tyndale, but to the Bishop utterly shewed himself to the contrary. The Bishop, desirous to have his purpose brought to pass, communed of the New Testaments and how gladly he would buy them. Packington then hearing what he wished for, said unto the Bishop, 'My Lord, if it be your pleasure, I can in this matter do more, I dare say, than most of the merchants of England that are here, for I know the Dutchmen and strangers that have bought them of Tyndale and have them here to sell, so that if it be your Lordship's pleasure to pay for them (for otherwise I cannot come by them but I must disburse money for them) I will then assure you to have every book of them that is imprinted and is here unsold.' The Bishop thinking that he had God by the toe, when indeed he had (as after he thought) the Devil by the fist, said, 'Gentle Master Packington, do your diligence and get them, and with all my heart I will pay for them whatsoever they cost you, for the books are erroneous and

[1] One of the names by which Geoffrey of Monmouth was known.

[2] i.e. that it should be translated at all. The Bishop was Cuthbert Tunstall (1474–1559).

naughts, and I intend surely to destroy them all and to burn them at Paul's Cross.'

Augustine Packington came to William Tyndale and said, 'William, I know thou art a poor man, and hast a heap of New Testaments and books by thee for the which thou hast both endangered thy friends and beggared thyself, and I have now gotten thee a merchant which with ready money shall dispatch thee of all that thou hast, if you think it so profitable for yourself.'—'Who is the merchant?' said Tyndale—'The Bishop of London,' said Packington.—'Oh, that is because he will burn them,' said Tyndale.—'Yea, Mary,' quoth Packington.—'I am the gladder,' said Tyndale, 'for these two benefits shall come thereof: I shall get money of him for these books to bring myself out of debt (and the whole world shall cry out upon the burning of God's word). And the overplus of the money that shall remain to me shall make me more studious to correct the said New Testament, and so newly to imprint the same once again, and I trust the second will much better like you[1] than ever did the first.' And so forward went the bargain: the Bishop had the books, Packington the thanks, and Tyndale had the money.

Afterwards, when more New Testaments were imprinted, they came thick and threefold into England. The Bishop of London, hearing that still there were so many New Testaments abroad, sent for Augustine Packington and said unto him: 'Sir, how cometh this, that there are so many New Testaments abroad and you promised and assured me that you had bought all?' Then said Packington, 'I promise you I bought all that then was to be had; but I perceive they have made more since, and it will never be better as long as they have the letters and stamps.[2] Therefore it were best for your Lordship to buy the stamps too, and then are you sure.' The Bishop smiled at him and said, 'Well, Packington, well,' and so ended the matter.

6
JOHN STOW (1525?–1605)

STOW had devoted his life, and exhausted his patrimony, in the study of English antiquities; he had travelled on foot throughout the Kingdom, inspecting all monuments of antiquity, and rescuing what he could from the dispersed libraries of the monasteries. . . . Late in life, worn out with study and the cares of poverty, neglected by that proud metropolis of which he had been the historian, yet his good-humour did not desert him; for, being afflicted with sharp pains in his aged feet, he observed that 'his

[1] i.e. please you. [2] The founts of type and printing presses.

affliction lay in that part which formerly he had made so much use of'. Many a mile had he wandered, many a pound had he yielded, for those treasures of antiquities which had exhausted his fortune, and with which he had formed works of great public utility. It was in his eightieth year that Stow at length received a public acknowledgement of his services, which will appear to us of a very extraordinary nature. He was so reduced in his circumstances that he petitioned James I for a *licence to collect alms* for himself, 'as a recompense for his labour and travel of *forty-five years*, in setting forth the *Chronicles of England*, and *eight years* taken up in the *Survey of the Cities of London and Westminster*, towards his relief now in his old age; having left his former means of living, and only employing himself for the service and good of his country'. Letters patent under the great seal were granted. After no penurious commendation of Stow's labours, he is permitted 'to gather the benevolence of well-disposed people within this realm of England: to ask, gather, and take the alms of all our loving subjects'. These letters patent were to be published by the clergy from their pulpit; they produced so little that they were renewed for another twelvemonth: one entire parish in the city contributed seven shillings and sixpence! Such, then, was the patronage received by Stow, to be a licensed beggar throughout the kingdom for one twelvemonth. Such was the public remuneration of a man who had been useful to his nation, but not to himself.

7
JOHN STUBBS, OR STUBBE (1543?–91)

[In 1578 it appeared likely that Queen Elizabeth intended to marry the Catholic Duke of Anjou. The prospect of this marriage dismayed her Protestant subjects, and in August 1579 John Stubbs voiced their apprehensions in a pamphlet called *The Discoverie of a Gaping Gulf*. . ., which, as William Camden makes clear below, gave great offence to the Queen.]

HER Majesty . . . burned with choler that there was a book published in print inveighing against the marriage, as fearing the alteration of religion, which was intituled *A gaping gulf to swallow England by a French marriage*. . . . Neither would Queen Elizabeth be persuaded that the author of the book had any other purpose but to bring her into hatred with her subjects, and to open a gap to some prodigious innovation. . . .

She began to be the more displeased with Puritans than she had been before-time, persuading herself that such a thing had not passed without their privity; and within a few days after, John Stubbs of Lincoln's Inn, a zealous professor of religion, the author of this relative pamphlet (whose sister Thomas Cartwright the arch-Puritan had married), William Page the disperser of the copies, and Singleton the printer were apprehended: against whom sentence was given that their right hands should be cut off by a law in the time of Philip and Mary against the authors of *seditious writings*, and those that disperse them. . . .

Not long after, upon a stage set up in the market place at Westminster, Stubbs and Page had their right hands cut off by the blow of a butcher's knife with a mallet struck through their wrists. The printer had his pardon. I can remember that, standing by John Stubbs, so soon as his right hand was cut off he put off his hat with the left, and cried aloud, 'God save the Queen!' The people round him stood mute, whether stricken with fear at the first sight of this strange kind of punishment, or for commiseration of the man whom they reputed honest, or out of a secret inward repining they had at this marriage, which they suspected would be dangerous to religion.

8

EDMUND SPENSER (1552?–99)

IT is said that upon his presenting some poems to the Queen she ordered him a gratuity of one hundred pounds, but the Lord Treasurer Burleigh objecting to it, said with some scorn of the poet, of whose merit he was totally ignorant, 'What, all this for a song?' The Queen replied, 'Then give him what is reason.' Spenser for some time waited, but had the mortification to find himself disappointed of Her Majesty's bounty. Upon this he took a proper opportunity to present a paper to Queen Elizabeth, in which he reminded her of the order she had given, in the following lines:

> I was promised on a time
> To have reason for my rhime.
> From that time, unto this season,
> I received nor rhime, nor reason.

The paper produced the intended effect, and the Queen, after sharply reproving the Treasurer, immediately directed the payment of the hundred pounds she had first ordered.

9

[William Camden commemorates a great contemporary.]

EDMUND SPENSER, born at London, and a student in Cambridge, . . . had so happy a genius for poetry that he outwent all the poets before him, not excepting his fellow-Londoner, Chaucer himself; but through a fate common to that fraternity he was always poor, though he had been Secretary to the Lord Grey, Lord-Deputy of Ireland. For he had scarce fixed himself in his new retirement, and had got a little leisure to pursue his studies, but the rebels rifled and threw him out of house and home, so that he returned into England in a bare condition, where he died not long after, and was interred in Westminster not far from Chaucer, at the Earl of Essex's charge.

His hearse was attended by the gentlemen of his faculty, who cast into his tomb some funeral elegies, and the pens they were wrote with.

10

SIR WALTER RALEGH (1552?–1618)

HE loved a wench well; and one time getting one of the Maids of Honour up against a tree in a wood ('twas his first lady) who seemed at first boarding to be something fearful of her honour, and modest, she cried, 'Sweet Sir Walter, what do you me ask? Will you undo me? Nay, sweet Sir Walter! Sweet Sir Walter! Sir Walter!' At last, as the danger and the pleasure at the same time grew higher, she cried in the ecstasy, 'Swisser Swatter, Swisser Swatter!' She proved with child, and I doubt not but this hero took care of them both, as also that the product was more than an ordinary mortal.

[For the 'product', see No. 26 below.]

11

RICHARD HOOKER (1554?–1600)

MR. HOOKER in his college . . . continued his studies with all quietness for the space of three years; about which time he entered into sacred orders, being then made deacon and priest; and, not long after, was appointed to preach at St. Paul's Cross.

In order to which sermon, to London he came, and immediately to the Shunamite's house (which is a house so called, for that, besides the stipend paid the preacher, there is provision made also for his lodging and diet two days before and one day after his sermon). This house was then kept by John Churchman, sometime a draper of good note in Watling Street, upon whom poverty had at last come like an armed man, and brought him into a necessitous condition; which, though it be a punishment, is not always an argument of God's disfavour, for he was a virtuous man. I shall not yet give the like testimony of his wife, but leave the reader to judge by what follows. But to this house Hooker came so wet, so weary, and weather-beaten, that he was never known to express more passion than against a friend that dissuaded him from footing it to London, and for finding him no easier a horse, supposing the horse trotted when he did not. And at this time also such a faintness and fear possessed him that he would not be persuaded two days' rest and quietness, or any other means could be used to make him able to preach his Sunday sermon; but a warm bed and rest, and drink proper for a cold given him by Mrs. Churchman, and her diligent attendance added unto it, enabled him to perform the office of the day, which was in or about the year 1581. . . .

The kindness of Mrs. Churchman's curing him of his late distemper and cold . . . was so gratefully apprehended by Mr. Hooker that he thought himself bound in conscience to believe all that she said; so that the good man came to be persuaded by her that he was a man of a tender constitution, and that it was best for him to have a wife that might prove a nurse to him; such an one as might both prolong his life and make it more comfortable; and such an one she could and would provide for him if he thought fit to marry. And he, not considering that the children of this world are wiser in their generation than the children of light, but, like a true Nathaniel, fearing no guile because he meant none, did give her such a power as Eleazar was trusted with (you may read it in the book of Genesis) when he was sent to choose a wife for Isaac; for even so he trusted her to choose for him, promising upon a fair summons to return to London and accept of her choice; and he did so in that or about the year following. Now the wife provided for him was her daughter Joan, who brought him neither beauty nor portion; and for her conditions, they were too like that wife's which is by Solomon compared to a dripping house; so that the good man had no reason to rejoice in the wife of his youth, but too just cause to say with the holy prophet, 'Woe is me that I am constrained to have my habitation in the tents of Kedar.'

This choice of Mr. Hooker's (if it were his choice) may be wondered at; but let us consider that the prophet Ezekiel says, 'There is a wheel within a wheel,' a secret sacred wheel of providence (most visible in marriages) guided by his hand, that allows not the race to the swift, nor bread to the wise, nor good wives to good men. . . .

And by this marriage the good man was drawn from the tranquillity of his college, from that garden of piety, of pleasure, of peace, and a sweet conversation, into the thorny wilderness of a busy world, into those corroding cares that attend a married priest and a country parsonage, which was Drayton Beauchamp in Buckinghamshire, not far from Aylesbury. . . .

And in this condition he continued about a year, in which time his two pupils, Edwin Sandys and George Cranmer, took a journey to see their tutor, where they found him with a book in his hand (it was the Odes of Horace), he being then, like humble and innocent Abel, tending his small allotment of sheep in a common field, which he told his pupils he was forced to do then, for that his servant was gone home to dine, and assist his wife to do some necessary household business. When his servant returned and released him, then his two pupils attended him unto his house, where their best entertainment was his quiet company, which was presently denied them, for *Richard was called to rock the cradle*; and the rest of their welcome was so like this that they stayed but till next morning, which was time enough to discover and pity their tutor's condition; and they having in that time rejoiced in the remembrance, and then paraphrased on[1] many of the innocent recreations of their younger days, and other like diversions, and thereby given him as much present comfort as they were able, they were forced to leave him to the company of his wife Joan, and seek themselves a quieter lodging for next night. But at their parting from him Mr. Cranmer said, 'Good tutor, I am sorry your lot is fallen in no better ground as to your parsonage; and more sorry that your wife proves not a more comfortable companion after you have wearied yourself in your restless studies.' To whom the good man replied, 'My dear George, if saints have usually a double share in the miseries of this life, I that am none ought not to repine at what my wise Creator hath appointed for me, but labour (as indeed I do daily) to submit mine to his will, and possess my soul in patience and peace.'

12
FRANCIS BACON (1561–1626)

MR. HOBBES told me that the cause of his lordship's death was trying an experiment: viz. as he was taking the air in a coach with Dr. Witherborne (a Scotchman, physician to the King) towards Highgate, snow lay on the

[1] Commented upon.

ground, and it came into my Lord's thoughts why flesh might not be preserved in snow, as in salt. They were resolved they would try the experiment presently. They alighted out of the coach and went into a poor woman's house at the bottom of Highgate Hill, and bought a hen, and made the woman exenterate it, and then stuffed the body with snow, and my Lord did help to do it himself. The snow so chilled him that he immediately fell so extremely ill that he could not return to his lodgings (I suppose then at Gray's Inn), but went to the Earl of Arundel's house at Highgate, where they put him into a good bed warmed with a pan, but it was a damp bed that had not been lain in about a year before, which gave him such a cold that in two or three days, as I remember he[1] told me, he died of suffocation.

13

WILLIAM SHAKESPEARE (1564–1616)

UPON a time when Burbage played Richard III, there was a citizen grew so far in liking with him that before she went from the play she appointed him to come that night unto her by the name of Richard the Third. Shakespeare overhearing their conclusion went before, was entertained, and at his game ere Burbage came. Then message being brought that Richard the Third was at the door, Shakespeare caused return to be made that William the Conqueror was before Richard the Third.

14

SHAKESPEARE was godfather to one of Ben Jonson's children, and after the christening, being in a deep study, Jonson came to cheer him up, and asked him why he was so melancholy. 'No, faith, Ben,' says he, 'not I, but I have been considering a great while what should be the fittest gift for me to bestow upon my godchild, and I have resolved at last.'—'I prithee what?' says he.—'I'faith, Ben, I'll e'en give him a dozen good Lattin[2] spoons, and thou shalt translate them.'

[1] i.e. Thomas Hobbes, who was talking to John Aubrey.

[2] *Lattin*: 'a mixed metal of yellow colour, either identical with, or closely resembling, brass' (*O.E.D.*).

15

SHAKESPEARE, in his frequent journeys between London and his native place Stratford-upon-Avon, used to lie at Davenant's, at the Crown, in Oxford. He was very well acquainted with Mrs. Davenant; and her son (afterwards Sir William) was supposed to be more nearly related to him than as a godson only.

One day, when Shakespeare was just arrived, and the boy sent for from school to him, a head of one of the colleges (who was pretty well acquainted with the affairs of the family) met the child running home, and asked him whither he was going in so much haste? The boy said, 'To my godfather, Shakespeare.' 'Fie, child,' says the old gentleman, 'why are you so superfluous? Have not you learned yet that you should not use the name of God in vain?'

16

THE Duke of Marlborough talking over some point of English history with Bishop Burnet, and advancing some anachronisms and strange matters of fact, his Lordship, in a great astonishment at this new history, inquired of his Grace where he had met with it. The Duke, equally surprised on his side to be asked that question by so knowing a man in history as the Bishop, replied, 'Why, don't you remember? It is in the only English history of those times that I ever read, in Shakespeare's plays.'

17

KINGS must be crowned, and it is fitting that Shakespeare's belated coronation should have been held in the town of his birth. The Stratford Jubilee (as its sponsors called it) took place, oddly, not on the bicentenary of the poet's birth in 1764 but five years later, and not, as one might expect, in April when he was born but in irrelevant September. . . .

The most celebrated Shakespearean authority of the age did not attend; Johnson's absence was noted and regretted. Nor did the other intellectuals make the journey. But Boswell, delighted, was there, and as he set foot in that drowsy borough of 2,287 souls he experienced (he tells us) such emotions as stirred Cicero in Athens. On the first morning, Wednesday, 5 September, the thirty cannon roared, bells rang through all Stratford, and the serenaders—fantastically garbed actors—sang, to the accompaniment of clarinets, flutes, hautboys, and guitars:

Let beauty with the sun arise,
To Shakespeare tribute pay.

During the public breakfast in the Town Hall the country militia played Dibdin's 'Warwickshire', and Boswell joined in the chorus, 'The Will of all Wills was a Warwickshire Will.' Even the deer-poaching escapade made for local glory: 'The thief of all thieves was a Warwickshire thief.' . . .

But the next morning the rains came, first in a drizzle, then a torrent. The procession of Shakespearean characters, with a satyr-drawn triumphal chariot containing Melpomene, Thalia, and the Graces, was called off. Cancelled too was the crowning of the Bard. There were murmurs of complaint that the managers of the Jubilee had not provided any awning or covering of some sort in anticipation of such an accident. Now two thousand revellers crowded into the Rotunda built to accommodate half that many. Dr. Arne led the musicians in Garrick's 'Ode to Shakespeare'. During the encore of Mrs. Baddeley's solo, 'Thou soft-flowing Avon', Garrick in a sudden gesture flung open the doors to reveal the swollen waters surging against the flimsy structure. The effect (according to one observer) was 'irresistible, electrical'. The crowd laughed, but laughter turned to tears as Mrs. Baddeley, that beautiful insinuating creature, went on to sing in her haunting soprano:

Thou soft-flowing Avon, by thy silver stream,
Of things more than mortal, sweet Shakespeare would dream . . .

That night there was a masquerade, at which Corsica Boswell, resplendent in his scarlet breeches and grenadier cap embroidered with *Vive la Libertà* in gold letters, danced the minuet with water coming over his shoe-tops. Some departing merrymakers regrettably fell into flooded ditches; the more prudent stayed on until daybreak, when they retreated over planks stretching from the entrance to their waiting carriages. Several avowed that the deluge was the judgement of God on the idolatry of the Jubilee.

18

SOME time in 1863, after several hole-and-corner meetings of a few literary enthusiasts, it was announced in the newspapers that a National Shakespeare committee had been formed with the object of celebrating in some unexplained fashion the tercentenary of Shakespeare's birth. Hepworth Dixon, the then editor of the *Athenaeum*, who was always hungering after notoriety, seeing the chance of a little cheap popularity, joined the movement, and speedily placed himself at its head. It was commonly rumoured that Dixon aspired to the honours of knighthood, and hoped to secure these if, when matters were ripe, the Prince of Wales accepted the office of president. His first step was to persuade his friend the Duke of Manchester, whose Kimbolton papers he had edited for him, to act as chairman of the committee. His next was to strengthen the latter by adding many notable individuals to it; after which he autocratically appointed his principal satellites as secretaries, nominating no less than a round dozen of them. He then chose a council who submitted their own names for the approval of the general committee, and were elected by the narrow majority of two, which they thought warranted them in describing themselves as the representatives of the 'intellect, wealth, and commercial enterprise of the nation'. Vice-presidents were next appointed, including a string of noblemen, and three distinguished literary men—Sir Edward Bulwer Lytton, Alfred Tennyson, and Charles Dickens.

A section of the committee was strongly of the opinion that Mr. Thackeray should be joined to the foregoing, and at an ensuing meeting I[1] proposed inviting him to become one of our vice-presidents. Colonel Sykes, who presided, intimated that in the case of so distinguished a personage as Mr. Thackeray, there could be no question as to the propriety of the proposed course, and was about to declare the motion carried *nem. con.*, when Hepworth Dixon—who had not forgotten a former snubbing Thackeray had given him—interposed with the objection that a circular sent to Thackeray asking him to join the committee had not been responded to. Nothing being thought of this, Dixon's henchman, J. Cordy Jeaffreson, came to his aid, and, after talking vaguely about the inordinate opinion which he knew Mr. Thackeray to entertain of himself, suggested that the committee would be only demeaning themselves by again applying to him. As Dixon had a considerable following, composed of contributors to the *Athenaeum*, and timid literary men who trembled for their next book, he secured the rejection of my proposal and the carrying of a counter-resolution, little dreaming that he was bringing about the speedy effacement of the National Shakespeare committee at the same time.

It was in the large room at the Society of Arts that the committee meetings were held, but so little interest did the public take in the proceedings that the newspapers sent no reporter to chronicle what transpired, and the outrageous resolution only oozed out by degrees. I took the matter up warmly, and, supported merely by one or two friends, agitated it at one committee meeting after another, suggesting among other things the rescinding of the resolution, and thereby avoiding a public scandal, but to no purpose. I then published an account of the affair in the *Illustrated Times*,

[1] Henry Vizetelly.

which, as the other papers quoted it, led to the committee being vigorously assailed in all directions for their asinine resolution. Laurence Oliphant, in an indignant article in the *London Review*, called attention to the circumstance that the two most prominent members on the self-elected council were 'the David and Jonathan of a literary organ whose columns had been disfigured by a virulent and indecent criticism—needlessly cruel, offensive and unjust—on Miss Thackeray's charming novel, *The Story of Elizabeth*. To one or both of them,' said he, 'the father of the authoress attributed (rightly or wrongly) the slashing review, and was highly indignant at the cruel attack. This was known to the council, and yet, with exquisite taste, they put forward these two gentlemen to invite the adhesion of the greatest satirist of the day to the movement they had assumed the direction of.'

The sad part of the affair was that, within three weeks of this affront being put upon Mr. Thackeray by men unworthy of unloosing his shoestrings, London was startled by the news that the great novelist had been found dead in his bed on the morning of Christmas Eve. . . .

As may be supposed, the painful incident of Mr. Thackeray's death cast considerable gloom over the next meeting of the National Shakespeare committee. Hepworth Dixon figuratively wept crocodile tears, and gravely moved that all record of the slight put upon Mr. Thackeray should be erased from the minute book, which, at one time, he had fondly talked of depositing in the British Museum; and of course Jeaffreson again did vassal's service. The suggestion, however, was too much for the meeting, which peremptorily determined that the offensive resolution, together with the names of its supporters, should remain inscribed on the committee's minutes, but that the committee should record their expression of deep regret at such a resolution having ever been carried. This was the beginning of the end, and a few weeks afterwards a protest against the proceedings of the executive, signed by Theodore Martin, Shirley Brooks, Dr. Brewer, and others, appeared in the morning papers, and the grand National Shakespeare committee, with its superstructure of a dozen secretaries, toppled over like a house of cards.

19

As if to compensate for their shadowy and doubtful origins, traditions about Shakespeare would, over the centuries, attach themselves to the particular: to actual places and tangible objects. Tradition marked the pew in the Guild Chapel where sat Stratford's most illustrious son. In 1877 the master of the free school, like others before him, proudly displayed Shakespeare's desk to visitors: 'William was a studious lad,' he pointed out, 'and selected that corner of the room so that he might not be disturbed by the other boys.' The poet who left behind no personal papers nevertheless favoured posterity with innumerable baubles, gew-gaws, and toys to mock apes: his pencil-case, walking stick, gloves, brooch, table, spoon, and wooden salt cellars, not to mention a jug in the form of a large coffee pot, with a neat head of the owner, in his fortieth year, engraved on the silver lid. The proprietor of the Shakespeare Hotel took pleasure in showing his visitors Shakespeare's clock, before parting with it at a public auction in 1880: not to be outdone, the nearby Falcon Inn boasted the shovel-board at which he delighted to play. . . .

In the early nineteenth century, Mary Hornby, custodian of the Birthplace, imposed upon the credulous with her bogus treasures. With her 'frosty face, lighted up by a cold blue anxious eye, and garnished with artificial locks of flaxen hair, curling from under an exceedingly dirty cap' (so Washington Irving described her), this garrulous harridan showed off the shattered stock of the dramatist's matchlock, his tobacco box, the sword with which he played Hamlet, a 'curious piece of carving' representing David slaying Goliath, and—among other curiosities—'a Gold embroidered Box' presented to Shakespeare by the King of Spain in return for a goblet of great value. The presence of these relics must be regarded as miraculous, for when Samuel Vince visited Stratford in the summer of 1787, the only Shakespeare item remaining there was the poet's chair, 'fixed in one of the Chimnies'.

20
SIR HENRY WOTTON (1568–1639)

AT his first going ambassador into Italy, as he passed through Germany, he stayed some days at Augusta:[1] where having been in his former travels well known by many of the best note for learning and ingeniousness (those that are esteemed the *virtuosi* of that nation), with whom he passing an evening in merriments, was requested by Christopher Flecamore to write some sentence in his *albo* (a book of white paper which, for that purpose, many of the German gentry usually carry about them), and Sir Henry Wotton consenting to the motion, took an occasion from some accidental discourse of the present company to write a pleasant definition of an ambassador, in these very words:

Legatus est vir bonus peregrè missus ad mentiendum Reipublicae causâ.

[1] Augsburg.

Which Sir Henry Wotton could have been content should have been thus Englished:

An ambassador is an honest man sent to lie abroad for the good of his country.

But the word for *lie* being the hinge upon which the conceit was to turn was not so expressed in Latin as would admit (in the hands of an enemy especially) so fair a construction as Sir Henry thought in English. Yet as it was, it slept quietly among other sentences in this *albo* almost eight years, till by accident it fell into the hands of Jasper Scioppius, a Romanist, a man of a restless spirit and a malicious pen, who with books against King James prints this as a principle of that religion professed by the King and his ambassador, Sir Henry Wotton, then at Venice; and in Venice it was presently after written in several glass windows, and spitefully declared to be Sir Henry Wotton's.

This coming to the knowledge of King James, he apprehended it to be such an oversight, such a weakness or worse in Sir Henry Wotton, as caused the King to express much wrath against him; and this caused Sir Henry Wotton to write two apologies, one to Velserus (one of the chiefs of Augusta) in the universal language, which he caused to be printed and given and scattered in the most remarkable places both in Germany and Italy, as an antidote against the venomous books of Scioppius; and another apology to King James, which were both so ingenious, so clear, and so choicely eloquent, that his Majesty (who was a pure judge of it) could not forbear at the receipt thereof to declare publicly that Sir Henry Wotton had commuted sufficiently for a greater offence.

21

[Logan Pearsall Smith describes a notable find at Burley-on-the-Hill, Rutland.]

In examining the Seventh Report of the Historical Manuscripts Commission, I found a note by A. J. Horwood, who had been sent in 1878 to examine the manuscripts, at a great mansion near Oakham, of a manuscript volume which contained 'copies of letters seemingly by and to Sir Henry Wotton'. I found that this house was in the possession of a certain elderly colonel, and I began inquiring among the people I met if any of them knew him. At last I met an old lady who was his cousin, and who kindly said that I might write to him and make use of her name as an introduction. I therefore wrote, and received a most courteous answer from the colonel, saying that he knew nothing of the manuscript book, and did not believe he possessed it, but that he was quite willing for me to come and look for it myself.

I therefore went to Oakham, and took a cab up to an immense Italian villa, which is one of the biggest houses in England, if not the biggest. I drove into a great colonnaded courtyard of about twenty acres (larger, I believe, than the Great Court of Trinity College, Cambridge), and up to the splendid steps of the mansion—steps partially broken and partially overgrown with weeds, for the whole place looked ill-kept and considerably out of repair, as if funds were not abundant on that hilltop. I rang the great resounding front-door bell, and the stately portal was opened by an old gentleman in a shawl, who reminded me of the Duke of Wellington in his appearance. I introduced myself, and mentioned his cousin, of whom we talked awhile, and then I stated my errand, at which he gave me a somewhat malicious chuckle and showed me into an immense library, which occupied one wing of the great house and looked about a mile long. It was full of debris, pictures without frames, frames without pictures, old rocking-horses without heads, and was lined with immense old bookshelves that seemed to touch the sky. 'Now you can have a look, and you must let me give you luncheon later,' he said, and then he disappeared.

It was a cold day in November; the library was unheated, and I felt the beginnings of a violent cold upon me. My despair at the gigantic search in prospect (which would have required weeks at least for its satisfactory performance) can be imagined; but still I felt that, having come so far, I must at least take a look. While I was doing this, I happened to see the colonel with two maiden ladies (whom I afterwards found to be his daughters) staring at me through an immense window from the terrace outside. By great good fortune I found within half an hour the book I was looking for, and saw at once that it was of even greater interest than I had hoped, as it contained many copies of Wotton's unpublished letters, a number of documents concerning his first embassy at Venice (1604–10), and a large collection of notes of 'table-talk', kept by someone in his household at Venice during that period, with many anecdotes about Queen Elizabeth, James I, Henry IV, Bacon, and Essex, and various personages of the time, as well as a number of poems by Donne and others, a copy of Donne's *Paradoxes*, with a long unpublished letter which Donne sent with them, and a number of other early, unpublished letters by Donne, some signed and some unsigned, all of which had escaped Horwood's notice when he examined the manuscript.

I took the book to the colonel's study, where there was a good fire, and where the old gentleman sat reading *The Times*. Occasionally I caught his eye, staring at me over its pages as if he were asking himself what sort of creature I could be to take so great an interest in old papers.

When at last I hinted that it would take me more than an afternoon to master and copy out the contents of this volume, he most kindly asked me to come and pay him a visit for this purpose. I was, of course, delighted to accept this invitation, and spent several days in this great seventeenth-century palace, whose wide terraces overlooked perhaps the most famous of English hunting counties. I had my meals with the colonel and his daughters, and attended divine service with them in the chapel of the house. They all treated me with the perfect courtesy of their class, and made no attempt to find out who I was, or what motive had induced me to engage in this (to them) so incomprehensible a form of sport. They were much too polite to ask any questions.

When I found that the period of my visit was insufficient for an adequate study of the contents of this book, I arranged for the Oxford University Press to purchase its copyright, and to have the volume sent to Oxford for careful copies to be made. Sir Herbert Grierson came to Oxford to examine the poems, which he afterwards published in his masterly edition of Donne's poems. I remember that when he and I were shut up together to examine this volume in a big room at the top of the Clarendon Press, Satan tempted me to make the suggestion that it would be rather fun to insert among these perfectly unknown notes of table-talk some chance remark about Bacon as a playwright which might set the Baconians agog; and I remember Grierson's expression of horror at this suggestion, which it is indeed lucky we did not carry out, since, shortly after the volume was returned to the place where I had found it, the house was burnt down and the manuscript destroyed.

22
JOHN DONNE (1573?–1631)

DR. DONNE, the poet, in 1602 married the daughter of Sir George Moore privately against her father's consent, who was so enraged that he not only turned him and his wife out of his house, but got Lord Chancellor Egerton to turn him out of his office as Secretary to the Great Seal. Donne and his wife took refuge in a house in Pyrford, in the neighbourhood of his father-in-law, who lived at Losely, in the county of Surrey, where the first thing he did was to write on a pane of glass—

John Donne
An Donne
Undone.

These words were visible at that house in 1749. It should be remembered that Donne's name was formerly pronounced Dun.

23

It is observed that a desire of glory or commendation is rooted in the very nature of man; and that those of the severest and most mortified lives, though they may become so humble as to banish self-flattery, and such weeds as naturally grow there, yet they have not been able to kill this desire of glory, . . . which I mention, because Dr. Donne, by the persuasion of Dr. Fox, easily yielded at this very time to have a monument made for him; but Dr. Fox undertook not to persuade him how, or what monument it should be; that was left to Dr. Donne himself.

A monument being resolved upon, Dr. Donne sent for a carver to make him in wood the figure of an urn, giving him directions for the compass and height of it; and to bring with it a board of the just height of his body. 'These being got, then without delay a choice of painter was got to be in a readiness to draw his picture, which was taken as followeth. Several charcoal-fires being first made in his large study, he brought with him into that place his winding-sheet in his hand, and, having put off all his clothes, had this sheet put on him, and so tied with knots at his head and feet, and his hands so placed, as dead bodies are usually fitted to be shrouded and put into their coffin, or grave. Upon this urn he thus stood with his eyes shut, and with so much of the sheet turned aside as might shew his lean, pale, and death-like face, which was purposely turned towards the East, from whence he expected the second coming of his and our Saviour Jesus.' In this posture he was drawn at his just height; and when the picture was fully finished, he caused it to be set by his bedside, where it continued, and became his hourly object till his death.

24
BEN JONSON (1573?–1637)

At that time[1] the pest was in London, he being in the country at Sir Robert Cotton's house with old Camden, he saw in a vision his eldest son, then a child and at London, appear unto him with the mark of a bloody cross on his forehead, as if it had been cutted with a sword; at which amazed he prayed unto God, and in the morning he came to Mr. Camden's chamber to tell him, who persuaded him it was but an apprehension of his fantasy at which he should not be disjected. In the mean time comes

[1] 1603. The boy was his eldest son, Benjamin, who died at the age of seven. Jonson mourned him in a moving poem as 'Ben Jonson his best piece of poetry'.

there letters from his wife of the death of that boy in the plague. He appeared to him (he said) of a manly shape, and of that growth that he thinks he shall be at the resurrection.

25

JONSON was delated[1] by Sir James Murray to the King for writing something against the Scots in a play *Eastward Ho!*, and voluntarily imprisoned himself with Chapman and Marston, who had written it among them. The report was that they should then have had their ears cut and noses. . . . After their delivery, he banqueted all his friends; there was Camden, Selden, and others. At the midst of the feast his old mother drank to him, and shewed him a paper which she had (if the sentence had taken execution) to have mixed in the prison among his drink, which was full of lusty strong poison; and that she was no churl, she told him she minded first to have drunk of it herself.

26

SIR WALTER RALEGH sent him governor with his son, *anno* 1613, to France. This youth being knavishly inclined, among other pastimes (as the setting of the favour of damosells on a codpiece), caused him to be drunken, and dead drunk, so that he knew not where he was; thereafter laid him on a car, which he made to be drawn by pioners[2] through the streets, at every corner showing his governor stretched out, and telling them that was a more lively image of the crucifix than any they had. At which sport young Ralegh's mother delighted much (saying his father young was so inclined), though the father abhorred it.

27

ROBERT BURTON (1577–1640)

THE author of *The Anatomy of Melancholy* is said to have laboured long in the writing of this book to suppress his own melancholy, and yet did but improve it; and that some readers have found the same effect. In an interval of vapours he would be extremely pleasant, and raise laughter in any company. Yet I have heard that nothing at last could make him laugh but going down to the Bridge-foot in Oxford, and hearing the barge-men

[1] *delated*: informed against. [2] *pioners*: i.e. piners, *obs.*, labourers.

scold and storm and swear at one another, at which he would set his hands to his sides, and laugh most profusely. Yet in his college and chamber so mute and mopish that he was suspected to be *felo de se*.

28
BISHOP RICHARD CORBET (1582–1635)

AFTER he was Doctor of Divinity, he sang ballads at the Cross at Abingdon on a market-day. He and some of his comrades were at the tavern by the Cross (which, by the way, was then the finest of England; I remember it when I was a freshman: it was an admirable curious Gothic architecture, and fine figures in the niches . . .). The ballad singer complained he had no custom, he could not put off his ballads. The jolly Doctor puts off his gown, and puts on the ballad singer's leathern jacket, and being a handsome man, and had a rare full voice, he presently vended a great many, and had a great audience.

29
JOHN SELDEN (1584–1654)

HIS treatise that tithes were not *jure divino* drew a great deal of envy upon him from the clergy.[1] William Laud, Archbishop of Canterbury, made him make his recantation before the High Commission Court. . . . After, he would never forgive the Bishops, but did still in his writings level them with the Presbytery. . . .

He died of a dropsy. He had his funeral scutcheons all ready . . . months before he died. When he was near death, the minister (Mr. Johnson) was coming to him to assoil him. Mr. Hobbes happened then to be there: said he, 'What, will you that have wrote like a man now die like a woman?' So the minister was not let in.

30

IN the beginning of September 1659 the library of the learned Selden was brought into that of Bodley. Anthony Wood laboured several weeks with Mr. Thomas Barlow and others in sorting them, carrying them

[1] The work that aroused the envy (i.e. ill-will) of the clergy was Selden's *The History of Tithes*, published in 1618.

upstairs, and placing them. In opening some of the books they found several pairs of spectacles which Mr. Selden had put in and forgotten to take out, and Mr. Thomas Barlow gave Anthony Wood a pair, which he kept in memory of Selden to his last day.

31
THOMAS HOBBES (1588–1679)

HE was forty years old before he looked on Geometry; which happened accidentally. Being in a gentleman's library . . ., Euclid's *Elements* lay open, and 'twas the 47th El. *libri* 1. He read the proposition. 'By God!' said he (he would now and then swear by way of emphasis), 'this is impossible!' So he reads the demonstration of it, which referred him back to such a proposition; which proposition he read. That referred him back to another, which he also read. *Et sic deinceps*, that at last he was demonstratively convinced of that truth. This made him in love with Geometry . . . I have heard Mr. Hobbes say that he was wont to draw lines on his thigh and on the sheets, abed, and also multiply and divide.

32

[In 1646, when Charles II (then Prince of Wales) was an exile in Paris, Hobbes was engaged to teach him the elements of mathematics. Hobbes returned to England in 1651, and at the time of the Restoration was living in the household of his patron, the Earl of Devonshire.]

IT happened, about two or three days after His Majesty's happy return, that, as he was passing in his coach through the Strand, Mr. Hobbes was standing at Little Salisbury House gate (where his lord then lived). The King espied him, put off his hat very kindly to him, and asked him how he did. About a week after, he had oral conference with His Majesty at Mr. S. Cowper's,[1] where, as he sate for his picture, he was diverted by Mr. Hobbes's pleasant discourse. Here His Majesty's favours were redintegrated to him, and order was given that he should have free access to His Majesty, who was always much delighted in his wit and smart repartees.

The wits at Court were wont to bait him. But he feared none of them, and would make his part good. The King would call him the *bear*: 'Here comes the bear to be baited!'

[1] Samuel Cooper (1609–72), the miniature painter.

33

In his old age he was very bald (which claimed a veneration); yet within door he used to study and sit bare-headed, and said he never took cold in his head, but that the greatest trouble was to keep off the flies from pitching on the baldness. . . .

He had very few books. I never saw (nor Sir William Petty) above half a dozen about him in his chamber. Homer and Virgil were commonly on his table; sometimes Xenophon, or some probable history, and Greek Testament, or so. He had read much, if one considers his long life, but his contemplation was much more than his reading. He was wont to say that if he had read as much as other men he should have known no more than other men . . .

He had an inch-thick board about sixteen inches square, whereon paper was pasted. On this board he drew his lines (schemes). When a line came into his head, he would, as he was walking, take a rude memorandum of it, to preserve it in his memory till he came to his chamber. He was never idle; his thoughts were always working. . . .

He had always books of prick-song lying on his table (e.g. of Henry Lawes's, etc. *Songs*), which at night, when he was abed, and the doors made fast, and was sure nobody heard him, he sang aloud—not that he had a very good voice, but to clear his pipes. He did believe it did his lungs good, and conduced much to prolong his life.

34
GEORGE WITHER (1588–1667)

In 1639 Wither was a captain of horse in the expedition against the Scots, and quarter-master general of the regiment wherein he was captain. . . . But this our author, who was always from his youth puritanically affected (sufficiently evidenced in his satires), sided with the Presbyterians in the beginning of the civil wars raised by them, *anno* 1642, became an enemy to the King and regality, sold the estate he had, and with the moneys received for it raised a troop of horse for the parliament, was made a captain and soon after a major, having this motto on his colours, *Pro Rege, Lege, Grege*; but being taken prisoner by the cavaliers, Sir John Denham the poet (some of whose land at Egham in Surrey Wither had got into his clutches) desired His Majesty not to hang him, 'because that so long as Wither lived, Denham would not be accounted the worst poet in England'.

35
WILLIAM PRYNNE (1600–69)

He was a learned man, of immense reading, but is much blamed for his unfaithful quotations. His manner of study was thus: he wore a long quilt cap, which came two or three, at least, inches over his eyes, which served him as an umbrella to defend his eyes from the light. About every three hours his man was to bring him a roll and a pot of ale to refocillate his wasted spirits. So he studied and drank, and munched some bread; and this maintained him till night, and then he made a good supper. . . .

He was burgess of the City of Bath, before and since the King's restoration. . . . Upon the opening of the Parliament, viz. letting in the secluded members,[1] he girt on his old long rusty sword (longer than ordinary). Sir William Waller marching behind him, as he went to the House, William Prynne's long sword ran between Sir William's short legs and threw him down, which caused laughter.

36
EDWARD POCOCKE (1604–91)

[Pococke, an orientalist of great learning, became the first Professor of Arabic at Oxford in 1636. His editions and Latin translations of various Arabic works gave him a European reputation.]

In 1643 he was presented by his college to the rectory of Childrey, a living of very good value in Berkshire; and the military state of Oxford rendering the demands of his professorship impractical set him more at liberty to attend particularly to the duties of this new relation, which he discharged with the religious care of a worthy parish priest.

Among other instances of his prudent and pious care for the religious improvement of his flock, it is observable that though he was led, both by genius and inclination, to spend his whole life in the most recondite literature, yet his sermons were always composed in a plain style upon practical subjects, carefully avoiding all show and ostentation of learning. But from this very exemplary caution not to amuse[2] his hearers (contrary to the common method then in vogue) with what they could not understand, some of them took occasion to entertain very contemptible thoughts

[1] The members of parliament ejected in 'Pride's Purge' (1648) were enabled by General Monck to resume their seats on 21 February 1660. [2] *amuse*: bewilder.

of his learning, and to speak of him accordingly. So that one of his Oxford friends, as he travelled through Childrey, inquiring for his diversion of some of the people, Who was their minister, and how they liked him? received this answer: 'Our parson is one Mr. Pococke, a plain honest man. But Master,' said they, 'he is no Latiner.'

37

EDMUND WALLER (1606–87)

WALLER, who had been involved during the Civil War in a royalist plot to secure the City of London for the King, had his life spared on payment of a large fine, but was sentenced to be banished from the country. In 1651 he was allowed to return to England, and four years later he wrote and published *A Panegyric to my Lord Protector*. Shortly after the restoration of Charles II he published another poem, *To the King, Upon His Majesty's Happy Return*. When the King had read it, he told Waller that he thought it much inferior to his panegyric on Cromwell. 'Sir,' replied Waller, 'we poets never succeed so well in writing truth as in writing fiction.'

38

[About 1635 Edmund Waller fell in love with Dorothy Sidney, the daughter of the Earl of Leicester, whose family seat was Penshurst in Kent. She was the 'Sacharissa' of his poems, but she married another man.]

UPON the marriage of that lady to Lord Spencer, afterwards Earl of Sunderland, which was solemnized July 11, 1639, Mr. Waller wrote the following letter to Lady Lucy Sidney, her sister . . .

MADAM,

In this common joy at Penshurst, I know none to whom complaints may come less unseasonably than to your ladyship, the loss of a bedfellow being almost equal to that of a mistress; and therefore you ought at least to pardon, if you consent not to the imprecations of, the deserted, which just Heaven no doubt will hear. May my lady Dorothy, if we may yet call her so, suffer as much, and have the like passion for this young lord, whom she has preferred to the rest of mankind, as others have had for her; and may his love, before the year go about, make her taste of the first curse imposed upon womankind, the pains of becoming a mother. May her first born be none of her own sex, nor so like her but that he may resemble her lord as much as herself. May she that always affected silence and retirement have the house filled with the noise and number of her children, and hereafter of her grandchildren; and then may she arrive at that great curse, so much declined by fair ladies, old age; may she live to be very old and yet seem young; be told so by her glass, and have no aches to inform her of the truth; and when she shall appear to be mortal, may her lord not mourn for her, but go hand in hand with her to that place where we are told there is neither marrying nor giving in marriage, that being there divorced we may all have an equal interest in her again! My revenge being immortal, I wish all this may befall her posterity to the world's end and afterwards! To you, madam, I wish all good things, and that this loss may in good time be happily supplied with a more constant bedfellow of the other sex. Madam, I humbly kiss your hands, and beg pardon for this trouble, from

Your ladyship's
most humble servant,
E. Waller.

He lived to converse with Lady Sunderland when she was very old, but his imprecations relating to her glass did not succeed, for my lady knew she had the disease which nothing but death could cure; and in a conversation with Mr. Waller and some other company at Lady Wharton's she asked him in raillery, 'When, Mr. Waller, will you write such fine verses upon me again?' 'Oh Madam,' said he, 'when your ladyship is as young again.'

39
JOHN MILTON (1608–74)

By his third wife . . . he never had any child; and those he had by the first he made serviceable to him in that very particular in which he most wanted their service, and supplied his want of eyesight by their eyes and tongue; for though he had daily about him one or other to read to him, some persons of man's estate, who of their own accord greedily catched at the opportunity of being his readers, that they might as well reap the benefit of what they read to him as oblige him by the benefit of their reading, others of younger years sent by their parents to the same end; yet excusing only the eldest daughter by reason of her bodily infirmity, and difficult utterance of speech (which to say truth I doubt was the principal cause of excusing her), the other two were condemned to the performance of reading, and exactly pronouncing of all the languages of whatever book he should at one time or another think fit to peruse; viz. the Hebrew (and I think the Syriac), the Greek, the Latin, the Italian, Spanish, and French. All which sorts of books to be confined to read, without understanding one word, must needs be a trial of patience, almost beyond endurance; yet it was endured by both for a long time; yet the irksomeness of this employment could not always be concealed, but broke out more and more into expressions of uneasiness; so that at length they were all (even the eldest also) sent out to learn some curious and ingenious sorts of manufacture that are proper for women to learn, particularly embroideries in gold and silver.

40

WHEN the Plague was abated, and the city had become safely habitable, Milton returned to Artillery Row. He had not been long back when London was devastated by a fresh calamity, only less terrible than the plague, because it destroyed the home, and not the life. The Great Fire succeeded the Great Plague: 13,000 houses, two-thirds of the city, were reduced to ashes, and the whole current of life and business entirely suspended. Through these two overwhelming disasters Milton must have been supporting his solitary spirit by writing *Paradise Regained*, *Samson Agonistes*, and giving the final touches to *Paradise Lost*. . . .

For licenser there was now the Archbishop of Canterbury, to wit, for religious literature. Of course the Primate read by deputy, usually one of his chaplains. The reader into whose hands *Paradise Lost* came, though an Oxford man, and a cleric on his preferment, who had written his pamphlet against the dissenters, happened to be one whose antecedents, as Fellow of All Souls, and Proctor (in 1663), ensured his taking a less pedantic and bigoted view of his duties. Still, though Dryden's dirty plays would have encountered no objection before such a tribunal, the same facilities were not likely to be accorded to anything which bore the name of John Milton, ex-secretary to Oliver, and himself an austere republican. Tomkyns—that was the young chaplain's name—did stumble at a phrase in Book I, 598:

> With fear of change
> Perplexes monarchs

There had been in England, and were to be again, times when men had hanged for less than this. Tomkyns, who was sailing on the smooth sea of preferment with a fair wind, did not wish to get into trouble, but at last he let the book pass. Perhaps he thought it was only religious verse written for the sectaries, which would never be heard of at court, or among the wits, and that therefore it was of little consequence what it contained.

A publisher was found—notwithstanding that Paul's, or as it now was again, St. Paul's-Churchyard, had ceased to exist—in Aldersgate, which lay outside the circuit of the conflagration. The agreement, still preserved in the national museum, between the author, 'John Milton, gent. of the one parte, and Samuel Symons, printer, of the other parte', is among the curiosities of our literary history. The curiosity consists not so much in the illustrious name appended (not in autograph) to the deed, as in the contrast between the present fame of the book and the waste-paper price at which the copyright is being valued. The author received £5 down, was to receive a second £5 when the first edition should be sold, a third £5 when the second, and a fourth £5 when the third edition should be gone. Milton lived to receive the second £5, and no more: £10 in all, for *Paradise Lost.*

41

ONE day, probably in February of 1674, though possibly earlier, two of the most famous modern poets called upon Milton at his house in Bunhill. These distinguished visitors were John Dryden, the poet laureate, and old Edmund Waller, perennial Member of Parliament. Milton received them very civilly; he had heard, no doubt of Dryden's great admiration for *Paradise Lost.* Eventually, of course, the talk turned to matters of prosody. Dryden later reported that, on this or some other visit, Milton acknowledged to him that Spenser was his 'original'. . . . The poet laureate was concerned, however, about something of more immediate importance to him than problems of poetic influence. He had come, in fact, to ask the blind man's permission to turn *Paradise Lost* into 'an heroic opera'—to be written in rhyming couplets.[1]

Milton, we are told, considered this unexpected request, and replied: 'Well, Mr. Dryden, it seems you have a mind to tag my points, and you have my leave to tag them. But some of them are so awkward and old-fashioned that I think you had as good leave them as you found them.'

Thus, with gentle irony, and with an apposite reference to the then-fashionable metal knobs worn at the ends of laces, Milton put a witty schism between himself and the tinkling world of Restoration verse. Dryden, having got what he wanted, set to work, finishing his adaptation, he tells us, within a month.

42

[In the summer of 1790, when the parish church of St. Giles, Cripplegate, was undergoing extensive repairs, it was thought appropriate to search for the grave of Milton, who had been buried, according to tradition, in the chancel under the

[1] *The State of Innocence, and Fall of Man* (unacted) (1677). It sold much faster than *Paradise Lost*, reaching a ninth edition in 1695.

clerk's desk. On 3 August, Mr. Thomas Strong, vestry clerk, and Mr. John Cole were informed that the grave had been found, and passed on the information to Philip Neve, an antiquary, who was greatly interested in everything connected with Milton. Neve afterwards published *A Narrative of the Disinterment of Milton's Coffin in the Parish Church of St. Giles, Cripplegate.* The leaden coffin which had been found appeared to be old and much corroded, and there was no inscription or plate upon it. 'It was suggested that if they opened the leaden coffin they might find some inscription on the wooden one inside it, but with a just and laudable piety, they disdained to disturb the sacred ashes after a requiem of 116 years.' What followed, however, was very different. The account is based on Philip Neve's *Narrative*, as condensed by a contributor to *Notes & Queries.*]

ON that evening, however, Cole and others held what he called a merry meeting at the house of one Fountain, a publican, in Beech Lane, who was an overseer of the parish, the company including John Laming (pawnbroker), Taylor (a Derbyshire surgeon), and William Ascough (coffin maker). Of course one of the chief topics of conversation was the discovery of Milton's coffin on that day, and several of those assembled expressed a desire to see it. Cole, who had given orders that the ground should be closed, after satisfying himself that there was no doubt as to the coffin being Milton's, was willing to gratify their curiosity on the morrow, provided that the remains had not already been reinterred. Accordingly they went to the church the next day, and found this to be the case. Holmes, one of Ascough's journeymen, pulled the coffin from its place, that they might see it in the daylight, and with the aid of a chisel and mallet forced it open as far down as the breast, and discovered the corpse enveloped in a shroud, on disturbing which the ribs, which had remained standing, fell. Then followed the ghastly desecration of the remains, which Mr. Neve describes in detail from information which he received from the violators themselves. Fountain, the publican, for instance, said that 'he pulled hard at the teeth, which resisted, until someone hit them a knock with a stone, when they easily came out'. All the teeth in the upper jaw, of which there were only five, were taken by Fountain. Laming, the pawnbroker, took one, and Taylor two from the lower jaw; and, continues Mr. Neve, 'Mr. Laming told me that he had at one time a mind to bring away the whole under-jaw, with the teeth in it; he had it in his hand, but tossed it back again.' Laming afterwards reached his hand down and took out one of the leg-bones, but threw it back also. He likewise took a large quantity of the hair, which 'lay strait and even' just as it had been combed and tied together before interment. When they had finished their gruesome task they quitted the church. The coffin was replaced, but not covered; and Ascough, the clerk, having gone away, and the sexton, Mrs. Hoppey, being from home, Elizabeth Grant, the gravedigger, took possession of it, and kept a tinder-box at hand for striking a light by which to exhibit the remains to such as were curious to see them, for which she charged the sum of sixpence, afterwards reducing it to threepence and twopence. The workmen in the church considered they also had a right to some share in the plunder, for they refused admission to such as would not pay the 'price of a pot of beer', to avoid which it appears that a number of people got into the church by a window.

Mr. Neve spared no pains in his endeavours to discover those who had gained possession of relics taken from Milton's coffin, and succeeded in obtaining some of the hair, a tooth, and a piece of the coffin, for which he paid two shillings. These, he proceeds to state, he procured for the purpose of doing his share in making a restitution of all that had been taken, as being the only means of making atonement for the violation of the dead.

[Neve was quite convinced that the grave that had been violated was indeed Milton's, but others were sceptical, and a considerable controversy ensued. Cowper wrote some indignant stanzas 'On the Late Indecent Liberties taken with the Remains of Milton'.]

43
LUCIUS CARY, VISCOUNT FALKLAND (1610?–43)

I[1] BELIEVE the method observed by the famous Lord Falkland, in some of his writings, would not be an ill one for young divines: I was assured by an old person of quality who knew him well that when he doubted whether a word were perfectly intelligible or no, he used to consult one of his lady's chambermaids (not the waiting-woman, because it was possible she might be conversant in romances), and by her judgement was guided whether to receive or to reject it. And if that great person thought such a caution necessary in treatises offered to the learned world, it will be sure at least as proper in sermons, where the meanest hearer is supposed to be concerned, and where very often a lady's chambermaid may be allowed to equal half the congregation, both as to quality and understanding.

[1] The narrator is Jonathan Swift.

44
THOMAS KILLIGREW (1612–83)

[Samuel Pepys notes a bit of Court gossip.]

MR. COOLING told us how the King, once speaking of the Duke of York's being mastered by his wife, said to some of the company by, that he would go no more abroad with this Tom Otter,[1] meaning the Duke of York, and his wife. Tom Killigrew being by, said, 'Sir, pray which is the best for a man, to be a Tom Otter to his wife or to his mistress?'—meaning the King's being so to my Lady Castlemaine.

45
ABRAHAM COWLEY (1618–67)

I BELIEVE I can tell the particular little chance that filled my head first with such chimes of verse as have never since left ringing there: for I remember when I began to read, and to take some pleasure in it, there was wont to lie in my mother's parlour (I know not by what accident, for she herself never in her life read any book but of devotion), but there was wont to lie Spenser's works. This I happened to fall upon, and was infinitely delighted with the stories of the knights, and giants, and monsters, and brave houses which I found everywhere there (though my understanding had little to do with all this), and by degrees with the tinkling of the rhyme and dance of the numbers; so that I think I had read him all over before I was twelve years old, and was thus made a poet as immediately as a child is made an eunuch.

46

[Dryden indulges in some anecdotal banter at the expense of Cowley.]

WITHOUT being injurious to the memory of our English Pindar, I will presume to say that his metaphors are sometimes too violent, and his language is not always pure. But at the same time I must excuse him; for through the iniquity of the times he was forced to travel at an age when,

[1] Captain Otter, in Ben Jonson's *Epicœne: or The Silent Woman*, who is completely under the domination of Mrs. Otter.

instead of learning foreign languages, he should have studied the beauties of his mother-tongue, which, like all other speeches, is to be cultivated early, or we shall never write it with any kind of elegance. Thus, by gaining abroad, he lost at home; like the painter in the *Arcadia*, who, going to see a skirmish, had his arms lopped off, and returned, says Sir Philip Sidney, well-instructed how to draw a battle, but without a hand to perform his work.

47
ANDREW MARVELL (1621–78)

THE severe tracts which he was continually publishing against the state and popery, and the inflammatory literary fight which he had with Parker[1] and others, often made his life in danger; but no bribes, no offers of fortune or situation, though so very contrary to his private interests, could make him swerve from the virtuous path he had first set out upon, and in which he continued to walk invariably to the last.

A man of such excellent parts and facetious converse could not be unknown to Charles the Second, who loved the company of wits so much that he would suffer the severest jokes, rather than not enjoy them. Mr. Marvell had been honoured with an evening's entertainment by His Majesty, who was so charmed with the ease of his manners, the soundness of his judgement, and the nimbleness of his wit, that the following morning, to show him his regard, he sent the Lord Treasurer Danby to wait upon him with a particular message from himself. His lordship with some difficulty found his elevated retreat, which was in a second floor in a court in the Strand, the very *gradus ad Parnassum*. Lord Danby, from the darkness of the staircase, and the narrowness thereof, abruptly burst open the door, and suddenly entered the room, wherein he found Mr. Marvell writing. Astonished at the sight of so noble and so unexpected a visitor, he asked his lordship with a smile, if he had not mistook his way. 'No,' replied my Lord, with a bow, 'not since I have found Mr. Marvell'; continuing, that he came with a message from the King, who wished to do him some signal service, to testify his high opinion of his merits. He replied with his usual pleasantry that kings had it not in their power to serve him; he had no void left aching in his breast. But becoming more serious, he assured his lordship that he was highly sensible of this mark of His Majesty's affection; but he knew too well the

[1] Samuel Parker, author of *A Discourse of Ecclesiastical Politie*, to which Marvell replied in *The Rehearsal Transprosed* (1672).

nature of courts to accept of favours, which were expected to bind a man in the chains of their interest, which his spirit of freedom and independence would not suffer him to embrace. To take a place at the hands of His Majesty would be proving him guilty of the first sin, ingratitude, if he voted against him; and if he went in the smooth stream of his interest, it might be doing injustice to his country and his conscience. He therefore begged that His Majesty would allow him to enjoy a state of liberty, and to esteem him more his faithful and dutiful subject, and more in the true interest of his welfare, by this refusal of his munificence, than if he had embraced his royal bounty.

These royal offers proving vain, Lord Danby began to assure him that the King had ordered him a thousand guineas, which he hoped he would be pleased to receive till he could bring his mind to accept of something better and more durable. At this Mr. Marvell renewed his usual smile, and said, 'Surely, my good Lord, you do not mean to treat me ludicrously by these munificent offers, which seem to interpret a poverty on my part. Pray, my Lord Treasurer, do these apartments wear in the least the air and mark of need? And as for my living, that is plentiful and good, which you shall have from the mouth of the servant.—Pray, what had I to dinner yesterday?'—'A shoulder of mutton, sir.'—'And tomorrow, my Lord Danby, I shall have the sweet blade-bone broiled; and when your lordship makes honourable mention of my cook and my diet, I am sure His Majesty will be too tender in future to attempt to bribe a man with golden apples who lives so well on the viands of his native country.' The Lord Treasurer, unable to withstand this, withdrew with smiles; and Mr. Marvell sent to his bookseller for the loan of one guinea.

48
SIR WILLIAM PETTY (1623–87)

ABOUT 1660 there was a great difference between him and Sir Hierome Sankey (one of Oliver's knights).... They printed one against the other. (This knight was wont to preach at Dublin.) The knight had been a soldier, and challenged Sir William to fight with him. Sir William is extremely short-sighted, and being the challengee, it belonged to him to nominate place and weapon: he nominates for the place a dark cellar; and the weapon to be a great carpenter's axe. This turned the knight's challenge into ridicule, and so it came to naught.

49
JOHN CROWNE (*fl.* 1665–1700)

It was at the very latter end of King Charles's reign that Mr. Crowne being tired with the fatigue of writing, and shocked by the uncertainty of theatrical success, and desirous to shelter himself from the resentments of those numerous enemies which he had made by his *City Politics*, made his application immediately to the King himself; and desired his Majesty to establish him in some office that might be a security to him for life. The King had the goodness to assure him he should have an office, but added that he would first see another comedy. Mr. Crowne endeavouring to excuse himself, by telling the King that he plotted slowly and awkwardly, the King replied that he would help him to a plot, and so put into his hands the Spanish comedy called *Non pued Esser*. Mr. Crowne was obliged immediately to go to work upon it; but, after he had writ three Acts of it, found to his surprise that the Spanish play had some time before been translated, and acted, and damned, under the title of *Tarugo's Wiles, or the Coffee-house*. Yet, supported by the King's command, he went boldly on and finished it. . . .

The play was now just ready to appear to the world; and as everyone that had seen it rehearsed was highly pleased with it, everyone who had heard of it was big with the expectation of it, and Mr. Crowne was delighted with the flattering hope of being made happy for the rest of his life by the performance of the King's promise; when, upon the very last day of the rehearsal, he met Cave Underhill coming from the playhouse as he himself was going towards it. Upon which the poet reprimanding the player for neglecting so considerable a part as he had in the comedy, and neglecting it on a day of so much consequence as the very last day of rehearsal, 'Oh Lord, sir,' says Underhill, 'we are all undone.' 'Wherefore?' says Mr. Crowne. 'Is the playhouse on fire?' 'The whole nation,' replies. the player, 'will quickly be so, for the King is dead.' At the hearing which dismal words, the author was little better; for he who but the moment before was ravished with the thought of the pleasure which he was about to give to his King, and of the favours which he was afterwards to receive from him, this moment found, to his unspeakable sorrow, that his royal patron was gone for ever, and with him all his hopes. The King indeed revived from his apoplectic fit, but three days after died, and Mr. Crowne by his death was replunged in the deepest melancholy.

[Crowne's play, *Sir Courtly Nice*, was produced successfully early in the reign of James II.]

50
THE BIBLE, 1631

ROBERT BARKER and Martin Lucas, the King's printers at London, printed an edition of the Bible of one thousand copies, in which a serious mistake was made by leaving out the word *not* in the seventh commandment, causing it to read 'Thou shalt commit adultery.' His Majesty King Charles I being made acquainted with it by Dr. William Laud, Bishop of London, an order was given for calling the printers into the Star Chamber, where, upon the fact being proved, the whole impression was called in, and the printers fined £3,000. With this fine, or a part of it, a fount of fair Greek types and matrices were provided, for publishing such manuscripts as might be prepared, and should be judged worthy of publication. . . .

A prior circumstance, indeed, had occurred, which induced the government to be more vigilant on the biblical press. The learned Ussher 'one day hastening to preach at Paul's Cross, entered the shop of one of the stationers, as booksellers were then called, and inquiring for a Bible of the London edition, when he came to look for his text, to his astonishment and his horror he discovered that the verse was omitted in the Bible. This gave the first occasion of complaint to the King of the insufferable negligence and incapacity of the London press; and . . . first bred that great contest which followed between the University of Cambridge and the London stationers about the right of printing Bibles.'

51
JOHN DRYDEN (1631–1700)

DRYDEN has himself told us that he was of a grave cast and did not much excel in sallies of humour. One of his *bons mots*, however, has been preserved. He does not seem to have lived on very amicable terms with his wife, Lady Elizabeth, whom, if we may believe the lampoons of the time, he was compelled by one of her brothers to marry. Thinking herself neglected by the bard, and that he spent too much time in his study, she one day exclaimed, 'Lord, Mr. Dryden, how can you always be poring over those musty books? I wish I were a book, and then I should have more of your company.' 'Pray, my dear,' replied old John, 'if you do become a book let it be an almanack, for then I shall change you every year.'

52

EVEN Dryden was very suspicious of rivals. He would compliment Crowne when a play of his failed, but was cold to him if he met with success. He sometimes used to own that Crowne had some genius, but then he always added that his father and Crowne's mother were very well acquainted.

53
ROBERT SOUTH (1634–1716)

DR. SOUTH, when once preaching before Charles II, . . . observed that the monarch and his attendants began to nod, and as nobles are common men when they are asleep, some of them soon after snored; on which he broke off his sermon, and called, 'Lord Lauderdale, let me entreat you to rouse yourself; you snore so loud that you will wake the King!'

54

DR. SOUTH, when he resided at Caversham in Oxfordshire, was called out of bed on a cold winter's morning by his clerk, to marry a couple who were then waiting for him. The doctor hurried up, and went shivering to church; but seeing only an old man of seventy, with a woman about the same age, and his clerk, he asked the latter in a pet where the bridegroom and the bride were, and what that man and woman wanted. The old man replying that they came there to be married, the doctor looked sternly at him and exclaimed, 'Married!' 'Yes, married,' said the old man hastily; 'better marry than do worse.' 'Go, get you gone, you silly old fools!' said the doctor; 'get home and do your worst!' And then hobbled out of church in a great passion with his clerk for calling him out of bed on such a ridiculous errand.

55
EDWARD STILLINGFLEET (1635–99)

KING CHARLES II asked Stillingfleet, 'How it came about that he always read his sermons before him, when, he was informed, he always preached without book elsewhere?' He told the King that 'the awe of so noble an audience, where he saw nothing that was not greatly superior to him, but chiefly the seeing before him so great and wise a prince, made him afraid to trust himself'. With which answer the King was very well contented. 'But pray,' says Stillingfleet, 'will your majesty give me leave to ask a question too? Why do you read your speeches,[1] when you can have none of the same reason?' 'Why truly, doctor,' says the King, 'your question is a very pertinent one, and so will be my answer. I have asked them so often, and for so much money, that I am ashamed to look them in the face.'

56
THOMAS FLATMAN (1637–88)

THIS person . . . was in his younger days much against marriage, to the dislike of his father, and made a song describing the cumbrances of it, beginning thus:

> Like a dog with a bottle tied close to his tail,
> Like a tory in a bog, or a thief in a jail, etc.

But being afterwards smitten with a fair virgin, and more with her fortune, he did espouse her 26 November 1672; whereupon his ingenious comrades did serenade him that night, while he was in the embraces of his mistress, with the said song.

57
SIR CHARLES SEDLEY (1639–1701)

HE was extremely active in effecting the Revolution, which was thought the more extraordinary, as he had received favours from King James II. That Prince, it seems, had fallen in love with a daughter of Sir Charles's, who was not very handsome; for James was remarkable for dedicating his affections to women who were not great beauties; in consequence of his intrigue with her, and in order to give her greater lustre in life, he created Miss Sedley Countess of Dorchester. This honour, so far from pleasing, greatly shocked Sir Charles. However libertine himself had been, yet he could not bear the thoughts of his daughter's dishonour; and with regard

[1] i.e. to the House of Commons.

to this her exaltation, he only considered it as rendering her more conspicuously infamous. He therefore conceived a hatred to James, and readily joined to dispossess him of his throne and dominions.

Being asked one day, why he appeared so warm against the King, who had created his daughter a Countess, 'It is from a principle of gratitude I am so warm,' returns Sir Charles; 'for since his Majesty has made my daughter a Countess, it is fit I should do all I can to make his daughter[1] a Queen.'

58
WILLIAM WYCHERLEY (1641–1716)

UPON the writing of his first play, which was *St. James's Park*,[2] he became acquainted with several of the most celebrated wits both of the Court and Town. The writing of that play was likewise the occasion of his becoming acquainted with one of King Charles's mistresses after a very particular manner. As Mr. Wycherley was going through Pall Mall towards St. James's in his chariot, he met the foresaid lady in hers, who, thrusting half her body out of the chariot, cried out aloud to him, 'You, Wycherley, you are a son of a whore!', at the same time laughing aloud and heartily. . . . If you never heard of this passage before, you may be surprised at so strange a greeting from one of the most beautiful and best-bred ladies in the world. Mr. Wycherley was certainly very much surprised at it, yet not so much but he soon apprehended it was spoke with allusion to the latter end of a song in the forementioned play:

> When parents are slaves
> Their brats cannot be any other,
> Great wits and great braves
> Have always a punk to their mother.

As, during Mr. Wycherley's surprise, the chariots drove different ways, they were soon at a considerable distance from each other, when Mr. Wycherley, recovering from his surprise, ordered his coachman to drive back and to overtake the lady. As soon as he got over-against her, he said to her, 'Madam, you have been pleased to bestow a title on me which generally belongs to the fortunate. Will your ladyship be at the play tonight?' 'Well,' she replied, 'what if I am there?' 'Why then, I will be there to wait on your ladyship, though I disappoint a very fine woman who

[1] Mary, wife of William III, was the elder daughter of James II.

[2] *Love in a Wood, or, St. James's Park.* The lady was Barbara Villiers, Duchess of Cleveland.

has made me an assignation.' 'So,' said she, 'you are sure to disappoint a woman who has favoured you for one who has not.' 'Yes,' he replied, 'if she who has not favoured me is the finer woman of the two. But he who will be constant to your ladyship till he can find a finer woman is sure to die your captive.' The lady blushed, and bade her coachman drive away. As she was then in all her bloom, and the most celebrated beauty that was then in England, or perhaps that has been in England since, she was touched with the gallantry of that compliment. In short, she was that night in the first row of the King's box in Drury Lane, and Mr. Wycherley in the Pit under her, where he entertained her during the whole play. And this was the beginning of a correspondence between these two persons which afterwards made a great noise in the Town.

59

WYCHERLEY was in a bookseller's shop at Bath or Tunbridge when Lady Drogheda came in and happened to inquire for the *Plain Dealer*. A friend of Wycherley's who stood by him pushed him towards her and said, 'There's the plain dealer, Madam, if you want him.' Wycherley made his excuses, and Lady Drogheda said that 'she loved plain dealing best'. He afterwards visited that lady, and in some time married her. This proved a great blow to his fortunes. Just before the time of his courting he was designed for governor to the late Duke of Richmond, and was to have been allowed £1,500 a year from the government. His absence from court in the progress of this amour, and his being yet more absent after his marriage (for Lady Drogheda was very jealous of him), disgusted his friends there so much that he lost all his interest with them. His lady died; he got little by her, and his misfortunes were such that he was thrown into the Fleet and lay there seven years.

It was then that Colonel Brett got his *Plain Dealer* to be acted, and contrived to get the King (James II) to be there. The colonel attended him thither. The King was mightily pleased with the play, asked who was the author of it, and upon hearing it was one of Wycherley's, complained that he had not seen him for so many years, and inquired what was become of him. The colonel improved this opportunity so well that the King gave orders that his debts should be discharged out of the privy purse. Wycherley was so weak as to give in an account only of £500, and so was confined almost half a year longer, till his father was at last prevailed upon to pay the rest—between two and three hundred pounds more.

60
GILBERT BURNET (1643–1715)

BISHOP BURNET's absence of mind is well known. Dining with the Duchess of Marlborough, after her husband's disgrace, he compared this great general to Belisarius. 'But,' said the Duchess eagerly, 'how came it that such a man was so miserable, and universally deserted?' 'Oh, madam,' exclaimed the *distrait* prelate, 'he had such a brimstone of a wife!'

61
EDMUND BOHUN (1645–99)

[On the restoration of Charles II in 1660, printing and publishing came under strict control. Sir Roger L'Estrange was appointed Licenser of the Press in 1662, and held that office until the Revolution. He was succeeded by a Scots gentleman called Fraser, who was as zealous a Whig as L'Estrange was a Tory. In 1692, however, he gave great offence by licensing a book showing that the famous *Icon Basilike* was not the work of Charles I, but of Dr. John Gauden. Fraser was forced to resign his office, and was replaced by Edmund Bohun. The subsequent misfortunes of Bohun are here related by Macaulay.]

THIS change of men produced an immediate and total change of system: for Bohun was as strong a Tory as a conscientious man who had taken the oaths could possibly be. He had been conspicuous as a persecutor of Nonconformists and a champion of the doctrine of passive obedience. He had edited Filmer's absurd treatise on the origin of government, and had written an answer to the paper which Algernon Sydney had delivered to the Sheriffs on Tower Hill. Nor did Bohun admit that, in swearing allegiance to William and Mary, he had done anything inconsistent with his old creed. For he had succeeded in convincing himself that they reigned by right of conquest, and that it was the duty of an Englishman to serve them as faithfully as Daniel had served Darius, or as Nehemiah had served Artaxerxes. This doctrine, whatever peace it might bring to his own conscience, found little favour with any party. The Whigs loathed it as servile: the Jacobites loathed it as revolutionary. Great numbers of Tories had doubtless submitted to William on the ground that he was, rightfully or wrongfully, King in possession; but very few of them were disposed to allow that his possession had originated in conquest. Indeed the plea which had satisfied the weak and narrow mind of Bohun was a mere fiction, and, had it been a truth, would have been a truth not to be uttered by Englishmen without agonies of shame and mortification. He however clung to his favourite whimsy with a tenacity which the general disapprobation only made more intense. His old friends, the steadfast adherents of indefeasible hereditary right, grew cold and reserved. He asked Sancroft's blessing, and got only a sharp word and a black look. He asked Ken's blessing; and Ken, though not much in the habit of transgressing the rules of Christian charity and courtesy, murmured something about a little scribbler. Thus cast out by one faction, Bohun was not received by any other. . . .

As to the rest, Bohun was a man of some acuteness and learning, contracted understanding, and unpopular manners. He had no sooner entered on his functions than all Paternoster Row and Little Britain were in a ferment. The Whigs had, under Fraser's administration, enjoyed almost as entire a liberty as if there had been no censorship. They were now as severely treated as in the days of L'Estrange. A history of the Bloody Assizes was about to be published, and was expected to have as great a run as the *Pilgrim's Progress*. But the new licenser refused his Imprimatur. The book, he said, represented rebels and schismatics as heroes and martyrs; and he would not sanction it for its weight in gold. . . .

There was then about town a man of good family, of some reading, and of some small literary talent, named Charles Blount. In politics he belonged to the extreme section of the Whig party. . . . He was an infidel, and the head of a small school of infidels who were troubled with a morbid desire to make converts. He translated from the Latin translation part of the Life of Apollonius of Tyana, and appended to it notes of which the flippant profaneness called forth the severe censure of an unbeliever of a very different order, the illustrious Bayle. Blount also attacked Christianity in several original treatises, or rather in several treatises purporting to be original; for he was the most audacious of literary thieves, and transcribed, without acknowledgement, whole pages from authors who had preceded him. His delight was to worry the priests by asking them how light existed before the sun was made, how Paradise could be bounded by Pison, Gihon, Hiddekel, and Euphrates, how serpents moved before they were condemned to crawl, and where Eve found the thread to stitch her figleaves. . . .

Little as either the intellectual or the moral character of Blount may seem to deserve respect, it is in a great measure to him that we must attribute the emancipation of the English press. Between him and the licensers there was a feud of long standing. Before the Revolution one of his heterodox treatises had been grievously mutilated by L'Estrange, and at last suppressed by orders from L'Estrange's superior the Bishop of London. Bohun was a scarcely less severe critic than L'Estrange. Blount therefore began to make war on the censorship and the censor. The hostilities were commenced by a tract which came forth without any licence, and which was entitled *A Just Vindication of Learning and of the Liberty of the Press, by Philopatris.* Whoever reads this piece, and is not aware that Blount was one of the most unscrupulous plagiaries that ever lived, will be surprised to find, mingled with the poor thoughts and poor words of a third-rate pamphleteer, passages so elevated in sentiment and style that they would be worthy of the greatest name in letters. The truth is that the *Just Vindication* consists chiefly of garbled extracts from the *Areopagitica* of Milton. . . . The *Just Vindication* was well received. The blow was speedily followed up. There still remained in the *Areopagitica* many fine passages which Blount had not used in his first pamphlet. Out of these passages he constructed a second pamphlet entitled *Reasons for the Liberty of Unlicensed Printing.* To these Reasons he appended a postscript entitled 'A Just and True Character of Edmund Bohun'. This Character was written with extreme bitterness. Passages were quoted from the licenser's writings to prove that he held the doctrines of passive obedience and non-resistance. He was accused of using his power systematically for the purpose of favouring the enemies and silencing the friends of the Sovereigns whose bread he ate; and it was asserted that he was the friend and the pupil of his predecessor Sir Roger.

The 'Just and True Character of Bohun' could not be publicly sold; but it was widely circulated. While it was passing from hand to hand, and while the Whigs were everywhere exclaiming against the new censor as a second L'Estrange, he was requested to authorize the publication of an anonymous work entitled *King William and Queen Mary Conquerors.* He readily and eagerly complied. For there was between the doctrines which he had long professed and the doctrines which were propounded in this treatise a coincidence so exact that many suspected him of being the author; nor was this suspicion weakened by a passage in which a compliment was paid to his political writings. But the real author was that very Blount who was, at that time, labouring to inflame the public both against the Licensing Act and the licenser. Blount's motives may be easily divined. His own opinions were diametrically opposed to those which, on this occasion, he put forward in the most offensive manner. It is therefore impossible to doubt that his object was to ensnare and to ruin Bohun. It was a base and wicked scheme. But it cannot be denied that the trap was laid and baited with much skill. The republican succeeded in personating a high Tory. The atheist succeeded in personating a High Churchman. The pamphlet concluded with a devout prayer that the God of light and love would open the understanding and govern the will of Englishmen, so that they might see the things which belonged to their peace. The censor was in raptures. In every page he found his own thoughts expressed more plainly than he had ever expressed them. Never before, in his opinion, had the true claim of their Majesties to obedience been so clearly stated. Every Jacobite who read this admirable tract must inevitably be converted. The nonjurors would flock to take the oaths. The nation, so long divided, would at length be united. From these pleasing dreams Bohun was awakened by learning, a few hours after the appearance of the discourse which had charmed him, that the title-page had set all London in a flame, and that the odious words, 'King William and Queen Mary Conquerors', had moved the indignation of multitudes who had never read further. Only four days after the publication he heard that the House of Commons had taken the matter up, that the book had been called by some members a rascally book, and that, as the author was unknown, the Serjeant at Arms was in search of the licenser. Bohun's mind had never been strong; and he was entirely unnerved and bewildered by the fury and suddenness of the storm which had burst upon him. He went to the House. Most of the members whom he met in the passages and lobbies frowned on him. When he was put to the bar, and, after three profound obeisances, ventured to lift his head and look round him, he could read his doom in the angry and contemptuous looks which were cast on him from every side. He hesitated, blundered, contradicted himself, called the Speaker My Lord, and, by his confused way of speaking, raised a tempest of rude laughter which confused him still more. As soon as he had withdrawn, it was unanimously resolved that the obnoxious treatise should be burned in Palace Yard by the common hangman. It was also resolved, without a division, that the King should be requested to remove Bohun from the office of licenser. The poor man, ready to faint with grief and fear, was conducted by the officers of the House to a place of confinement.

[As a result of Bohun's foolish mistake the Licensing Act, when it was due for renewal, was extended for only two years. When it came up for consideration again in 1695, it was allowed to lapse, and the press was henceforth free.]

62
JOHN WILMOT, EARL OF ROCHESTER
(1647–80)

[In 1673 a rhymed heroic tragedy by Samuel Pordage, *Herod and Mariamne*, was produced at the theatre in Lincoln's Inn Fields. According to the prologue, it had been written much earlier.]

MR. PORDAGE (who at least has rendered himself famous for following the Muses, though he could never overtake them) seems not to have had interest enough among the players to usher his own performances on the theatre. He had taken infinite pains to make Herod an arrant Jew, and was very unwilling to lose his labour after the work had not only received the approbation of himself, but of several of his poetical friends also. A patron was still wanting; and after consulting some of his acquaintances, who should have the honour of patronizing so accomplished a play, it was resolved, *nemine contradicente*, that Wilmot, Earl of Rochester, was the most worthy of such a favour. To this end the author, though not personally or nominally known to my Lord Rochester, waited upon him and left the play for his lordship's perusal, and lived for some days on the expectation of his approaching applause. At the expiration of about a week he went a second time to my Lord's house, where he found the manuscript in the hands of the porter, with this distich writ upon the cover of it:

> Poet, whoe'er thou art, God damn thee,
> Go hang thyself, and burn thy Mariamne.

63

JOHN SHEFFIELD, EARL OF MULGRAVE AND DUKE OF BUCKINGHAM
(1648–1721)

THIS nobleman (a warrior, a politician, a courtier, and a poet) was not personally a tyrant to his Yorkshire tenants, whatever his steward might have been; for he never came near them if he could help it. But, before he had arrived at his dukedom, and when he was very young, the Great Plague broke out in London; and he thought it a less plague to visit his estate than to stay in the midst of the epidemic.

As soon as the pestilence was subdued, . . . he set out again for the metropolis: but, during his stay on the estate, he had been so affable to his dependents, and it was so much their interest to have him among them, that they used every effort in their power to seduce him into a liking for the country, and to inoculate him into a taste which, it was clear, he did not take naturally. They accompanied him, therefore, in a body, nearly through the first stage of his journey to town; and after having gone in procession with his carriage over Saltersgate Moor, a dismal waste of sundry miles, they then took their leaves, beseeching him to come back to them soon.

Many flowery speeches passed between the noble Earl and his adherents—of kindness and patronage on one side, and duty and devotion on the other; all ending, on the part of the tenantry, with 'At what time may we hope for the happiness of seeing Your Lordship again?' The answer was, for some time, ingeniously evaded; till at last this main desideratum was so strongly pushed that there was no parrying it, and his Lordship said, 'My worthy friends, I shall make a point of being with you again, *at the next Plague.*'

64
JEREMY COLLIER (1650–1726)

IN his *Short View of the Immorality and Profaneness of the English Stage* the Revd. Jeremy Collier singled out Congreve as one of the chief offenders, and took exception to a number of passages in *The Old Bachelor*. To this Congreve made a rather ineffective reply, in the course of which he remarked of his first comedy: 'When I wrote it, I had little thoughts of the stage; but did it, to amuse myself, in a slow recovery from a fit of sickness.' He regretted, he said, that he had allowed himself to be drawn in to the business of playwriting—'a difficult and thankless study'—and so to become involved 'in a perpetual war with knaves and fools'. If Congreve thought he had disposed of Collier satisfactorily, he was mistaken; for Collier had at his command the gift of witty repartee that was so much prized in the period. 'What his disease was,' Collier replied, 'I am not to inquire; but it must be a very ill one to be worse than the remedy.'

65
NATHANIEL LEE (1653?–92)

LEE, for aught we know, might have some noble flights of fancy, even in Bedlam; and it is reported of him that while he was writing one of his scenes by moon-light, a cloud intervening, he cried out in extacsy, 'Jove, snuff the moon!', but as this is only related upon common report, we desire no more credit may be given to it than its own nature demands.

66
JOHN DENNIS (1657–1734)

MR. DENNIS happened once to go to the play when a tragedy was acted in which the machinery of thunder was introduced, a new artificial method of producing which he had formerly communicated to the managers.

Incensed by this circumstance, he cried out in a transport of resentment, 'That is *my* thunder, by G—d; the villains will play my thunder, but not my plays.'

67

MR. DENNIS wrote many letters and pamphlets for the administration of the Earl of Godolphin and the Duke of Marlborough, and never failed to lash the French with all the severity natural to him. When the peace (which the Whigs reckoned the most inglorious that ever was made) was about to be ratified, Mr. Dennis, who certainly over-rated his importance, took it into his imagination that when the terms of peace should be stipulated, some persons who had been most active against the French would be demanded by that nation as hostages; and he imagined himself of importance enough to be made choice of, but dreaded his being given up to the French as the greatest evil that could befall him. Under the influence of this strong delusion, he actually waited on the Duke of Marlborough, and begged his grace's interposition, that he might not be sacrificed to the French, for, says he, 'I have always been their enemy.' To this strange request his grace very gravely replied, 'Do not fear, Mr. Dennis, you shall not be given up to the French: I have been a greater enemy to them than you, and you see I am not afraid of being sacrificed, nor am in the least disturbed.' Mr. Dennis upon this retired, well satisfied with his grace's answer, but there still remained upon his spirits a dread of his becoming a prey to some of the enemies of Great Britain.

68
DANIEL DEFOE (1660–1731)

[This incident, which took place 'about 80 years ago', was related by Richard Polwhele in a letter dated 1822.]

ABOUT 80 years ago, there was no place of worship at a large village to the west of Truro, distant at least five miles from its parish church; nor was there a Bible to be seen: but there were one Testament, and one Common Prayer-book, which were bound together. This valuable rarity was the property of an old woman who kept the village inn, and, with the celebrated history of *Robinson Crusoe*, was deposited on a shelf in the kitchen. On a summer's day, alarmed by a violent thunderstorm, the villagers sought shelter under the roof which contained this sacred deposit, as the only place of safety. To make assurance doubly sure, anxious inquiry was made for Jack, the landlady's apprentice, who had the rare good fortune to have learnt his letters. This lad was considered a prodigy; and, being found, was desired to commence reading prayers to the terrified auditory, who were on their knees in the common drinking room. Jack went to fetch the *Prayer-book* from the shelf, where it had long rested beside its *companion*. Unfortunately, as things were in a state of confusion, he took down the latter, and falling on his knees, began reading as fast as he could. And, from miscalling some words and mis-spelling others, the boy had continued some time before the error was discovered. At length, having stumbled upon the man *Friday*, his mistress cried out: 'Why, Jock! thee hast got the wrong book! sure thee'st reading prayers out of *Robinson Crusoe*!'—Jack felt this reproof as an insult offered to his superior understanding, and pertinaciously continued to read, declaring that '*Robinson Crusoe* would as soon stop the thunder as the prayer-book.'

69

A RESPECTABLE alderman of Oxford, Mr. Tawney, was so fascinated with *Robinson Crusoe* that he used to read it through every year, and thought every part of it as true as holy writ. Unfortunately for him, a friend at last told him that it was little more than a fiction; that Robinson Crusoe was but a Scottish sailor of the name of Alexander Selkirk, whose plain story of his shipwreck on the island of Juan Fernandez had been embellished and worked up into the narrative he so much admired, by an ingenious author, Daniel Defoe. 'Your information, sir,' said the alderman, 'may be very correct, but I wish you had withheld it; for in undeceiving me, you have deprived me of one of the greatest pleasures of my old age.'

70

BISHOP FRANCIS ATTERBURY (1662–1732)

IN 1715 I dined with the Duke of Ormonde at Richmond. . . . During the dinner there was a jocular dispute (I forget how it was introduced) concerning short prayers. Sir William Wyndham told us that the shortest prayer he had ever heard was the prayer of a common soldier just before the Battle of Blenheim, 'O God, if there be a God, save my soul, if I have a soul!' This was followed by a general laugh. I immediately reflected that such a treatment of the subject was too ludicrous, at least very improper, where a learned and religious prelate was one of the company. But I had soon an opportunity of making a different reflection. Atterbury, seeming to join in the conversation, and applying himself to Sir William Wyndham, said: 'Your prayer, Sir William, is indeed very short; but I remember another as short, but a much better, offered up likewise by a poor soldier in the same circumstances: 'O God, if in the day of battle I forget thee, do not thou forget me!' This, as Atterbury pronounced it with his usual grace and dignity, was a very gentle and polite reproof, and was immediately felt by the whole company. And the Duke of Ormonde, who was the best bred man of his age, suddenly turned the discourse to another subject.[1]

71
JONATHAN SWIFT (1667–1745)

In the yearly visits which he made to London . . . Swift passed much of his time at Lord Berkeley's, officiating as Chaplain to the family, and attending Lady Berkeley in her private devotions. After which, the Doctor, by her desire, used to read to her some moral or religious discourse. The Countess had at this time taken a great liking to Mr. Boyle's Meditations,[2] and was determined to go through them in that manner; but as Swift had by no means the same relish for that kind of writing which her Ladyship had, he soon grew weary of the task, and a whim coming into his head, resolved to get rid of it in a way which might occasion some sport in the family; for which they had as high a relish as himself.

The next time he was employed in reading one of those Meditations, he took an opportunity of conveying away the book, and dexterously inserted a leaf on which he had written his own Meditation on a Broom-stick; after which he took care to have the book restored to its proper place, and in his next attendance on my Lady, when he was desired to proceed to the next Meditation, Swift opened upon the place where the leaf had been inserted, and with great composure of countenance read the title, 'A Meditation on a Broom-stick'. Lady Berkeley, a little surprised at the oddity of the title, stopped him, repeating the words: 'A Meditation on a Broom-stick! Bless me, what a strange subject! But there is no knowing

[1] Bishop Atterbury's 'poor soldier' was the royalist commander Sir Jacob Astley, and his prayer was offered up before the battle of Edgehill (1642), in which he was wounded. Atterbury had almost certainly come across the story in the *Memoires* (1701) of Sir Philip Warwick, whose version of the prayer is even more moving: 'O Lord! thou knowest how busy I must be this day: if I forget thee, do not thou forget me.'

[2] The Hon. Robert Boyle, *Occasional Reflections upon Several Subjects* (1665).

what useful lessons of instruction this wonderful man may draw from things apparently the most trivial. Pray let us hear what he says upon it.' Swift then, with an inflexible gravity of countenance, proceeded to read the Meditation, in the same solemn tone which he had used in delivering the former. Lady Berkeley, not at all suspecting a trick, in the fullness of her prepossession was every now and then, during the reading of it, expressing her admiration of this extraordinary man, who could draw such fine moral reflections from so contemptible a subject; with which, though Swift must have been inwardly not a little tickled, yet he observed a most perfect composure of features, so that she had not the least room to suspect any deceit. Soon after, some company coming in, Swift pretended business and withdrew, foreseeing what was to follow. Lady Berkeley, full of the subject, soon entered upon the praises of those heavenly Meditations of Mr. Boyle. 'But', said she, 'the Doctor has been just reading one to me which has surprised me more than all the rest.' One of the company asked which of the Meditations she meant. She answered directly, in the simplicity of her heart, 'I mean that excellent Meditation on a Broomstick.' The company looked at each other with some surprise, and could scarce refrain from laughing. But they all agreed that they had never heard of such a Meditation before. 'Upon my word,' said my Lady, 'there it is, look into that book and convince yourselves.' One of them opened the book, and found it there indeed, but in Swift's handwriting; upon which a general burst of laughter ensued; and my Lady, when the first surprise was over, enjoyed the joke as much as any of them; saying 'What a vile trick has that rogue played me. But it is his way, he never baulks his humour in anything.' The affair ended in a great deal of harmless mirth, and Swift, you may be sure, was not asked to proceed any further in the Meditations.

72

THE knot of Wits used at this time [*c.* 1710] to assemble at Button's Coffee-house; and I had a singular account of Swift's first appearance there from Ambrose Philips, who was one of Mr. Addison's little senate. He said that they had for several successive days observed a strange clergyman come into the coffee-house, who seemed utterly unacquainted with any of those who frequented it; and whose custom it was to lay his hat down on a table, and walk backwards and towards at a good pace for half an hour or an hour, without speaking to any mortal, or seeming in the least to attend to anything that was going forward there. He then used to take up his hat, pay his money at the bar, and walk away without opening his lips. . . .

This made them more than usually attentive to his motions; and one evening, as Mr. Addison and the rest were observing him, they saw him cast his eyes several times on a gentleman in boots, who seemed to be just come out of the country, and at last advance towards him as intending to address him. They were all eager to hear what this dumb, mad parson had to say, and immediately quitted their seats to get near him. Swift went up to the country gentleman, and in a very abrupt manner, without any previous salute, asked him, 'Pray, sir, do you remember any good weather in the world?' The country gentleman, after staring a little at the singularity of his manner, and the oddity of the question, answered, 'Yes, sir, I thank God, I remember a great deal of good weather in my time.' 'That is more', said Swift, 'than I can say; I never remember any weather that was not too hot, or too cold; too wet, or too dry; but, however God Almighty contrives it, at the end of the year 'tis all very well.' Upon saying this, he took up his hat, and without uttering a syllable more, or taking the least notice of anyone, walked out of the coffee-house, leaving all those who had been spectators of this odd scene staring after him, and still more confirmed in the opinion of his being mad.

There is another anecdote recorded of him, of what passed between him and Dr. Arbuthnot in the same coffee-house. The Doctor had been scribbling a letter in great haste, which was much blotted; and seeing this odd parson near him, with a design to play upon him said, 'Pray, sir, have you any sand about you?' 'No,' replied Swift, 'but I have the gravel, and if you will give me your letter I'll p—ss upon it.' Thus singularly commenced an acquaintance between those two great wits, which afterwards ripened into the closest friendship.

73

In 1723 died Mrs. [i.e. Miss Esther] Van Homrigh, a woman made unhappy by her admiration of wit, and ignominiously distinguished by the name of *Vanessa*. . . . She was a young woman fond of literature, whom *Decanus*, the Dean (called *Cadenus* by transposition of the letters), took pleasure in directing and instructing; till, from being proud of his praise, she grew fond of his person. Swift was then about forty-seven, at an age when vanity is strongly excited by the amorous attention of a young woman. If it be said that Swift should have checked a passion which he never meant to gratify, recourse must be had to that extenuation which he so much despised, 'men are but men': perhaps, however, he did not at first know his own mind, and, as he represents himself, was undetermined. For his admission of her courtship, and his indulgence of her hopes after his marriage to Stella,[1] no other honest plea can be found than that he delayed a disagreeable discovery from time to time, dreading the immediate bursts of distress, and watching for a favourable moment. She thought herself neglected, and died of disappointment; having ordered by her will the poem to be published in which *Cadenus* had proclaimed her excellence, and confessed his love. The effect of the publication upon the Dean and Stella is thus related by Delany.

I have good reason to believe that they were both greatly shocked and distressed (though it may be differently) upon this occasion. The Dean made a tour to the South of Ireland, for about two months, at this time, to dissipate his thoughts, and give place to obloquy. And Stella retired (upon the earnest invitation of the owner) to the house of a cheerful, generous, good-natured friend of the Dean's, whom she also much loved and honoured. There my informer often saw her; and, I have reason to believe, used his utmost endeavours to relieve, support, and amuse her in this sad situation.

One little incident he told me of, on that occasion, I think I shall never forget. As her friend was an hospitable, open-hearted man, well-beloved and largely acquainted, it happened one day that some gentlemen dropped in to dinner who were strangers to Stella's situation; and as the poem of *Cadenus and Vanessa* was then the general topic of conversation, one of them said, 'Surely that Vanessa must be an extraordinary woman that could inspire the Dean to write so finely upon her.' Mrs. Johnson smiled, and answered 'that she thought that point not quite so clear; for it was well known the Dean could write finely upon a broomstick'.

74

[In the Spring of 1724 Swift published the first of his *Drapier's Letters* attacking the patent granted to William Wood for producing a new copper coinage for Ireland. He followed this up with three more letters, the fourth and severest of them appearing on 13 October. About a week later Lord Carteret, the new Lord Lieutenant, arrived in Ireland, and on the 27th he issued a proclamation offering a reward of £300 for a discovery of the authorship of the fourth letter.]

THE day after the Proclamation was issued out against the Drapier, there was a full levee at the Castle. The Lord Lieutenant was going round the circle, when Swift abruptly entered the chamber, and pushing his way through the crowd never stopped till he got within the circle; where, with marks of the highest indignation in his countenance, he addressed the Lord Lieutenant with the voice of a Stentor that re-echoed through the room: 'So, my Lord Lieutenant, this is a glorious exploit that you have

[1] It was widely believed that Swift had been privately married in his forty-ninth year to Esther Johnson ('Stella').

performed yesterday, in issuing a Proclamation against a poor shop-keeper whose only crime is an honest endeavour to save his country from ruin. You have given a noble specimen of what this devoted nation is to hope for from your government. I suppose you expect a statue of copper will be erected to you for this service done to Wood.' He then went on for a long time inveighing in the bitterest terms against the Patent, and displaying in the strongest colours all the fatal consequences of introducing that execrable coin. The whole assembly were struck mute with wonder at this unprecedented scene. The titled slaves and vassals of power felt and shrunk into their own littleness in the presence of this man of virtue. He stood super-eminent among them, like his own Gulliver amid a circle of Lilliputians. For some time a profound silence ensued; when Lord Carteret, who had listened with great composure to the whole speech, made this fine reply, in a line of Virgil's:

> *Res dura & regni novitas me talia cogunt*
> *moliri.*[1]

The whole assembly was struck with the beauty of this quotation, and the levee broke up in good humour....

75

SWIFT was known over the whole kingdom by the title of THE DEAN, given to him by way of pre-eminence, as it were by common consent; and when THE DEAN was mentioned, it always carried with it the idea of the first and greatest man in the kingdom. THE DEAN said this; THE DEAN did that; whatever he said or did was received as infallibly right, with the same degree of implicit credit given to it as was paid to the Stagyrite of old or to the modern Popes. We may judge of the greatness of his influence from a passage in a letter of Lord Carteret to him, 24 March 1733, who was at that time Chief Governor of Ireland: 'I know by experience how much the City of Dublin thinks itself under your protection; and how strictly they used to obey all orders fulminated from the sovereignty of St. Patrick's.' And in the postscript to another of 24 March 1737, he says: 'When people ask me how I governed Ireland, I say that I pleased Dr. Swift.'

[1] Hard fortune, and the newness of my reign, compel me to such measures.

76

SWIFT was delighted with the stir caused by the publication of *Gulliver's Travels*, and from Dublin he wrote gaily to Pope about some of the first reactions to his book. Among the less favourable comments he had to report were those of a real or apocryphal Irish bishop who said 'that book was full of improbable lies, and for his part he hardly believed a word of it'.

77

DEAN SWIFT, in one of his pedestrian journeys from London towards Chester, took shelter from a summer tempest under a large oak on the roadside, at no great distance from Lichfield. Presently a man, with a pregnant woman, were driven by the like impulse to avail themselves of the same covert. The dean, entering into conversation, found the parties were destined for Lichfield to be married. As the situation of the woman indicated no time should be lost, a proposition was made on his part to save them the rest of the journey by performing the ceremony on the spot. The offer was gladly accepted, and thanks being duly returned, the bridal pair, as the sky brightened, were about to return; but the bridegroom suddenly recollecting that a certificate was requisite to authenticate the marriage, requested one, which the dean wrote in these words:

Under an oak, in stormy weather,
I joined this rogue and whore together;
And none but he who rules the thunder
Can put this rogue and whore asunder.

78

I NEVER wake without finding life a more insignificant thing than it was the day before: which is one great advantage I get by living in this country,[1] where there is nothing I shall be sorry to lose; but my greatest misery is recollecting the scene of twenty years past, and then all on a sudden dropping into the present. I remember when I was a little boy, I felt a great fish at the end of my line which I drew up almost on the ground, but it dropped in, and the disappointment vexeth me to this very day, and I believe it was the type of all my future disappointments.

[1] Swift was writing from Dublin, in his sixty-second year.

79
MRS. SUSANNA CENTLIVRE (1667–1723)

MRS. CENTLIVRE dedicated *The Gotham Election* to Mr. Secretary Craggs, who made her a present of twenty guineas by the hands of Mrs. Bracegirdle, who had got leave for her to dedicate it to him; and when she told him he was very liberal, and sent the author more than she could reasonably expect, especially as her farce had never been acted, he told her he considered not so much the merit of the piece as what was proper to be done by a Secretary of State.

80
WILLIAM CONGREVE (1670–1729)

[Voltaire recalls his meeting with Congreve.]

MR. CONGREVE raised the glory of comedy to a greater height than any English writer before or since his time. . . . He was infirm and come to the verge of life when I knew him. Mr. Congreve had one defect, which was his entertaining too mean an idea of his own first profession, that of a writer, though it was to this he owed his fame and fortune. He spoke of his works as trifles that were beneath him, and hinted to me in our first conversation that I should visit him upon no other foot than that of a gentleman who led a life of plainness and simplicity. I answered that had he been so unfortunate as to be a mere gentleman, I should never have come to see him; and I was very much disgusted at so unseasonable a piece of vanity.

81
COLLEY CIBBER (1671–1757)

CIBBER and Verbruggen were two dissipated young fellows who determined, in opposition to the advice of friends, to become great actors. Much about the same time they were constant attendants upon Downs, the prompter of Drury-Lane, in expectation of employment. What the first part was in which Verbruggen distinguished himself cannot now be known. But Mr. Richard Cross, late prompter of Drury-Lane theatre, gave me the following history of Colley Cibber's first establishment as a hired actor. He was known only, for some years, as Master Colley. After waiting impatiently for a long time for the prompter's notice, by good fortune he obtained the honour of carrying a message on the stage, in some play, to Betterton. Whatever was the cause, Master Colley was so terrified that the scene was disconcerted by him. Betterton asked, in some anger, who the young fellow was that had committed the blunder. Downs replied, 'Master Colley.'—'Master Colley! then forfeit him.'—'Why, sir,' said the prompter, 'he has no salary.'—'No?' said the old man; 'why then, put him down ten shillings a week, and forfeit him five shillings.'

82

COLLEY CIBBER, they say, was extremely haughty as a theatrical manager, and very insolent to dramatists. When he had rejected a play, if the author desired him to point out the particular parts of it which displeased him, he took a pinch of snuff, and answered in general terms—'Sir, there is nothing in it *to coerce my passions.*'

83
JOSEPH ADDISON (1672–1719)

[Pope writes to a friend in the country about the reception of Addison's *Cato* in the spring of 1713.]

CATO was not so much the wonder of Rome itself in his days as he is of Britain in ours; and though all the foolish industry possible has been used to make it a party play, yet what the author once said of another may be the most properly in the world applied to him on this occasion:

> Envy it self is dumb, in wonder lost,
> And factions strive, who shall applaud him most.[1]

The numerous and violent claps of the Whig party on the one side the theatre were echoed back by the Tories on the other, while the author sweated behind the scenes with concern to find their applause proceeded more from the hand than the head. This was the case too of the prologue-writer,[2] who was clapped into a staunch Whig sore against his will, at almost every two lines. I believe you have heard that after all the applause

[1] Addison, *The Campaign*, ll. 45–6. [2] Pope himself.

of the opposite faction, my Lord Bolingbroke sent for Booth who played Cato, into the box, between one of the acts and presented him with 50 guineas; in acknowledgement (as he expressed it) for his defending the cause of liberty so well against a *perpetual dictator*.[1] The Whigs are unwilling to be distanced this way, as 'tis said, and therefore design a present to the said Cato very speedily; in the meantime they are getting ready as good a sentence as the former on their side. So betwixt them, 'tis probable that Cato (as Dr. Garth expressed it) may have something to live upon after he dies.

This play was published but this Monday, and Mr. Lewis tells me it is not possible to convey it to you before Friday next. The town is so fond of it that the orange wenches and fruit women in the Park offer the books at the side of the coaches, and the Prologue and Epilogue are cried about the streets by the common hawkers.

84

FREE and elegant as was the accustomed style of Addison, it is well known that on many occasions he could not satisfy the fastidiousness of his taste in his own compositions. It was his official business to write to Hanover that Queen Anne was dead: he found it so difficult to express himself suitably to his own notions of the importance of the event that the Lords of the Regency were obliged to employ a Mr. Southwell, one of the clerks. Southwell stated the fact, as he was ordered, in the ordinary perspicuity of business; and then boasted of his superiority to Addison, in having readily done that which Addison, attempting to do, had failed.

85

[Edward Young's *Conjectures on Original Composition*, from which this celebrated anecdote is taken, was published in the form of a letter to Samuel Richardson. The 'youth nearly related' whom Addison summoned to his deathbed was the Earl of Warwick, the dissolute son of Addison's wife by her former marriage, whose only other contact with literature is that he once, in Pope's words, 'carried me and Cibber in his coach to a bawdy-house'.]

YOU know, indeed, the value of his writings, and close with the world in thinking them immortal; but I believe you know not that his name would have deserved immortality though he had never written; and that, by a

[1] The Duke of Marlborough's request to be made Captain-General for life had been much resented by the Tories.

better title than the pen can give: you know, too, that his life was amiable; but perhaps you are still to learn that his death was triumphant . . .

For, after a long and manly but vain struggle with his distemper, he dismissed his physicians, and with them all hopes of life: but with his hopes of life he dismissed not his concern for the living, but sent for a youth nearly related, and finely accomplished, yet not above being the better for good impressions from a dying friend. He came; but life now glimmering in the socket, the dying friend was silent. After a decent and proper pause, the youth said, 'Dear Sir! you sent for me: I believe, and I hope, that you have some commands; I shall hold them most sacred.' May distant ages not only hear, but feel, the reply! Forcibly grasping the youth's hand, he softly said, 'See in what peace a Christian can die.' He spoke with difficulty, and soon expired. Through grace divine, how great is man! Through divine mercy, how stingless is death! Who would not thus expire?

86
RICHARD STEELE (1672–1729)

MR. SAVAGE was once desired by Sir Richard Steele, with an air of the utmost importance, to come very early to his house the next morning. Mr. Savage came as he had promised, found the chariot at the door, and Sir Richard waiting for him, and ready to go out. What was intended, and whither they were to go, Savage could not conjecture, and was not willing to inquire, but immediately seated himself with Sir Richard; the coachman was ordered to drive, and they hurried with the utmost expedition to Hyde-Park Corner, where they stopped at a petty tavern, and retired to a private room. Sir Richard then informed him that he intended to publish a pamphlet, and that he had desired him to come thither that he might write for him. They soon sat down to the work. Sir Richard dictated, and Savage wrote, till the dinner that had been ordered was put upon the table. Savage was surprised at the meanness of the entertainment, and after some hesitation ventured to ask for wine, which Sir Richard, not without reluctance, ordered to be brought. They then finished their dinner, and proceeded in their pamphlet, which they concluded in the afternoon.

Mr. Savage then imagined his task over, and expected that Sir Richard would call for the reckoning, and return home; but his expectations deceived him, for Sir Richard told him that he was without money, and that the pamphlet must be sold before the dinner could be paid for; and Savage was therefore obliged to go and offer their new production to sale for two guineas, which with some difficulty he obtained. Sir Richard then returned home, having retired that day only to avoid his creditors, and composed the pamphlet only to discharge his reckoning.

87

SIR RICHARD STEELE having one day invited to his house a great number of persons of the first quality, they were surprised at the number of liveries which surrounded the table; and after dinner, when wine and mirth had set them free from the observation of rigid ceremony, one of them inquired of Sir Richard how such an expensive train of domestics could be consistent with his fortune. Sir Richard very frankly confessed that they were fellows of whom he would very willingly be rid. And being then asked why he did not discharge them, declared that they were bailiffs who had introduced themselves with an execution, and whom, since he could not send them away, he had thought it convenient to embellish with liveries that they might do him credit while they stayed.

His friends were diverted with the expedient, and, by paying the debt, discharged their attendance, having obliged Sir Richard to promise that they should never again find him graced with a retinue of the same kind.

88

NICHOLAS ROWE (1674–1718)

AN English gentleman[1] . . . being very much noticed for his wit and poetry, and withal a man of no fortune, was recommended by a great many of the nobility of that kingdom, and being introduced to the Lord of Oxford, he asked him if he understood Spanish. The gentleman replied, No, but that in a little time he could still be master of it in such a degree as to qualify to serve in any station when His Lordship thought fit to employ him; and away he went and employed six or seven months in the close study of that language. And having acquired what he thought necessary (not doubting but he'd be employed in some business abroad, which he most desired), he waited on His Lordship and told him that he now believed he understood the Spanish language tolerably well. 'Well then,' replied my Lord, 'you'll have the pleasure of reading *Don Quixote* in the original, and 'tis the finest book in the world'; which was all that gentleman got for his long attendance and hard study.

[1] i.e. Rowe.

89

At twenty-five Rowe produced *The Ambitious Stepmother*, which was received with so much favour that he devoted himself from that time wholly to elegant literature. . . . He once (1704) tried to change his hand. He ventured on a comedy, and produced *The Biter*, with which, though it was unfavourably treated by the audience, he was himself delighted; for he is said to have sat in the house, laughing with great vehemence whenever he had in his own opinion produced a jest. But finding that he and the public had no sympathy of mirth he tried at lighter scenes no more.

90
SIR ROBERT WALPOLE (1676–1745)

When Sir Robert Walpole was dismissed from all his employments he retired to Houghton and walked into the Library; when, pulling down a book and holding it some minutes to his eyes, he suddenly and seeming sullenly exchanged it for another. He held that about half as long, and looking out a third returned it instantly to its shelf and burst into tears. 'I have led a life of business so long,' said he, 'that I have lost my taste for reading, and now—what shall I do?'

91
JOHN WARBURTON (1682–1759)

There is, among the Lansdowne manuscripts at the British Museum, a folio volume of no great bulk, which, if we believe the story it tells, is perhaps the most pitiful of all monuments to the vanity of antiquarian endeavour. For it embraces, or at least purports to embrace, the entire remains of that extensive collection of the unprinted drama of the earlier seventeenth century brought together, or supposed to have been brought together, about a hundred years later by John Warburton, Somerset Herald, prefaced by a long list of the treasures that have perished. The story of that disaster is one of the best known of literary anecdotes: how the zealous antiquary laboriously gathered together this unique collection of pieces by Shakespeare and others; how he handed it over for safe custody to his cook, who made use of the precious leaves for some obscure process connected with her trade, and how the owner made no further inquiry on the subject till he had devoured all but three and a half out of a total of some fifty or sixty plays. The story has been told over and over again with every kind of facetious adornment, till no history of literature is complete without it, and our national biography has to take serious account of the eccentric herald and his cook Elizabeth B. . . .

My own idea of what happened is somewhat as follows. Warburton in the course of his antiquarian researches came across a few manuscript plays and grew interested in the subject. He collected notes, probably from various sources, but chiefly from Humphrey Moseley's entries, and made out a list containing the titles of such pieces as he thought it might be possible to recover, in addition to those of the plays of which he had already become possessed. Some he actually did succeed in finding, and a few further manuscripts coming into his hands were added at the end of the list. The collection and list were then laid aside, a few manuscripts finding their way among the rest of the collection's archaeological litter, the bulk, however, within reach of the parsimonious fingers of Betsy the baker of pies. Long afterwards her master discovered his loss, and no longer in the least remembering either the extent of his collection or the nature of his list, added in a fit of not unnatural vexation the famous memorandum:

'After I had been many years Collecting these MSS Playes, through my own carelessness and the Ignorace [*sic*] of my Ser. in whose hands I had lodgd them they was unluckely burnd or put under Pye bottoms, excepting ye three which followes.' J.W.

If this be so, we have undoubtedly to lament the loss of a few pieces, perhaps of considerable interest, but not by any means the dramatic holocaust that has made famous the name of 'the pie-eating Somerset Herald'.

92
EUSTACE BUDGELL (1686–1737)

[Eustace Budgell, a cousin of Addison's, was probably always eccentric, but after he lost most of his money in South Sea stock his behaviour became more and more extravagant. In 1733 he was accused of forging the will of Dr. Matthew Tindal, and in his last years he was involved in numerous lawsuits which he defended unsuccessfully himself.]

AT last, after being cast in several of his own suits, and being distressed to the utmost, he determined to make away with himself. He had always thought very loosely of revelation, and latterly became an avowed deist; which, added to his pride, greatly disposed him to this resolution.

Accordingly, within a few days after the loss of his great cause, and his estates being decreed for the satisfaction of his creditors, in the year 1736 he took a boat at Somerset-Stairs (after filling his pockets with stones upon the beach), ordered the waterman to shoot the bridge, and while the boat was going under it threw himself over-board. Several days before, he had been visibly distracted in his mind, and almost mad, which makes such an action less wonderful. . . .

It has been said, Mr. Budgell was of opinion that when life becomes uneasy to support, and is overwhelmed with clouds and sorrows, that a man has a natural right to take it away, as it is better not to live than live in pain. The morning before he carried his notion of self-murder into execution he endeavoured to persuade his daughter to accompany him, which she very wisely refused. His argument to induce her was: life is not worth the holding.—Upon Mr. Budgell's bureau was found a slip of paper, in which were written these words:

> What Cato did, and Addison approv'd,
> Cannot be wrong.

93
ALEXANDER POPE (1688–1744)

THE famous Lord Halifax was rather a pretender to taste than really possessed of it. When I had finished the two or three first books of my translation of the *Iliad*, that Lord 'desired to have the pleasure of hearing them read at his house'. Addison, Congreve, and Garth were there at the reading. In four or five places Lord Halifax stopped me very civilly, and with a speech each time of much the same kind: 'I beg your pardon, Mr. Pope, but there is something in that passage that does not quite please me. Be so good as to mark the place and consider it a little at your leisure. I'm sure you can give it a better turn.'

I returned from Lord Halifax's with Dr. Garth in his chariot, and as we were going along was saying to the Doctor that my Lord had laid me under a good deal of difficulty by such loose and general observations; that I had been thinking over the passages almost ever since, and could not guess at what it was that offended his lordship in either of them. Garth laughed heartily at my embarrassment, said I had not been long enough acquainted with Lord Halifax to know his way yet, that I need not puzzle myself in looking those places over and over when I got home. 'All you need do', says he, 'is to leave them just as they are, call on Lord Halifax two or three months hence, thank him for his kind observation on those passages, and then read them to him as altered. I have known him much longer than you have, and will be answerable for the event.'

I followed his advice, waited on Lord Halifax some time after, said 'I hoped he would find his objections to those passages removed,' read them to him exactly as they were at first, and his lordship was extremely pleased with them and cried out: 'Ay, now they are perfectly right! Nothing can be better.'

94

[Pope to the Earl of Burlington: November 1716.]

My Lord—If your mare could speak, she would give you an account of the extraordinary company she had on the road; which since she cannot, I will.

It was the enterprising Mr. Lintott, the redoubtable rival of Mr. Tonson, who mounted on a stone-horse (no disagreeable companion to your Lordship's mare) overtook me in Windsor Forest. He said he heard I designed for Oxford, the seat of the muses, and would, as my bookseller, accompany me thither.

I asked him where he got his horse? He answered, he got it of his publisher. 'For that rogue, my printer', said he, 'disappointed me: I hoped to put him in a good humour by a treat at the tavern, of a brown fricassee of rabbits which cost two shillings, with two quarts of wine, besides my conversation. I thought myself cocksure of his horse, which he readily promised me, but said that Mr. Tonson had just such another design of going to Cambridge, expecting there the copy of *A Comment upon the Revelations*; and if Mr. Tonson went, he was pre-engaged to attend him, being to have the printing of the said copy. So in short, I borrowed this stone-horse of my publisher, which he had of Mr. Oldmixon for a debt; he lent me too the pretty boy you see after me; he was a smutty dog yesterday, and cost me near two hours to wash the ink off his face: but the devil is a fair-conditioned devil, and very forward in his catechise: if you have any more bags, he shall carry them.'

I thought Mr. Lintott's civility not to be neglected, so gave the boy a small bag, containing three shirts and an Elzevir Virgil; and mounting in an instant proceeded on the road, with my man before, my courteous stationer beside, and the aforesaid devil behind.

Mr. Lintott began in this manner: 'Now damn them! what if they should put it into the newspaper how you and I went together to Oxford? Why, what would I care? If I should go down into Sussex, they would say I was gone to the Speaker.[1] But what of that? If my son were but big enough to go on with the business, by God I would keep as good company as old Jacob.'[2]

Hereupon I inquired of his son. 'The lad', says he, 'has fine parts, but is somewhat sickly, *much as you are*—I spare for nothing in his education at Westminster. Pray, don't you think Westminster to be the best school in England? Most of the late ministry came out of it; so did many of this ministry. I hope the boy will make his fortune.'

'Don't you design to let him pass a year at Oxford?'—'To what purpose?' said he. 'The universities do but make pedants, and I intend to breed him a man of business.'

As Mr. Lintott was talking, I observed he sate uneasy on his saddle, for which I expressed some solicitude. 'Nothing,' says he, 'I can bear it well enough; but since we have the day before us, methinks it would be very pleasant for you to rest awhile under the woods.' When we were alighted, 'See here, what a mighty pretty Horace I have in my pocket! What if you amused yourself in turning an ode till we mount again? Lord! if you pleased, what a clever Miscellany might you make at leisure hours.' 'Perhaps I may,' said I, 'if we ride on; the motion is an aid to my fancy; a round trot very much awakens my spirits. Then jog on apace, and I'll think as hard as I can.'

Silence ensued for a full hour; after which Mr. Lintott lugged the reins, stopt short, and broke out, 'Well, sir, how far have you gone?' I answered, 'Seven miles.' 'Zounds, sir,' said Lintott, 'I thought you had done seven stanzas. Oldsworth in a ramble round Wimbledon-hill would translate a whole ode in half this time. I'll say that for Oldsworth (though I lost by his *Timothy*'s),[3] he translates an ode of Horace the *quickest* of any man in England. I remember Dr. King would write verses in a tavern three hours after he couldn't speak: and there's Sir Richard[4] in that rumbling old chariot of his, between Fleet-ditch and St. Giles's pound shall make you half a *Job*.'

'Pray, Mr. Lintott,' said I, 'now you talk of translators, what is your method of managing them?'—'Sir,' replied he, 'those are the saddest pack of rogues in the world. In a hungry fit, they'll swear they understand all the languages in the universe. I have known one of them take down a Greek book upon my counter and cry, "Ay, this is Hebrew, I must read it from the latter end." By God, I can never be sure in these fellows,

[1] Sir Spencer Compton, who lived in Eastbourne.

[2] Jacob Tonson, Lintott's chief rival.

[3] William Oldisworth wrote *A Dialogue between Timothy and Philatheus* (an answer to Matthew Tindal's *The Rights of the Christian Church*), which Lintott published in three volumes (1709–11).

[4] Sir Richard Blackmore, whose long poem, *A Paraphrase on the Book of Job*, was published in 1700.

for I neither understand Greek, Latin, French, nor Italian myself. But this is my way: I agree with them for ten shillings per sheet, with a proviso, that I will have their doings corrected by whom I please; so by one or other they are led at last to the true sense of an author; my judgement giving the negative to all my translators.'—'But how are you secure that those correctors may not impose upon you?'—'Why, I get any civil gentleman (especially any Scotchman) that comes into my shop to read the original to me in English; by this I know whether my first translator be deficient, and whether my corrector merits his money or no. I'll tell you what happened to me last month: I bargained with Sewell for a new version of Lucretius to publish against Tonson's; agreeing to pay the author so many shillings at his producing so many lines. He made a great progress in a very short time, and I gave it to the corrector to compare with the Latin; but he went directly to Creech's translation, and found it the same word for word, all but the first page. Now, what d'ye think I did? I arrested the translator for a cheat; nay, and I stopped the *corrector's pay* too, upon this proof that he had made use of Creech instead of the original.'

'Pray tell me next how you deal with the critics.'—'Sir,' said he, 'nothing more easy. I can silence the most formidable of them; the rich ones for a sheet apiece of the blotted manuscript, which costs me nothing. They'll go about with it to their acquaintance, and pretend they had it from the author, who submitted to their correction: this has given some of them such an air that in time they come to be consulted with, and dedicated to, as the top critics of the town.—As for the poor critics, I'll give you one instance of my management, by which you may guess the rest. A lean man that looked like a very good scholar came to me t'other day; he turned over Homer, shook his head, shrugged up his shoulders, and pished at every line of it. "*One would wonder*," says he, "*at the strange presumption of men; Homer is no such easy task that* every *stripling*, every *versifier*—" He was going on when my wife called to dinner. "Sir," said I, "will you please to eat a *piece of beef* with me?"—"Mr. Lintott," said he, "*I am sorry you should be at the expense of this great book, I am really concerned on your account.*"—"Sir, I am obliged to you: if you can dine upon a piece of beef, together with a slice of pudding—"—"Mr. Lintott, *I do not say but Mr. Pope, if he would condescend to advise with men of learning*—"—"Sir, the *pudding* is upon the table, if you please to go in—." My critic complies, he comes to a taste of your poetry, and tells me in the same breath that the book is commendable, and the pudding is excellent. Now, sir,' concluded Mr. Lintott, 'in return to the frankness I have shown, pray tell me, Is it the opinion of your friends at Court that my Lord Lansdowne will be brought to the bar or not?' I told him I heard *not*, and I hoped it, my Lord being one I had particular obligations to. 'That may be,' replied

Mr. Lintott, 'but by God if he is not, I shall lose the printing of a very good trial.'

These, my Lord, are a few traits by which you may discern the genius of my friend Mr. Lintott, which I have chosen for the subject of a letter. I dropped him as soon as I got to Oxford, and paid a visit to my Lord Carlton at Middleton.

95

'WHO is this Pope that I hear so much about?' said George II; 'I cannot discover what is his merit. Why will not my subjects write in prose? I hear a great deal, too, of Shakespeare, but I cannot read him, he is such a *bombast* fellow.'

96

SAMUEL RICHARDSON (1689–1761)

I WAS not eleven years old when I wrote, spontaneously, a letter to a widow of near fifty, who, pretending to a zeal for religion, and who was a constant frequenter of church ordinances, was continually fomenting quarrels and disturbances by backbiting and scandal among all her acquaintance. I collected from the Scripture texts that made against her. Assuming the style and address of a person in years, I exhorted her; I expostulated with her. But my hand-writing was known: I was challenged with it, and owned the boldness; for she complained of it to my mother with tears. My mother chid me for the freedom taken by such a boy with a woman of her years. But knowing that her son was not of a pert or forward nature, but, on the contrary, shy and bashful, she commended my principles, though she censured the liberty taken.

As a bashful and not forward boy, I was an early favourite with all the young women of taste and reading in the neighbourhood. Half a dozen of them then met to work with their needles, used, when they got a book they liked, and thought I should, to borrow me to read to them, their mothers sometimes with them; and both mothers and daughters used to be pleased with the observations they put me upon making.

I was not more than thirteen when three of these young women, unknown to each other, having an high opinion of my taciturnity, revealed to me their love secrets in order to induce me to give them copies to write after, or correct, for answer to their lovers' letters. Nor did any one of them ever know that I was the secretary to the others. I have been directed to chide, and even repulse, when an offence was either taken or given, at the very time that the heart of the chider or repulser was open before me, overflowing with esteem and affection; and the fair repulser dreading to be taken at her word, directing *this* word, or *that* expression, to be softened or changed. One, highly gratified with her lover's fervour and vows of everlasting love, has said, when I have asked her direction: 'I cannot tell you what to write; but (her heart on her lips) you cannot write too kindly.' All her fear only that she should incur slight for her kindness.

I recollect that I was early noted for having invention. I was not fond of play, as other boys: my schoolfellows used to call me *Serious* and *Gravity*. And five of them particularly delighted to single me out, either for a walk, or at their fathers' houses or at mine, to tell them stories, as they phrased it. Some I told them from my reading as true; others from my head, as mere invention; of which they would be most fond, and often were affected by them. One of them, particularly, I remember, was for putting me to write a history, as he called it, on the model of Tommy Potts. I now forget what it was; only, that it was of a servant-man preferred by a fine young lady (for his goodness) to a lord who was a libertine. All my stories carried with them, I am bold to say, a useful moral.

97

WHEN his story of *Pamela* first came out, some extracts got into the public papers, and used by that means to find their way down as far as Preston in Lancashire, where my aunt who told me the story then resided. One morning as she rose, the bells were set ringing and the flag was observed to fly from the great steeple. She rang her bell and inquired the reason of these rejoicings, when her maid came in bursting with joy, and said, 'Why, madam, poor Pamela's married at last; the news came down to us in this morning's paper.'

98

ONE day, as Mrs. Barbauld was going to Hampstead in the stage-coach, she had a Frenchman for her companion; and entering into conversation with him, she found that he was making an excursion to Hampstead for the express purpose of *seeing the house in the Flask Walk* where Clarissa Harlowe lodged. What a compliment to the genius of Richardson!

99

ONE day at his country-house at Northend, where a large company was assembled at dinner, a gentleman who was just returned from Paris, willing to please Mr. Richardson, mentioned to him a very flattering circumstance—that he had seen his *Clarissa* lying on the King's brother's table. Richardson observing that part of the company were engaged in talking to each other, affected then not to attend to it. But by and by, when there was a general silence, and he thought that the flattery might be fully heard, he addressed himself to the gentleman, 'I think, Sir, you were saying something about—', pausing in a high flutter of expectation. The gentleman, provoked at his inordinate vanity, resolved not to indulge it, and with an exquisitely sly air of indifference answered, 'A mere trifle, Sir, not worth repeating.' The mortification of Richardson was visible, and he did not speak ten words more the whole day. Dr. Johnson was present, and appeared to enjoy it much.

100

[An entry in Byron's diary, dated 'Ravenna, January 4, 1821'.]

I WAS out of spirits—read the papers—thought what *fame* was, on reading, in a case of murder, that Mr. Wych, grocer, at Tunbridge, sold some bacon, flour, cheese, and, it is believed, some plums, to some gipsy woman accused. He had on his counter (I quote faithfully) 'a *book*, the Life of *Pamela*, which he was *tearing* for *waste paper*, etc. etc. In the cheese was found, etc., and a *leaf* of *Pamela wrapt round the bacon.*' What would Richardson, the vainest and luckiest of *living* authors (i.e. while alive)—he who, with Aaron Hill, used to prophesy and chuckle over the presumed fall of Fielding (the *prose* Homer of human nature) and of Pope (the most beautiful of poets)—what would he have said, could he have traced his pages from their place on the French prince's toilets (see Boswell's *Johnson*) to the grocer's counter and the gipsy-murderess's bacon! ! !

101
LORD CHESTERFIELD (1694–1773)

I KNEW a gentleman who was so good a manager of his time that he would not even lose that small portion of it which the calls of nature obliged him to pass in the necessary-house; but gradually went through all the Latin poets in those moments. He bought, for example, a common edition of Horace, of which he tore off gradually a couple of pages, carried them with him to that necessary place, read them first, and then sent them down as a sacrifice to Cloacina: this was so much time fairly gained, and I recommend you to follow his example. . . . Books of science and of a grave sort must be read with continuity; but there are very many, and even very useful ones, which may be read with advantage by snatches and unconnectedly: such are all the good Latin poets, except Virgil in his *Æneid*, and such are most of the modern poets, in which you will find many pieces worth reading that will not take up above seven or eight minutes.

102
BISHOP WILLIAM WARBURTON (1698–1779)

[James Quin, Garrick's chief rival and a noted wit, retired from the stage at the close of the 1752 season. Warburton, whose marriage to the favourite niece of Ralph Allen (the original of Fielding's Squire Allworthy) had accelerated his rise in the Church, and who managed to combine arrogance, self-approval, and a belief in his own omniscience with an eye to the main chance, was one of the least liked ecclesiastics of the eighteenth century.]

MR. WARBURTON, about the year 1750 or 1752, being in company with Quin the player at Mr. Allen's, near Bath, took several opportunities of being sharp upon him on the subject of his love of eating and his voluptuous life. However, in the course of the evening, he said he should be obliged to Quin for 'a touch of his quality', as he could never again see him on the stage. Quin said that plays were then quite out of his head; however, he believed he remembered a few lines of Pierre;[1] on which he got up, and looking directly at Mr. Allen, repeated *ore rotunda*—

Honest men
Are the soft easy cushions on which knaves
Repose and fatten.

Warburton gave him no further trouble for the rest of the evening.

[1] In Otway's *Venice Preserved*, Act I, lines 126–8.

103
JAMES THOMSON (1700–48)

In the year 1730, about six years after he had been in London, he brought a tragedy upon the stage called *Sophonisba*. . . . Mr. Thomson makes one of his characters address Sophonisba in a line which some critics reckoned the false pathetic:

O! Sophonisba, Sophonisba, oh!

Upon which a smart from the pit cried out,

Oh! Jamey Thomson, Jamey Thomson, oh!

104
JOHN DYER (1700?–58)

[By a statute of Charles II, designed to encourage the wool trade, it was made illegal for the dead to be buried in anything but woollen.]

In 1757 Dyer published *The Fleece*, his greatest poetical work, of which I will not suppress a ludicrous story. Dodsley the bookseller was one day mentioning it to a critical visitor, with more expectation of success than the other could easily admit. In the conversation the author's age was asked, and being represented as advanced in life, 'He will', said the critic, 'be buried in woollen.'

105
RICHARD SAVAGE (d. 1743)

[Richard Savage, who claimed to be the son of the fourth Earl Rivers and the Countess of Macclesfield, lived a precarious existence for the greater part of his life. From time to time he was assisted by various friends (among whom Alexander Pope was one of the most patient and persistent); but his improvidence and his quickness to take offence defeated their attempts to help him. In his *Life of Mr. Richard Savage*, Johnson described the final effort made to provide for Savage, and its inevitable failure.]

SUCH were his misfortunes, which he yet bore, not only with decency, but with cheerfulness; nor was his gaiety clouded even by his last disappointments, though he was in a short time reduced to the lowest degree of distress, and often wanted both lodging and food. At this time he gave another instance of the insurmountable obstinacy of his spirit: his clothes were worn out, and he received notice that at a coffee-house some clothes and linen were left for him—the person who sent them did not, I believe, inform him to whom he was obliged, that he might spare the perplexity of acknowledging the benefit—but though the offer was so far generous it was made with some neglect of ceremonies, which Mr. Savage so much resented that he refused the present, and declined to enter the house till the clothes that were designed for him were taken away.

His distress was now publicly known, and his friends, therefore, thought it proper to concert some measures for his relief; and one of them[1] wrote a letter to him, in which he expressed his concern 'for the miserable withdrawing of his pension'; and gave him hopes that in a short time he should find himself supplied with a competence, 'without any dependence on those little creatures which we are pleased to call the Great'.

The scheme proposed for this happy and independent subsistence was that he should retire into Wales, and receive an allowance of fifty pounds a year, to be raised by a subscription, on which he was to live privately in a cheap place, without aspiring any more to affluence, or having any further care of reputation.

This offer Mr. Savage gladly accepted, though with intentions very different from those of his friends; for they proposed that he should continue an exile from London for ever, and spend all the remaining part of his life at Swansea; but he designed only to take the opportunity, which this scheme offered him, of retreating for a short time that he might prepare his play for the stage and his other works for the press, and then to return to London to exhibit his tragedy, and live upon the profits of his own labour. . . .

While this scheme was ripening his friends directed him to take a lodging in the liberties of the Fleet, that he might be secure from his creditors, and sent him every Monday a guinea, which he commonly spent before the next morning, and trusted, after his usual manner, the remaining part of the week to the bounty of fortune.

He now began very sensibly to feel the miseries of dependence. Those by whom he was to be supported began to prescribe to him with an air of authority, which he knew not how decently to resent nor patiently to bear; and he soon discovered from the conduct of most of his subscribers that he was yet in the hands of 'little creatures'. . . .

[1] Pope.

After many alterations and delays, a subscription was at length raised, which did not amount to fifty pounds a year, though twenty were paid by one gentleman:[1] such was the generosity of mankind that what had been done by a player[2] without solicitation could not now be effected by application and interest; and Savage had a great number to court and to obey for a pension less than that which Mrs. Oldfield paid him without exacting any servilities.

Mr. Savage, however, was satisfied and willing to retire, and was convinced that the allowance, though scanty, would be more than sufficient for him, being now determined to commence a rigid œconomist, and to live according to the exactest rules of frugality; for nothing was in his opinion more contemptible than a man who, when he knew his income, exceeded it; and yet he confessed that instances of such folly were too common, and lamented that such men were not to be trusted with their own money.

Full of these salutary resolutions he left London in July 1739, having taken leave with great tenderness of his friends, and parted from the author of this narrative[3] with tears in his eyes. He was furnished with fifteen guineas, and informed that they would be sufficient not only for the expense of his journey, but for his support in Wales for some time, and that there remained but little more of the first collection. He promised a strict adherence to his maxims of parsimony, and went away in the stage-coach; nor did his friends expect to hear from him till he informed them of his arrival at Swansea.

But when they least expected arrived a letter dated the fourteenth day after his departure, in which he sent them word that he was yet upon the road, and without money, and that he therefore could not proceed without a remittance. They then sent him the money that was in their hands, with which he was enabled to reach Bristol, from whence he was to go to Swansea by water.

At Bristol he found an embargo laid upon the shipping, so that he could not immediately obtain a passage; and being therefore obliged to stay there some time he, with his usual felicity, ingratiated himself with many of the principal inhabitants, was invited to their houses, distinguished at their public feasts, and treated with a regard that gratified his vanity, and therefore easily engaged his affection.

He began very early after his retirement to complain of the conduct of his friends in London, and irritated many of them so much by his letters that they withdrew, however honourably, their contributions; and it is

[1] Pope.

[2] Anne Oldfield, who 'allowed him a settled pension of fifty pounds a year, which was during her life regularly paid' (Johnson).

[3] Johnson.

believed that little more was paid him than the twenty pounds a year which were allowed him by the gentleman who proposed the subscription.

After some stay at Bristol he retired to Swansea, the place originally proposed for his residence, where he lived about a year, very much dissatisfied with the diminution of his salary. . . .

It may be alleged, and perhaps justly, that he was petulant and contemptuous; that he more frequently reproached his subscribers for not giving him more, than thanked them for what he received; but it is to be remembered that his conduct, and this is the worst charge that can be drawn up against him, did them no real injury, and that it therefore ought rather to have been pitied than resented; at least, the resentment it might provoke ought to have been generous and manly: epithets which his conduct will hardly deserve that starves the man whom he has persuaded to put himself in his power. . . .

He endeavoured, indeed, to release himself, and, with an intent to return to London, went to Bristol, where a repetition of the kindness which he had formerly found invited him to stay. He was not only caressed and treated, but had a collection made for him of about thirty pounds, with which it had been happy if he had immediately departed for London; but his negligence did not suffer him to consider that such proofs of kindness were not often to be expected, and that this ardour of benevolence was in a great degree the effect of novelty, and might, probably, be every day less; and therefore he took no care to improve the happy time, but was encouraged by one favour to hope for another, till at length generosity was exhausted and officiousness wearied.

Another part of his misconduct was the practice of prolonging his visits to unseasonable hours, and disconcerting all the families into which he was admitted. This was an error in a place of commerce which all the charms of his conversation could not compensate; for what trader would purchase such airy satisfaction by the loss of solid gain, which must be the consequence of midnight merriment, as those hours which were gained at night were generally lost in the morning?

Thus Mr. Savage, after the curiosity of the inhabitants was gratified, found the number of his friends daily decreasing, perhaps without suspecting for what reason their conduct was altered; for he still continued to harass with his nocturnal intrusions those that yet countenanced him and admitted him to their houses. . . .

He was always full of his design of returning to London to bring his tragedy upon the stage; but, having neglected to depart with the money that was raised for him, he could not afterwards procure a sum sufficient to defray the expenses of his journey: nor perhaps would a fresh supply have had any other effect than, by putting immediate pleasures in his power, to have driven the thoughts of his journey out of his mind.

While he was thus spending the day in contriving a scheme for the morrow, distress stole upon him by imperceptible degrees. His conduct had already wearied some of those who were at first enamoured of his conversation; but he might, perhaps, still have devolved to others, whom he might have entertained with equal success, had not the decay of his clothes made it no longer consistent with their vanity to admit him to their tables or to associate with him in public places. He now began to find every man from home at whose house he called; and was therefore no longer able to procure the necessaries of life, but wandered about the town, slighted and neglected, in quest of a dinner, which he did not always obtain.

To complete his misery he was pursued by the officers for small debts which he had contracted; and was therefore obliged to withdraw from the small number of friends from whom he had still reason to hope for favours. His custom was to lie in bed the greatest part of the day and to go out in the dark with the utmost privacy, and after having paid his visit return again before morning to his lodging, which was in the garret of an obscure inn.

[At last, on 10 January 1743, when he was returning to his lodging, he was arrested for a debt of about eight pounds which he owed at a coffee-house, and was taken into custody. He was treated 'with great humanity' by the keeper of the prison, and Pope continued to send him some financial support. In the summer of 1743, however, Savage became seriously ill.]

The symptoms grew every day more formidable, but his condition did not enable him to procure any assistance. The last time that the keeper saw him was on July the 31st, 1743, when Savage, seeing him at his bed-side, said, with an uncommon earnestness, 'I have something to say to you, Sir'; but, after a pause, moved his head in a melancholy manner, and, finding himself unable to recollect what he was going to communicate, said, ''Tis gone!' The keeper soon after left him; and the next morning he died. He was buried in the churchyard of St. Peter, at the expense of the keeper.

Such were the life and death of Richard Savage, a man equally distinguished by his virtues and vices; and at once remarkable for his weaknesses and abilities. . . .

Those are no proper judges of his conduct who have slumbered away their time on the down of plenty, nor will any wise man presume to say, 'Had I been in Savage's condition, I should have lived or written better than Savage.'

106
THOMAS BIRCH (1705–66)

[Birch, an industrious scholar, was in turn biographer, historian, and editor; a notable collector of facts and a determined preserver of biographical anecdotes.]

DR. BIRCH was very fond of angling, and devoted much time to that amusement. In order to deceive the fish, he had a dress constructed, which, when he put it on, made him appear like an old tree. His arms he conceived would appear like branches, and the line like a long spray. In this sylvan attire he used to take root by the side of a favourite stream, and imagined that his motions might seem to the fish to be the effect of the wind. He pursued this amusement for some years in the same habit, till he was ridiculed out of it by his friends.

107
DAVID MALLET (1705?–65)

DAVID MALLET being in company with Bishop Warburton, to whom Pope had consigned the care of his works, and who, he thought, had some intention of writing Mr. Pope's life, told him he had an anecdote which he believed nobody knew but himself. 'I was sitting one day with Mr. Pope in his last illness. "Mr. Mallet," said he, "I have had an odd kind of a vision; methought I saw my own head open, and Apollo come out of it; then I saw your head open, and Apollo went into it; after which our heads closed up again." ' Warburton replied: 'Why, Sir, if I had an intention of writing your life this might, perhaps, be a proper anecdote; but I do not see that in Mr. Pope's it will be of any consequence whatever.'

108
SAMUEL BOYSE (1708–49)

IT was about the year 1740 that Mr. Boyse, reduced to the last extremity of human wretchedness, had not a shirt, a coat, or any kind of apparel to put on; the sheets in which he lay were carried to the pawnbroker's, and he was obliged to be confined to bed, with no other covering than a blanket. He had little support but what he got by writing letters to his friends in the most abject style. He was perhaps ashamed to let this instance of distress be known to his friends, which might be the occasion of his remaining six weeks in that situation. During this time he had some employment in writing verses for the Magazines; and whoever had seen him in his study, must have thought the object singular enough. He sat up in bed with the blanket wrapt about him, through which he had cut a hole large enough to admit his arm, and placing the paper upon his knee, scribbled in the best manner he could the verses he was obliged to make. Whatever he got by those, or any of his begging letters, was but just sufficient for the preservation of life. And perhaps he would have remained much longer in this distressful state, had not a compassionate gentleman, upon hearing this circumstance related, ordered his clothes to be taken out of pawn, and enabled him to appear again abroad.

This six weeks' penance one would imagine sufficient to deter him for the future from suffering himself to be exposed to such distresses; but by a long habit of want it grew familiar to him, and as he had less delicacy than other men, he was perhaps less afflicted with his exterior meanness. For the future, whenever his distresses so pressed as to induce him to dispose of his shirt, he fell upon an artificial method of supplying one. He cut some white paper in slips, which he tied round his wrists, and in the same manner supplied his neck. In this plight he frequently appeared abroad, with the additional inconvenience of want of breeches.

109
JOHN CAMPBELL (1708–75)

DR. CAMPBELL, looking once into a pamphlet at a bookseller's shop, liked it so well as to purchase it; and it was not till he had read it half through that he discovered it to be of his own composition. . . .

Campbell was a prolific miscellaneous writer of considerable ability and wide general knowledge. Dr. Johnson was well acquainted with him, and had a sort of amused respect for a man who wrote at once so much and so well, and whom he once described as 'the richest author that ever grazed the common of literature'. He was prepared to concede that Campbell was not always rigidly truthful in his conversation, but he found no such carelessness in his books ('Campbell will lie, but he never lies on paper'). At one time Johnson was a frequent visitor at Campbell's house: 'I used to go pretty often to Campbell's on a Sunday evening, till I began to consider that the shoals of Scotchmen who flocked about him might probably say, when anything of mine was well done "Ay, ay, he has learnt this of CAWMELL!" '

110

ONCE, when the conversation turned on Campbell, Johnson mentioned that he had married 'a printer's devil'. REYNOLDS. 'A printer's devil, Sir! Why, I thought a printer's devil was a creature with a black face and in rags.' JOHNSON. 'Yes, Sir. But I suppose he had her face washed, and put clean clothes on her. (Then looking very serious, and very earnest.) And she did not disgrace him;—the woman had a bottom of good sense.' The word *bottom*, thus introduced, was so ludicrous when contrasted with his gravity that most of us could not forbear tittering and laughing; though I recollect that the Bishop of Killaloe kept his countenance with perfect steadiness, while Miss Hannah More slyly hid her face behind a lady's back who sat on the same settee with her. His pride could not bear that any expression of his should excite ridicule when he did not intend it; he therefore resolved to assume and exercise despotic power, glanced sternly around, and called out in a strong tone, 'Where's the merriment?' Then collecting himself, and looking aweful, to make us feel how he could impose restraint, and as it were searching his mind for a still more ludicrous word, he slowly pronounced, 'I say the *woman* was *fundamentally* sensible;' as if he had said, Hear this now, and laugh if you dare. We all sat composed as at a funeral.

111
HENRY FIELDING (1707–54)

FIELDING, hearing that a friend of his was dejected because he was so deeply in debt, said to his informant, 'Is that all? How happy I should be if I could only get £500 deeper in debt than I am already.'

112

HENRY FIELDING being once in company with the Earl of Denbigh, and the conversation turning on Fielding's being of the Denbigh family, the Earl asked the reason why they spelt their names differently; the Earl's family doing it with the E first (Feilding), and Mr. Henry Fielding with the I first (Fielding). 'I cannot tell, my Lord,' answered Harry, 'except it be that my branch of the family were the first that knew how to spell.'

113
SAMUEL JOHNSON (1709–84)

It is told that, when a child of three years old, Dr. Johnson chanced to tread upon a duckling, the eleventh of a brood, and killed it; upon which, it is said, he dictated to his mother the following epitaph:

> Here lies good master duck
> Whom Samuel Johnson trod on;
> If it had liv'd, it had been *good luck*,
> For then we'd had an *odd one*.

There is surely internal evidence that this little composition combines in it what no child of three years could produce, without an extension of its faculties by immediate inspiration; yet Mrs. Lucy Porter, Dr. Johnson's step-daughter, positively maintained to me, in his presence, that there could be no doubt of the truth of this anecdote, for she had heard it from his mother. So difficult is it to obtain an authentic relation of facts, and such authority may there be for error; for he assured me that his father made the verses, and wished to pass them for his child's. He added, 'My father was a foolish old man; that is to say, foolish in talking of his children.'

114

Guthrie, the historian, had from July 1736 composed the parliamentary speeches for the magazines;[1] but, from the beginning of the session which opened on the 19th of November 1740, Johnson succeeded to that department and continued it from that time to the debate on spirituous liquors, which happened in the House of Lords in February, 1742–3. The eloquence, the force of argument, and the splendour of language displayed in the several speeches are well known, and universally admired. The whole has been collected in two volumes by Mr. Stockdale, and may form a proper supplement to this edition. That Johnson was the author of the debates during that period was not generally known; but the secret transpired several years afterwards, and was avowed by himself on the following occasion. Mr. Wedderburne (now Lord Loughborough), Dr. Johnson, Dr. Francis (the translator of Horace), the present writer,[2] and

[1] William Guthrie (1708–70), who wrote the parliamentary reports in the *Gentleman's Magazine*.

[2] Arthur Murphy (1727–1805).

others dined with the late Mr. Foote. An important debate towards the end of Sir Robert Walpole's administration being mentioned, Dr. Francis observed that 'Mr. Pitt's speech on that occasion was the best he had ever read.' He added that 'he had employed eight years of his life in the study of Demosthenes, and finished a translation of that celebrated orator, with all the decorations of style and language within the reach of his capacity; but he had met with nothing equal to the speech above-mentioned.' Many of the company remembered the debate; and some passages were cited, with the approbation and applause of all present. During the ardour of conversation Johnson remained silent. As soon as the warmth of praise subsided, he opened with these words: 'That speech I wrote in a garret in Exeter-street.' The company was struck with astonishment. After staring at each other in silent amaze, Dr. Francis asked how that speech could be written by him. 'Sir,' said Johnson, 'I wrote it in Exeter-street. I never had been in the gallery of the House of Commons but once. Cave had interest with the door-keepers. He, and the persons employed under him, gained admittance; they brought away the subject of discussion, the names of the speakers, the side they took, and the order in which they rose, together with notes of the arguments advanced in the course of the debate. The whole was afterwards communicated to me, and I composed the speeches in the form which they now have in the Parliamentary Debates.' To this discovery Dr. Francis made answer: 'Then, Sir, you have exceeded Demosthenes himself; for to say that you have exceeded Francis's Demosthenes would be saying nothing.' The rest of the company bestowed lavish encomiums on Johnson: one, in particular, praised his impartiality; observing that he dealt out reason and eloquence with an equal hand to both parties. 'That is not quite true,' said Johnson: 'I saved appearances tolerably well; but I took care that the WHIG DOGS should not have the best of it.'

115

IN 1743–4, Osborne the bookseller, who kept a shop in Gray's-Inn, purchased the Earl of Oxford's library, at the price of thirteen thousand pounds. He projected a catalogue in five octavo volumes, at five shillings each. Johnson was employed in that painful drudgery. He was likewise to collect all such small tracts as were in any degree worth preserving, in order to reprint and publish the whole in a collection, called 'The Harleian Miscellany'. The catalogue was completed; and the Miscellany in 1749 was published in eight quarto volumes. In this business Johnson was a day-labourer for immediate subsistence, not unlike Gustavus Vasa working in the mines of Dalecarlia. What Wilcox, a bookseller of eminence in the Strand, said to Johnson, on his first arrival in town, was now confirmed. He lent our author five guineas, and then asked him, 'How do you mean to earn your livelihood in this town?' 'By my literary labours,' was the answer. Wilcox, staring at him, shook his head: 'By your literary labours!—You had better buy a porter's knot.' Johnson used to tell this anecdote to Mr. Nichols; but he said, 'Wilcox was one of my best friends, and he meant well.' In fact, Johnson, while employed in Gray's-Inn, may be said to have carried a porter's knot. He paused occasionally to peruse the book that came to his hand. Osborne thought that such curiosity tended to nothing but delay, and objected to it with all the pride and insolence of a man who knew that he paid daily wages. In the dispute that of course ensued, Osborne, with that roughness which was natural to him, enforced his argument by giving the lie. Johnson seized a folio, and knocked the bookseller down.

116

SOON after the publication of Johnson's Life of Savage, which was anonymous, Mr. Walter Harte, dining with Mr. Cave at St. John's Gate,[1] took occasion to speak very handsomely of the work. Cave told Harte, when they next met, that he had made a man very happy the other day at his house by the encomiums he bestowed on the author of Savage's Life. 'How could that be?' says Harte; 'none were present but you and I.' Cave replied, 'You might observe I sent a plate of victuals behind the screen. There skulked the Biographer, one Johnson, whose dress was so shabby that he durst not make his appearance. He overheard our conversation; and your applauding his performance delighted him exceedingly.'

117

JOHNSON received from some unknown source a letter deriving the word 'curmudgeon' from *cœur méchant*, or wicked heart—a wild enough guess, which pleased the doctor so much that he adopted it in his *Dictionary*, giving due credit to 'unknown correspondent'. Twenty years later, Dr. Ash, preparing a dictionary of his own,[2] was struck by this gem, and

[1] The printing office in Clerkenwell of Edward Cave, who published the *Gentleman's Magazine*. At this time (1744) Johnson, who was working for Cave, found it difficult to make ends meet.

[2] John Ash (1727?–79) published his *New and Complete Dictionary of the English Language* in 1775.

transferred it to his own pages. But, wishing all the glory of the discovery for himself, he gave no credit to Johnson, and informed a wondering world that curmudgeon was formed from *cœur*, 'unknown', and *méchant*, 'correspondent'.

118

LORD CHESTERFIELD, to whom Johnson had paid the high compliment of addressing to his Lordship the Plan of his Dictionary, had behaved to him in such a manner as to excite his contempt and indignation. . . . When the Dictionary was upon the eve of publication, Lord Chesterfield, who, it is said, had flattered himself with expectations that Johnson would dedicate the work to him, attempted in a courtly manner to sooth, and insinuate himself with the Sage, conscious, as it should seem, of the cold indifference with which he had treated its learned author; and further attempted to conciliate him by writing two papers in *The World* in recommendation of the work; and it must be confessed that they contain some studied compliments, so finely turned, that if there had been no previous offence, it is probable that Johnson would have been highly delighted. Praise in general was pleasing to him; but by praise from a man of rank and elegant accomplishments he was peculiarly gratified. . . .

This courtly device failed of its effect. Johnson, who thought that 'all was false and hollow', despised the honeyed words, and was even indignant that Lord Chesterfield should, for a moment, imagine that he could be the dupe of such an artifice. His expression to me concerning Lord Chesterfield upon this occasion was, 'Sir, after making great professions, he had for many years taken no notice of me; but when my Dictionary was coming out, he fell a scribbling in *The World* about it. Upon which, I wrote him a letter expressed in civil terms, but such as might shew him that I did not mind what he said or wrote, and that I had done with him.' . . .

TO THE RIGHT HONOURABLE THE EARL OF CHESTERFIELD.

February 7, 1755.

My Lord,

I have been lately informed, by the proprietor of *The World*, that two papers, in which my Dictionary is recommended to the public, were written by your Lordship. To be so distinguished is an honour, which, being very little accustomed to favours from the great, I know not well how to receive, or in what terms to acknowledge.

When, upon some slight encouragement, I first visited your Lordship, I was overpowered, like the rest of mankind, by the enchantment of your address; and could not forbear to wish that I might boast myself *Le vainqueur du vainqueur de la terre*;—that I might obtain that regard for which I saw the world contending; but I found my attendance so little encouraged, that neither pride nor modesty would suffer me to continue it. When I had once addressed your Lordship in public, I had exhausted all the art of pleasing which a retired and uncourtly scholar can possess. I had done all that I could; and no man is well pleased to have his all neglected, be it ever so little.

Seven years, my Lord, have now passed since I waited in your outward rooms, or was repulsed from your door; during which time I have been pushing on my work through difficulties, of which it is useless to complain, and have brought it, at last, to the verge of publication, without one act of assistance, one word of encouragement, or one smile of favour. Such treatment I did not expect, for I never had a Patron before.

The shepherd in Virgil grew at last acquainted with Love, and found him a native of the rocks.

Is not a Patron, my Lord, one who looks with unconcern on a man struggling for life in the water, and, when he has reached the ground, encumbers him with help? The notice which you have been pleased to take of my labours, had it been early, had been kind; but it has been delayed till I am indifferent, and cannot enjoy it; till I am solitary, and cannot impart it;[1] till I am known, and do not want it. I hope it is no very cynical asperity not to confess obligations where no benefit has been received, or to be unwilling that the Public should consider me as owning that to a Patron which Providence has enabled me to do for myself.

Having carried on my work thus far with so little obligation to any favourer of learning, I shall not be disappointed though I should conclude it, if less be possible, with less; for I have been long wakened from that dream of hope, in which I once boasted myself with so much exultation,

My Lord,
Your Lordship's most humble,
Most obedient servant,
SAM. JOHNSON.

119

MRS. DIGBY told me that when she lived in London with her sister Mrs. Brooke, they were, every now and then, honoured by the visits of Dr. Samuel Johnson. He called on them one day, soon after the publication of his immortal dictionary. The two ladies paid him due compliments on the occasion. Among other topics of praise, they very much commended the omission of all naughty words. 'What! my dears! then you have been looking for them?' said the moralist. The ladies, confused at being caught, dropped the subject of the dictionary.

[1] Johnson's wife had died on 17 March 1752.

120

[Boswell arranges a confrontation.]

My desire of being acquainted with celebrated men of every description had made me, much about the same time [1776], obtain an introduction to Dr. Samuel Johnson and to John Wilkes, Esq. Two men more different could perhaps not be selected out of all mankind. They had even attacked one another with some asperity in their writings; yet I lived in habits of friendship with both. I could fully relish the excellence of each; for I have ever delighted in that intellectual chemistry which can separate good qualities from evil in the same person. . . . I conceived an irresistible wish, if possible, to bring Dr. Johnson and Mr. Wilkes together. How to manage it was a nice and difficult matter.

My worthy booksellers and friends, Messieurs Dilly in the Poultry, at whose hospitable and well-covered table I have seen a greater number of literary men than at any other, except that of Sir Joshua Reynolds, had invited me to meet Mr. Wilkes and some more gentlemen on Wednesday, 15 May. 'Pray,' said I, 'let us have Dr. Johnson.'—'What, with Mr. Wilkes? not for the world,' said Mr. Edward Dilly: 'Dr. Johnson would never forgive me.' 'Come,' said I, 'if you'll let me negotiate for you, I will be answerable that all will go well.' Dilly. 'Nay, if you will take it upon you, I am sure I shall be very happy to see them both here.'

Notwithstanding the high veneration which I entertained for Dr. Johnson, I was sensible that he was sometimes a little actuated by the spirit of contradiction, and by means of that I hoped I should gain my point. I was persuaded that if I had come upon him with a direct proposal, 'Sir, will you dine in company with Jack Wilkes?' he would have flown into a passion, and would probably have answered, 'Dine with Jack Wilkes, sir! I'd as soon dine with Jack Ketch.' I therefore, while we were sitting quietly by ourselves at his house in an evening, took occasion to open my plan thus:—'Mr. Dilly, sir, sends his respectful compliments to you, and would be happy if you would do him the honour to dine with him on Wednesday next along with me, as I must soon go to Scotland.' Johnson. 'Sir, I am obliged to Mr. Dilly. I will wait upon him—' Boswell. 'Provided, sir, I suppose, that the company which he is to have is agreeable to you.' Johnson. 'What do you mean, sir? What do you take me for? Do you think I am so ignorant of the world as to imagine that I am to prescribe to a gentleman what company he is to have at his table?' Boswell. 'I beg your pardon, sir, for wishing to prevent you from meeting people whom you might not like. Perhaps he may have some of what he calls his patriotic friends with him.' Johnson. 'Well, sir, and what then? What care *I* for his *patriotic friends*? Poh!' BOSWELL. 'I should not be surprised to find Jack Wilkes there.' JOHNSON. 'And if Jack Wilkes *should* be there, what is that to *me*, sir? My dear friend, let us have no more of this. I am sorry to be angry with you; but really it is treating me strangely to talk to me as if I could not meet any company whatever, occasionally.' BOSWELL. 'Pray forgive me, sir: I meant well. But you shall meet whoever comes, for me.' Thus I secured him, and told Dilly that he would find him very well pleased to be one of his guests on the day appointed.

Upon the much-expected Wednesday, I called on him about half an hour before dinner, as I often did when we were to dine out together, to see that he was ready in time, and to accompany him. I found him buffeting his books, as upon a former occasion, covered with dust, and making no preparation for going abroad. 'How is this, sir?' said I. 'Don't you recollect that you are to dine at Mr. Dilly's?' JOHNSON. 'Sir, I did not think of going to Dilly's: it went out of my head. I have ordered dinner at home with Mrs. Williams.'[1] BOSWELL. 'But, my dear sir, you know you were engaged to Mr. Dilly, and I told him so. He will expect you, and will be much disappointed if you don't come. JOHNSON. 'You must talk to Mrs. Williams about this.'

Here was a sad dilemma. I feared that what I was so confident I had secured would yet be frustrated. He had accustomed himself to show Mrs. Williams such a degree of humane attention as frequently imposed some restraint upon him; and I knew that if she should be obstinate he would not stir. I hastened downstairs to the blind lady's room, and told her I was in great uneasiness, for Dr. Johnson had engaged to me to dine this day at Mr. Dilly's, but that he had told me he had forgotten his engagement, and had ordered dinner at home. 'Yes, sir,' said she, pretty peevishly, 'Dr. Johnson is to dine at home.'—'Madam,' said I, 'his respect for you is such that I know he will not leave you unless you absolutely desire it. But as you have so much of his company, I hope you will be good enough to forgo it for a day; as Mr. Dilly is a very worthy man, has frequently had agreeable parties at his house for Dr. Johnson, and will be vexed if the Doctor neglects him today. And then, madam, be pleased to consider my situation; I carried the message, and I assured Mr. Dilly that Dr. Johnson was to come, and no doubt he has made a dinner, and invited a company, and boasted of the honour he expected to have. I shall be quite disgraced if the Doctor is not there.' She gradually softened to my solicitations, which were certainly as earnest as most entreaties to ladies upon any occasion, and was graciously pleased to empower me to tell Dr. Johnson, 'That all things considered, she thought he should certainly go.' I flew

[1] Miss Anna Williams (1706–83), the blind lady who had an apartment in Johnson's house. On 22 September 1783, Johnson wrote to Mrs. Montagu: 'Thirty years and more she has been my companion, and her death has left me very desolate.'

back to him still in dust, and careless of what should be the event, 'indifferent in his choice to go or stay'; but as soon as I had announced to him Mrs. Williams's consent, he roared, 'Frank, a clean shirt,' and was very soon dressed. When I had him fairly seated in a hackney-coach with me, I exulted as much as a fortune-hunter who has got an heiress into a post-chaise with him to set out for Gretna-Green.

When we entered Mr. Dilly's drawing room, he found himself in the midst of a company he did not know. I kept myself snug and silent, watching how he would conduct himself. I observed him whispering to Mr. Dilly, 'Who is that gentleman, sir?'—'Mr. Arthur Lee.'—JOHNSON. 'Too, too, too' (under his breath), which was one of his habitual mutterings. Mr. Arthur Lee could not but be very obnoxious to Johnson, for he was not only a *patriot* but an *American*. He was afterwards minister from the United States at the court of Madrid. 'And who is the gentleman in lace?' —'Mr. Wilkes, sir.' This information confounded him still more; he had some difficulty to restrain himself, and taking up a book, sat down upon a window-seat and read, or at least kept his eye upon it intently for some time, till he composed himself. His feelings, I dare say, were awkward enough. But he no doubt recollected his having rated me for supposing that he could be at all disconcerted by any company, and he therefore resolutely set himself to behave quite as an easy man of the world, who could adapt himself at once to the disposition and manners of those whom he might chance to meet.

The cheering sound of 'Dinner is upon the table' dissolved his reverie, and we *all* sat down without any symptom of ill humour. There were present, besides Mr. Wilkes and Mr. Arthur Lee, who was an old companion of mine when he studied physic at Edinburgh, Mr. (now Sir John) Miller, Dr. Lettsom, and Mr. Slater the druggist. Mr. Wilkes placed himself next to Dr. Johnson, and behaved to him with so much attention and politeness, that he gained upon him insensibly. No man eat more heartily than Johnson, or loved better what was nice and delicate. Mr Wilkes was very assiduous in helping him to some fine veal. 'Pray give me leave, sir:—it is better here. A little of the brown—some fat, sir—a little of the stuffing—some gravy.—Let me have the pleasure of giving you some butter.—Allow me to recommend a squeeze of this orange;—or the lemon, perhaps, may have more zest.'—'Sir, sir, I am obliged to you, sir,' cried Johnson, bowing, and turning his head to him with a look for some time of 'surly virtue', but, in a short while, of complacency. . . .

Mr. Arthur Lee mentioned some Scotch who had taken possession of a barren part of America, and wondered why they should choose it. JOHNSON. 'Why, sir, all barrenness is comparative. The *Scotch* would not know it to be barren.' BOSWELL. 'Come, come, he is flattering the English. You have now been in Scotland, sir, and say if you did not see meat and drink enough there.' JOHNSON. 'Why yes, sir; meat and drink enough to give the inhabitants sufficient strength to run away from home.' All these quick and lively sallies were said sportively, quite in jest, and with a smile, which showed that he meant only wit. Upon this topic he and Mr. Wilkes could perfectly assimilate; here was a bond of union between them, and I was conscious that as both of them had visited Caledonia, both were fully satisfied of the strange narrow ignorance of those who imagine that it is a land of famine. But they amused themselves with persevering in the old jokes. When I claimed a superiority for Scotland over England in one respect, that no man can be arrested there for a debt merely because another swears it against him, but there must first be the judgement of a court of law ascertaining its justice; and that a seizure of the person, before judgement is obtained, can take place only if his creditor should swear that he is about to fly from the country, or, as it is technically expressed, is *in meditatione fugae*—WILKES. 'That, I should think, may be safely sworn of all the Scotch nation.' JOHNSON (to Mr. Wilkes). 'You must know, sir, I lately took my friend Boswell and shewed him genuine civilized life in an English provincial town. I turned him loose at Lichfield, my native city, that he might see for once real civility: for you know he lives among savages in Scotland, and among rakes in London.' WILKES. 'Except when he is with grave, sober, decent people like you and me.' JOHNSON (smiling). 'And we ashamed of him.'

. . . I attended Dr. Johnson home, and had the satisfaction to hear him tell Mrs. Williams how much he had been pleased with Mr. Wilkes's company, and what an agreeable day he had passed.

121

A VERY accomplished young lady who became in process of time the Hon. Mrs. Digby, related to her former tutor the following anecdote. This lady was present at the introduction of Dr. Johnson at one of the late Mrs. Montagu's literary parties, when Mrs. Digby herself, with several still younger ladies, almost immediately surrounded our Colossus of literature (an odd figure sure enough) with more wonder than politeness, and while contemplating him, as if he had been some monster from the deserts of Africa, Johnson said to them, 'Ladies, I am tame; you may stroke me.'

122

AFTER breakfast we walked to the top of a very steep hill behind the house. When we arrived at the summit, Mr. Langton said, 'Poor dear Dr. Johnson, when he came to this spot, turned back to look down the hill, and said he was determined "to take a roll down". When we understood what he meant to do, we endeavoured to dissuade him; but he was resolute, saying, "he had not had a roll for a long time"; and taking out of his lesser pockets whatever might be in them—keys, pencil, purse, or pen-knife—and laying himself parallel with the edge of the hill, he actually descended, turning himself over and over, till he came to the bottom.'

123

ADMIRAL WALSINGHAM, who sometimes resided at Windsor, and sometimes in Portugal Street, frequently boasted that he was the only man to bring together miscellaneous parties, and make them all agreeable; and, indeed, there never before was so strange an assortment as I have occasionally met there. At one of his dinners were the Duke of Cumberland, Dr. Johnson, Mr. Nairn the optician, and Mr. Leoni the singer: at another, Dr. Johnson, etc., and a young dashing officer, who determined, he whispered, to attack the old bear that we all seemed to stand in awe of. There was a good dinner, and during that important time Johnson was deaf to all impertinence. However, after the wine had passed rather freely, the young gentleman was resolved to bait him, and venture out a little further. 'Now, Dr. Johnson, do not look so glum, but be a little gay and lively like others: what would you give, old gentleman, to be as young and sprightly as I am?' 'Why, Sir,' said he, 'I think I would almost be content to be as foolish.'

124

DURING the last visit which the Doctor made to Lichfield, the friends with whom he was staying missed him one morning at the breakfast-table. On inquiring after him of the servants, they understood he had set off from Lichfield at a very early hour, without mentioning to any of the family whither he was going. The day passed without the return of the illustrious guest, and the party began to be very uneasy on his account, when, just before the supper-hour, the door opened, and the Doctor stalked into the room. A solemn silence of a few minutes ensued, nobody daring to inquire the cause of his absence, which was at length relieved by Johnson addressing the lady of the house in the following manner: 'Madam, I beg your pardon for the abruptness of my departure from your house this morning, but I was constrained to it by my conscience. Fifty years ago, Madam, on this day, I committed a breach of filial piety, which has ever since lain heavy on my mind, and has not till this day been expiated. My father, you recollect, was a bookseller, and had long been in the habit of attending Uttoxeter market, and opening a stall for the sale of his books during that day. Confined to his bed by indisposition, he requested me, this time fifty years ago, to visit the market, and attend the stall in his place. But, Madam, my pride prevented me from doing my duty, and I gave my father a refusal. To do away the sin of this disobedience, I this day went in a postchaise to Uttoxeter, and going into the market at the time of high business, uncovered my head, and stood with it bare an hour before the stall which my father had formerly used, exposed to the sneers of the standers-by and the inclemency of the weather; a penance by which I trust I have propitiated heaven for this only instance, I believe, of contumacy towards my father.'

125

JAMES HARRIS (1709–80)

[James Harris was the author of a once celebrated book, *Hermes, or a Philosophical Inquiry concerning Universal Grammar* (1751). The book on 'virtue' mentioned below is presumably his dissertation 'Concerning Happiness' in *Three Treatises* (1744).]

WHEN the late Mr. Harris of Salisbury made his first speech in the House of Commons, Charles Townshend asked, with an affected surprise, who he was? He had never seen him before.—'Ah! you must at least have heard of him. That's the celebrated Mr. Harris of Salisbury, who has written a very ingenious book on *grammar*, and another on *virtue*.'—'What the devil then brings him here? I am sure he will find neither the one nor the other in the House of Commons.'

126

A GENTLEMAN applied to his friend to lend him some amusing book, and he recommended Harris's *Hermes*. The gentleman, from the title, conceived it to be a novel, but turning it over and over, could make nothing of it, and at last coldly returned it with thanks. His friend asked him how he had been entertained. 'Not much,' he replied; 'he thought that all these imitations of *Tristram Shandy* fell far short of the original.'

127
DAVID HUME (1711–76)

DURING his intimacy with Lord Kames, Mr. Smellie[1] went one summer evening to sup with his Lordship; and the company was soon afterwards joined by the late Dr. John Warden McFarlane, the worthy, respectable, and highly useful minister of the Canongate, one of the suburbs of Edinburgh, and by Mr. David Hume, the celebrated philosopher and historian. The conversation went on for some time very agreeably; till Dr. Warden happened to mention that he had read a sermon just published by one Edwards under the strange title of the *Usefulness of Sin*. Mr. Hume repeated the words 'Usefulness of Sin'.—'I suppose,' said he, 'Mr. Edwards has adopted the system of Leibniz, that "all is for the best".' To this he added, with a peculiar keenness of eye, and forcible manner of expression which was unusual with him: 'But what the devil does the fellow make of hell and damnation?' Dr. Warden immediately took his hat and left the room; and though followed by Lord Kames, who anxiously pressed him to return, he positively refused to rejoin the company.

128

MR. HUME's cheerfulness was so great, and his conversation and amusements continued so much in their accustomed strain, that, notwithstanding many bad symptoms, few of his friends could believe his dissolution to be so fast approaching. Dr. Dundas, when taking leave of Mr. Hume one day, said to him, 'I shall tell your friend Colonel Edmonstone that I left you much better, and in a fair way of recovery.'—'Doctor,' Mr. Hume replied, 'as I believe you would not choose to tell anything but the truth, you had better tell him that I am dying as fast as my enemies, if I have any, could wish, and as easily and cheerfully as my best friends could desire.'

Soon afterwards Colonel Edmonstone went to see Mr. Hume, and to take a last farewell of him. But, on his way home, he could not refrain from writing a letter, bidding him once more an eternal adieu. Such were Mr. Hume's magnanimity and fortitude of mind, that his most intimate and affectionate friends knew they hazarded no offence in talking or writing to him as a dying man. Mr. Adam Smith happened to call upon Mr. Hume when he was reading Colonel Edmonstone's letter, which he immediately showed to Mr. Smith. After perusing this letter, Mr. Smith

[1] William Smellie, Scottish printer, naturalist, and antiquary (1740–95).

remarked that appearances were against Mr. Hume. 'Still, however,' he said, 'your cheerfulness is so great, and your spirit of life so strong, that I must entertain some faint hopes of your recovery.' Mr. Hume answered, 'Your hopes are groundless . . .' Mr. Smith replied, 'If it must be so, you have at least the satisfaction of leaving all your friends, your brother's family in particular, in great prosperity.' Mr. Hume said he felt that satisfaction so sensibly that, a few days before, when reading Lucian's Dialogues of the Dead, among all the excuses which are usually made to Charon by souls who are backward to be ferried in his boat over the river Styx, he could not find one that suited him. He had no house to furnish, no children to provide for, nor any enemies upon which he wished to be revenged. 'I could not well imagine', said he, 'what excuse I could make to Charon, in order to obtain a little delay. I have done every thing of consequence which I ever meant to do, and I could at no time expect to leave my relations and friends in a better situation than that in which I am now likely to leave them: I, therefore, have all reason to die contented.'

He then amused himself with some whimsical excuses which he supposed he might make to Charon, and with imagining the surly answers which it might suit the character of Charon to return to them. 'Upon further consideration,' said he, 'I thought I might say to him, "Good Charon, I have been correcting my works for a new edition. Allow me a little time that I may see how the public receives the alterations." But Charon would answer, "When you have seen the effect of these, you will be for making other alterations. There will be no end of such excuses; so, honest friend, please step into the boat." ' But Mr. Hume said, 'I might still urge, "Have a little patience, good Charon, I have been endeavouring to open the eyes of the public. If I live a few days longer, I may have the satisfaction of seeing the downfall of some of the prevailing systems of superstition." But Charon would then lose his temper and decency.—"You loitering rogue, that will not happen these many hundred years. Do you fancy I will grant you a lease for so long a term? Get into the boat this instant, you lazy loitering rogue!" '

129

LAURENCE STERNE (1713–68)

[The author of this anecdote is John Macdonald, whose account of his life as a footman was published in 1790.]

IN the month of January 1768, we set off for London. We stopped for some time at Almack's House in Pall Mall. My master afterwards took Sir

James Gray's house in Clifford Street, who was going Ambassador to Spain. He now began housekeeping, hired a French cook, a housemaid, and kitchenmaid, and kept a great deal of the best company. My master and Henry had words, and the valet had warning to provide for himself.

About this time Mr. Sterne, the celebrated author, was taken ill at the silk-bag shop in Old Bond Street. He was sometimes called 'Tristram Shandy', and sometimes 'Yorick'—a very great favourite of the gentlemen's. One day my master had company to dinner who were speaking about him; the Duke of Roxburgh, the Earl of March, the Earl of Ossory, the Duke of Grafton, Mr. Garrick, Mr. Hume, and a Mr. James. 'John,' said my master, 'go and inquire how Mr. Sterne is today.' I went, returned, and said: 'I went to Mr. Sterne's lodging; the mistress opened the door; I inquired how he did. She told me to go up to the nurse. I went into the room, and he was just a-dying. I waited ten minutes; but in five he said: "*Now it is come.*" He put up his hand as if to stop a blow, and died in a minute.' The gentlemen were all very sorry, and lamented him very much.

130
WILLIAM SHENSTONE (1714–63)

FROM his earliest infancy he was remarkable for his great fondness for reading, so that when any of his family went to distant markets or fairs, he constantly importuned them to bring him presents of books; which, if they returned home later than his usual hour of going to rest, were always taken up to bed to him; and sometimes when they had been forgotten, his mother had no other means to allure him to sleep but by wrapping a piece of wood in paper like a book, which he would then hug to his pillow till the morning discovered the deception.

131
JAMES BURNETT, LORD MONBODDO (1714–99)

ALL things considered, Monboddo was treated fairly gently in Boswell's *Journal of a Tour to the Hebrides* as it was published. To be sure, the estate of which Monboddo was so proud was called 'a wretched place, wild and naked, with a poor old house', and in a note Boswell referred to Samuel Foote's calling Monboddo an 'Elzevir edition of Johnson'[1] as a compliment, where Monboddo might have counted it an insult. . . .

[1] Monboddo was under five feet tall.

How far Monboddo took offence for himself is not clear, but that he did take offence, either for himself or for other men who had been less kindly treated, cannot be doubted. Certainly he would have disapproved in principle of a man's writing such things as Boswell had included in the printed *Journal*, for they constituted at the very least a transgression against the hospitality of men of good family. In the furor which followed Boswell's *Life of Johnson*, he was asked what he now thought of Boswell. He replied, 'Before I read his Book I thought he was a Gentleman who had the misfortune to be mad: I now think he is a madman who has the misfortune not to be a Gentleman.'

132

MONBODDO and Lord Kames had a sovereign contempt for each other's studies and works. . . . Soon after the *Elements of Criticism* were published, Lord Kames met Monboddo, then at the Bar, on the street. 'Well,' said he, 'have you read my book?'—'I have not, my lord. You write a great deal faster than I am able to read.'

133
THOMAS GRAY (1716–71)

MR. GRAY, our elegant poet, and delicate Fellow-Commoner of Peterhouse, has just removed to Pembroke Hall, in resentment of some usage he met with at the former place. The case is much talked of, and is this. He is much afraid of fire, and was a great sufferer in Cornhill;[1] he has ever since kept a ladder of ropes by him, soft as the silky cords by which Romeo ascended to his Juliet, and has had an iron machine fixed to his bedroom window. The other morning Lord Percival and some Petrenchians, going a hunting, were determined to have a little sport before they set out, and thought it would be no bad diversion to make Gray bolt, as they called it, so ordered their man Joe Draper to roar out fire. A delicate white night-cap is said to have appeared at the window; but finding the mistake, retired again to the couch. The young fellows, had he descended, were determined, they said, to have whipped the butterfly up again.

[1] In March 1748 the house in Cornhill where Gray was born was destroyed, along with many others, in a disastrous fire.

134
SAMUEL FOOTE (1720–77)

CHARLES HOWARD of Greystock published a silly book he called 'Thoughts'. He meets Foote at a coffee-house. 'And have you read my *Thoughts*?' says he. 'No,' replies the other, 'I wait for the second volume.' —'And why so?'—'Because I have heard', says Foote, 'that Second Thoughts were best.'

135

MY lord Sandwich had dined one day in Foote's company, in Covent Garden, at the famous Beef Steak Club. The glass had gone profusely round; and at the unguarded time, when the bold idea of the moment sallies forth without any regard to good manners—'Foote,' said Lord Sandwich, 'I have often wondered what catastrophe would bring *you* to your end; but I think you must either die of the pox, or the halter.'—'My Lord,' replied Foote instantaneously, '*that* will depend upon one of two contingencies—whether I embrace your lordship's mistress, or your lordship's principles.'

136
TOBIAS SMOLLETT (1721–71)

MANY petty squabbles which occurred to tease and embitter the life of Smollett, and to diminish the respectability with which his talents must otherwise have invested him, had their origin in his situation as editor of the *Critical Review*. He was engaged in one controversy with the notorious Shebbeare, in another with Dr. Grainger, the elegant author of the beautiful Ode to Solitude, and in several wrangles and brawls with persons of less celebrity.

But the most unlucky controversy in which his critical office involved our author was that with Admiral Knowles, who had published a pamphlet vindicating his own conduct in the secret expedition against Rochfort, which disgracefully miscarried, in 1757. This defence was examined in the *Critical Review*; and Smollett, himself the author of the article, used the following intemperate expressions concerning Admiral Knowles: 'He is an admiral without conduct, an engineer without knowledge, an officer without resolution, and a man without veracity.' The admiral commenced a prosecution against the printer of the *Review*, declaring at the same time that he desired only to discover the author of the paragraph, and, should he prove a gentleman, to demand satisfaction of a different nature. This decoy, for such it proved, was the most effectual mode which could have been devised to draw the high-spirited Smollett within the danger of the law. When the court were about to pronounce judgement in the case, Smollett appeared, and took the consequences upon himself, and Admiral Knowles redeemed the pledge he had given, by enforcing judgement for a fine of one hundred pounds, and obtaining a sentence against the defendant of three months' imprisonment. How the admiral reconciled his conduct to the rules usually observed by gentlemen, we are not informed; but the proceeding seems to justify even Smollett's strength of expression when he terms him an officer without resolution, and a man without veracity.

137
JAMES GRAINGER (1721?–66)

HAVING talked of Dr. Grainger's *Sugar-Cane*,[1] I mentioned to him Mr. Langton's having told me that this poem, when read in manuscript at Sir Joshua Reynolds's, had made all the assembled wits burst into a laugh, when, after much blank-verse pomp, the poet began a new paragraph thus:

Now, Muse, let's sing of *rats*.

And what increased the ridicule was, that one of the company, who slyly overlooked the reader, perceived that the word had been originally *mice*, and had been altered to *rats*, as more dignified.

This passage does not appear in the printed work, Dr. Grainger, or some of his friends, it should seem, having become sensible that introducing even *Rats* in a grave poem might be liable to banter. He, however, could not bring himself to relinquish the idea; for they are thus, in a still more ludicrous manner, periphrastically exhibited in his poem as it now stands:

Nor with less waste the whisker'd vermin race,
A countless clan, despoil the lowland cane.

[1] Boswell is talking to Johnson.

138
JOHN HOME (1722–1808)

At the first performance of *Douglas*,[1] when Young Norval was busily employed giving out one of his rodomontading speeches, a canny Scot, who had been observed to grow more and more excited as the piece progressed, unable longer to contain his feelings, called out with evident pride, 'Whaur's yer Wully Shakspere noo!'

139
CHRISTOPHER SMART (1722–71)

'Madness frequently discovers itself merely by unnecessary deviation from the usual modes of the world.[2] My poor friend Smart showed the disturbance of his mind by falling upon his knees and saying his prayers in the street, or in any other unusual place. Now although, rationally speaking, it is greater madness not to pray at all than to pray as Smart did, I am afraid there are so many who do not pray, that their understanding is not called in question.'

Concerning this unfortunate poet, Christopher Smart, who was confined in a mad-house, he had, at another time, the following conversation with Dr. Burney.—Burney. 'How does poor Smart do, sir; is he likely to recover?' Johnson. 'It seems as if his mind had ceased to struggle with the disease; for he grows fat upon it.' Burney. 'Perhaps, sir, that may be from want of exercise.' Johnson. 'No, sir; he has partly as much exercise as he used to have, for he digs in the garden. Indeed, before his confinement, he used for exercise to walk to the alehouse; but he was *carried* back again. I did not think he ought to be shut up. His infirmities were not noxious to society. He insisted on people praying with him; and I'd as lief pray with Kit Smart as anyone else. . . .'

[1] Edinburgh, 14 December 1756.
[2] Johnson is talking to Boswell.

140
MOSES MENDES (d. 1758)

HAYMAN, the painter, though but an ordinary artist, had some humour. . . . Mendes, the Jew poet, sat to him for his picture, but requested he would not put it in his show-room, as he wished to keep the matter a secret. However, as Hayman had but little business in portraits, he could not afford to let his new work remain in obscurity, so out it went with the few others that he had to display. A new picture being a rarity in Hayman's room, the first friend that came in took notice of it and asked whose portrait it was? 'Mendes.' 'Good heavens!' said the friend, 'you are wonderfully out of luck here. It has not a trait of his countenance.' 'Why, to tell you the truth,' said the painter, 'he desired *it might not be known*.'

141
JOHN GILBERT COOPER (1723–69)

MR. GILBERT COOPER[1] was the last of the *benevolists*, or sentimentalists, who were much in vogue between 1750 and 1760, and dealt in *general* admiration of virtue. They were all tenderness in *words*; their finer feelings evaporated in the moment of expression, for they had no connection with their practice. He was the person whom, when lamenting most piteously that his son then absent might be ill or even dead, Mr. Fitzherbert so grievously disconcerted by saying, in a growling tone, 'Can't you take a postchaise, and go and see him?'

142
ADAM SMITH (1723–90)

MR. BOSWELL has chosen to omit, for reasons which will be presently obvious, that Johnson and Adam Smith met at Glasgow; but I have been assured by Professor John Miller that they did so, and that Smith, leaving the party in which he had met Johnson, happened to come to another company where Miller was. Knowing that Smith had been in Johnson's society, they were anxious to know what had passed, and the more so

[1] Poet and miscellaneous writer; author of *Letters concerning Taste* (1754).

as Dr. Smith's temper seemed much ruffled. At first Smith would only answer, 'He's a brute—he's a brute;' but on closer examination, it appeared that Johnson no sooner saw Smith than he attacked him for some point of his famous letter on the death of Hume. Smith vindicated the truth of his statement. 'What did Johnson say?' was the universal inquiry. 'Why, he said,' replied Smith, with the deepest impression of resentment, 'he said, *you lie*!' 'And what did you reply?' 'I said, *you* are the son of a —.' On such terms did these two great moralists meet and part, and such was the classical dialogue between two great teachers of philosophy.

143
MRS. FRANCES BROOKE (1724–89)

MRS. BROOKE having repeatedly desired Johnson to look over her new play of 'The Siege of Sinope' before it was acted, he always found means to evade it; at last she pressed him so closely that he actually refused to do it, and told her that she herself, by carefully looking it over, would be able to see if there was anything amiss as well as he could. 'But, sir,' said she, 'I have no time. I have already so many irons in the fire.' 'Why then, Madam,' said he (quite out of patience), 'the best thing I can advise you to do is, to put your tragedy along with your irons.'

144
ARTHUR MURPHY (1727–1805)

THE way Johnson and Murphy got acquainted was an odd one. Mr. Murphy was engaged in a periodical paper called, I think, the *Gray's Inn Journal*, but he was in the country with his friend Foote, and said he must go to Town to publish his sheet for the day. 'Hang it,' says Foote, 'can't you do it here, and I'll send a man and horse—'tis but ten miles—up to the printer?' This was settled; and Murphy, impatient to join the company and unwilling to pump his own brains, just then snatched up a French journal that he saw lying about, translated a story which he liked in it, and sent it to the press. When he came to Town two days after, he soon found what he had done—that the story was a 'Rambler' written by Johnson and translated into French, and that he had been doing it back again. He flew to Johnson's lodging, catched him making of aether,[1] told him the truth, and commenced an acquaintance which has lasted with mutual esteem, I suppose near twenty years.

145

MURPHY and Burke were of different sides in the great question concerning literary property, settled as I remember in the year 1775.[2] 'But,' says Burke, 'you must remember the booksellers deal in commodities they are not supposed to understand.'—'True,' replies Murphy, 'some of 'em do deal in morality.'

146
DR. JOSEPH BLACK (1728–99)

DR. JOSEPH BLACK[3] was a striking and beautiful person; tall, very thin, and cadaverously pale; his hair carefully powdered, though there was little of it except what was collected into a long thin queue; his eyes dark, clear, and large, like deep pools of pure water. He wore black speckless clothes, silk stockings, silver buckles, and either a slim green silk umbrella, or a genteel brown cane. The general frame and air were feeble and slender. The wildest boy respected Black. No lad could be irreverent towards a man so pale, so gentle, so elegant, and so illustrious. So he glided, like a spirit, through our rather mischievous sportiveness, unharmed. He died, seated, with a bowl of milk on his knee, of which his ceasing to live did not spill a drop; a departure which it seemed, after the event happened, might have been foretold of this attenuated philosophical gentleman.

[1] When Boswell had his first glimpse of Johnson's library on 19 July 1763, he 'observed an apparatus for chymical experiments, of which Johnson was all his life very fond' (Boswell, *Life of Johnson*, ed. Hill–Powell, 1934–50, i. 436).

[2] For many years the English booksellers had been seeking to establish the principle of perpetual copyright, but the House of Lords decided against it on 22 February 1774. Murphy, who was a barrister, had drawn up the plea of the appellants against a perpetual right.

[3] Professor of Medicine and Chemistry at Edinburgh University.

147
OLIVER GOLDSMITH (1730–74)

GOLDSMITH told me[1] that he had sold a novel for four hundred pounds. This was his *Vicar of Wakefield*. But Johnson informed me that he had made the bargain for Goldsmith, and the price was sixty pounds . . . I shall give it authentically from Johnson's own exact narration: 'I received one morning a message from poor Goldsmith that he was in great distress, and as it was not in his power to come to me, begging that I would come to him as soon as possible. I sent him a guinea, and promised to come to him directly. I accordingly went as soon as I was dressed and found that his landlady had arrested him for his rent, at which he was in a violent passion. I perceived that he had already changed my guinea, and had got a bottle of Madeira and a glass before him. I put the cork into the bottle, desired he would be calm, and began to talk to him of the means by which he might be extricated. He then told me that he had a novel ready for the press, which he produced to me. I looked into it, and saw its merit; told the landlady I should soon return, and having gone to a bookseller, sold it for sixty pounds. I brought Goldsmith the money, and he discharged his rent, not without rating his landlady in a high tone for having used him so ill.'

148

[Richard Cumberland recalls the first night of *She Stoops to Conquer*.]

THE whole company pledged themselves to support the ingenious poet, and faithfully kept their promise to him. In fact he needed all that could be done for him, as Mr. Colman, the manager of Covent-Garden theatre, protested against the comedy when as yet he had not struck upon a name for it. Johnson at length stood forth in all his terrors as champion for the piece, and backed by us his clients and retainers demanded a fair trial. Colman again protested, but, with that salvo for his own reputation, liberally lent his stage to one of the most eccentric productions that ever found its way to it, and *She Stoops to Conquer* was put into rehearsal. We were not oversanguine of success, but perfectly determined to struggle hard for our author. . . .

We had among us a very worthy and efficient member, long since lost to his friends and the world at large, Adam Drummond of amiable

[1] James Boswell.

memory, who was gifted by nature with the most sonorous, and at the same time most contagious, laugh that ever echoed from the human lungs. The neighing of the horse of the son of Hystaspes was a whisper to it; the whole thunder of the theatre could not drown it. This kind and ingenuous friend fairly fore-warned us that he knew no more when to give his fire than the cannon did that was planted on a battery. He desired therefore to have a flapper at his elbow, and I had the honour to be deputed to that office. I planted him in an upper box, pretty nearly over the stage, in full view of the pit and galleries, and perfectly well situated to give the echo all its play through the hollows and recesses of the theatre. The success of our manoeuvres was complete. All eyes were upon Johnson, who sate in a front row of a side box, and when he laughed everybody thought themselves warranted to roar. In the meantime my friend followed signals with a rattle so irresistibly comic that, when he had repeated it several times, the attention of the spectators was so engrossed by his person and performances that the progress of the play seemed likely to become a secondary object, and I found it prudent to insinuate to him that he might halt his music without any prejudice to the author; but alas, it was now too late to rein him in; he had laughed upon my signal where he found no joke, and now unluckily he fancied that he found a joke in almost everything that was said; so that nothing in nature could be more malapropos than some of his bursts every now and then were. These were dangerous moments, for the pit began to take umbrage; but we carried our play through, and triumphed not only over Colman's judgement, but our own.

149

GOLDSMITH was often very fortunate in his witty contests, even when he entered the lists with Johnson himself. Sir Joshua Reynolds was in company with them one day, when Goldsmith said that he thought he could write a good fable, mentioned the simplicity which that kind of composition requires, and observed that in most fables the animals introduced seldom talk in character. 'For instance,' said he, 'the fable of the little fishes who saw birds fly over their heads, and envying them, petitioned Jupiter to be changed into birds. The skill', continued he, 'consists in making them talk like little fishes.' While he indulged himself in this fanciful reverie, he observed Johnson shaking his sides and laughing. Upon which he smartly proceeded, 'Why, Dr. Johnson, this is not so easy as you seem to think; for if you were to make little fishes talk, they would talk like WHALES.'

150
JAMES BRUCE (1730–94)

BRUCE's book[1] is both dull and dear. We join in clubs of five, each pays a guinea, draw lots who shall have it first, and the last to keep it for his patience.

Bruce's overbearing manner has raised enmity and prejudices; and he did wrong in retailing the most wonderful parts of his book in companies. A story may be credible when attended with circumstances, which seems false if detached.

I was present in a large company at dinner, when Bruce was talking away. Someone asked him what musical instruments were used in Abyssinia. Bruce hesitated, not being prepared for the question; and at last said, 'I think I saw one *lyre* there.' George Selwyn whispered his next man, 'Yes; and there is one less since he left the country.'

151
WILLIAM COWPER (1731–1800)

[Cowper complies with a request to write some mortuary verses.]

ON Monday morning last Sam brought me word that there was a man in the kitchen who desired to speak with me. I ordered him in. A plain, decent, elderly figure made its appearance, and, being desired to sit, spoke as follows: 'Sir, I am a clerk of the parish of All Saints, in Northampton; brother of Mr. Cox, the upholsterer. It is customary for the person in my office to annex to a bill of mortality, which he publishes at Christmas, a copy of verses. You will do me a great favour, sir, if you would furnish me with one.' To this I replied, 'Mr. Cox, you have several men of genius in your town, why have you not applied to some of them? There is a namesake of yours in particular, Cox the statuary, who, everybody knows, is a first-rate maker of verses. He surely is the man of all the world for your purpose.' 'Alas! sir, I have heretofore borrowed help from him; but he is a gentleman of so much reading that the people of our town cannot understand him.' I confess to you, my dear, I felt all the force of the compliment implied in this speech, and was almost ready to answer, 'Perhaps, my good friend, they may find me unintelligible too, for

[1] *Travels to discover the source of the Nile* (5 vols., 1790).

the same reason.' But on asking him whether he had walked over to Weston on purpose to implore the assistance of my Muse, and on his replying in the affirmative, I felt my mortified vanity a little consoled, and pitying the poor man's distress, which appeared to be considerable, promised to supply him. The wagon has accordingly gone this day to Northampton, loaded in part with my effusions in the mortuary style. A fig for poets who write epitaphs upon individuals! I have written *one* that serves *two hundred* persons.

[One of the stanzas of Cowper's poem is often quoted, that commencing—
Like crowded forest-trees we stand,
And some are marked to fall.]

152
RICHARD CUMBERLAND (1732–1811)

WHEN the *School for Scandal* came out, Cumberland's children prevailed upon their father to take them to see it;—they had the stage-box—their father was seated behind them; and as the story was told by a gentleman, a friend of Sheridan's, who was close by, every time the children laughed at what was going on on the stage, he pinched them, and said, 'What are you laughing at, my dear little folks? You should not laugh, my angels; there is nothing to laugh at'—and then, in an undertone, 'Keep still, you little dunces.'

Sheridan having been told of this long afterwards, said, 'It was very ungrateful in Cumberland to have been displeased with his poor children for laughing at my comedy; for I went the other night to see his tragedy, and laughed at it from beginning to end.'

153
GEORGE STEEVENS (1736–1800)

THE contributions of Steevens to Shakespearean learning were substantial and valuable. But he had a devil of perversity, which sufficiently accounts for Gifford's description of him as 'the Puck of commentators'. He is said to have ascribed his notes on the more indecent passages of Shakespeare to two clergymen, Richard Amner and John Collins, who had offended him. Nor do I think that he can have been altogether serious when he wrote on the 'parish top' in *Twelfth Night*, I. iii. 44, to be solemnly followed by later annotators down to the *Arden* edition, 'This is one of the old customs now laid aside. A large top was formerly kept in every village, to be whipped in frosty weather, that the peasants might be kept warm by exercise, and out of mischief, while they could not work.' Whether he was ever responsible for a deliberate fabrication is less clear.

154

George Steevens usually commenced his operations by opening some pretended discovery in the evening papers, which were then of a more literary cast; the *St. James's Chronicle*, the *General Evening Post*, or the *Whitehall*, were they not dead in body and in spirit, would now bear witness to his successful efforts. . . . The marvellous narrative of the upas-tree of Java, which Darwin adopted in his plan of 'enlisting imagination under the banner of science', appears to have been another forgery which amused our 'Puck'. It was first given in the *London Magazine*, as an extract from a Dutch traveller, but the extract was never discovered in the original author, and 'the effluvia of this noxious tree, which through a district of twelve or fourteen miles had killed all vegetation, and had spread the skeletons of men and animals, affording a scene of melancholy beyond what poets have described, or painters delineated', is perfectly chimerical! A splendid flim-flam!

When Dr. Berkenhout was busied in writing, without much knowledge or skill, a history of our English authors, Steevens allowed the good man to insert a choice letter by George Peele, giving an account of 'a merry meeting at the Globe', wherein Shakespeare and Ben Jonson and Ned Alleyne are admirably made to perform their respective parts. As the nature of the *Biographia Literaria* required authorities, Steevens ingeniously added, 'Whence I copied this letter I do not recollect.' However, he well knew that it came from *The Theatrical Mirror*, where he had first deposited the precious original, to which he had unguardedly ventured to affix the date of 1600; unluckily, Peele was discovered to have died two years before he wrote his own letter! The *date* is adroitly dropped in Berkenhout. Steevens did not wish to refer to his original, which I have often seen quoted as authority. . . .

One of the sort of inventions which I attribute to Steevens has been got up with a deal of romantic effect to embellish the poetical life of Milton; and unquestionably must have sadly perplexed his last matter-of-fact editor[1], who is not a man to comprehend a flim-flam!—for he has sanctioned the whole fiction by preserving it in his biographical narrative. The first impulse of Milton to travel in Italy is ascribed to the circumstance of his having been found asleep at the foot of a tree in the vicinity

[1] Henry John Todd (1763-1845).

of Cambridge, when two foreign ladies, attracted by the loveliness of the youthful poet, alighted from their carriage, and having admired him for some time as they imagined unperceived, the youngest, who was very beautiful, drew a pencil from her pocket, and having written some lines, put the paper with her trembling hand into his own! But it seems—for something was to account how the sleeping youth could have been aware of these minute particulars, unless he had been dreaming them—that the ladies had been observed at a distance by some friends of Milton, and they explained to him the whole silent adventure. Milton, on opening the paper, read *four verses* from Guarini, addressed to those 'human stars', his own eyes. On this romantic adventure, Milton set off for Italy, to discover the fair 'incognita', to which undiscovered lady we are told we stand indebted for the most impassioned touches in the *Paradise Lost*! We know how Milton passed his time in Italy, with Dati, and Gaddi, and Frescobaldi, and other literary friends, amidst its academies, and often busied in book-collecting. Had Milton's tour in Italy been an adventure of knight-errantry, to discover a lady whom he had never seen, at least he had not the merit of going out of the direct road to Florence and Rome, nor of having once alluded to this *Dame de ses pensées* in his letters or inquiries among his friends, who would have thought themselves fortunate to have introduced so poetical an adventure in the numerous *canzoni* they showered on our youthful poet.

This *historiette*, scarcely fitted for a novel, first appeared where generally Steevens's literary amusements were carried on, in the *General Evening Post* or the *St. James's Chronicle*: and Mr. Todd, in the improved edition of Milton's Life, obtained this spurious original, where the reader may find it; but the more curious part of the story remains to be told. Mr. Todd proceeds: 'The preceding highly-coloured relation, however, is *not singular*; my friend, Mr. Walker, points out to me a counterpart in the extract from the preface to *Poésies de Marguerite-Eleanore Clotilde, depuis Madame de Surville, Poète François du XV. Siècle. Paris*, 1803.'

And true enough we find among 'the family traditions' of this same Clotilde that Justine de Levis, great-grandmother of this unknown poetess of the fifteenth century, walking in a forest, witnessed the same beautiful *spectacle* which the Italian Unknown had at Cambridge; never was such an impression to be effaced, and she could not avoid leaving her tablets by the side of the beautiful sleeper, declaring her passion in her tablets by *four Italian verses*. The very number our Milton had meted to him! . . . The 'Poésies' of Clotilde are as genuine a fabrication as Chatterton's; subject to the same objections, having many ideas and expressions which were unknown in the language at the time they are pretended to have been composed, and exhibiting many imitations of Voltaire and other poets . . . A pretended editor is said to have found by mere accident the precious manuscript, and while he was copying for the press, in 1793, these pretty poems, for such they are, of his *grande tante*, was shot in the reign of terror, and so completely expired that no one could ever trace his existence! The real editor, whom we must presume to be the poet, published them in 1803.

155

STEEVENS, in 1789, having procured a block of marble, and having engraved upon it by means of aquafortis some Anglo-Saxon letters, placed it in the window of a shop in Southwark, and caused it to be represented to the Society of Antiquaries that it had been dug up in Kennington Lane, and was the tombstone of Hardecanute. Jacob Schnebbelie produced in good faith a drawing, which was engraved by Basire and published in the *Gentleman's Magazine*. Samuel Pegge, falling into the trap, read a paper on the inscription before the Society of Antiquaries on 10 December 1789; but the deception was discovered before the disquisition was printed in the *Archæologia*. An acrimonious correspondence between Steevens and those he hoped to dupe followed in the daily and monthly journals. Steevens finally committed the stone to the custody of Sir Joseph Banks, and it was regularly exhibited at his assemblies in Soho Square.

156

TALKING of an acquaintance of ours [Steevens], whose narratives, which abounded in curious and interesting topics, were unhappily found to be very fabulous, I[1] mentioned Lord Mansfield's having said to me, 'Suppose we believe one *half* of what he tells.' JOHNSON. 'Ay; but we don't know *which* half to believe.'

157
JOHN HORNE TOOKE (1736–1812)

WHEN Horne Tooke was about fourteen or fifteen years old, at Eton, in construing a passage in a Latin author, the Master asked him *why* some ordinary construction, the rule of which was very familiar, obtained in the passage. The pupil replied he did not know, on which the Master, pro-

[1] Boswell

voked by his ignorance or perverseness, caused him to be flogged, a punishment which he received with perfect *sang froid* and without a murmur. The Master then put the question to the next boy in the class, who readily gave the answer, whatever it was, as laid down among the common rules in the Eton Grammar. The Master said, 'Take him down—a blockhead,' on which Horne burst into tears, which the Master observing as something not readily intelligible, exclaimed, 'Why, what is the meaning of this?' Horne replied, 'I knew the rule as well as he did, but you asked me the Reason, which I did not know.'—'My boy, I am afraid I have done you some wrong. I will make the best reparation I can,' and, taking down a Virgil from his bookcase, he subscribed it as a presentation copy with his own name, and presented it to Tooke, at the same time taking him back to the class and restoring him the place he had apparently lost.

This anecdote Sharp[1] received from the mouth of Horne Tooke himself, who showed the Virgil when he told the story. The boy was father to the man. The youthful logical precision of Eton was quite worthy of the author of the *Diversions of Purley*.

158
EDWARD GIBBON (1737–94)

AFTER leaving Florence I compared the solitude of Pisa with the industry of Lucca and Leghorn, and continued my journey through Sienna to Rome, where I arrived in the beginning of October. My temper is not very susceptible of enthusiasm, and the enthusiasm which I do not feel I have ever scorned to affect. But, at the distance of twenty-five years, I can neither forget nor express the strong emotions which agitated my mind as I first approached and entered the *eternal city*. After a sleepless night, I trod, with a lofty step, the ruins of the Forum; each memorable spot where Romulus *stood*, or Tully spoke, or Caesar fell, was at once present to my eye; and several days of intoxication were lost or enjoyed before I could descend to a cool and minute investigation. . . . It was at Rome, on the 15th of October, 1764, as I sat musing amidst the ruins of the Capitol, while the barefooted friars were singing vespers in the Temple of Jupiter, that the idea of writing the decline and fall of the city first started to my mind. But my original plan was circumscribed to the decay of the city rather than of the empire: and, though my reading and reflections began to point towards that object, some years elapsed, and

[1] Richard ('Conversation') Sharp (1759–1835).

several avocations intervened, before I was seriously engaged in the execution of that laborious work.

. . . I have presumed to mark the moment of conception: I shall now commemorate the hour of my final deliverance. It was on the day, or rather night, of the 27th of June, 1787, between the hours of eleven and twelve, that I wrote the last lines of the last page, in a summer-house in my garden.[1] After laying down my pen, I took several turns in a *berceau*, or covered walk of acacias, which commands a prospect of the country, the lake, and the mountains. The air was temperate, the sky was serene, the silver orb of the moon was reflected from the waters, and all nature was silent. I will not dissemble the first emotions of joy on recovery of my freedom, and, perhaps, the establishment of my fame.

159

THE Duke of Gloucester, brother of King George III, permitted Mr. Gibbon to present to him the first volume of *The History of the Decline and Fall of the Roman Empire*. When the second volume of that work appeared, it was quite in order that it should be presented to His Royal Highness in like manner. The prince received the author with much good nature and affability, saying to him, as he laid the quarto on the table, 'Another d—mn'd thick, square book! Always scribble, scribble, scribble! Eh! Mr. Gibbon?'

160

GIBBON took very little exercise. He had been staying some time with Lord Sheffield in the country; and when he was about to go away, the servants could not find his hat. 'Bless me,' said Gibbon, 'I certainly left it in the hall on my arrival here.' He had not stirred out of doors during the whole of the visit.

161

HERE is an anecdote of William Spencer's which has just occurred to me. The *dramatis personae* were Lady Elizabeth Foster, Gibbon the historian, and an eminent French physician whose name I forget; the historian and doctor being rivals in courting the lady's favour. Impatient at Gibbon's occupying so much of her attention by his conversation, the doctor said

[1] At Lausanne.

crossly to him, 'Quand milady Elizabeth Foster sera malade de vos fadaises, je la guérirai.' On which Gibbon, drawing himself up grandly, and looking disdainfully at the physician, replied, 'Quand milady Elizabeth Foster sera morte de vos reçettes, je l'im-mor-taliserai.' The pompous lengthening of the last word, while at the same time a long sustained pinch of snuff was taken by the historian, brought, as mimicked by Spencer, the whole scene most livelily before one's eyes.

162
TOM PAINE (1737–1809)

[The father of Charles Knight, publisher and author, kept a bookshop at Windsor at the close of the eighteenth century.]

SOON after the publication of Paine's *Rights of Man*, in 1791,—before the work was declared libellous—the King[1] was wandering about Windsor early on a summer morning, and was heard calling out 'Knight, Knight!' in the shop whose shutters were just opened. My father made his appearance as quickly as possible at the sound of the well-known voice, and he beheld his Majesty quietly seated, reading with marked attention. Late on the preceding evening a parcel from Paternoster Row had been opened, and its miscellaneous contents were exposed on the counter. Horror! the King had taken up the dreadful *Rights of Man*, which advocated the French Revolution in reply to Burke. Absorbed Majesty continued reading for half an hour. The King went away without a remark; but he never afterwards expressed his displeasure, or withdrew his countenance. Peter Pindar's incessant endeavours to represent the King as a garrulous simpleton were more likely to provoke the laughter of his family than to suggest any desire to stifle the poor jests by those terrors of the law which might have been easily commanded.

163
JOHN WOLCOT ('PETER PINDAR'), 1738–1819

THAT so keen a satirist as himself should have many enemies was natural, especially as his exposure of the foibles of George III had made him be set down for a Jacobin, which he was not . . .

[1] George III.

When an old lady asked him if he did not think he was a very bad subject of our most pious king George, he replied, 'I do not know anything about that, Madam, but I *do* know that the king has been a devilish good subject for me.'

164
JAMES BOSWELL (1740–95)

THIS is to me a memorable year;[1] for in it I had the happiness to obtain the acquaintance of that extraordinary man whose memoirs I am now writing; an acquaintance which I shall ever esteem as one of the most fortunate circumstances in my life. Though then but two-and-twenty, I had for several years read his works with delight and instruction, and had the highest reverence for their author, which had grown up in my fancy into a kind of mysterious veneration, by figuring to myself a state of solemn elevated abstraction in which I supposed him to live in the immense metropolis of London . . .

Mr. Thomas Davies the actor, who then kept a bookseller's shop in Russell Street, Covent-garden, told me that Johnson was very much his friend, and came frequently to his house, where he more than once invited me to meet him; but by some unlucky accident or other he was prevented from coming to us.

Mr. Thomas Davies was a man of good understanding and talents, with the advantage of a liberal education. Though somewhat pompous, he was an entertaining companion; and his literary performances have no inconsiderable share of merit. . . . Mr. Davies recollected several of Johnson's remarkable sayings, and was one of the best of the many imitators of his voice and manner while relating them. He increased my impatience more and more to see the extraordinary man whose works I highly valued, and whose conversation was reported to be so peculiarly excellent.

At last, on Monday the 16th of May, when I was sitting in Mr. Davies's back-parlour, after having drunk tea with him and Mrs. Davies, Johnson unexpectedly came into the shop; and Mr. Davies having perceived him through the glass-door in the room in which we were sitting, advancing towards us—he announced his awful approach to me somewhat in the manner of an actor in the part of Horatio when he addresses Hamlet on the appearance of his father's ghost, 'Look, my lord, it comes.' I found that I had a very perfect idea of Johnson's figure, from the portrait of him painted by Sir Joshua Reynolds soon after he had published his Dictionary,

[1] 1763.

in the attitude of sitting in his easy chair in deep meditation, which was the first picture his friend did for him, which Sir Joshua very kindly presented to me, and from which an engraving has been made for this work. Mr. Davies mentioned my name, and respectfully introduced me to him. I was much agitated; and recollecting his prejudice against the Scotch, of which I had heard much, I said to Davies, 'Don't tell him where I come from.'—'From Scotland,' cried Davies, roguishly. 'Mr. Johnson,' said I, 'I do indeed come from Scotland, but I cannot help it.' I am willing to flatter myself that I meant this as light pleasantry to soothe and conciliate him, and not as an humiliating abasement at the expense of my country. But however that might be, this speech was somewhat unlucky; for with that quickness of wit for which he was so remarkable, he seized the expression 'come from Scotland', which I used in the sense of being of that country; and, as if I had said that I had come away from it, or left it, retorted, 'That, Sir, I find is what a very great number of your countrymen cannot help.' This stroke stunned me a good deal; and when we had sat down, I felt myself not a little embarrassed, and apprehensive of what might come next. He then addressed himself to Davies: 'What do you think of Garrick? He has refused me an order for the play for Miss Williams because he knows the house will be full, and that an order would be worth three shillings.' Eager to take any opening to get into conversation with him, I ventured to say, 'O, Sir, I cannot think Mr. Garrick would grudge such a trifle to you.' 'Sir,' (said he, with a stern look) 'I have known David Garrick longer than you have done: and I know no right you have to talk to me on the subject.' Perhaps I deserved this check; for it was rather presumptuous in me, an entire stranger, to express any doubt of the justice of his animadversion upon his old acquaintance and pupil. I now felt myself much mortified, and began to think that the hope which I had long indulged of obtaining his acquaintance was blasted. And, in truth, had not my ardour been uncommonly strong, and my resolution uncommonly persevering, so rough a reception might have deterred me for ever from making any further attempts. Fortunately, however, I remained upon the field not wholly discomfited; and was soon rewarded by hearing some of his conversation. . . .

I was highly pleased with the extraordinary vigour of his conversation, and regretted that I was drawn away from it by an engagement at another place. I had, for a part of the evening, been left alone with him, and had ventured to make an observation now and then, which he received very civilly; so that I was satisfied that though there was a roughness in his manner, there was no ill-nature in his disposition. Davies followed me to the door, and when I complained to him a little of the hard blows which the great man had given me, he kindly took upon him to console me by saying, 'Don't be uneasy. I can see he likes you very well.'

165

[On 24 December 1764 Boswell succeeded in having his first interview with Voltaire at Ferney.]

I WAS in true spirits; the earth was covered with snow; I surveyed wild nature with a noble eye. I called up all the grand ideas which I have ever entertained of Voltaire. The first object that struck me was his church with the inscription: 'Deo erexit Voltaire MDCCLXI.' His château was handsome, I was received by two or three footmen, who showed me into a very elegant room. I sent by one of them a letter to Monsieur de Voltaire which I had from Colonel Constant at the Hague. He returned and told me, 'Monsieur de Voltaire is very much annoyed at being disturbed. He is abed.' I was afraid that I should not see him. Some ladies and gentlemen entered, and I was entertained for some time. At last Monsieur de Voltaire opened the door of his apartment, and stepped forth. I surveyed him with eager attention, and found him just as his print had made me conceive him. He received me with dignity, and that air of the world which a Frenchman acquires in such perfection. He had a slate-blue, fine frieze night-gown, and a three-knotted wig. He sat erect upon his chair, and simpered when he spoke. He was not in spirits, nor I neither. All I presented was the 'foolish face of wondering praise'.

We talked of Scotland. He said the Glasgow editions were 'très belles'. I said, 'An Academy of Painting was also established there, but it did not succeed. Our Scotland is no country for that.' He replied with a keen archness, 'No; to paint well it is necessary to have warm feet. It's hard to paint when your feet are cold.' Another would have given a long dissertation on the coldness of our climate. Monsieur de Voltaire gave the very essence of raillery in half a dozen words. . . .

I told him that Mr. Johnson and I intended to make a tour through the Hebrides, the Northern Isles of Scotland. He smiled, and cried, 'Very well; but I shall remain here. You will allow me to stay here?' 'Certainly.' 'Well then, go. I have no objections at all.'

I asked him if he still spoke English. He replied, 'No. To speak English one must place the tongue between the teeth, and I have lost my teeth.' . . .

I returned yesterday to this enchanted castle. The magician appeared a little before dinner. But in the evening he came into the drawing room in great spirits. I placed myself by him. I touched the keys in unison with his imagination. I wish you had heard the music. He was all brilliance. He gave me continued flashes of wit. I got him to speak English, which he does in a degree that made me now and then start up and cry, 'Upon my soul this is astonishing!' When he talked our language he was animated with the soul of a Briton. He had bold flights. He had humour. He had an extravagance; he had a forcible oddity of style that the most comical of our *dramatis personae* could not have exceeded. He swore bloodily, as was the fashion when he was in England. He hummed a ballad; he repeated nonsense. Then he talked of our Constitution with a noble enthusiasm. I was proud to hear this from the mouth of an illustrious Frenchman. At last we came upon religion. Then did he rage. The company went to supper. Monsieur de Voltaire and I remained in the drawing room with a great Bible before us; and if ever two mortal men disputed with vehemence, we did. Yes, upon that occasion he was one individual and I another. . . . I demanded of him an honest confession of his real sentiments. He gave it me with candour and with a mild eloquence which touched my heart. I did not believe him capable of thinking in the manner that he declared to me was 'from the bottom of his heart'. He expressed his veneration—his love—of the Supreme Being, and his entire resignation to the will of Him who is All-wise. He expressed his desire to resemble the Author of Goodness by being good himself. His sentiments go no further. He does not inflame his mind with grand hopes of the immortality of the soul. He says it may be, but he knows nothing of it. And his mind is in perfect tranquillity. I was moved; I was sorry. I doubted his sincerity. I called to him with emotion, 'Are you sincere? are you really sincere?' He answered, 'Before God, I am.' Then with the fire of him whose tragedies have so often shone on the theatre of Paris, he said, 'I suffer much. But I suffer with patience and resignation; not as a Christian—but as a man.'

166

[On 30 August 1773, Johnson and Boswell passed Loch Ness on their way to the Hebrides, and near the shore of the loch they came upon the first Highland hut that Johnson had seen. In his *Journey to the Western Islands of Scotland* Johnson remarks that 'as our business was with life and manners, we were willing to visit it.' Johnson describes the hut in some detail, and gives some account of the circumstances of the occupant; but in his *Journal of a Tour to the Hebrides* Boswell records an aspect of life and manners that Johnson had discreetly passed over.]

WHEN we had advanced a good way by the side of Loch Ness, I perceived a little hut, with an old-looking woman at the door of it. I thought here might be a scene that would amuse Dr. Johnson; so I mentioned it to him. 'Let's go in,' said he. We dismounted, and we and our guides entered the hut. It was a wretched little hovel of earth only, I think, and for a window had only a small hole, which was stopped with a piece of turf, that was taken out occasionally to let in light. In the middle of the room or space which we entered was a fire of peat, the smoke going out at a hole in the roof. She had a pot upon it, with goat's flesh, boiling. There was at one end under the same roof, but divided by a kind of partition made of wattles, a pen or fold in which we saw a good many kids.

Dr. Johnson was curious to know where she slept. I asked one of the guides, who questioned her in Erse. She answered with a tone of emotion, saying (as he told us), she was afraid we wanted to go to bed to her. This *coquetry*, or whatever it may be called, of so wretched a being was truly ludicrous. Dr. Johnson and I afterwards were merry upon it. I said, it was he who alarmed the poor woman's virtue.—'No, sir,' said he, 'she'll say, "There came a wicked young fellow, a wild dog, who I believe would have ravished me, had there not been with him a grave old gentleman who repressed him: but when he gets out of the sight of his tutor, I'll warrant you he'll spare no woman he meets, young or old." '—'No, sir,' I replied, 'she'll say, "There was a terrible ruffian who would have forced me, had it not been for a civil decent young man, who, I take it, was an angel sent from heaven to protect me." '

167

IT was Boswell's custom during the sessions to dine daily with the Judges, invited or not. He obtruded himself everywhere. Lowe[1] (mentioned by him in his life of Johnson) once gave me a humorous picture of him. Lowe had requested Johnson to write him a letter, which Johnson did, and Boswell came in while it was writing. His attention was immediately fixed; Lowe took the letter, retired, and was followed by Boswell.

'Nothing,' said Lowe, 'could surprise me more. Till that moment he had so entirely overlooked me, that I did not imagine he knew there was such a creature in existence; and he now accosted me with the most overstrained and insinuating compliments possible:

'How do you do, Mr. Lowe? I hope you are very well, Mr. Lowe? Pardon my freedom, Mr. Lowe, but I think I saw my dear friend, Dr. Johnson, writing a letter for you.'

'Yes, sir.'

'I hope you will not think me rude, but if it would not be too great a favour, you would infinitely oblige me, if you would just let me have a sight of it. Every thing from that hand, you know, is so inestimable.'

'Sir, it is on my own private affairs, but—'

[1] Mauritius Lowe (1746–93), painter.

'I would not pry into a person's affairs, my dear Mr. Lowe, by any means, I am sure you would not accuse me of such a thing, only if it were no particular secret.'

'Sir, you are welcome to read the letter.'

'I thank you, my dear Mr. Lowe, you are very obliging, I take it exceedingly kind. (Having read) It is nothing, I believe, Mr. Lowe, that you would be ashamed of.'

'Certainly not.'

'Why then, my dear sir, if you would do me another favour, you would make the obligation eternal. If you would but step to Peele's coffee-house with me, and just suffer me to take a copy of it, I would do anything in my power to oblige you.'

'I was overcome', said Lowe, 'by this sudden familiarity and condescension, accompanied with bows and grimaces. I had no power to refuse; we went to the coffee-house, my letter was presently transcribed, and as soon as he had put his document in his pocket, Mr. Boswell walked away, as erect and proud as he was half an hour before, and I ever afterward was unnoticed. Nay, I am not certain', added he sarcastically, 'whether the Scotchman did not leave me, poor as he knew I was, to pay for my own dish of coffee.'

168

JAMES LACKINGTON, Bookseller (1746–1815)

AT the time we were purchasing household goods we kept ourselves very short of money, and on Christmas eve we had but half-a-crown left to buy a Christmas dinner. My wife desired that I would go to market and purchase this festival dinner, and off I went for that purpose; but in the way I saw an old bookshop, and I could not resist the temptation of going in; intending only to spend sixpence or ninepence out of my half-a-crown. But I stumbled upon Young's *Night Thoughts*—forgot my dinner—down went my half-crown—and I hastened home, vastly delighted with the acquisition. When my wife asked me where was our Christmas dinner, I told her it was in my pocket.—'In your pocket,' said she; 'that is a strange place! How could you think of stuffing a joint of meat into your pocket?' I assured her that it would take no harm. But as I was in no haste to take it out, she began to be more particular, and inquired what I had got, etc. On which I began to harangue on the superiority of intellectual pleasures over sensual gratifications, and observed that the brute creation enjoyed the latter in a much higher degree than man. And that a man, that was not possessed of intellectual enjoyments, was but a two-legged brute.

I was proceeding in this strain: 'And so,' said she, 'instead of buying a dinner, I suppose you have, as you have done before, been buying books with the money?' I confessed I had bought Young's *Night Thoughts*. 'And I think', said I, 'that I have acted wisely; for had I bought a dinner we should have eaten it tomorrow, and the pleasure would have been soon over, but should we live fifty years longer, we shall have the *Night Thoughts* to feast upon.' This was too powerful an argument to admit of any further debate; in short, my wife was convinced.

169
SAMUEL PARR (1747–1825)

[Samuel Parr and Sir James Mackintosh, both strong Whigs, were in sympathy with the French Revolution, and Mackintosh answered Burke's *Reflections* with his *Vindiciæ Gallicæ* (1791). But whereas Parr always stuck to his revolutionary principles, Mackintosh became more conservative in later years. Father O'Coighly, or O'Quigley, an Irish priest, was arrested at Margate as he was leaving for France. In his pocket was found a paper urging the French to invade England. He was found guilty of high treason, and hanged on 7 June 1798.]

ABOUT the time of the trial of O'Quigley, who was hanged at Maidstone for treason, in 1798, some articles appeared in the *Morning Chronicle*, apparently reflecting on Fox. Dr. Parr read them, and was much displeased. He attributed them to Mackintosh (not then Sir James) because they contained some literary criticism or remark which Parr thought he had communicated to Mackintosh exclusively. In point of fact he was wrong, as it turned out in the sequel that Mackintosh had nothing to do with them; but while in the state of wrath which his belief that Mackintosh was the author occasioned, he (Dr. Parr) and Mackintosh dined together at the table of Sir William Milner, in Manchester Street, Manchester Square. In the course of conversation, after dinner, Mackintosh observed that O'Quigley was one of the *greatest villains that ever was hanged*. Dr. Parr had been watching for an opening, and immediately said, 'No, Jemmy! bad as he was, he might have been a great deal worse. He was an Irishman; he might have been a Scotchman! He was a priest; he might have been a lawyer! He stuck to his principles'— (*giving a violent rap on the table*)—'he might have betrayed them!'

170
JEREMY BENTHAM (1748–1832)

BENTHAM lived next door.[1] We used to see him bustling away, in his sort of half-running walk, in the garden. Both Hazlitt and I often looked with a longing eye from the windows of the room at the white-haired philosopher in his leafy shelter, his head the finest and most venerable ever placed on human shoulders.

The awe which his admirers had of Bentham was carried so far as to make them think everything he said or thought a miracle. Once, I remember, he came to see Leigh Hunt in Surrey Gaol, and played battledore and shuttlecock with him. Hunt told me after of the prodigious power of Bentham's mind. 'He proposed', said Hunt, 'a reform in the handle of battledores!' 'Did he?' said I with awful respect. 'He did,' said Hunt, 'taking in everything, you see, like the elephant's trunk, which lifts alike a pin or twelve hundredweight. Extraordinary mind!' 'Extraordinary,' I echoed.

171
RICHARD BRINSLEY SHERIDAN (1751–1816)

CONVERSING about dramatic literature, Sheridan furnished us with some particulars relative to the first night's performance of *The Rivals*. During the violent opposition in the fifth act, an apple hitting Lee, who performed Sir Lucius O'Trigger, he stepped forward, and with a genuine rich brogue, angrily cried out, 'By the pow'rs, is it *personal*?—is it me, or the matter?'

172

INSTEAD of being annoyed, Sheridan seemed rather amused when one of the company inadvertently alluded to Merry's remark, on the night of the first performance of *The School for Scandal*, at the close of the second act: 'I wish the *dramatis personae* would leave off talking, and let the play begin.'

[1] The writer is Benjamin Robert Haydon.

173

TWO days previous to the performance of *The Critic*, the last scene was not written; Dr. Ford and Mr. Linley, the joint proprietors, began to get nervous and fidgety, and the actors were absolutely *au désespoir*, especially King, who was not only stage-manager, but had to play Puff. To him was assigned the duty of hunting down and worrying Sheridan about the last scene; day after day passed, until . . . the last day but two arrived, and it made not its appearance.

At last Mr. Linley, who being his father-in-law was pretty well aware of his habits, hit upon a stratagem. A night rehearsal of *The Critic* was ordered, and Sheridan, having dined with Linley, was prevailed upon to go; while they were on the stage, King whispered Sheridan that he had something particular to communicate, and begged he would step into the second green-room. Accordingly Sheridan went, and there found a table, with pens, ink, and paper, a good fire, an armed chair at the table, and two bottles of claret, with a dish of anchovy sandwiches. The moment he got into the room, King stepped out, and locked the door; immediately after which, Linley and Ford came up and told the author that, until he had written the scene, he would be kept where he was.

Sheridan took this decided measure in good part; he ate the anchovies, finished the claret, wrote the scene, and laughed heartily at the ingenuity of the contrivance.

174

ONE evening that their late Majesties honoured Drury Lane with their presence, the play, by royal command, was *The School for Scandal.* When Mr. Sheridan was in attendance to light their Majesties to their carriage, the King said to him, 'I am much pleased with your comedy of *The School for Scandal*; but I am still more so with your play of *The Rivals*—that is my favourite, and I will never give it up.'

Her Majesty, at the same time, said, 'When, Mr. Sheridan, shall we have another play from your masterly pen?' He replied that he was writing a comedy, which he expected very shortly to finish.

I[1] was told of this; and the next day, walking with him along Piccadilly, I asked him if he had told the Queen that he was writing a play. He said he had, and that he was actually about one.

[1] Michael Kelly (1764?–1826), actor and composer.

'Not you,' said I to him; 'you will never write again; you are afraid to write.'

He fixed his penetrating eye on me, and said, 'Of whom am I afraid?'

I said, 'You are afraid of the author of *The School for Scandal*.'

175

I[1] WAS present on the second day of Hastings' trial in Westminster Hall; when Sheridan was listened to with such attention that you might have heard a pin drop.—During one of those days Sheridan, having observed Gibbon among the audience, took occasion to mention 'the luminous author of *The Decline and Fall*'. After he had finished, one of his friends reproached him with flattering Gibbon. 'Why, what did I say of him?' asked Sheridan.—'You called him the luminous author,' etc.—'Luminous! oh, I meant—*vol*uminous.'

176

ON the night of the 24th of February 1809, when the House of Commons was occupied with Mr. Ponsonby's motion on the Conduct of the War in Spain, and Mr. Sheridan was in attendance, with the intention, no doubt, of speaking, the House was suddenly illuminated by a blaze of light; and, the Debate being interrupted, it was ascertained that the Theatre of Drury Lane was on fire. A motion was made to adjourn; but Mr. Sheridan said, with much calmness, that 'whatsoever might be the extent of the private calamity, he hoped it would not interfere with the public business of the country'. He then left the House; and, proceeding to Drury Lane, witnessed, with a fortitude which strongly interested all who observed him, the entire destruction of his property. It is said that, as he sat at the Piazza Coffee-house during the fire, taking some refreshment, a friend of his having remarked on the philosophic calmness with which he bore his misfortune, Sheridan answered, 'A man may surely be allowed to take a glass of wine *by his own fireside*.'

177

JOSEPH RITSON (1752–1803)

[Ritson was a painstaking, accurate, irritable, and exceptionally quarrelsome scholar, whose editions of metrical romances and ballads still have value. His eccentricities, which increased with age, culminated in mental derangement,

[1] Samuel Rogers.

and he died insane. One of his more reputable eccentricities was vegetarianism, which led him to write *An Essay on Abstinence from Animal Food as a Moral Duty* (1802).]

HE found a vegetarian printer for the work: Richard Phillips of St. Paul's Churchyard. And not content with espousing one unpopular cause, he had it printed, as he was determined all his books should henceforth be printed, in his most advanced etymological spelling.

While Ritson was about professing his 'vegetable love'—or rather, faith—thus publicly, a lamentable but ludicrous incident occurred. It must be told in the words of Frederick Madden, who declares he got the story from Francis Douce[1] himself:

Ritson was sitting in Mr. Douce's house eating some bread and cheese for luncheon, when a little girl who was in the room very innocently looked up in Mr. Ritson's face and said, 'La! Mr. Ritson, what a quantity of mites you are eating!' Ritson absolutely trembled with passion—laid down his knife—and abruptly quitted the room! On Mr. Douce following him, he said in a tone of excitement, 'You have done this on purpose to insult me.' The only answer Mr. Douce made was, 'Sir, there is the door, and I never wish to see you again within it.'

What made the little girl's remark hurt was the fact that Ritson had given especial praise to the Brahmins: 'for, not confineing murder to the killing of a man, they religiously abstain from takeing away the life of the meanest animal, mite or flea'. Was he now, after a life of scrupulous and humane self-denial, to be forbidden his favourite food, or convicted of sin against his own doctrines—by a child? His shattered nerves would not stand the shock. Douce wrote to Ellis, soon afterwards, that Ritson and he had parted: 'We have taken a formal leave of each other—under our hands and seals, probably forever. . . .'

178
DUGALD STEWART (1753–1828)

DUGALD STEWART, in the true absence of mind of a philosopher, often forgot, it was alleged, to return books which he had borrowed to read. On its being said that, eminent as he was in many branches of knowledge, he confessed himself deficient in Arithmetic, a punster said, 'That, tho' very improbable, might be true; but he certainly excelled in book-keeping.'

[1] Francis Douce (1757–1834), antiquary and bibliophile.

179
GEORGE CRABBE (1754–1832)

ONE gloomy day in 1779, as Crabbe strolled up the bleak and cheerless cliff at Aldeburgh, he stopped opposite a muddy piece of water, and taking it for the waters of Helicon, said, 'I will go to London.' To effect this, he applied himself to his neighbour, the late Mr. Dudley North, for the loan of £5, which was immediately sent, and after paying his debts, he found £3 in his pocket when he set off to make his fortune in the metropolis. 'Without black velvet breeches what is man?' says the author of *The Man of Taste*; but let us ask what *was* man in Crabbe's day without a tie-wig? Accordingly, our youthful bard, not wishing to meet the Muses in an undress, out of his £3 purchased a fashionable tie-wig, and then took lodgings at Mr. Vickery's, opposite the Exchange.

Here he lived in great seclusion, and in great privation of course; but steadily pursuing his inflexible purpose of improving his talents, preserving the most honourable feelings of independence, and keeping his wig in excellent buckle. Sometimes he was reduced even to a very few shillings, and was in much woeful perplexity. He wrote to Lord Shelbourne, who did *not* answer him, and to Lord Thurlow, who *did*. He tried Messrs. Dodsley and Beckett in vain, and he must either have starved, or parted with his peruke, or returned to Slaughden and the butter firkins, when he fortunately thought of addressing himself to *Edmund Burke*. This was in 1781. Politics were raging, the blazing fires of London[1] were scarcely extinct in their ashes, and Burke was employed in 'wielding the wild democracy of the House'—but he heard the youthful Poet with smiles of benevolence—he attended to his history with patience and benignity—he encouraged him, advised him, soothed his misfortunes, opened his house, and spread his table for him—made Dodsley publish his poem, *The Library*, and got him into orders. Crabbe was a long and frequent guest at Beaconsfield, and nothing could exceed the friendly hospitality, and the delicate and polite attentions which he received there.

We must give an instance that may be instructive to some *great persons of our acquaintance in their treatment of poets*. 'One day some company of rank not having arrived as expected, the servants kept back some costly dish that had been cooked. Mrs. Burke asked for it. The butler said, "It was kept back, as the company had not come."—"*What, is not Mr. Crabbe here?* Let it be brought up immediately." ' Now, if this is not real politeness, arising from delicacy of mind, good feeling, and a genuine sense of what is right and decorous, we never met with it.

[1] i.e. in the riots fomented by Lord George Gordon in June 1780.

180

[The Revd George Crabbe recalls his father]

NUMBERLESS were the manuscripts which he completed; and not a few of them were never destined to see the light. I can well remember more than one grand incremation—not in the chimney, for the bulk of the paper to be consumed would have endangered the house—but in the open air—and with what glee his children vied in assisting him, stirring up the fire, and bringing him fresh loads of the fuel as fast as their little legs would enable them. What the various works thus destroyed treated of, I cannot tell; but among them was an Essay on Botany in English; which, after he had made great progress in it, my father laid aside, in consequence merely, I believe, of the remonstrance of the late Mr. Davies, vice-master of Trinity College, Cambridge, with whom he had become casually acquainted, and who, though little tinged with academical peculiarities, could not stomach the notion of degrading such a science by treating it in a modern language. My father used to say that, had this treatise come out at the time when his friend arrested its progress, he might perhaps have had the honour of being considered as the first discoverer of more than one addition to the British Flora, since those days introduced to notice, classed and named, by other naturalists. . . . But among other prose writings of the same period some were of a class which, perhaps, few have ever suspected Mr. Crabbe of meddling with, though it be one in which so many of his poetical contemporaries have earned high distinction. During one or two of his winters in Suffolk, he gave most of his evening hours to the writing of *Novels*, and he brought not less than three such works to a conclusion. . . . I forget the title of his third novel; but I clearly remember that it opened with a description of a wretched room, similar to some that are presented in his poetry, and that, on my mother's telling him frankly that she thought the effect very inferior to that of the corresponding pieces in verse, he paused in his reading, and, after some reflection, said, 'Your remark is just.' The result was a leisurely examination of all these manuscript novels, and another of those grand incremations which, at an earlier period, had been sport to his children.

181

WE happened to be on a visit at Aldeburgh, when the dread of a French invasion was at its height. The old artillery of the fort had been replaced by cannon of a large calibre; and one, the most weighty I remember to have seen, was constantly primed, as an alarm gun. About one o'clock one dark morning, I heard a distant gun at sea; in about ten minutes another, and at an equal interval a third; and then at last, the tremendous roar of the great gun on the fort, which shook every house in the town. After inquiring into the state of affairs, I went to my father's room, and, knocking at the door, with difficulty waked the inmates, and said, 'Do not be alarmed, but the French are landing.' I then mentioned that the alarm gun had been fired, that horsemen had been dispatched for the troops at Ipswich, and that the drum on the quay was then beating to arms. He replied, 'Well, my old fellow, you and I can do no good, or we would be among them; we must wait the event.' I returned to his door in about three-quarters of an hour, to tell him that the agitation was subsiding, and found him fast asleep. Whether the affair was a mere blunder, or there had been a concerted manoeuvre to try the fencibles, we never could learn with certainty; but I remember that my father's coolness on the occasion, when we mentioned it next day, caused some suspicious shakings of the head among the ultra-loyalists at Aldeburgh.

182

WOULD the reader like to follow my father into his library?—a scene of unparalleled confusion—windows rattling, paint in great request, books in every direction but the right—the table—but no, I cannot find terms to describe it, though the counterpart might be seen, perhaps, not one hundred miles from the study of the justly-famed and beautiful rectory of Bremhill[1]. Once, when we were staying at Trowbridge, in his absence for a few days at Bath, my eldest girl thought she should surprise and please him by putting every book in perfect order, making the best bound the most prominent; but, on his return, thanking her for her good intention, he replaced every volume in its former state; 'for', said he, 'my dear, grandpapa understands his own confusion better than your order and neatness'.

183
MARTIN JOSEPH ROUTH (1755–1854)

[These recollections of the aged President of Magdalen College, Oxford, were recorded by John William Burgon (see No. 333), who matriculated at Worcester College at the age of twenty-eight, became Vicar of St. Mary's, Oxford, in 1863, and Dean of Chichester in 1876. He managed to get the interview because he

[1] From 1804-50 the incumbent was the poet William Lisle Bowles.

'had been charged with a book for him, and having obtained his permission to bring it in person, presented [himself] at his gate'.]

AVAILING myself of a pause after he had inquired after my intended pursuits, I leaned forward (for he was more than slightly deaf) and remarked that perhaps he would allow me to ask him a question. 'Eh, sir?' 'I thought that perhaps you would allow me to ask a question about Divinity, sir.' He told me to go on. I explained that I desired a few words of counsel, if he would condescend to give them—some directions as to the best way of pursuing the study which he had himself cultivated with such signal success. Aware that my request was almost as vague as the subject was vast, and full of genuine consideration for the aged oracle, I enlarged for a minute on the matter, chiefly in order to give him time to adjust his thoughts before making reply. He inquired what I had read. 'Pearson and Eusebius, carefully.'

The gravity which by this time his features had assumed was very striking. He lay back in his chair. His head sank forward on his chest, and he looked like one absorbed in thought. 'Yes—I think, sir' (said he after a long pause, which, besides raising my curiosity, rather alarmed me by the contrast it presented to his recent animated manner) 'I think, sir, were I you, sir—that I would—first of all—read the—the Gospel according to St. Matthew.' Here he paused. 'And after I had read the Gospel according to St. Matthew—I would—were I you, sir—go on to read—the Gospel according to St.—Mark.' I looked at him anxiously to see whether he was serious. One glance was enough. He was giving me (but at a very slow rate) the outline of my future course. 'I think, sir, when I had read the Gospel according to St. Mark, I would go on, sir—yes! go on to—to the—the Gospel—according to—St. Luke, sir.' (Another pause, as if the reverend speaker were reconsidering the matter.) 'Well, sir, and when I had read those three gospels, sir, were I in your place, I would go on—yes, I would certainly go on to read the Gospel according to St. John.'

For an instant I had felt an inclination to laugh. But by this time a very different set of feelings came over me. Here was a theologian of ninety-one, who, after surveying the entire field of sacred science, had come back to the point he had started from; and had nothing better to advise me to read than the Gospel! . . .

A full year elapsed before I ventured to repeat the intrusion. . . . I ventured to address him somewhat as follows: 'Mr. President, give me leave to ask you a question I have sometimes asked of aged persons, but never of any so aged or so learned as yourself.' He looked so kindly at me that I thought I might go on. 'Every studious man, in the course of a long and thoughtful life, has had occasion to experience the special value of some axiom or precept. Would you mind giving me the benefit of such a word of advice?' He bade me explain, evidently to gain time. I quoted an instance. He nodded and looked thoughtful. Presently he brightened up and said, 'I think, sir, since you care for the advice of an old man, sir, you will find it a very good practice' (here he looked me in the face) '*always to verify your references*, sir!'

184
WILLIAM BLAKE (1757–1827)

[From 1790 to 1800 Blake lived with his wife at Number 13 Hercules Buildings, Lambeth.]

AT the end of the little garden in Hercules Buildings there was a summer-house. Mr. Butts calling one day found Mr. and Mrs. Blake sitting in this summer-house, freed from 'those troublesome disguises' which have prevailed since the Fall. '*Come in!*' cried Blake; '*it's only Adam and Eve, you know!*' Husband and wife had been reciting passages from *Paradise Lost*, in character, and the garden of Hercules Buildings had to represent the Garden of Eden: a little to the scandal of wondering neighbours, on more than one occasion.

185

HIS wife was an excellent cook—a talent which helped to fill out Blake's waistcoat a little, as he grew old. She could even prepare a made dish, when need be. As there was no servant, he fetched the porter for dinner himself, from the house at the corner of the Strand. Once, pot of porter in hand, he espied coming along a dignitary of art—that highly respectable man, William Collins, R.A., whom he had met in society a few evenings before. The Academician was about to shake hands, but seeing the porter, drew up, and did not know him. Blake would tell the story very quietly, and without sarcasm. . . . His habits were very temperate. It was only in later years that he took porter regularly. He then fancied it soothed him, and would sit and muse over his pint after a one o'clock dinner. When he drank wine, which, at home, of course, was seldom, he professed a liking to drink off good draughts from a tumbler, and thought the wine glass system absurd: a very heretical opinion in the eyes of your true wine drinkers. Frugal and abstemious on principle, he was sometimes rather imprudent, and would take anything that came in his way. A nobleman once sent him some oil of walnuts he had had expressed[1] purposely for an

[1] i.e. pressed, squeezed.

artistic experiment. Blake tasted it, and went on tasting, till he had drunk the whole. When his lordship called to ask how the experiment prospered, the artist had to confess what had become of the ingredients. It was ever after a standing joke against him.

186

BLAKE, who always saw in fancy every form he drew, believed that angels descended to painters of old, and sat for their portraits. When he himself sat to Phillips for that fine portrait so beautifully engraved by Schiavonetti, the painter, in order to obtain the most unaffected attitude, and the most poetic expression, engaged his sitter in a conversation concerning the sublime in art. 'We hear much', said Phillips, 'of the grandeur of Michael Angelo; from the engravings, I should say he has been over-rated; he could not paint an angel so well as Raphael.' 'He has not been over-rated, Sir,' said Blake, 'and he could paint an angel better than Raphael.' 'Well, but', said the other, 'you never saw any of the paintings of Michael Angelo, and perhaps speak from the opinions of others; your friends may have deceived you.' 'I never saw any of the paintings of Michael Angelo,' replied Blake, 'but I speak from the opinion of a friend who could not be mistaken.' 'A valuable friend truly,' said Phillips, 'and who may he be I pray?' 'The arch-angel Gabriel, Sir,' answered Blake.—'A good authority surely, but you know evil spirits love to assume the looks of good ones; and this may have been done to mislead you.' 'Well now, Sir,' said Blake, 'this is really singular: such were my own suspicions; but they were soon removed—I will tell you how. I was one day reading Young's *Night Thoughts*, and when I came to that passage which asks "who can paint an angel?", I closed the book and cried, "Aye! who can paint an angel?" A voice in the room answered, "Michael Angelo could." "And how do *you* know?" I said, looking round me, but I saw nothing save a greater light than usual. "I *know*," said the voice, "for I sat to him: I am the arch-angel Gabriel." "Oho!" I answered, "you are, are you? I must have better assurance than that of a wandering voice; you may be an evil spirit—there are such in the land." "You shall have good assurance," said the voice; "can an evil spirit do this?" I looked whence the voice came, and was then aware of a shining shape, with bright wings, who diffused much light. As I looked, the shape dilated more and more: he waved his hands; the roof of my study opened; he ascended into heaven; he stood in the sun, and beckoning to me, moved the universe. An angel of evil could not have *done that*—it was the arch-angel Gabriel.' The painter marvelled much at this wild story;

but he caught from Blake's looks, as he related it, that rapt poetic expression which has rendered his portrait one of the finest of the English school.

187

THE friend who obliged me[1] with these anecdotes on observing the interest which I took in the subject, said, 'I know much about Blake—I was his companion for nine years. I have sat beside him from ten at night till three in the morning, sometimes slumbering and sometimes waking, but Blake never slept; he sat with a pencil and paper drawing portraits of those whom I most desired to see. I will show you, Sir, some of these works.' He took out a large book filled with drawings, opened it, and continued: 'Observe the poetic fervour of that face—it is Pindar as he stood a conqueror in the Olympic games. And this lovely creature is Corinna, who conquered in poetry in the same place. That lady is Lais, the courtesan —with the impudence which is part of her profession, she stept in between Blake and Corinna, and he was obliged to paint her to get her away. . . .'

He closed the book, and taking out a small panel from a private drawer, said, 'This is the last which I shall show you; but it is the greatest curiosity of all. Only look at the splendour of the colouring and the original character of the thing!' 'I see', said I, 'a naked figure with a strong body and a short neck—with burning eyes which long for moisture, and a face worthy of a murderer, holding a bloody cup in his clawed hands, out of which it seems eager to drink. I never saw any shape so strange, nor did I ever see any colouring so curiously splendid—a kind of glistening green and dusky gold, beautifully varnished. But what in the world is it?' 'It is a ghost, Sir—the ghost of a flea—a spiritualization of the thing!' 'He saw this in a vision then,' I said. 'I'll tell you all about it, Sir. I called on him one evening, and found Blake more than usually excited. He told me he had seen a wonderful thing—the ghost of a flea! "And did you make a drawing of him?" I inquired. "No, indeed," said he, "I wish I had, but I shall, if he appears again!" He looked earnestly into a corner of the room, and then said, "Here he is—reach me my things—I shall keep my eye on him. There he comes! his eager tongue whisking out of his mouth, a cup in his hand to hold blood, and covered with a scaly skin of gold and green." —As he described him so he drew him.'

[1] Allan Cunningham.

188

[Frederick Tatham (1805–78) became the friend of Blake and his wife in their old age. On Blake's death, Mrs. Blake stayed for some time with Tatham and his wife, and was apparently very fond of them. Tatham's account of Blake's last hours must be based on what Mrs. Blake told him, and although there are signs of dramatization in his narrative, the facts are probably authentic.]

ABOUT a year before he died he was seized with a species of ague (as it was then termed), of which he was alternately better and worse. He was at times very ill, but rallied, and all had hopes of him; indeed, such was his energy that even then, though sometimes confined to bed, he sat up drawing his most stupendous works. In August he gradually grew worse, and required much more of his wife's attention; indeed, he was decaying fast; his patience during his agonies of pain is described to have been exemplary.

Life, however, like a dying flame flashed once more, gave one more burst of animation, during which he was cheerful, and free from the tortures of his approaching end. He thought he was better, and as he was sure to do, asked to look at the work over which he was occupied when seized with his last attack: it was a coloured print of the Ancient of Days, striking the first circle of the Earth, done expressly by commission for the writer of this. After he had worked upon it he exclaimed: 'There, I have done all I can; it is the best I have ever finished. I hope Mr. Tatham will like it.' He threw it suddenly down, and said, 'Kate, you have been a good wife, I will draw your portrait.' She sat near his bed and he made a drawing, which, though not a likeness, is finely touched and expressed. He then threw that down, after having drawn for an hour, and began to sing Hallelujahs and songs of joy and triumph, which Mrs. Blake described as being truly sublime in music and in verse. He sang loudly and with true ecstatic energy, and seemed too happy that he had finished his course, that he had run his race, and that he was shortly to arrive at the goal, to receive the prize of his high and eternal calling. After having answered a few questions concerning his wife's means of living after his decease, and after having spoken of the writer of this as a likely person to become the manager of her affairs, his spirit departed like the sighing of a gentle breeze, and he slept in company with the mighty ancestors he had formerly depicted. He passed from death to an immortal life on the 12th of August 1827. . . . Such was the entertainment of the last hour of his life. His bursts of gladness made the room peal again. The walls rang and resounded with the beatific symphony. It was a prelude to the hymns of saints. It was an overture to the choir of Heaven. It was a chaunt for the response of angels.

189
ROBERT BURNS (1759–96)

THE young ladies of Harvieston were, according to Dr. Currie, surprised with the calm manner in which Burns contemplated their fine scenery on Devon water; and the Doctor enters into a little dissertation on the subject, showing that a man of Burns's lively imagination might probably have formed anticipations which the realities of the prospect might rather disappoint. This is possible enough; but I suppose few will take it for granted that Burns surveyed any scenes either of beauty or of grandeur without emotion, merely because he did not choose to be ecstatic for the benefit of a company of young ladies. He was indeed very impatient of interruption on such occasions; I have heard that riding one dark night near Carron, his companion teased him with noisy exclamations of delight and wonder, whenever an opening in the wood permitted them to see the magnificent glare of the furnaces; 'Look, Burns! Good Heaven! look! look! what a glorious sight!'—'Sir,' said Burns, clapping spurs to Jenny Geddes, 'I would not *look*! *look*! at your bidding, if it were the mouth of hell!'

190

[On 6 August 1844, a festival 'in honour of the genius of the poet Burns' was held at Ayr. What happened is described by Charles Mackay, the Scottish poet and journalist.]

THE Festival took place . . . in a large pavilion erected in a meadow nearly opposite Alloway Kirk, and within sight of the poet's monument. The pavilion, richly decorated with flags and other ornaments, was planned for the accommodation of 2,000 guests, and all the tickets to the banquet, charged fifteen shillings for the gentlemen and ten shillings for the ladies, were speedily taken up. . . . The procession was composed of the magistrates and baillies of many important towns, with deputations of their townspeople, of the Masonic bodies, among whom, when living, Burns stood high in rank and repute, and who were proud of his brotherhood in the craft; and of Foresters, Odd Fellows, and many other societies, preceded by bands of music, and bearing, many of them, not merely the customary flags and banners of Great Britain, but the ancient historic flag of Scotland, under the gleam and glamour of which Bruce fought and won the battle of Bannockburn. There was also a grand procession of peasants and farm labourers, assembled in honour of the greatest peasant—next perhaps to King David of the Jews, a peasant, a poet, a patriot, and a king—whom any age had produced, and who bore high erected in the midst of them a gigantic thistle, eight or nine feet high, and with a profusion of flowers, which must have been the result of high cultivation. As this national emblem made its appearance, with the proud motto, 'Nemo me impune lacessit' emblazoned on a banner streaming over it, the applause of the immense assemblage was loud and unrestrained, and was repeated again and again as Christopher North took off his hat in reverence to the symbol as it was borne past. At two o'clock in the afternoon the banquet was served in the pavilion, and I had the good fortune, as an invited guest, to be assigned a seat of honour on the platform, to the left hand of the distinguished vice-chairman[1] of the day. I was unable, from the distance and the want of acoustic facility in the tent, to hear a word said by Lord Eglinton on the occasion; but I saw from the newspapers in due time, that he had made a very eloquent and appreciative speech, and done justice to the genius of the bard whose memory they had all assembled to honour. Professor Wilson's speech, of which I heard every word that he was permitted to deliver, was still more eloquent, and as the literary effort of a literary man, on a great literary occasion, was equal to the Professor's reputation. But he made a great mistake. He took no account of time or space, and painting his picture of the poet on too extensive a canvas, fairly exhausted the patience of his auditory before he had advanced beyond the threshold of his argument. He dwelt upon the errors of Burns: upon his over passionate youth, and Samson-like enslavement to many Delilahs; and to the excessive conviviality that brought him into bad company, and overclouded his day ere the noon had fairly come. The long speech of Lord Eglinton, excellent though it was, had not disposed the audience for a second speech of equal dimensions, and after the Professor had expatiated for about half-an-hour or more on the frailties of the bard, the sounds of impatience, dissent, and disapprobation grew so loud, so prolonged, and so often repeated, that the Professor, seeing the hopelessness of proceeding, sat down with the best part of his speech unspoken. He turned to me, as he resumed his place, and said, 'It is a pity they won't hear me out. I only dwelt upon the errors of Burns, that I might lift him out of them in power and glory, as one of the very greatest of Scotsmen who ever conferred honour upon his country.'

'Fortunately', I replied, 'you can publish your speech, as you intended to speak it, and so put yourself right.'

'Yes,' he replied, 'I'll shame the fools and print it.'

[1] Professor John Wilson, 1785–1854 ('Christopher North').

191
RICHARD PORSON (1759–1808)

PORSON thought Gibbon's *Decline and Fall* beyond all comparison the greatest literary production of the eighteenth century, and was in the habit of repeating long passages from it. Yet I have heard him say that 'there could not be a better exercise for a schoolboy than to turn a page of it into English.'

192

PORSON was walking with a Trinitarian friend; they had been speaking of the Trinity. A buggy came by with three men in it: 'There', says he, 'is an illustration of the Trinity.' 'No,' said his friend Porson, 'you must show me one man in *three* buggies, if you can.'

193

A MAN of such habits as Porson was little fitted for the office of Librarian to the London Institution.[1] He was very irregular in his attendance there; he never troubled himself about the purchase of books which ought to have been added to the library; and he would frequently come home dead-drunk long after midnight. I have good reason to believe that, had he lived, he would have been requested to give up the office—in other words, he would have been dismissed. I once read a letter which he received from the Directors of the Institution, and which contained, among other severe things, this cutting remark: 'We only know that you are our Librarian by seeing your name attached to the receipts for your salary.' . . . As Librarian to the Institution, he had £200 a year, apartments rent-free, and the use of a servant. Yet he was eternally railing at the Directors, calling them 'mercantile and mean beyond merchandize and meanness'.

[1] These reminiscences were communicated to Samuel Rogers by William Maltby, who succeeded Porson as Principal Librarian to the London Institution.

194
WILLIAM BECKFORD (1760–1844)

A DISTANT connection of mine, who, I must presume, was a person of an inquiring mind, found himself involved in a curious adventure. . . .[1] There was one house, and that the most interesting of all, that shut its door against my inquisitive friend and everybody else. Fonthill Abbey, or Fonthill Splendour as it was sometimes called, situated a few miles from Bath, was a treasure-house of beauty. Every picture was said to be a gem, and the gardens were unequalled by any in England, the whole being guarded by a dragon in the form of Mr. Beckford. 'Not only', says an authority, 'had the art-treasures of that princely place been sealed against the public, but the park itself—known by rumour as a beautiful spot—had for several years been inclosed by a most formidable wall, about seven miles in circuit, twelve feet high, and crowned by a *chevaux-de-frise*.' These formidable obstacles my distant cousin undertook to surmount, and he laid a wager of a considerable sum that he would walk in the gardens, and even penetrate into the house itself.

Having nothing better to do, he spent many an anxious hour in watching the great gate in the wall, in the hope that by some inadvertence it might be left open and unguarded; and one day the happy moment arrived. The porter was ill, and his wife opened the gate to a tradesman, who, after depositing his goods at the lodge (no butcher or baker was permitted to go to the Abbey itself), retired, leaving the gate open, relying probably upon the woman's shutting it. Quick as thought my relative passed the awful portals, and made his way across the park. Guided by the high tower—called 'Beckford's Folly'—my inquisitive friend made his way to the gardens, and not being able immediately to find the entrance, was leaning on a low wall that shut the gardens from the park, and taking his fill of delight at that gorgeous display—the gardens being in full beauty—when a man with a spud in his hand—perhaps the head-gardener—approached, and asked the intruder how he came there, and what he wanted.

'The fact is, I found the gate in the wall open, and having heard a great deal about this beautiful place, I thought I should like to see it.'

'Ah,' said the gardener, 'you would, would you? Well, you can't see much where you are. Do you think you could manage to jump over the wall? If you can, I will show you the gardens.'

My cousin looked over the wall, and found such a palpable obstacle—in the shape of a deep ditch—that he wondered at the proposal.

[1] The narrator is the Victorian painter, W. P. Frith (1819–1909).

'Oh, I forgot the ditch! Well, go to the door; you will find it about a couple of hundred yards to your right, and I will admit you.'

In a very short time, to his great delight, my cousin found himself listening to the learned names of rare plants, and inhaling the perfume of lovely flowers. Then the fruit-gardens and hot-houses—'acres of them', as he afterwards declared—were submitted to his inspection. After the beauties of the gardens and grounds had been thoroughly explored, and the wager half won, the inquisitive one's pleasure may be imagined when his guide said:

'Now, would you like to see the house and its contents? There are some rare things in it—fine pictures and so on. Do you know anything about pictures?'

'I think I do, and should, above all things, like to see those of which I have heard so much; but are you sure that you will not get yourself into a scrape with Mr. Beckford? I've heard he is so very particular.'

'Oh no!' said the gardener, 'I don't think Mr. Beckford will mind what I do. You see, I have known him all my life, and he lets me do pretty well what I like here.'

'Then I shall be only too much obliged.'

'Follow me, then,' said the guide.

My distant cousin was really a man of considerable taste and culture, a great lover of art, with some knowledge of the old masters and the different schools; and he often surprised his guide, who, catalogue in hand, named the different pictures and their authors, by his acute and often correct criticism. . . . When the pictures had been thoroughly examined, there remained bric-à-brac of all kinds, costly suits of armour, jewelry of all ages, bridal coffers beautifully painted by Italian artists, numbers of ancient and modern musical instruments, with other treasures, all to be carefully and delightfully examined, till, the day nearing fast towards evening, the visitor prepared to depart, and was commencing a speech of thanks in his best manner, when the gardener said, looking at his watch:

'Why, bless me, it's five o'clock! ain't you hungry? You must stop and have some dinner.'

'No, really, I couldn't think of taking such a liberty. I am sure Mr. Beckford would be offended.'

'No, he wouldn't. You must stop and dine with me; I am Mr. Beckford.'

My far-off cousin's state of mind may be imagined. He had won his wager, and he was asked, actually asked, to dine with the man whose name was a terror to the tourist, whose walks abroad were so rare that his personal appearance was unknown to his neighbours. What a story to relate to his circle at Bath! How Mr. Beckford had been belied, to be sure! The dinner was magnificent, served on massive plate—the wines of the rarest vintage. Rarer still was Mr. Beckford's conversation. He entertained his guest with stories of Italian travel, with anecdotes of the great in whose society he had mixed, till he found the shallowness of it; in short, with the outpouring of a mind of great power and thorough cultivation. My cousin was well read enough to be able to appreciate the conversation and contribute to it, and thus the evening passed delightfully away. Candles were lighted, and host and guest talked till a fine Louis Quatorze clock struck eleven. Mr. Beckford rose and left the room. The guest drew his chair to the fire, and waited the return of his host. He thought he must have dozed, for he started to find the room in semi-darkness, and one of the solemn powdered footmen putting out the lights.

'Where is Mr. Beckford?' said my cousin.

'Mr. Beckford is gone to bed,' said the man, as he extinguished the last candle.

The dining-room door was open, and there was a dim light in the hall.

'This is very strange,' said my cousin; 'I expected Mr. Beckford back again. I wished to thank him for his hospitality.'

This was said as the guest followed the footman to the front-door. That functionary opened it wide and said:

'Mr. Beckford ordered me to present his compliments to you, sir, and I am to say that as you found your way into Fonthill Abbey without assistance, you may find your way out again as best you can; and he hopes you will take care to avoid the bloodhounds that are let loose in the gardens every night. I wish you good-evening. No, thank you, sir: Mr. Beckford never allows vails.'

My cousin climbed into the branches of the first tree that promised a safe shelter from the dogs, and there waited for daylight; and it was not till the sun showed itself that he made his way, terror attending each step, through the gardens into the park, and so to Bath. 'The wager was won,' said my relative; 'but not for fifty million times the amount would I again pass such a night as I did at Fonthill Abbey.'

195
WILLIAM COBBETT (1762–1835)

AT eleven years of age my employment was clipping of box-edgings and weeding beds of flowers in the garden of the Bishop of Winchester, at the Castle of Farnham, my native town. I had always been fond of beautiful gardens; and a gardener, who had just come from the King's gardens at Kew, gave such a description of them as made me instantly resolve to work in these gardens. The next morning, without saying a word to anyone, off I set, with no clothes except those upon my back, and with thirteen half-pence in my pocket. I found that I must go to Richmond, and I accordingly went on, from place to place, inquiring my way thither. A long day (it was in June) brought me to Richmond in the afternoon. Twopennyworth of bread and cheese and a pennyworth of small beer which I had on the road, and one half-penny that I had lost somehow or other, left three pence in my pocket. With this for my whole fortune, I was trudging through Richmond in my blue smock frock and my red garters tied under my knees, when, staring about me, my eye fell upon a little book in a bookseller's window, on the outside of which was written: 'TALE OF A TUB; Price 3*d*.' The title was so odd that my curiosity was excited. I had the 3*d*., but, then, I could have *no supper*. In I went, and got the little book, which I was so impatient to read that I got over into a field, at the upper corner of Kew Gardens, where there stood a *hay-stack*. The book was so different from anything that I had ever read before: it was something so *new* to my mind, that, though I could not at all understand some of it, it delighted me beyond description; and it produced what I have always considered a sort of birth of intellect.

I read on till it was dark, without any thought of supper or bed. When I could see no longer I put my little book in my pocket, and tumbled down by the side of the stack, where I slept till the birds in Kew Gardens awaked me in the morning; when off I started to Kew, reading my little book. The singularity of my dress, the simplicity of my manner, my confident and lively air, and, doubtless, his own compassion besides, induced the gardener, who was a Scotsman, I remember, to give me victuals, find me lodging, and set me to work. And it was during the period that I was at Kew that the present king and two of his brothers laughed at the oddness of my dress, while I was sweeping the grass plot round the foot of the Pagoda. The gardener, seeing me fond of books, lent me some gardening books to read; but these I could not relish after my *Tale of a Tub*, which I carried about with me wherever I went, and when I, at about twenty years old, lost it in a box that fell overboard in the Bay of Fundy in North America, the loss gave me greater pain than I have ever felt at losing thousands of pounds.

196

WILLIAM LISLE BOWLES (1762–1850)

WHEN Madame de Staël was here[1] Mr. Bowles the poet, or as Lord Byron calls him, the sonneteer, was invited to dine here. She admired his 'Sonnets' and his *Spirit of Maritime Discovery* and ranked him high as an

[1] Bowood, the seat of the Lansdowne family.

English genius. In riding to Bowood that day he fell from his horse and sprained his shoulder but still came on. Lord Lansdowne, willing to show him to advantage, alluded to this in presenting him before dinner to Madame de Staël. He is a simple country-curate-looking man and rather blunt, and when Madame de Staël in the midst of the listening circle in the drawing room began to compliment him and herself upon the effort he had made to come and see her, he replied, 'Oh, Ma'am, say no more about it, for I would have done a great deal more to see so great a *curiosity*.' Lord Lansdowne says it is impossible to describe the shock in Madame de Staël's face—the breathless astonishment—and the total change produced in her opinion of the man, and her manner towards him. She said afterwards to Lord Lansdowne, 'Je vois bien que ce n'est qu'un curé qui n'a pas le sens commun—quoique grand poète.' She never forgot it. Two years afterwards she spoke of it to Lord Lansdowne at Geneva, and wondered how it was possible that *un tel homme* could exist.

197
SAMUEL ROGERS (1763–1855)

MY friend Maltby and I, when we were very young men, had a strong desire to see Dr. Johnson; and we determined to call upon him and introduce ourselves. We accordingly proceeded to his house in Bolt Court; and I had my hand on the knocker, when our courage failed us, and we retreated. Many years afterwards, I mentioned this circumstance to Boswell, who said, 'What a pity you did not go boldly in! he would have received you with all kindness.'

198

MR. ROGERS told me that when the *Pleasures of Memory* was first published, one of those busy gentlemen who are vain of knowing everybody came up to him at a party, and said, 'Lady — is dying to be introduced to the author of the *Pleasures of Memory*.'—'Pray let her live', said Rogers, and with difficulty they made their way through the crowd to the lady.—'Mr. Rogers, madam, author of the *Pleasures of Memory*.'—'Pleasures of what?'—'I felt for my friend', said Rogers.

199

HIS wit was perhaps in higher repute than any in his time, except that of Sydney Smith; but while Sydney's wit was genial and good-humoured, and even his mockeries gave no offence, that of Rogers was sarcastic and bitter; and the plea which I have heard him advance for its bitterness was, in itself, a satire: 'They tell me I say ill-natured things', he observed in his slow, quiet, deliberate way; 'I have a weak voice; if I did not say ill-natured things, no one would hear what I said.'

200

ROGERS was aghast at the rapidity with which the Scotts, Byrons, and Moores poured out their works; and even Campbell was too quick for him—he, with all his leisure, and being always at it, producing to the amount of two octavo volumes in his whole life. The charge of haste and incompleteness alleged against his *Columbus* in the *Edinburgh Review*, forty years since, was very exasperating to him; and so absurd that one cannot but suspect Sydney Smith of being the author of it, for the sake of contrast with his conversational description of Rogers's method of composition. Somebody asked one day whether Rogers had written anything lately. 'Only a couplet', was the reply—(the couplet being his celebrated epigram on Lord Dudley). '*Only* a couplet!' exclaimed Sydney Smith. 'Why, what would you have? When Rogers produces a couplet, he goes to bed, and the knocker is tied—and straw is laid down—and caudle is made—and the answer to inquiries is that Mr. Rogers is as well as can be expected.'

201

ON a certain day we went to call at Mrs. Procter's with our father.[1] We found an old man standing in the middle of the room, taking leave of his hostess, nodding his head—he was a little like a Chinese mandarin with an ivory face. His expression never changed but seemed quite fixed. He knew my father and spoke to him and to us too, still in this odd fixed way. Then he looked at my sister. 'My little girl,' he said to her, 'will you come and live with me? You shall be as happy as the day is long; you shall have

[1] This is a reminiscence of Thackeray's daughter, Anne, Lady Ritchie. Mrs. Procter, the wife of Bryan Waller Procter, the poet, was a well-known literary hostess of the day.

a white pony to ride, and feed upon red-currant jelly.' This prospect was so alarming and unexpected that the poor little girl suddenly blushed up and burst into tears. The old man was Mr. Samuel Rogers, but happily he did not see her cry, for he was already on his way to the door.

202
MARIA EDGEWORTH (1767–1849)

[In 1849 Macaulay paid a visit to Ireland. What follows is an extract from his diary.]

August 24. *Killarney.*—A busy day. I found that I must either forgo the finest part of the sight or mount a pony. Ponies are not much in my way. However, I was ashamed to flinch, and rode twelve miles, with a guide, to the head of the Upper Lake, where we met the boat which had been sent forward with four rowers. One of the boatmen gloried in having rowed Sir Walter Scott and Miss Edgeworth, twenty-four years ago. It was, he said, a compensation to him for having missed a hanging which took place that very day.

203
WILLIAM WORDSWORTH (1770–1850)

[Wordsworth as a Cambridge undergraduate.]

AMONG the band of my Compeers was one
My class-fellow at School, whose chance it was
To lodge in the Apartments which had been,
Time out of mind, honor'd by Milton's name;
The very shell reputed of the abode
Which he had tenanted. O temperate Bard!
One afternoon, the first time I set foot
In this thy innocent Nest and Oratory,
Seated with others in a festive ring
Of common-place convention, I to thee
Pour'd out libations, to thy memory drank,
Within my private thoughts, till my brain reel'd
Never so clouded by the fumes of wine

Before that hour, or since. Thence forth I ran
From that assembly, through a length of streets,
Ran, Ostrich-like, to reach our Chapel Door
In not a desperate or opprobrious time,
Albeit long after the importunate Bell
Had stopp'd, with wearisome Cassandra voice
No longer haunting the dark winter night. . . .
Empty thoughts!
I am ashamed of them; and that great Bard,
And thou, O Friend![1] who in thy ample mind
Hast station'd me for reverence and love,
Ye will forgive the weakness of that hour
In some of its unworthy vanities,
Brother of many more.

204

Mr. Coleridge arrived in Bristol from Germany, and as he was about to pay Mr. Wordsworth a visit, he pressed me[2] to accompany him. I had intended a journey to London, and now determined on proceeding with so agreeable a companion, and on so pleasant a journey and tour, taking the metropolis on my return. To notice the complicated incidents which occurred on this tour would occupy a large space. I therefore pass it all over, with the remark, that in this interview with Mr. Wordsworth the subject of the *Lyrical Ballads* was mentioned but once, and that casually, and only to account for its failure! which Mr. Wordsworth ascribed to two causes; first the *Ancient Mariner*, which, he said, no one seemed to understand; and secondly, the unfavourable notice of most of the Reviews.

On my reaching London, having an account to settle with Messrs. Longman and Rees, the booksellers, of Paternoster Row, I sold them all my copyrights, which were valued as one lot by a third party. On my next seeing Mr. Longman, he told me that in estimating the value of the copyrights Fox's *Achmed*[3] and Wordsworth's *Lyrical Ballads* were 'reckoned as nothing'. 'That being the case,' I replied, 'as both these authors are my personal friends, I should be obliged if you would return me again these two copyrights, that I may have the pleasure of presenting them to their respective writers.' Mr. Longman answered, with his customary liberality, 'You are welcome to them.' . . . On Mr. Coleridge's

[1] Coleridge.
[2] Joseph Cottle.
[3] A volume of poems by the Persian scholar, Charles Fox (1749–1809).

return from the north, I gave him Mr. Wordsworth's receipt for his thirty guineas; so that whatever advantage has arisen subsequently from the sale of this volume of the *Lyrical Ballads* has pertained exclusively to Mr. W.

I have been the more particular in these statements, as it furnishes, perhaps, the most remarkable instance on record of a volume of poems remaining for so long a time almost totally neglected, and afterwards acquiring, and that almost rapidly, so much deserved popularity.

205

ONE day Wordsworth at a large party leaned forward to Sir Humphrey Davy at a moment of silence and said: 'Davy, do you know the reason I published my "White Doe" in quarto?' 'No', said Davy, slightly blushing at the attention this awakened. 'To express my own opinion of it', replied Wordsworth.

Once as I was walking with Wordsworth in Pall Mall we ran into Christie's, where there was a very good copy of 'The Transfiguration', which he abused through thick and thin. In the corner stood the group of Cupid and Psyche kissing. After looking some time he turned round to me with an expression I shall never forget, and said, 'The Dev-ils!'

206

SOMEONE having observed that the next Waverley novel was to be 'Rob Roy', Wordsworth took down his volume of Ballads, and read to the company 'Rob Roy's Grave'; then, returning it to the shelf, observed, 'I do not know what more Mr. Scott can have to say upon the subject.'

207

[Carlyle recalls his memories of Wordsworth.]

DURING the last seven or ten years of his life, Wordsworth felt himself to be a recognized lion, in certain considerable London circles, and was in the habit of coming up to town with his wife for a month or two every season, to enjoy his quiet triumph and collect his bits of tribute *tales quales*. . . . Wordsworth generally spoke a little with me on those occasions; sometimes, perhaps, we sat by one another; but there came from him nothing considerable, and happily at least nothing with an effort. 'If you think me dull, be it just so!'—this seemed to a most respectable extent to be his inspiring humour. Hardly above once (perhaps at the Stanleys') do I faintly recollect something of the contrary on his part for a little while, which was not pleasant or successful while it lasted.

The light was always afflictive to his eyes; he carried in his pocket something like a skeleton brass candlestick, in which, setting it on the dinner-table, between him and the most afflictive or nearest of the chief lights, he touched a little spring, and there flirted out, at the top of his brass implement, a small vertical green circle which prettily enough threw his eyes into shade, and screened him from that sorrow. In proof of his equanimity as lion I remember, in connection with this green shade, one little glimpse which shall be given presently as finis. But first let me say that all these Wordsworth phenomena appear to have been indifferent to me, and have melted to steamy oblivion in a singular degree. Of his talk to others in my hearing I remember simply nothing, not even a word or gesture. To myself it seemed once or twice as if he bore suspicions, thinking I was not a real worshipper, which threw him into something of embarrassment, till I hastened to get them laid by frank discourse on some suitable thing; nor, when we did talk, was there on his side or on mine the least utterance worth noting. The tone of his voice, when I got him afloat on some Cumberland or other matter germane to him, had a braced rustic vivacity, willingness, and solid precision, which alone rings in my ear when all else is gone. Of some Druid circle, for example, he prolonged his response to me with the addition, 'And there is another some miles off, which the country people call Long Meg and her Daughters'; as to the now ownership of which 'It', etc; 'and then it came into the hands of a Mr. Crackanthorpe'; the sound of those two phrases is still lively and present with me; meaning or sound of absolutely nothing more.

Still more memorable is an ocular glimpse I had in one of these Wordsworthian lion-dinners, very symbolic to me of his general deportment there. . . . Dinner was large, luminous, sumptuous; I sat a long way from Wordsworth; dessert I think had come in, and certainly there reigned in all quarters a cackle as of Babel (only politer perhaps), which far up in Wordsworth's quarter (who was leftward on my side of the table) seemed to have taken a sententious, rather louder, logical, and quasi-scientific turn, heartily unimportant to gods and men, so far as I could judge of it and of the other babble reigning. I looked upwards, leftwards, the coast being luckily for a moment clear; there, far off, beautifully screened in the shadow of his vertical green circle, sate Wordsworth, silent, slowly but steadily gnawing some portion of what I judged to be raisins, with his eye and attention placidly fixed on these and these alone.

The sight of whom, and of his rock-like indifference to the babble, quasi-scientific and other, with attention turned on the small practical alone, was comfortable and amusing to me, who felt like him but could not eat raisins. This little glimpse I could still paint, so clear and bright is it, and this shall be symbolical of all.

208

[Sir Charles Gavan Duffy, a friend and admirer of Carlyle, published in 1892 *Conversations with Thomas Carlyle.* Carlyle's observations on Wordsworth were made on one of his visits to Ireland, in 1846 or 1849.]

HE said that when he met Wordsworth first he had been assured that he talked better than any man in England. It was his habit to speak whatever was in his mind at the time, with total indifference to the impression it produced on his hearers; on that occasion he kept discoursing on how far you could get carried out of London on this side or on that for sixpence. One was disappointed, perhaps; but, after all, that was the only healthy way of talking, to say what was actually in your mind, and let sane creatures make what they can of it. Wordsworth maintained a stern composure, and went his way, content that the world should go quite another road. . . .

But though Wordsworth was the man of most practical mind of any of the persons connected with literature whom he had encountered, his pastoral pipings were far from being of the importance his admirers imagined. He was essentially a cold, hard, silent, practical man, who, if he had not fallen into poetry, would have done effectual work of some sort in the world. This was the impression one got of him as he looked out of his stern blue eyes, superior to men and circumstances.

I said I expected to hear of a man of softer mood, more sympathetic and less taciturn.

Carlyle said, 'No, no, not at all; he was a man quite other than that; a man of an immense head and great jaws like a crocodile's, cast in a mould designed for prodigious work.'

209

AT a friend's house, after dinner the conversation turned upon wit and humour. The author of *Lalla Rookh*, who was present, gave some illustrations from Sheridan's 'sayings, doings, and writings'. Starting from his reverie, Wordsworth said that he did not consider himself to be a witty poet. 'Indeed,' continued he, 'I do not think I was ever witty but *once* in my life.' A great desire was naturally expressed by all to know what this special drollery was. After some hesitation the old poet said—'Well, well, I will tell you. I was standing some time ago at the entrance of my cottage at Rydal Mount. A man accosted me with the question—"Pray, sir, have you seen my wife pass by?"; whereupon I said, "Why, my good friend, I didn't know till this moment that you had a wife!"' The company stared, and finding that the old bard had discharged his entire stock, burst into a roar of laughter, which the facetious Wordsworth, in his simplicity, accepted as a genuine compliment to the brilliancy of his wit.

210

I[1] CALLED afterwards at Rogers's house to ask permission for some friends, who are coming to town for the day, to see his house and pictures tomorrow afternoon. He was at home, and sent word that he particularly wished to see me. I got out of the carriage and was shown into the drawing room, where, to my great surprise, I found him and dear old Wordsworth in court dresses, with swords and cocked hats dancing the *minuet de la cour*. Wordsworth said he was rehearsing his bows for the Queen's ball, and getting a lesson from Rogers about it. Wordsworth's dress did very well, except his thick grey worsted stockings which we all exclaimed against. He declared that he could not wear any other kind, so I persuaded him to put a black silk pair over them. This solved the difficulty; he consented, and we had the satisfaction of seeing the dear old poet in the evening looking very picturesque in his court dress.

211

JAMES HOGG (1770–1835)

THE personal history of James Hogg must have interested Scott. . . . Under the garb, aspect, and bearing of a rude peasant—and rude enough he was in most of these things, even after no inconsiderable experience of society—Scott found a brother poet, a true son of nature and genius, hardly conscious of his powers. He had taught himself to write by copying the letters of a printed book as he lay watching his flock on the hillside, and had probably reached the utmost pitch of his ambition when

[1] Georgiana, Lady Chatterton (1806–76), novelist and miscellaneous writer.

he first found that his artless rhymes could touch the heart of the ewe-milker who partook the shelter of his mantle during the passing storm . . .

Shortly after their first meeting, Hogg, coming into Edinburgh with a flock of sheep, was seized with a sudden ambition of seeing himself in print, and wrote out that same night 'William and Katie', and a few other ballads already famous in the Forest, which some obscure bookseller gratified him by putting forth accordingly; but they appear to have attracted no notice beyond their original sphere. . . .

The next time that Hogg's business carried him to Edinburgh he waited upon Scott, who invited him to dinner in Castle Street, in company with William Laidlaw, who happened also to be in town, and some other admirers of the rustic genius. When Hogg entered the drawing-room, Mrs. Scott, being at the time in a delicate state of health, was reclining on a sofa. The Shepherd, after being presented, and making his best bow, forthwith took possession of another sofa placed opposite to hers, and stretched himself thereupon at all his length; for, as he said afterwards, 'I thought I could never do wrong to copy the lady of the house.' As his dress at this period was precisely that in which any ordinary herdsman attends cattle to the market, and as his hands, moreover, bore most legible marks of a recent sheep-smearing, the lady of the house did not observe with perfect equanimity the novel usage to which her chintz was exposed. The Shepherd, however, remarked nothing of all this—dined heartily and drank freely, and, by jest, anecdote, and song, offered plentiful merriment to the more civilized part of the company. As the liquor operated, his familiarity increased and strengthened; from 'Mr. Scott' he advanced to 'Sherra', and thence to 'Scott', 'Walter', and 'Wattie'—until, at supper, he fairly convulsed the whole party by addressing Mrs. Scott as 'Charlotte'.

The collection entitled *The Mountain Bard* was eventually published by Constable, in consequence of Scott's recommendation, and this work did at last afford Hogg no slender share of the popular reputation for which he had so long thirsted.

212

SIR WALTER SCOTT (1771–1832)

HENRY WEBER, a poor German scholar, . . . escaping to this country in 1804 from misfortunes in his own, excited Scott's compassion, and was thenceforth furnished, through his means, with literary employment of various sorts. Weber was a man of considerable learning; but Scott, as was his custom, appears to have formed an exaggerated notion of his capacity, and certainly countenanced him, to his own severe cost, in several most unfortunate undertakings. When not engaged in things of a more ambitious character, he had acted for ten years as his protector's amanuensis, and when the family were in Edinburgh, he very often dined with them. There was something very interesting in his appearance and manners; he had a fair, open countenance, in which the honesty and the enthusiasm of his nation were alike visible; his demeanour was gentle and modest; and he had not only a stock of curious antiquarian knowledge, but the reminiscences, which he detailed with amusing simplicity, of an early life chequered with many strange enough adventures. He was, in short, much a favourite with Scott and all the household, and was invited to dine with them so frequently, chiefly because his friend was aware that he had an unhappy propensity to drinking, and was anxious to keep him away from places where he might have been more likely to indulge it. This vice, however, had been growing on him; and of late Scott had found it necessary to make some rather severe remonstrances about habits which were at once injuring his health and interrupting his literary industry.

They had, however, parted kindly when Scott left Edinburgh at Christmas 1813—and the day after his return Weber attended him as usual in his library, being employed in transcribing extracts during several hours, while his friend, seated over against him, continued working at the Life of Swift. The light beginning to fail, Scott threw himself back in his chair, and was about to ring for candles, when he observed the German's eyes fixed upon him with an unusual solemnity of expression. 'Weber,' said he, 'what's the matter with you?' 'Mr. Scott,' said Weber rising, 'you have long insulted me, and I can bear it no longer. I have brought a pair of pistols with me, and must insist on your taking one of them instantly;' and with that he produced the weapons, which had been deposited under his chair, and laid one of them on Scott's manuscript. 'You are mistaken, I think', said Scott, 'in your way of setting about this affair—but no matter. It can, however, be no part of your object to annoy Mrs. Scott and the children; therefore, if you please, we will put the pistols into the drawer till after dinner, and then arrange to go out together like gentlemen.' Weber answered with equal coolness, 'I believe that will be better', and laid the second pistol also on the table. Scott locked them both in his desk, and said, 'I am glad you have felt the propriety of what I suggested—let me only request further that nothing may occur while we are at dinner to give my wife any suspicion of what has been passing.' Weber again assented, and Scott withdrew to his dressing room, from which he immediately dispatched a message to one of Weber's intimate companions—and then dinner was served, and Weber joined the family circle as usual. He conducted himself with perfect composure, and everything seemed to go on in the ordinary way, until whisky and hot water being produced, Scott, instead of inviting his guest to help himself, mixed two moderate tumblers of toddy, and handed one of them to Weber, who, upon that, started up with a furious countenance, but instantly sat down again, and when Mrs. Scott expressed her fear that he was ill, answered placidly that he was liable to spasms, but that the pain was gone. He then took the glass, eagerly gulped down its contents, and pushed it back to Scott. At this moment the friend who had been sent for made his appearance, and Weber, on seeing him enter the room, rushed past him and out of the house, without stopping to put on his hat. The friend, who pursued instantly, came up with him at the end of the street, and did all he could to soothe his agitation, but in vain. The same evening he was obliged to be put into a strait waistcoat; and though, in a few days, he exhibited such symptoms of recovery that he was allowed to go by himself to pay a visit in the north of England, he there soon relapsed, and continued ever afterwards a hopeless lunatic, being supported to the end of his life in June 1818, at Scott's expense in an asylum at York.

213

HAPPENING to pass through Edinburgh in June 1814 I[1] dined one day with William Menzies (now the Honourable William Menzies, one of the Supreme Judges at the Cape of Good Hope), whose residence was then in George Street, situated very near to, and at right angles with, North Castle Street. It was a party of very young persons, most of them, like Menzies and myself, destined for the bar of Scotland, all gay and thoughtless, enjoying the first flush of manhood, with little remembrance of the yesterday or care of the morrow. When my companion's worthy father and uncle, after seeing two or three bottles go round, left the juveniles to themselves, the weather being hot, we adjourned to a library which had one large window looking northwards. After carousing here for an hour or more, I observed that a shade had come over the aspect of my friend, who happened to be placed immediately opposite to myself, and said something that intimated a fear of his being unwell. 'No,' said he, 'I shall be well enough presently, if you will only let me sit where you are, and take my chair; for there is a confounded hand in sight of me here, which has often bothered me before, and now it won't let me fill my glass with a good will.' I rose to change places with him accordingly, and he pointed out this hand which, like the writing on Belshazzar's wall, disturbed his hour of hilarity. 'Since we sat down,' he said, 'I have been watching it—it fascinates my eye—it never stops—page after page is

[1] John Gibson Lockhart, Scott's biographer.

finished and thrown on that heap of MS., and still it goes on unwearied—and so it will be till candles are brought in, and God knows how long after that. It is the same every night—I can't stand the sight of it when I am not at my books.' 'Some stupid, dogged engrossing clerk, probably,' exclaimed myself, or some other giddy youth in our society. 'No, boys,' said our host, 'I well know what hand it is—'tis Walter Scott's.' This was the hand that, in the evenings of three summer weeks, wrote the two last volumes of *Waverley*.

214

BEFORE breakfast was over the post-bag arrived, and its contents were so numerous that Lord Melville asked Scott what election was on hand, not doubting that there must be some very particular reason for such a shoal of letters. He answered that it was much the same most days, and added, 'Though no one has kinder friends in the franking line, and though Freeling and Croker[1] especially are always ready to stretch the point of privilege in my favour, I am nevertheless a fair contributor to the revenue, for I think my bill for letters seldom comes under £150 a year; and as to coach-parcels, they are a perfect ruination.' He then told with high merriment a disaster that had lately befallen him. 'One morning last spring', he said, 'I opened a huge lump of a dispatch, without looking how it was addressed, never doubting that it had travelled under some omnipotent frank like the First Lord of the Admiralty's, when, lo and behold, the contents proved to be a MS. play, by a young lady of New York, who kindly requested me to read and correct it, equip it with prologue and epilogue, procure for it a favourable reception from the manager of Drury Lane, and make Murray or Constable bleed handsomely for the copyright; and on inspecting the cover, I found that I had been charged five pounds odd for the postage. This was bad enough, but there was no help, so I groaned and submitted. A fortnight or so after, another packet of not less formidable bulk arrived, and I was absent enough to break its seal too without examination. Conceive my horror when out jumped the same identical tragedy of *The Cherokee Lovers*, with a second epistle from the authoress, stating that, as the winds had been boisterous, she feared the vessel entrusted with her former communication might have foundered, and therefore judged it prudent to forward a duplicate.'

[1] Sir Francis Freeling, Secretary of the General Post Office, and John William Croker, Secretary of the Admiralty.

215

[Since 1817 Scott had been suffering from violent fits of cramp in the stomach, caused by undiagnosed gall-stones.]

THE accounts of Scott's condition circulated in Edinburgh in the course of this April[1] were so alarming that I should not have thought of accepting his invitation to revisit Abbotsford unless John Ballantyne had given me better tidings about the end of the month. He informed me that his 'illustrious friend' (for so both the Ballantynes usually spoke of him) was so much recovered as to have resumed his usual literary tasks, though with this difference, that he now, for the first time in his life, found it necessary to employ the hand of another. I have now before me a letter of the 8th April, in which Scott says to Constable, 'Yesterday I began to dictate, and did it easily and with comfort. This is a great point, but I must proceed by little and little; last night I had a slight return of the enemy, but baffled him;' and he again writes to the bookseller on the 11th —'John Ballantyne is here, and returns with copy, which my increasing strength permits me to hope I may now furnish regularly.'

The *copy* (as MS. for the press is technically called) which Scott was thus dictating, was that of *The Bride of Lammermoor*; and his amanuenses were William Laidlaw and John Ballantyne, of whom he preferred the latter when he could be at Abbotsford, on account of the superior rapidity of his pen, and also because John kept his pen to the paper without interruption, and though with many an arch twinkle in his eyes, and now and then an audible smack of his lips, had resolution to work on like a well-trained clerk; whereas good Laidlaw entered with such keen zest into the interest of the story as it flowed from the author's lips, that he could not suppress exclamations of surprise and delight—'Gude keep us a'!—the like o' that!—eh sirs!'—and so forth, which did not promote dispatch. I have often, however, in the sequel, heard both these secretaries describe the astonishment with which they were equally affected when Scott began this experiment. The affectionate Laidlaw beseeching him to stop dictating, when his audible suffering filled every pause, 'Nay, Willie,' he answered, 'only see that the doors are fast. I would fain keep all the cry as well as all the wool to ourselves; but as to giving over work, that can only be when I am in woollen.' John Ballantyne told me that after the first day he always took care to have a dozen of pens made before he seated himself opposite to the sofa on which Scott lay, and that though he often turned himself on his pillow with a groan of torment, he usually continued the sentence in the same breath. But when dialogue of

[1] 1819. The narrator is Lockhart.

peculiar animation was in progress, spirit seemed to triumph altogether over matter; he arose from his couch and walked up and down the room, raising and lowering his voice, and as it were acting the parts. It was in this fashion that Scott produced the far greater portion of *The Bride of Lammermoor*, the whole of *The Legend of Montrose*, and almost the whole of *Ivanhoe*.

216

[In the summer of 1822 George IV paid a visit to Edinburgh, anchoring on August 14 in the Roads of Leith. Although it was a day of pouring rain, Scott, who had taken charge of the arrangements for entertaining the royal visitor, had himself rowed out to the *Royal George* to welcome him.]

ON receiving the poet on the quarter-deck, his Majesty called for a bottle of Highland whisky, and having drunk his health in this national liquor, desired a glass to be filled for him. Sir Walter, after draining his own bumper, made a request that the King would condescend to bestow on him the glass out of which his Majesty had just drunk his health; and this being granted, the precious vessel was immediately wrapped up and carefully deposited in what he conceived to be the safest part of his dress. So he returned with it to Castle Street; but, to say nothing at this moment of graver distractions, on reaching his house he found a guest established there of a sort rather different from the usual visitors of the time. The poet Crabbe, to whom he had been introduced when last in London by Mr. Murray of Albemarle Street, after repeatedly promising to follow up the acquaintance by an excursion to the north, had at last arrived in the midst of these tumultuous preparations for the royal advent. Notwithstanding all such impediments, he found his quarters ready for him, and Scott entering, wet and hurried, embraced the venerable man with brotherly affection. The royal gift was forgotten—the ample skirt of the coat within which it had been packed, and which he had hitherto held cautiously in front of his person, slipped back to its more usual position—he sat down beside Crabbe, and the glass was crushed to atoms. His scream and gesture made his wife conclude that he had sat down on a pair of scissors, or the like; but very little harm had been done except the breaking of the glass, of which alone he had been thinking.

217

[Ever since his bankruptcy in 1826 Scott had been making heroic efforts to pay off his creditors. Early in 1830 he suffered a severe stroke as the result of constant overwork, and in the winter of 1831–2 he was in Italy vainly trying to recover his health. He was brought back to Abbotsford in July, and died about two months later.]

SOON after his arrival at Naples, Sir Walter went with his physician and one or two friends to the great museum. It happened that on the same day a large collection of students and Italian literati were assembled in one of the rooms to discuss some newly discovered manuscripts. It was soon known that the 'Wizard of the North' was there, and a deputation was sent immediately to request him to honour them by presiding at their session. At this time Scott was a wreck, with a memory that retained nothing for a moment, and limbs almost as helpless as an infant's. He was dragging about among the relics of Pompeii, taking no interest in any thing he saw, when the request was made known to him through his physician. 'No, no,' said he, 'I know nothing of their lingo. Tell them I am not well enough to come.' He loitered on, and in about half an hour he turned to Dr. H. and said, 'Who was that you said wanted to see me?' The doctor explained. 'I'll go,' said he, 'they shall see me if they wish it;' and against the advice of his friends, who feared it would be too much for his strength, he mounted the staircase, and made his appearance at the door. A burst of enthusiastic cheers welcomed him on the threshold, and forming two lines, many of them on their knees, they seized his hands as he passed, kissed them, thanked him in their passionate language for the delight with which he had filled the world, and placed him in the chair with the most fervent expressions of gratitude for his condescension. The discussion went on; but not understanding a syllable of the language Scott was soon wearied, and his friends observing it, pleaded the state of his health as an apology, and he rose to take his leave. These enthusiastic children of the south crowded once more around him, and with exclamations of affection and even tears kissed his hands once more, assisted his tottering steps, and sent after him a confused murmur of blessings as the door closed on his retiring form. It is described by the writer[1] as the most affecting scene he had ever witnessed.

[1] Sir William Gell (1777–1836), who left an account of Scott's visit to Naples.

218
SYDNEY SMITH (1771–1845)

THE story of Jeffrey and the North Pole, as told by Sydney Smith, . . . happened while the Jeffreys were my near neighbours in London; and Mrs. Sydney Smith related the incident to me at the time.[1] Captain (afterwards Sir John) Ross had just returned from an unsuccessful polar expedition, and was bent upon going again. He used all his interest to get the government stirred up to fit out another expedition; and among others, the Lord Advocate[2] was to be applied to, to bespeak his good offices. The mutual friend who undertook to do Captain Ross's errand to Jeffrey arrived at an unfortunate moment. Jeffrey was in delicate health at that time, and made a great point of his daily ride; and when the applicant reached his door, he was putting his foot in the stirrup and did not want to be detained. So he pished and pshawed, and cared nothing for the North Pole, and at length 'damned' it. The applicant spoke angrily about it to Sydney Smith, wishing that Jeffrey would take care what he was about, and use more civil language. 'What do you think he said to me?' cried the complainant. 'Why, he damned the North Pole!'—'Well, never mind! never mind!' said Sydney Smith soothingly. 'Never mind his damning the North Pole. *I* have heard him speak disrespectfully of the equator.'

219

SYDNEY SMITH was a frequent guest at the home of Samuel Rogers, and the old poet liked to repeat his witty remarks. 'At one time,' he recalled, 'when I gave a dinner, I used to have candles placed all round the dining room, and high up, in order to show off the pictures. I asked Smith how he liked that plan. "Not at all," he replied; "above, there is a blaze of light, and below, nothing but darkness and gnashing of teeth."'

220

SOMEONE speaking of Macaulay, Smith remarked: 'Yes, I take great credit to myself; I always prophesied his greatness from the first moment I saw him, then a very young and unknown man, on the Northern Circuit. There are no limits to his knowledge, on small subjects as well as great;

[1] The writer is Harriet Martineau.
[2] Francis Jeffrey was appointed Lord Advocate in the Whig government of 1830.

he is like a book in breeches. . . . Yes, I agree, he is certainly more agreeable since his return from India. His enemies might perhaps have said before (though I never did so) that he talked rather too much; but now he has occasional flashes of silence that make his conversation perfectly delightful.'

221

HE was writing one morning in his favourite bay-window, when a pompous little man, in rusty black, was ushered in . 'May I ask what procures me the honour of this visit?' said my father.[1] 'Oh,' said the little man, 'I am compounding a history of the distinguished families in Somersetshire, and have called to obtain the Smith arms.' 'I regret, sir,' said my father, 'not to be able to contribute to so valuable a work; but the Smiths never had any arms, and have invariably sealed their letters with their thumbs.'

222

SAMUEL TAYLOR COLERIDGE (1772–1834)

[Coleridge recalls his childhood.]

MY father's sister kept an *every-thing* shop at Crediton—and there I read through all the gilt-cover little books that could be had at that time, and likewise all the uncovered tales of *Tom Hickathrift*, *Jack the Giant-killer*, etc. and etc. etc. etc.—and I used to lie by the wall, and *mope*—and my spirits used to come upon me suddenly, and in a flood—and then I was accustomed to run up and down the church-yard, and act over all I had been reading on the docks, the nettles, and the rank-grass. At six years old I remember to have read *Belisarius*,[2] *Robinson Crusoe*, and *Philip Quarll*[3]—and then I found the *Arabian Nights*' entertainments—one tale of which (the tale of a man who was compelled to seek for a pure virgin) made so deep an impression on me (I had read it in the evening while my mother was mending stockings) that I was haunted by spectres whenever I was in the dark—and I distinctly remember the anxious and fearful eagerness with which I used to watch the window in which the books lay—and whenever the sun lay upon them, I would seize it, carry it by the wall, and bask, and read. My father found out the effect which these books had produced—and burnt them. So I became a *dreamer*—and acquired an indisposition to all bodily activity—and I was fretful, and

[1] The writer is Sydney Smith's daughter, Lady Holland. [2] Possibly a translation of Marmontel's *Bélisaire* (1766), but more probably John Oldmixon's *Life of Belisarius* (1713). [3] *The English Hermit: or The Adventures of Philip Quarll* (1727).

inordinately passionate, and as I could not play at any thing, and was slothful, I was despised and hated by the boys; and because I could read and spell, and had, I may truly say, a memory and understanding forced into almost an unnatural ripeness, I was flattered and wondered at by all the old women—and so I became very vain, and despised most of the boys that were at all near my own age, and before I was eight years old I was a *character*: sensibility, imagination, vanity, sloth, and feelings of deep and bitter contempt for almost all who traversed the orbit of my understanding were even then prominent and manifest.

223

AT school I enjoyed the inestimable advantage of a very sensible, though at the same time a very severe master. . . . In our own English compositions (at least for the last three years of our school education) he showed no mercy to phrase, metaphor, or image unsupported by a sound sense, or where the same sense might have been conveyed with equal force and dignity in plainer words. Lute, harp, and lyre, muse, muses, and inspirations, Pegasus, Parnassus, and Hippocrene were all abominations to him. In fancy I can almost hear him now, exclaiming '*Harp? Harp? Lyre? Pen and ink, boy, you mean! Muse, boy, Muse? Your nurse's daughter, you mean! Pierian spring? Oh aye! the cloister-pump, I suppose!*' Nay, certain introductions, similes, and examples were placed by name on a list of interdiction. Among the similes, there was, I remember, that of the Manchineel fruit, as suiting equally well with too many subjects; in which however it yielded the palm at once to the example of Alexander and Clytus, which was equally good and apt, whatever might be the theme. Was it ambition? Alexander and Clytus! Flattery? Alexander and Clytus! Anger? Drunkenness? Pride? Friendship? Ingratitude? Late repentance? Still, still Alexander and Clytus! At length, the praises of agriculture having been exemplified in the sagacious observation that, had Alexander been holding the plough, he would not have run his friend Clytus through with a spear, this tried and serviceable old friend was banished by public edict *in secula seculorum*.

224

MR. COLERIDGE now told us of one of his Cambridge eccentricities, which highly amused us. He said that he had paid his addresses to some young woman (I think, a Mary E—)[1] who rejecting his offer, he took it

[1] Mary Evans. The narrator is Joseph Cottle.

so much in dudgeon, that he ran away from the University to London, when, in a reckless state of mind, he enlisted himself as a common man in a regiment of horse. No objection having been taken to his height, or age, and being thus accepted, he was asked his name. He had previously determined to give one that was thoroughly Kamschatkian, but having noticed that morning over a door in Lincoln's Inn Fields (or the Temple) the name 'Cumberbatch' (not 'Comberback'), he thought this word sufficiently outlandish, and replied, 'Silas Tomken Cumberbatch', and such was the entry into the regimental book. . . .

Mr. Coleridge, in the midst of all his deficiencies, it appeared, was liked by the men, although he was the butt of the whole company; being esteemed by them as next kin to a natural, though of a peculiar kind—a talking natural. This fancy of theirs was stoutly resisted by the love-sick swain, but the regimental logic prevailed; for whatever they could do, with masterly dexterity, he could not do at all, ergo, must he not be a natural? There was no man in the regiment who met with so many falls from his horse as Silas Tomken Cumberbatch! He often calculated with so little precision his due equilibrium, that, in mounting on one side (perhaps the wrong stirrup), the probability was, especially if his horse moved a little, that he lost his balance, and, if he did not roll back on this side, came down ponderously on the other! when the laugh spread among the men, 'Silas is off again!' Mr. C. had often heard of campaigns, but he never before had so correct an idea of hard service.

Some mitigation was now in store for Mr. C. arising out of a whimsical circumstance. He had been placed as a sentinel at the door of a ball-room, or some public place of resort, when two of his officers, passing in, stopped for a moment near Mr. C., talking about Euripides, two lines from whom one of them repeated. At the sound of Greek, the sentinel instinctively turned his ear; when he said, with all deference, touching his lofty cap, 'I hope your honour will excuse me, but the lines you have repeated are not quite accurately cited. These are the lines,' when he gave them in their more correct form. 'Besides,' said Mr. C., 'instead of being in Euripides, the lines will be found in the second antistrophe of the *Œdipus* of Sophocles.' 'Why, who the d— are you?' said the officer, 'old Faustus ground[1] young again?' 'I am only your honour's humble sentinel,' said Mr. C. again touching his cap.

The officers hastened into the room, and inquired of one another about that 'odd fish' at the door; when one of the mess (it is believed, the surgeon) told them that he had had his eye upon him, but he would neither tell where he came from, nor anything about his family of the Cumberbatches. 'But,' continued he, 'instead of being an "odd fish", I suspect he must be a "stray-bird" from the Oxford, or Cambridge

[1] i.e. grown.

aviary.' They learned also the laughable fact that he was bruised all over by frequent falls from his horse. 'Ah,' said one of the officers, 'we have had, at different times, two or three of these "University birds" in our regiment.' They, however, kindly took pity on the 'poor scholar', and had Mr. C. removed to the medical department, where he was appointed 'assistant' in the regimental hospital. This change was a vast improvement in Mr. C'.s condition; and happy was the day also on which it took place, for the sake of the sick patients; for Silas Tomken Cumberbatch's amusing stories, they said, did them more good than all the 'doctor's physic'! . . .

In one of these interesting conversaziones, when Mr. C. was sitting at the foot of a bed, surrounded by his gaping comrades (who were always solicitous of, and never wearied with, his stories), the door suddenly burst open, and in came two or three gentlemen (his friends), amid the uniform dresses in vain, for some time, looking for their man. At length they pitched on Mr. C., and taking him by the arm, led him in silence out of the room (a picture, indeed, for a Wilkie!). As the supposed *deserter* passed the threshold, one of the astonished auditors uttered, with a sigh, 'Poor Silas! I wish they may let him off with a cool five hundred!' Mr. C.'s ransom being soon adjusted, his friends had the pleasure of placing him, once more, safe in the University. . . .

The inspecting officer of his regiment, on one occasion, was examining the guns of the men, and coming to one piece which was rusty, he called out in an authoritative tone, 'Whose rusty gun is this?', when Mr. C. said, 'Is it *very* rusty, sir?' 'Yes, Cumberbatch, it *is*,' said the officer, sternly. 'Then, sir,' replied Mr. C., 'it must be mine!' The oddity of the reply disarmed the officer, and the 'poor scholar' escaped without punishment.

225

[In 1795, with their plan for establishing a 'pantisocracy' on the banks of the Susquehanna indefinitely postponed, Coleridge and Southey were living in Bristol. Southey announced, and started to deliver, a course of twelve lectures on history.]

THESE lectures of Mr. Southey were numerously attended, and their composition was greatly admired; exhibiting, as they did, a succinct view of the various subjects commented upon, so as to chain the hearer's attention. They, at the same time, evinced great self-possession in the lecturer; a peculiar grace in the delivery; with reasoning so judicious and acute as to excite astonishment in the auditory, that so young a man should concentrate so rich a fund of valuable matter in lectures comparatively so brief, and which clearly authorized the anticipation of his future eminence.

From this statement it will justly be inferred that no public lecturer could have received stronger proofs of approbation than Mr. S. from a polite and discriminating audience. Mr. Coleridge now solicited permission of Mr. Southey to deliver his fourth lecture, 'On the Rise, Progress, and Decline of the Roman Empire,' as a subject 'to which he had devoted much attention.' The request was immediately granted, and, at the end of the third lecture, it was formally announced to the audience that the next lecture would be delivered by 'Mr. Samuel Taylor Coleridge, of Jesus College, Cambridge.'

At the usual hour the room was thronged. The moment of commencement arrived. No lecturer appeared! Patience was preserved for a quarter, extending to half an hour!—but still no lecturer! At length it was communicated to the impatient assemblage that 'a circumstance, exceedingly to be regretted, would prevent Mr. Coleridge from giving his lecture that evening, as intended'. Some few present learned the truth, but the major part of the company retired, not very well pleased, and under the impression that Mr. C. had either broken his leg, or that some severe family affliction had occurred. Mr. C.'s rather habitual absence of mind, with the little importance he generally attached to engagements, renders it likely that at this very time he might have been found at No. 48 College Street composedly smoking his pipe, and lost in profound musings on his divine Susquehanna! . . .,

Wishing to gratify my two young friends (and their ladies elect) with a pleasant excursion, I invited them to accompany me in a visit to the Wye, including Piercefield and Tintern Abbey; objects new to us all. It so happened, the day we were to set off was that immediately following the woeful disappointment, but here all was punctuality. . . . After dinner, an unpleasant altercation occurred between—no other than the two Pantisocratians! When feelings are accumulated in the heart, the tongue will give them utterance. Mr. Southey, whose regular habits scarcely rendered it a virtue in him never to fail in an engagement, expressed to Mr. Coleridge his deep feelings of regret that his audience should have been disappointed on the preceding evening; reminding him that unless he had determined punctually to fulfil his voluntary engagement, he ought not to have entered upon it. Mr. C. thought the delay of the lecture of little or no consequence. This excited a remonstrance, which produced a reply. At first I interfered with a few conciliatory words, which were unavailing; and these two friends, about to exhibit to the world a glorious example of the effects of concord and sound principles, with an exemption from all the selfish and unsocial passions, fell, alas! into the common lot of humanity, and in so doing must have demonstrated, even to themselves, the rope of sand to which they had confided their destinies!

In unspeakable concern and surprise, I retired to a distant part of the room, and heard with dismay the contention continued, if not extending; for now the two young ladies entered into the dispute (on adverse sides, as might be supposed), each confirming or repelling the arguments of the belligerents. A little cessation in the storm afforded me the opportunity of stepping forward, and remarking that 'however much the disappointment was to be regretted, it was an evil not likely again to occur' (Mr. S. shook his head), and that 'the wisest way was to forget the past, and to remember only the pleasant objects before us.' In this opinion the ladies concurred, when, placing a hand of one of the dissentients in that of the other, the hearty salutation went round, and, with our accustomed spirits, we prepared once more for Piercefield and the Abbey.

226

[Coleridge's account of how he wrote 'Kubla Khan'.]

IN the summer of 1797, the Author, then in ill health, had retired to a lonely farm-house between Porlock and Linton, on the Exmoor confines of Somerset and Devonshire. In consequence of a slight indisposition, an anodyne had been prescribed, from the effects of which he fell asleep in his chair at the moment that he was reading the following sentence, or words of the same substance, in 'Purchas's Pilgrimage':

> Here the Khan Kubla commanded a palace to be built, and a stately garden thereunto. And thus ten miles of fertile ground were inclosed with a wall.

The Author continued for about three hours in a profound sleep, at least of the external senses, during which time he has the most vivid confidence that he could not have composed less than from two to three hundred lines; if that indeed can be called composition in which all the images rose up before him as *things*, with a parallel production of the correspondent expressions, without any sensation or consciousness of effort. On awaking he appeared to himself to have a distinct recollection of the whole, and taking his pen, ink, and paper, instantly and eagerly wrote down the lines that are here preserved. At this moment he was unfortunately called out by a person on business from Porlock, and detained by him above an hour, and on his return to his room, found, to his no small surprise and mortification, that though he still retained some vague and dim recollection of the general purport of the vision, yet, with the exception of some eight or ten scattered lines and images, all the rest had passed away like the images on the surface of a stream into which a stone has been cast, but, alas! without the restoration of the latter!

227

[In 1797 Coleridge was living with his wife and baby son in a cottage at Nether Stowey, while Wordsworth with his sister Dorothy was staying a few miles away at Alfoxden House, which he had rented furnished since the middle of July. England and France had been at war since 1793, and in 1797 there were widespread fears of a possible French invasion. In the resulting excitement the arrival of two odd strangers at Alfoxden House appears to have aroused suspicion among the local inhabitants; and when Coleridge was visited by John Thelwall, a revolutionary agitator who had been tried on a charge of high treason only three years earlier, suspicion became almost certainty. Acting on information received, the government sent down a detective called Walsh to report on what was going on. The fortunate preservation of some part of the relevant correspondence will show how near the unsuspecting poets came to being arrested.]

Copy of Mr. Lyson's second letter to the Duke of Portland

Bath, 11. Aug. 1797

My Lord Duke—On the 8th instant I took the liberty to acquaint your Grace with a very suspicious business concerning an emigrant family, who have contrived to get possession of a Mansion House at Alfoxton, late belonging to the Revd. Mr. St. Albyn, under Quantock Hills. I am since informed, that the Master of the house has no wife with him, but only a Woman who passes for his Sister. The man has Camp Stools, which he and his visitors take with them when they go about the country upon their nocturnal or diurnal excursions, and have also a Portfolio in which they enter their observations, which they have been heard to say were almost finished. They have been heard to say they should be rewarded for them, and were very attentive to the River near them—probably the River coming within a mile or two of Alfoxton from Bridgewater. These people may *possibly* be under Agents to some principal at Bristol . . .

D. Lysons.

Report from G. Walsh to Mr. J. King, Permanent Under-Secretary of State for the Home Department

Bear Inn, Hungerford, Berks: 11 Aug. 1797

Sir—Charles Mogg says that he was at Alfoxton last Saturday was a week, that he there saw Thomas Jones who lives in the Farm House at

Alfoxton, who informed Mogg that some French people had got possession of the Mansion House and that they were washing and Mending their cloaths all Sunday, that He Jones would not continue there as he did not like It. That Christopher Trickie and his Wife who live at the Dog pound at Alfoxton, told Mogg that the French people had taken the plan of Their House, and that They had also taken the plan of all the places round that part of the Country, that a Brook runs in front of Trickie's House and the French people inquired of Trickie whether the Brook was Navigable to the Sea, and upon being informed by Trickie that It was not, They were afterwards seen examining the Brook quite down to the Sea. That Mrs. Trickie confirmed everything her husband had said. Mogg spoke to some other persons inhabitants of that Neighbourhood, who all told him they thought these French people very suspicious persons and that They were doing no good there . . .

As Mr. Mogg is by no means the most intelligent Man in the World, I thought it my duty to send You the whole of his Story as he related It . . .

I shall wait here your further Orders and am
Sir, Your most obedient Humble Servt.
G. Walsh.

Copy of Mr. King's letter to Walsh
Whitehall Aug. 12th, 1797

Sir—I have considered the contents of your letter to me from the Bear Inn, Hungerford, of yesterday's date. You will immediately proceed to Alfoxton or its neighbourhood yourself, taking care on your arrival so to conduct yourself as to give no cause of suspicion to the Inhabitants of the Mansion house there. You will narrowly watch their proceedings, and observe how they coincide with Mogg's account and that contained in the within letter from Mr. Lysons to the Duke of Portland. . . . Should they however move, you must follow their track and give me notice thereof, and of the place to which they have betaken themselves. I herewith transmit you a bank note of £20.

J. King.

Letter of G. Walsh to J. King.
Globe Inn, Stowey, Somerset: 15th Augst 1797

Sir—In consequence of Your orders which I rec'd Yesterday, I immediately set out for this Place, which altho it is five Miles from Alfoxton, is the nearest house I can get any accommodation at.

I had not been many minutes in this house before I had an opportunity of entering upon my Business, By a Mr. Woodhouse asking the Landlord, If he had seen any of those Rascalls from Alfoxton. To which the Landlord reply'd, He had seen two of them Yesterday. Upon which Woodhouse asked the Landlord, If Thelwall was gone. I then asked if they meant the famous Thelwall. They said Yes. That he had been down some time, and that there were a Nest of them at Alfoxton House who were protected by a Mr. Poole a Tanner of this Town, and that he supposed Thelwall was there (Alfoxton House) at this time. I told Woodhouse that I had heard somebody say at Bridgewater that They were French people at the Manor House. The Landlord and Mr. Woodhouse answered, No, No. They are not French, But they are people that will do as much harm as All the French can do.

I hope To-morrow to be able to give you some information, in the mean time I shall be very attentive to your instructions.

I think this will turn out no French affair, but a mischiefuous gang of disaffected Englishmen. I have just procured the Name of the person who took the House. His name is *Wordsworth* a name I think known to Mr. Ford.

I have the honor to be Sir,
Your most obedient Humble Sert.
G. Walsh.

Letter of G. Walsh to J. King.

Stowey: 16th Augt 1797

Sir,—The inhabitants of Alfoxton House are a Sett of violent Democrats. The House was taken for a Person of the name of Wordsworth, who came to it from a Village near Honiton in Devonshire, about five Weeks since. The Rent of the House is secured to the Landlord by a Mr. Thomas Poole of this Town. Mr. Poole is a Tanner and a Man of some property. He is a most Violent Member of the Corresponding Society and a strenuous supporter of Its Friends. He has with him at this time a Mr. Coldridge and his wife both of whom he has supported since Christmas last. This Coldridge came last from Bristol and is reckoned a Man of Superior Ability. He is frequently publishing, and I am told is soon to produce a new work. He has a Press in the House and I am informed He prints as well as publishes his own productions . . .

By the direction on a letter that was going to the Post Yesterday, It appears that Thelwall is now at Bristol.

I last Night saw Thomas Jones who lives at Alfoxton House. He exactly confirms Mogg of Hungerford, with this addition that the Sunday after Wordsworth came, he Jones was desired to wait at table, that there were 14 persons at Dinner, Poole and Coldridge were there, And there was a little Stout Man with dark cropt Hair and wore a White Hat and Glasses (Thelwall) who after Dinner got up and talked so loud and was in such a passion that Jones was frightened and did not like to go near them since. That Wordsworth has lately been to his former House and brought back with him a Woman Servant, that Jones has seen this Woman who is very Chatty, and that she told him that Her Master was a Phylosopher . . .

Your most obedient Humble Sert.
G. Walsh.

[In *Biographia Literaria* Coleridge gives his own account of this odd episode, based apparently on what the friendly landlord of The Globe Inn had told him after the government spy had left Nether Stowey. Walsh, it appears, was finally convinced that the whole business was only a case of local gossip.]

The dark guesses of some zealous Quidnunc met with so congenial a soil in the grave alarm of a titled Dogberry of our neighbourhood, that a SPY was actually sent down from the government *pour surveillance* of myself and friend. There must have been not only abundance, but *variety* of these 'honourable men' at the disposal of Ministers: for this proved a very honest fellow. After three weeks' truly Indian perseverance in tracking us (for we were commonly together), during all which time seldom were we out of doors, but he contrived to be within hearing (and all the while utterly unsuspected; how indeed *could* such a suspicion enter our fancies?) he not only rejected Sir Dogberry's request that he would try yet a little longer, but declared to him his belief that both my friend and myself were as good subjects, for aught he could discover to the contrary, as any in His Majesty's dominions. He had repeatedly hid himself, he said, for hours together behind a bank at the sea-side (our favourite seat), and overheard our conversation. At first he fancied that we were aware of our danger; for he often heard me talk of one *Spy Nozy*, which he was inclined to interpret of himself, and of a remarkable feature belonging to him; but he was speedily convinced that it was the name of a man who had made a book and lived long ago. Our talk ran most upon books, and we were perpetually desiring each other to look at *this*, and to listen to *that*; but he could not catch a word about politics. Once he had joined me on the road; (this occurred as I was returning home alone from my friend's house, which was about three miles from my own cottage), and, passing himself off as a traveller, he had entered into conversation with me, and talked of purpose in a *democrat* way in order to draw me out. The result, it appears, not only convinced him that I was no friend of Jacobinism, but (he added), I had 'plainly made it out to be such a silly as well as wicked thing, that he felt ashamed though he had only *put it on*'. I distinctly remembered the occurrence, and had mentioned it immediately on my return, repeating what the traveller with his Bardolph nose had said, with my own answer; and so little did I suspect the true object of my 'tempter ere accuser', that I expressed with no small pleasure my hope and belief that the conversation had been of some service to the poor misled malcontent. This incident therefore prevented all doubt as to the truth of the report, which through a friendly medium came to me from the master of the village inn, who had been ordered to entertain the *Government Gentleman* in his best manner, but above all to be silent concerning such a person being in his house. At length he received Sir Dogberry's commands to accompany his guest at the final interview; and, after the absolving suffrage of the *gentleman honoured with the confidence of Ministers*, answered, as follows, to the following queries. D. Well, landlord! and what do you know of the person in question? . . . Has he not been seen wandering on the hills towards the Channel, and along the shore, with books and papers in his hand, taking charts and maps of the country? L. Why, as to that, your honour! I own I have heard—I am sure I would not wish to speak ill of anybody; but it is certain that I have heard— D. Speak out, man! don't be afraid, you are doing your duty to your King and Government. L. Why, folks do say, your honour! as how he is a *Poet*, and that he is going to put Quantock and all about here in print; and as they be so much together, I suppose that the strange gentleman has some *consarn* in the business.

So ended this formidable inquisition. . . .

228

COLERIDGE came to Rose[1] one day early, obviously in great trouble: he sat down without saying a word, and tears even began to flow down his cheeks. Rose inquired earnestly what was the matter—what was weighing upon his mind? but for some time he could get no answer. At last, Coleridge told him he was come to consult him about something relating to the conduct of his wife. Rose was startled, yet he could not think that she had been guilty of any serious misconduct, and told him so. Coleridge answered that what she had done, if he yielded to it, would embitter the rest of his life. Rose was alarmed, and besought Coleridge to tranquillize himself, and to tell him what had happened: he hinted a hope that it was nothing affecting her moral character as a wife. 'Oh no,' said Coleridge, 'nothing of that kind, but it is something that I cannot think of without the deepest pain.'—'Well,' said Rose, 'let us hear it: perhaps it is not so

[1] Hugh James Rose (1795–1838), classical scholar and theologian. See note, p. 362.

bad as you at this moment consider it.'—'I came to you,' added Coleridge, 'as a friend and a clergyman, to ask you what I ought under the circumstances to do.'—'Let me have the circumstances,' rejoined Rose, 'and then I may be better able to judge. Calm yourself.'

Again Coleridge wiped his 'large grey eyes', and went on to apologize for the trouble he was giving. Rose assured him that his main trouble was to see a friend so unhappy; and, after beating about the bush for some time longer, Coleridge declared that he could never live with his wife again, if she were not brought to her senses. Rose here began to fear that Mrs. Coleridge had literally gone out of her mind; but Coleridge reassured him upon that head, adding, however, that a sane woman could hardly have required of her husband what she had expected from him; viz., that on the coldest mornings, even when the snow was on the ground, and icicles hanging from the eves of their cottage, she compelled him to get out of bed in his night-shirt, and light the fire, before she began to dress herself and the baby.

229

[Frederic Mansel Reynolds, editor of *The Keepsake*, and a son of Frederic Reynolds the dramatist, 'had hired, for the autumn months, the upper portion of a small gardener's cottage at Highgate, a shell of a place, the first floor of which supplied two little cabins, just big enough for coziness, fun, and revel'. Here one evening he gave a dinner for eight friends, who included Lockhart, Theodore Hook, Henry Luttrell, and Coleridge.]

OUR host had replenished his sideboard with fine wines from his father's cellars and wine merchants in town; but having, unluckily, forgotten port, a few bottles of black-strap[1] had been obtained for the nonce from the adjacent inn at Highgate; and sooth to say it was not of the first quality. To add to this grievance, the glasses appertaining to the lodgings were of a diminutive capacity, and when they came to be addressed to champagne and hock, were only tolerable and not to be endured. Thus, in the midst of dinner, or rather more towards the close, we were surprised by Hook's rising, and asking us to fill our bumpers to a toast. It was not difficult to fill these glasses, and we were pledged to follow the example of our leader in draining them. In a brief but most entertaining address he described the excellent qualities of Reynolds, and above all his noble capacity for giving rural dinners, but—there was always a but, not a butt of wine, but a but, a something *manqué*. On this occasion it was but too notorious in the size of those miserable pigmies, out of which we were

[1] An inferior kind of port wine.

trying to drink his health etc. etc. etc. The toast was drunk with acclamation, and then followed the exemplary cannikin clink, hob-nobbing, and striking the poor little glasses on the table till every one was broken save one, and that was reserved for a poetical fate.

Tumblers were substituted, and might possibly contribute their share to the early hilarity and consecutive frolic of the night; for ere long Coleridge's sonorous voice was heard declaiming on the extraordinary ebullitions of Hook—'I have before in the course of my time met with men of admirable promptitude of intellectual power and play of wit, which, as Stillingfleet tells,

> The rays of wit gild whereso'er they strike;

but I never could have conceived such amazing readiness of mind, and resources of genius to be poured out on the mere subject and impulse of the moment.' Having got the poet into this exalted mood, the last of the limited wine-glasses was mounted upon the bottom of a reversed tumbler, and, to the infinite risk of the latter, he was induced to shy at the former with a silver fork, till after two or three throws he succeeded in smashing it into fragments, to be tossed into the basket with its perished brethren. . . . The exhibition was remembered for years afterwards by all who partook of it; and I have a letter of Lockhart's alluding to the date of our witnessing the roseate face of Coleridge, lit up with animation, his large grey eye beaming, his white hair floating, and his whole frame, as it were, radiating with intense interest, as he poised the fork in his hand, and launched it at the fragile object (the last glass of dinner) distant some three or four feet from him on the table!

230

THE tragedy of *Remorse* was written while Coleridge lived with Mr. Morgan, and I believe would never have been completed but for the importunities of Mrs. Morgan. A few days after the appearance of his piece, he was sitting in the coffee-room of a hotel, and heard his name coupled with a coroner's inquest, by a gentleman who was reading a newspaper to a friend. He asked to see the paper, which was handed to him with the remark that 'It was very extraordinary that Coleridge the poet should have hanged himself just after the success of his play; but he was always a strange mad fellow.'—'Indeed, sir,' said Coleridge, 'it is a *most extraordinary* thing that he should have hanged himself, be the subject of an inquest, and yet that he should at this moment be speaking to you.' The astonished stranger hoped he had 'said nothing to hurt his feelings', and was made easy on that point. The newspaper related that a gentleman in black had been cut down from a tree in Hyde Park, without money or papers in his pockets, his shirt being marked 'S. T. Coleridge'; and Coleridge was at no loss to understand how this might have happened, since he seldom travelled without losing a shirt or two.

231

[From the diary of Thomas Moore, August 4 1833.]

DROVE to Regent's Park; told of Coleridge riding about in a strange shabby dress, with I forget whom, at Keswick, and on some company approaching them, Coleridge offered to fall behind and pass for his companion's servant. 'No,' said the other, 'I am proud of you as a friend; but, I must say, I should be ashamed of you as a servant.'

232

[Samuel Rogers recalls Coleridge's conversation.]

COLERIDGE was a marvellous talker. One morning, when Hookham Frere also breakfasted with me, Coleridge talked for three hours without intermission about poetry, and so admirably, that I wish every word he uttered had been written down.

But sometimes his harangues were quite unintelligible, not only to myself, but to others. Wordsworth and I called upon him one forenoon, when he was in a lodging off Pall Mall. He talked uninterruptedly for about two hours, during which Wordsworth listened to him with profound attention, every now and then nodding his head as if in assent. On quitting the lodging, I said to Wordsworth, 'Well, for my own part, I could not make head or tail of Coleridge's oration: pray, did you understand it?' 'Not one syllable of it', was Wordsworth's reply.

233

JAMES MILL (1773–1836)

THE eighteenth-century quality in the elder Utilitarians comes out in their extraordinary positiveness on psychological and metaphysical points. In 1817 James Mill was beginning to plan the *Analysis of the Human Mind*, which he published in 1829. 'If I had time to write a book,' he says, 'I would make the human mind as plain as the road from Charing Cross to St. Paul's.' A year earlier he wrote, 'I am reading, at least I have begun to read, the *Critique of Pure Reason*. I see clearly enough what poor Kant is about.'

234

FRANCIS JEFFREY, LORD JEFFREY (1773–1850)

MRS. HENRY SIDDONS, a neighbour and intimate friend of the late Lord Jeffrey, who had free licence to enter his house at all hours unannounced and come and go as she listed, opened his library door one day very gently to look if he was there, and saw enough at a glance to convince her that her visit was ill-timed. The hard critic of the 'Edinburgh' was sitting in his chair, with his head on the table, in deep grief. As Mrs. Siddons was delicately retiring, in the hope that her entrance had been unnoticed, Jeffrey raised his head, and kindly beckoned her back. Perceiving that his cheek was flushed, and his eyes suffused with tears, she apologized for her intrusion, and begged permission to withdraw. When he found that she was seriously intending to leave him, he rose from his chair, took her by both hands, and led her to a seat.

Lord Jeffrey (*loq.*). 'Don't go, my dear friend. I shall be right again in another minute.'

Mrs. H. Siddons. 'I had no idea that you had had any bad news or cause for grief, or I would not have come. Is anyone dead?'

Lord Jeffrey. 'Yes, indeed. I'm a great goose to have given way so; but I could not help it. You'll be sorry to hear that little Nelly, Boz's little Nelly, is dead.'

The fact was, Jeffrey had just received the last number then out of *The Old Curiosity Shop*, and had been thoroughly overcome by its pathos.

235

ROBERT SOUTHEY (1774–1843)

IN associating with Southey, not only was it necessary to salvation to refrain from touching his books, but various rites, ceremonies, and usages must be rigidly observed. At certain appointed hours only was he open to conversation; at the seasons which had been predestined from all eternity for holding intercourse with his friends. Every hour of the day had its commission—every halfhour was assigned to its own peculiar, undeviating function. The indefatigable student gave a detailed account of his most painstaking life, every moment of which was fully employed and strictly pre-arranged, to a certain literary Quaker lady.

'I rise at five throughout the year; from six till eight I read Spanish; then French, for one hour: Portuguese, next, for half an hour—my watch lying on the table; I give two hours to poetry; I write prose for two hours; I translate so long; I make extracts so long'; and so of the rest, until the poor fellow had fairly fagged himself into his bed again.

'And, pray, when dost thou think, friend?' she asked, drily, to the great discomfiture of the future Laureate.

236

ON returning from a visit to the Lakes, I[1] told Porson that Southey had said to me, 'My *Madoc* has brought me in a mere trifle; but that poem will be a valuable possession to my family.' Porson answered, '*Madoc* will be read—when Homer and Virgil are forgotten.'

237

[Carlyle, a lonely widower in his seventy-second year, recalls the first and only visit of Southey to Cheyne Row.]

I FORGET how often we met; it was not very often; it was always at H. Taylor's, or through Taylor.[2] One day, for the first and last time, he made us a visit at Chelsea; a certain old lady cousin of Taylor's, who sometimes presided in his house for a month or two in the town season—a Miss Fenwick,[3] of provincial accent and type, but very wise, discreet, and well-bred—had come driving down with him. Their arrival, and loud thundering knock at the door, is very memorable to me;—the moment being unusually critical in our poor household! My little Jeannie was in hands with the marmalade that day: none ever made such marmalade for me, pure as liquid amber, in taste and in look almost poetically delicate, and it was the only one of her pretty and industrious confitures

[1] William Maltby. Cf. p. 132 n.

[2] Sir Henry Taylor (1800–86), author of *Philip van Artevelde* and other plays.

[3] Miss Isabella Fenwick (d. 1856). To her in 1842–3 Wordsworth dictated many interesting notes to his poems.

that I individually cared for; which made her doubly diligent and punctual about it. (Ah me, ah me!) The kitchen fire, I suppose, had not been brisk enough, free enough, so she had had the large brass pan and contents brought up to the brisker parlour fire; and was there victoriously boiling it, when it boiled over, in huge blaze, set the chimney on fire—and I (from my writing upstairs I suppose) had been suddenly summoned to the rescue. What a moment! what an outlook! The kindling of the chimney soot was itself a grave matter, involving fine of £10 if the fire-engines had to come. My first and immediate step was to parry this, by at once letting down the grate valve, and cutting quite off the supply of oxygen or atmosphere; which of course was effectual, though at the expense of a little smoke in the room meanwhile. The brass pan and remaining contents (not much wasted or injured) she had herself snatched off and set on the hearth; I was pulling down the back-windows, which would have completed the temporary settlement, when, hardly three yards from us, broke out the thundering door-knocker: and before the brass pan could be got away, Miss Fenwick and Southey were let in. Southey, I don't think my darling had yet seen; but her own fine modest composure, and presence of mind, never in any greatest other presence forsook her. I remember how daintily she made the salutations, brief quizzical bit of explanation, got the wreck to vanish; and sate down as member of our little party. Southey and I were on the sofa together; she nearer Miss Fenwick, for a little of feminine 'aside' now and then. The colloquy did not last long:—I recollect no point of it, except that Southey and I got to speaking about Shelley (whom perhaps I remembered to have lived in the Lake country for some time, and had started on Shelley as a practicable topic). Southey did not rise into admiration of Shelley either for talent or conduct; spoke of him and his life, without bitterness, but with contemptuous sorrow, and evident aversion mingled with his pity. To me also poor Shelley always was, and is, a kind of ghastly object, colourless, pallid, without health or warmth or vigour; the sound of him shrieky, frosty, as if a ghost were trying to 'sing to us'; the temperament of him spasmodic, hysterical, instead of strong or robust; with fine affections and aspirations, gone all such a road:—a man infinitely too weak for that solitary scaling of the Alps which he undertook in spite of all the world. At some point of the dialogue I said to Southey, 'a haggard existence that of his'. I remember Southey's pause, and the tone and air with which he answered, 'It is a haggard existence!' His look, at this moment, was unusually gloomy and heavy-laden, full of confused distress;—as if in retrospect of his own existence, and the haggard battle it too had been.[1]

[1] If, as Carlyle goes on to say, Southey was 'now about sixty-three', the first symptoms of the mental collapse which soon followed were probably already visible.

238

CHARLES LAMB (1775–1834)

COLERIDGE was one evening running before the wind. He had talked about everything, from Moses downwards. At last he came to his own doings at Shrewsbury, and was swinging on, nineteen knots to the hour. 'At this place, at Shrewsbury (which is not only remarkable for its celebrated cakes, and for having been the point of rendezvous for Falstaff's regiment of foot, but also, if I may presume to speak of it, for the first development of the imaginative faculty in myself, by which faculty I would be understood to mean, etc. etc.)—at Shrewsbury I was accustomed to preach.—I believe, Charles Lamb, that you have heard me preach?' pursued he, turning round to his fatigued friend, who rapidly retorted—'I—I—never heard you do anything else.'

239

In December[1] Wordsworth was in town, and as Keats wished to know him I made up a party to dinner of Charles Lamb, Wordsworth, Keats, and Monkhouse, his friend; and a very pleasant party we had. . . .

On December 28th the immortal dinner came off in my painting-room, with Jerusalem[2] towering up behind us as a background. Wordsworth was in fine cue, and we had a glorious set-to—on Homer, Shakespeare, Milton, and Virgil. Lamb got exceedingly merry and exquisitely witty; and his fun in the midst of Wordsworth's solemn intonations of oratory was like the sarcasm and wit of the fool in the intervals of Lear's passion. He made a speech and voted me absent, and made them drink my health. 'Now,' said Lamb, 'you old Lake poet, you rascally poet, why do you call Voltaire dull?' We all defended Wordsworth, and affirmed there was a state of mind when Voltaire would be dull. 'Well,' said Lamb, 'here's Voltaire—the Messiah of the French nation, and a very proper one too.'

He then, in a strain of humour beyond description, abused me for putting Newton's head into my picture; 'a fellow', said he, 'who believed nothing unless it was as clear as the three sides of a triangle.' And then he and Keats agreed he had destroyed all the poetry of the rainbow by reducing it to the prismatic colours. It was impossible to resist him, and we all drank 'Newton's health and confusion to mathematics'. It

[1] 1817. The host was Benjamin Robert Haydon, the painter.

[2] Haydon's painting of 'Christ's Entry into Jerusalem', not finished till 1820.

was delightful to see the good humour of Wordsworth in giving in to all our frolics without affectation and laughing as heartily as the best of us.

By this time other friends joined, among them poor Ritchie,[1] who was going to penetrate by Fezzan to Timbuctoo. I introduced him to all as 'a gentleman going to Africa'. Lamb seemed to take no notice; but all of a sudden he roared out: 'Which is the gentleman we are going to lose?' We then drank the victim's health, in which Ritchie joined.

In the morning of this delightful day, a gentleman, a perfect stranger, had called on me. He said he knew my friends, had an enthusiasm for Wordsworth, and begged I would procure him the happiness of an introduction. He told me he was a comptroller of stamps, and often had correspondence with the poet.[2] I thought it a liberty; but still, as he seemed a gentleman, I told him he might come.

When we retired to tea we found the comptroller. In introducing him to Wordsworth I forgot to say who he was. After a little time the comptroller looked down, looked up, and said to Wordsworth: 'Don't you think, sir, Milton was a great genius?' Keats looked at me, Wordsworth looked at the comptroller. Lamb who was dozing by the fire turned round and said: 'Pray, sir, did you say Milton was a great genius?' 'No, sir: I asked Mr. Wordsworth if he were not.' 'Oh,' said Lamb, 'then you are a silly fellow.' 'Charles! my dear Charles!' said Wordsworth; but Lamb, perfectly innocent of the confusion he had created, was off again by the fire.

After an awful pause the comptroller said: 'Don't you think Newton a great genius?' I could not stand it any longer. Keats put his head into my books. Ritchie squeezed in a laugh. Wordsworth seemed asking himself: 'Who is this?' Lamb got up, and taking a candle said: 'Sir, will you allow me to look at your phrenological development?' He then turned his back on the poor man, and at every question of the comptroller he chaunted:

> Diddle, diddle dumpling, my son John
> Went to bed with his breeches on.

The man in office, finding Wordsworth did not know who he was, said in a spasmodic and half-chuckling anticipation of assured victory: 'I have had the honour of some correspondence with you, Mr. Wordsworth.' 'With me, sir?' said Wordsworth, 'not that I remember.' 'Don't you, sir? I am a comptroller of stamps.' There was a dead silence, the

[1] Joseph Ritchie (1788?–1819), African traveller, who died on an expedition to the Sudan. [2] Wordsworth was Distributor of Stamps for Westmorland.

comptroller evidently thinking that was enough. While we were waiting for Wordsworth's reply, Lamb sung out:

Hey diddle diddle,
The cat and the fiddle.

'My dear Charles!' said Wordsworth.

Diddle diddle dumpling, my son John,

chaunted Lamb, and then rising, exclaimed: 'Do let me have another look at that gentleman's organs.' Keats and I hurried Lamb into the painting-room, shut the door, and gave way to inextinguishable laughter. Monkhouse followed and tried to get Lamb away. We went back, but the comptroller was irreconcilable. We soothed and smiled, and asked him to supper. He stayed, though his dignity was sorely affected. However, being a good-natured man, we parted all in good humour, and no ill effects followed.

All the while, until Monkhouse succeeded, we could hear Lamb struggling in the painting-room, and calling at intervals: 'Who is that fellow? Allow me to see his organs once more.'

It was indeed an immortal evening. Wordsworth's fine intonation as he quoted Milton and Virgil, Keats' eager inspired look, Lamb's quaint sparkle of lambent humour, so speeded the stream of conversation, that in my life I never passed a more delightful time. All our fun was within bounds. Not a word passed that an apostle might not have listened to. It was a night worthy of the Elizabethan age, and my solemn Jerusalem flashing up by the flame of the fire, with Christ hanging over us like a vision, all made up a picture which will long glow upon

that inward eye
Which is the bliss of solitude.

240

JUST before the Lambs quitted the metropolis for the voluntary banishment of Enfield Chase, they came to spend a day with me[1] at Fulham, and brought with them a companion, who, 'dumb animal' though it was, had for some time past been in the habit of giving play to one of Charles Lamb's most amiable characteristics—that of sacrificing his own feelings and inclinations to those of others. This was a large and very handsome dog, of a rather curious and singularly sagacious breed, which had belonged to Thomas Hood, and at the time I speak of, and to oblige both

[1] P. G. Patmore (1786–1855), miscellaneous writer.

dog and master, had been transferred to the Lambs—who made a great pet of him, to the entire disturbance and discomfiture, as it appeared, of all Lamb's habits of life, but especially of that most favourite and salutary of all, his long and heretofore solitary suburban walks: for Dash (that was the dog's name) would never allow Lamb to quit the house without him, and, when out, would never go anywhere but precisely where it pleased himself. The consequence was, that Lamb made himself a perfect slave to this dog—who was always half-a-mile off from his companion, either before or behind, scouring the fields and roads in all directions, up and down 'all manner of streets', and keeping his attendant in a perfect fever of anxiety and irritation, from his fear of losing him on the one hand, and his reluctance to put the needful restraint upon him on the other. Dash perfectly well knew his host's amiable weakness in this respect, and took a due dog-like advantage of it. In the Regent's Park in particular Dash had his quasi-master completely at his mercy; for the moment they got within the Ring, he used to squeeze himself through the railing, and disappear for half-an-hour together in the enclosed and thickly planted greensward, knowing perfectly well that Lamb did not dare to move from the spot where he (Dash) had disappeared till he thought proper to show himself again. And they used to take this walk oftener than any other, precisely because Dash liked it and Lamb did not.

The performance of the Pig-driver that Leigh Hunt describes so capitally in the 'Companion' must have been an easy and straightforward thing compared with this enterprise of the dear couple in conducting Dash from Islington to Fulham. It appeared, however, that they had not undertaken it this time purely for Dash's gratification; but (as I had often admired the dog) to ask me if I would accept him—'if only out of charity', said Miss Lamb, 'for if we keep him much longer, he'll be the death of Charles.'

I readily took charge of the unruly favourite, and soon found, as I suspected, that his wild and wilful ways were a pure imposition upon the easy temper of Lamb; for as soon as he found himself in the keeping of one who knew what dog-decorum was, he subsided into the best-bred and best-behaved of his species.

A few weeks after I had taken charge of Dash, I received the following letter from Lamb, who had now removed to Enfield Chase. . . .

Dear Patmore—Excuse my anxiety—but how is Dash? (I should have asked if Mrs. Patmore kept her rules and was improving—but Dash came uppermost. The order of our thoughts should be the order of our writing.) Goes he muzzled, or *aperto ore*? Are his intellects sound, or does he wander a little in *his* conversation? You cannot be too careful to watch the first symptoms of incoherence.

The first illogical snarl he makes, to St. Luke's with him. All the dogs here are going mad, if you believe the overseers; but I protest they seem to me very rational and collected. But nothing is so deceitful as mad people to those who are not used to them. Try him with hot water. If he won't lick it up, it is a sign he does not like it. Does his tail wag horizontally or perpendicularly? That has decided the fate of many dogs at Enfield. Is his general deportment cheerful? I mean when he is pleased—for otherwise there is no judging. You can't be too careful. Has he bit any of the children yet? If he has, have them shot, and keep *him* for curiosity, to see if it was the hydrophobia. . . . If the slightest suspicion arises in your breast that all is not right with him (Dash), muzzle him, and lead him in a string (common packthread will do; he don't care for twist) to Hood's, his quondam master, and he'll take him in at any time. You may mention your suspicions or not, as you like, or as you may think it will wound or not Mr. H's feelings. Hood, I know, will wink at a few follies in Dash, in consideration of his former sense. Besides, Hood is deaf, and if you hinted anything, ten to one he would not hear you. Besides, you will have discharged your conscience, and laid the child at the right door, as they say. . . .

[Patmore replies to this in the same facetious spirit: Dash is 'very mad indeed', and has bitten one of the kittens. His letter concludes with the dog's latest escapade.]

He was out at near dusk, down the lane, a few nights ago, with his mistress, . . . when Dash attacked a carpenter, armed with a large saw—not Dash, but the carpenter—and a 'wise saw' it turned out, for its teeth protected him from Dash's, and a battle royal ensued, worthy the Surrey Theatre. Mrs. Patmore says that it was really frightful to see the saw, and the way in which it and Dash gnashed their teeth at each other. . . .

241

FROM Colebrooke Lamb removed to Enfield Chase—a painful operation at all times, for as he feelingly misapplied Wordsworth, 'the moving accident was not his trade'. . . . There were no pastoral yearnings concerned in this Enfield removal. There is no doubt which of Captain Morris's 'Town and Country Songs' would have been most to Lamb's taste. 'The sweet shady side of Pall Mall' would have carried it hollow. In courtesy to a friend, he would select a green lane for a ramble, but left to himself, he took the turnpike road as often as otherwise. 'Scott,' says Cunningham, 'was a stout walker.' Lamb was a porter one. He calculated distances, not by long measure, but by ale and beer measure. 'Now I have walked a pint.' Many a time I[1] have accompanied him in these matches against Meux, not without sharing in the stake, and then, what cheerful

[1] Thomas Hood.

and profitable talk! For instance, he once delivered to me orally the substance of the 'Essay on the Defect of Imagination in Modern Artists', subsequently printed in the *Athenaeum*. But besides the criticism, there were snatches of old poems, golden lines, and sentences culled from old books, and anecdotes of men of note. Marry, it was like going a ramble with gentle Izaak Walton, minus the fishing.

242

ACCORDING to his promise, Mr. Lamb honoured us with a visit, accompanied by his sister, Mr. and Mrs. Hood,[1] and a few others hastily gathered together for the occasion. On entering the room, Mr. Lamb seemed to have forgotten that any previous introduction had taken place. 'Allow me, madam,' said he, 'to introduce to you my sister Mary; she's a very good woman, but she drinks!' 'Charles, Charles,' said Miss Lamb imploringly (her face at the same time covered with blushes), 'how can you say such a thing?' 'Why,' rejoined he, 'you know it's a fact; look at the redness of your face. Did I not see you in your cups at nine o'clock this morning?' 'For shame, Charles,' returned his sister; 'what will our friends think?' 'Don't mind him, my dear Miss Lamb,' said Mrs. Hood soothingly, 'I will answer that the cups were only breakfast-cups full of coffee.'

Seeming much delighted with the mischief he had made, he turned away, and began talking quite comfortably on indifferent topics to someone else. For my own part I could not help telling Mrs. Hood I longed to shake 'Charles'. 'Oh,' replied she smiling, 'Miss Lamb is so used to his unaccountable ways that she would be miserable without them.' Once, indeed, as Mr. Lamb told Hood, 'having really gone a little too far', and seeing her, as he thought, quite hurt and offended, he determined to amend his manners, 'behave politely, and leave off joking altogether'. For a few days he acted up to this resolution, behaving, as he assured Hood, 'admirably, and what do you think I got for my pains?' 'I have no doubt,' said Hood, 'you got sincere thanks.' 'Bless you, no!' rejoined Lamb; 'why, Mary did nothing but keep bursting into tears every time she looked at me, and when I asked her what she was crying for, when I was doing all I could to please her, she blubbered out: "You're changed, Charles, you're changed; what have I done that you should treat me in this cruel manner?" "Treat you! I thought you did not like my jokes, and therefore tried to please you by strangling them down." "Oh, oh," cried she, sobbing as if her heart would break; "joke again, Charles—I

[1] i.e. Mr. and Mrs. Thomas Hood. The narrator is Mary Balmanno.

don't know you in this manner. I am sure I should die if you behaved as you have done for the last few days." So you see I joke for her good'; adding, with a most elfish expression, 'it saved her life then, anyhow.'

243
MATTHEW GREGORY ('MONK') LEWIS (1775–1818)

LEWIS at Oatlands was observed one morning to have his eyes red, and his air sentimental. Being asked why, he replied, 'that when people said anything *kind* to him, it affected him deeply; and just now the Duchess[1] has said something *so* kind to me that. . . .' Here tears began to flow again. 'Never mind, Lewis,' said Colonel Armstrong to him, 'never mind, don't cry. *She could not mean it.*'

244
JANE AUSTEN (1775–1817)

From James Stanier Clarke, 27 March 1816

Dear Miss Austen,

I have to return you the thanks of His Royal Highness, the Prince Regent, for the handsome copy you sent him of your last excellent novel.[2] . . . The Prince Regent has just left us for London; and having been pleased to appoint me Chaplain and Private English Secretary to the Prince of Cobourg, I remain here with His Serene Highness and a select party until the marriage. Perhaps when you again appear in print you may chuse to dedicate your volumes to Prince Leopold: any historical romance, illustrative of the history of the august House of Coburg, would just now be very interesting.

Believe me at all times,
Dear Miss Austen,
Your obliged friend,
J. S. Clarke.

[1] The Duchess of York. [2] *Emma*.

JANE AUSTEN

To James Stanier Clarke, 1 April 1816

My dear Sir,

I am honoured by the Prince's thanks and very much obliged to yourself for the kind manner in which you mention the work. . . . You are very kind in your hints as to the sort of composition which might recommend me at present, and I am fully sensible that an historical romance, founded on the House of Saxe Cobourg, might be much more to the purpose of profit or popularity than such pictures of domestic life in country villages as I deal in. But I could no more write a romance than an epic poem. I could not sit seriously down to write a serious romance under any other motive than to save my life; and if it were indispensable for me to keep it up and never relax into laughing at myself or other people, I am sure I should be hung before I had finished the first chapter. No, I must keep to my own style and go on in my own way; and though I may never succeed again in that, I am convinced that I should totally fail in any other.

I remain, my dear Sir,
Your very much obliged, and very sincere friend,
J. Austen.

245
THOMAS CAMPBELL (1777–1844)

AT a literary dinner Campbell asked leave to propose a toast, and gave the health of Napoleon Bonaparte. The war was at its height, and the very mention of Napoleon's name, except in conjunction with some uncomplimentary epithet, was in most circles regarded as an outrage. A storm of groans broke out, and Campbell with difficulty could get a few sentences heard. 'Gentlemen,' he said, 'you must not mistake me. I admit that the French Emperor is a tyrant. I admit that he is a monster. I admit that he is the sworn foe of our nation, and, if you will, of the whole human race. But, gentlemen, we must be just to our great enemy. We must not forget that he once shot a bookseller.' The guests, of whom two out of every three lived by their pens, burst into a roar of laughter, and Campbell sat down in triumph.

246

TAKING a walk with Campbell one day up Regent Street, we[1] were accosted by a wretched-looking woman with a sick infant in her arms, and another starved little thing creeping at its mother's side. The woman begged for a copper. I had no change, and Campbell had nothing but a sovereign. The woman stuck fast to the Poet, as if she read his heart in his face, and I could feel his arm beginning to tremble. At length, saying something about its being his *duty* to assist such poor creatures, he told the woman to wait; and, hastening into a mercer's shop, asked, rather impatiently, for change. You know what an excitable being he was; and now he fancied all business must give way until the change was supplied! The shopman thought otherwise; the Poet insisted; an altercation ensued; and in a minute or two the master jumped over the counter and collared him, telling us he would turn us both out—that he believed we came there to kick up a row, for some dishonest purpose. So here was a pretty dilemma. We defied him, but said we would go out instantly on his apologizing for his gross insult. All was uproar. Campbell called out, 'Thrash the fellow—thrash him!' 'You will not go out then?' said the mercer. 'No, never, until you apologize.' 'Well, we shall soon see—John, go to Vine-street and fetch the police.'

In a few minutes two policemen appeared; one went close up to Mr. Campbell, the other to myself. The Poet was now in such breathless indignation that he could not articulate a sentence. I told the policeman the object he had in asking change; and that the shopman had most unwarrantably insulted us. 'This gentleman', I added by way of climax, 'is Mr. Thomas Campbell, the distinguished Poet—a man who would not hurt a fly, much less act with the dishonest intention that person has insinuated.' The moment I uttered the name, the policeman backed away two or three paces, as if awe-struck, and said, 'Guid G—d, mon, is that Maister Cammel, the Lord Rector o' Glasgow?' 'Yes, my friend, he is, as this card may convince you,' handing it to him; 'all this commotion has been caused by a mistake.' By this time the mercer had cooled down to a moderate temperature, and in the end made every reparation in his power, saying he was very busy at the time, and 'had he but known the gentleman, he would have changed *fifty* sovereigns for him!' 'My dear fellow,' said the Poet (who had recovered his speech), 'I am not at all offended'; and it was really laughable to see them shaking hands long and vigorously, each with perfect sincerity and mutual forgiveness.

[1] The narrator is William Beattie, Campbell's biographer.

247
WILLIAM HAZLITT (1778–1830)

JOHN LAMB (the brother of Charles) once knocked down Hazlitt, who was impertinent to him; and on those who were present interfering and begging Hazlitt to shake hands and forgive him, Hazlitt said, 'Well, I don't care if I do. I am a metaphysician, and do not mind a blow; nothing but an *idea* hurts *me*.'

248
BISHOP HENRY PHILLPOTTS (1778–1869)

THE Bishop was renowned for his suave and courtly manners, his charming voice, and the subtle precision of its modulations . . .

At one of his luncheon-parties he was specially kind to a country clergyman's wife, who knew none of the company, and he took her out on a terrace in order to show her the view—a view of the sea shut in by the crags of a small cove. 'Ah, my lord,' gasped the lady, 'it reminds one so much of Switzerland.' 'Precisely,' said the Bishop, 'except that there we have the mountains without the sea, and here we have the sea without the mountains.'

249
THOMAS MOORE (1779–1852)

IN the month of July 1806, I had come up to London from a visit to Donington Park, having promised my dear and most kind friend, the late Dowager Lady Donegal, to join her and her sister at Worthing. The number of the *Edinburgh* containing the attack on my *Odes and Epistles* had been just announced. . . .The *Review* did not, however, reach me in London; for I have a clear recollection of having, for the first time, read the formidable article in my bed one morning at the inn in Worthing, where I had taken up my sleeping quarters during my short visit to the Donegals. Though, on the first perusal of the article, the contemptuous language applied to me by the reviewer a good deal roused my Irish blood, the idea of seriously noticing the attack did not occur to me, I think, till some time after. I remember, at all events, having talked over the article with my friends, Lady Donegal and her sister, in so light and careless a tone as to render them not a little surprised at the explosion which afterwards took place. I also well remember that, when the idea of calling out Jeffrey first suggested itself to me, the necessity I should be under of proceeding to Edinburgh for the purpose was a considerable drawback on my design, not only from the difficulty I was likely to experience in finding anyone to accompany me in so Quixotic an expedition, but also from the actual and but too customary state of my finances, which rendered it doubtful whether I should be able to compass the expense of so long a journey.

In this mood of mind I returned to London, and there, whether by *good* or *ill* luck, but in my own opinion the *former*, there was the identical Jeffrey himself just arrived on a short visit to his London friends. From Rogers, who had met Jeffrey the day before at dinner at Lord Fincastle's, I learned that the conversation in the course of the day having happened to fall upon me, Lord F. was good enough to describe me as possessing 'great amenity of manners'; on which Jeffrey said laughingly, 'I am afraid he would not show much amenity to *me*.'

. . . I accordingly applied to my old friend Hume, who without hesitation agreed to be the bearer of my message. It is needless to say that, feeling as I then did, I liked him all the better for his readiness, nor indeed am I at all disposed to like him a whit the less for it now. Having now secured my second, I lost no time in drawing up the challenge which he was to deliver; and as actual combat, not parley, was my object, I took care to put it out of the power of my antagonist to explain or retract, even if he was so disposed. Of the short note which I sent, the few first lines have long escaped my memory; but after adverting to some assertion contained in the article, accusing me, if I recollect aright, of a deliberate intention to corrupt the minds of my readers, I thus proceeded: 'To this I beg leave to answer, You are a liar; yes, sir, a liar; and I choose to adopt this harsh and vulgar mode of defiance in order to prevent at once all equivocation between us, and to compel you to adopt for your own satisfaction that alternative which you might otherwise have hesitated in affording to mine.' I am not quite sure as to the exact construction of this latter part of the note, but it was as nearly as possible, I think, in this form.

There was of course but one kind of answer to be given to such a cartel. Hume had been referred by Jeffrey to his friend Mr. Horner, and the meeting was fixed for the following morning at Chalk Farm. Our great difficulty now was where to procure a case of pistols; for Hume, though he had been once, I think, engaged in mortal affray, was possessed of no such implements; and as for *me*, I had once nearly blown off my thumb by discharging an over-loaded pistol, and that was the whole, I believe, of my previous acquaintance with fire-arms. William Spencer, being the only one of all my friends whom I thought likely to furnish me with these *sine-qua-nons*, I hastened to confide to him my wants, and request his assistance on this point. He told me if I would come to him in the evening, he would have the pistols ready for me. . . .

I must have slept pretty well; for Hume, I remember, had to wake me in the morning, and the chaise being in readiness, we set off for Chalk Farm. Hume had also taken the precaution of providing a surgeon to be within call. On reaching the ground we found Jeffrey and his party already arrived. I say his 'party', for although Horner only was with him, there were, as we afterwards found, two or three of his attached friends (and no man, I believe, could ever boast of a greater number) who, in their anxiety for his safety, had accompanied him, and were hovering about the spot. And then was it that, for the first time, my excellent friend Jeffrey and I met face to face. He was standing, with the bag which contained the pistols in his hand, while Horner was looking anxiously around.

It was agreed that the spot where we found them, which was screened on one side by large trees, would be as good for our purpose as any we could select; and Horner, after expressing some anxiety respecting some men whom he had seen suspiciously hovering about, but who now appeared to have departed, retired with Hume behind the trees for the purpose of loading the pistols, leaving Jeffrey and myself together.

All this had occupied but a very few minutes. We, of course, had bowed to each other on meeting; but the first words I recollect to have passed between us was Jeffrey's saying, on our being left together, 'What a beautiful morning it is!' 'Yes,' I answered with a slight smile, 'a morning made for better purposes'; to which his only response was a sort of assenting sigh. As our assistants were not, any more than ourselves, very expert at warlike matters, they were rather slow in their proceedings; and as Jeffrey and I walked up and down together, we came once in sight of their operations: upon which I related to him, as rather *à propos* to the purpose, what Billy Egan, the Irish barrister, once said, when, as he was sauntering about in like manner while the pistols were loading, his antagonist, a fiery little fellow, called out to him angrily to keep his ground. 'Don't make yourself unaisy, my dear fellow,' said Egan; 'sure, isn't it bad enough to take the dose, without being by at the mixing up?'

Jeffrey had scarcely time to smile at this story, when our two friends, issuing from behind the trees, placed us at our respective posts (the distance, I suppose, having been previously measured by them), and put the pistols into our hands. They then retired to a little distance; the pistols were on both sides raised; and we waited but the signal to fire, when some police officers, whose approach none of us had noticed, and who were within a second of being too late, rushed out from a hedge behind Jeffrey; and one of them, striking at Jeffrey's pistol with his staff, knocked it to some distance into the field, while another running over to me, took possession also of mine. We were then replaced in our respective carriages, and conveyed, crest-fallen, to Bow Street.

On our way thither Hume told me that from Horner not knowing anything about the loading of pistols he had been obliged to help him in the operation, and in fact to take upon himself chiefly the task of loading both pistols. When we arrived at Bow Street, the first step of both parties was to dispatch messengers to procure some friends to bail us; and as William Spencer was already acquainted with the transaction, to him I applied on my part, and requested that he would lose no time in coming to me. In the meanwhile we were all shown into a sitting-room, the people in attendance having first inquired whether it was our wish to be separated, but neither party having expressed any desire to that effect, we were all put together in the same room. Here conversation upon some literary subject, I forget what, soon ensued, in which I myself took only the brief and occasional share beyond which, at that time of my life, I seldom ventured in general society. But whatever was the topic, Jeffrey, I recollect, expatiated upon it with all his peculiar fluency and eloquence; and I can now most vividly recall him to my memory, as he lay upon his back on a form which stood beside the wall, pouring volubly forth his fluent but most oddly pronounced diction, and dressing this subject out in every variety of array that an ever rich and ready wardrobe of phraseology could supply. I have been told of his saying, soon after our rencontre, that he had taken a fancy to me from the first moment of our meeting together in the field; and I can truly say that my liking for him is of the same early date.

250
GEORGE CROLY (1780–1860)

CROLY once asked me if I had read a certain book. I said, 'Yes, I had reviewed it.' 'What!' he exclaimed, 'do you read the books you review?' 'Yes,' I replied, 'as a rule I do.' 'That's wrong,' replied the Doctor, 'it creates a prejudice.'

251
LEIGH HUNT (1784–1859)

[A reminiscence by George Smith, the publisher.]

LEIGH HUNT was of a small stature, with sallow not to say yellow complexion. His mouth lacked refinement and firmness, but he had large expressive eyes. His manner, however, had such fascination that, after he had spoken for five minutes, one forgot how he looked. . . .

Business was by no means Leigh Hunt's strong point. In this respect, but not otherwise, he may have suggested Skimpole to Charles Dickens. On one of my first visits I found him trying to puzzle out the abstruse questions of how he should deduct some small sum such as thirteen shillings and ninepence from a sovereign. On another occasion I had to pay him a sum of money, £100 or £200, and I wrote him a cheque for the amount. 'Well,' he said, 'what am I to do with this little bit of paper?' I told him that if he presented it at the bank they would pay him cash for it, but I added, 'I will save you that trouble.' I sent to the bank and cashed the cheque for him. He took the notes away carefully enclosed in an envelope. Two days afterwards Leigh Hunt came in a state of great agitation to tell me that his wife had burned them. He had thrown the envelope with the bank-notes inside carelessly down and his wife had flung it into the fire. Leigh Hunt's agitation while on his way to bring this news had not prevented him from purchasing on the road a little statuette of Psyche which he carried, without any paper round it, in his hand. I told him I thought something might be done in the matter; I sent to the bankers and got the numbers of the notes, and then in company with Leigh Hunt went off to the Bank of England. I explained our business and we were shown into a room where three old gentlemen were sitting at tables. They kept us waiting some time, and Leigh Hunt, who had meantime been staring all round the room, at last got up, walked up to one of the staid officials, and addressing him said in wondering tones, 'And this is the Bank of England! And do you sit here all day, and never see the green woods and the trees and flowers and the charming country?' Then in a tone of remonstrance he demanded, 'Are you contented with such a life?' All this time he was holding the little naked Psyche in one hand, and with his long hair and flashing eyes made a surprising figure. I fancy I can still see the astonished faces of the three officials; they would have made a delightful picture. I said, 'Come away, Mr. Hunt, these gentlemen are very busy.' I succeeded in carrying Leigh Hunt off, and after entering into certain formalities, we were told that the value of the notes would be paid in twelve months. I gave Leigh Hunt the money at once, and he went away rejoicing.

252

JAMES HANNAY[1] knew Carlyle well, and often went to see him, but it was in his poorer days. One day when Mr. Hannay went to the house, he saw two gold sovereigns lying exposed in a little vase on the chimney-piece. He asked Carlyle what they were for. Carlyle looked—for him—embarrassed, but gave no definite answer. 'Well, now, my dear fellow,' said Hannay, 'neither you nor I are quite in a position to play ducks and drakes with sovereigns: what *are* these for?'—'Well,' said Carlyle, 'the fact is, Leigh Hunt likes better to find them there than that I should give them to him.'

253
THOMAS LOVE PEACOCK (1785–1866)

MR. PEACOCK talked . . . at much length about Jeremy Bentham, with whom he had been extremely intimate—dining with him *tête-à-tête* once a week for years together. He mentioned among other things that when experiments were being made with Mr. Bentham's body after his death,[2] Mr. James Mill had one day come into Mr. Peacock's room at the India House and told him that there had exuded from Mr. Bentham's head a kind of oil, which was almost unfreezable, and which he conceived might be used for the oiling of chronometers which were going into high latitudes. 'The less you say about that, Mill,' said Peacock, 'the better it will be for *you*; because if the fact once becomes known, just as we see now in the newspapers that a fine bear is to be killed for his grease, we shall be having advertisements to the effect that a fine philosopher is to be killed for his oil.'

[1] Scottish novelist and miscellaneous writer (1827–73).
[2] In his will Bentham left his body to be dissected.

254
HARRIETTE WILSON (1786–1846)

[Harriette Wilson, the daughter of a Swiss clockmaker, was born in London, and at the age of about fifteen became the mistress of Lord Craven. He was succeeded by the Hon. Frederick Lamb, and by a long series of distinguished lovers and acquaintances, including Lord Hertford (Thackeray's 'Marquis of Steyne'), Beau Brummell, and the Duke of Wellington. About 1820 she went to live in Paris, and being in need of money, partly owing to 'the ill-timed parsimony of the Duke of Beaufort, who thought to compound a promised annuity of £500 by a single payment of £1,200', she decided to write her memoirs.]

HER manuscript found its way into the hands of one J. J. Stockdale, of No. 24 Opera Colonnade. Julia Johnstone[1] . . . calls Stockdale 'a hackneyed vendor of obscenity', and the nature of his shop's contents may be guessed from the titles of several other of his publications: *The Beauty, Marriage Ceremonies and Intercourse of the Sexes, in all Nations; The New Art of Love*, and Dr. Robertson's *Anatomy of Physiology*. If he also sold an ill-printed Boccaccio, an abbreviated Voltaire (with all the philosophy left out) and the Works of Aristotle with coloured plates, it would not be surprising. The immortal novels of Paul de Kock had unfortunately not yet been written.

Thomas Little, who edited most of the works at 24 Opera Colonnade, was probably Stockdale himself. He had the impudence in his postscript to Harriette's volumes to claim that 'this publication cannot fail to produce the greatest moral effect on the present and future generations. [For] if

> Vice is a monster, of such hideous mien
> That, to be hated, needs but to be seen,

when has Vice ever been so unsparingly exposed?'

Unfortunately the authoress was quite unable to rise to the heights of such Apocalyptic fervour, and made no secret throughout her narrative of having, on the whole, enjoyed herself very much. It is pleasant to think that the lapse of a hundred years has elevated the book to the level of an historical document, and made such humbug for ever unnecessary.

The work appeared in 1825, and was instantly a success. Harriette had hoped for twenty editions. Stockdale sold thirty within the year; and a French version in six volumes carried the notoriety of the authoress to her new place of residence. The happy publisher was compelled to erect a barricade in front of his premises to prevent the public from storming the

[1] She wrote *Confessions of Julia Johnstone . . .* (1825).

shop. He was, however, not without his troubles. Frederick Lamb called to threaten prosecution, and two of Harriette's victims did prosecute, and involved Stockdale in considerable expense. But as he and the authoress between them fingered, as Julia puts it, £10,000 of the public money, they had little reason to complain.

The fashionable world was in great agitation, especially as further instalments of the damaging record were threatened. Meetings were held at White's, Brooks's, and the United Service Clubs in order to decide what could be done. It is probable that the action brought by Blore, the stone-mason of Piccadilly, was financed from these aristocratic institutions, as a kind of *ballon d'essai*. Harriette had held the unfortunate Blore up to ridicule for the boorishness of his alleged advances, and the stone-mason, now married and the father of a family, claimed damages. In spite of the eloquence of Stockdale he won his case, and was awarded £300. Another plaintiff, one Hugh Evans Fisher, received even more; but although both actions were successful, Harriette's former wealthy admirers decided that it would be safer to go no further. They seem to have bought her silence, and Harriette troubled them no more.

255
RICHARD WHATELY (1787–1863)

WHATELY never wasted a thought upon his dignity.[1] If he had, the dignity would have been an unwelcome weight; but, without any intentional arrogance, he was accustomed to assume the intellectual dictatorship of every company in which he found himself. There could be no greater mistake than to infer from this that there was any tincture in him of ecclesiastical intolerance. He was in reality intolerant of intolerance, and of not many things beside. He lived upon easy terms with the young men about the Viceregal Court, and one of them, a young nobleman who was Aide-de-camp to the Lord-Lieutenant, made a little mistake in assuming that a scoff at the Roman Catholic Bishops would be acceptable: 'My Lord Archbishop,' said the Aide-de-camp, 'do you know what is the difference between a Roman Catholic Bishop and a donkey?' 'No,' said the Archbishop. 'The one has a cross on his breast and the other on his back,' said the Aide-de-camp. 'Ha!' said the Archbishop; 'do you know the difference between an Aide-de-camp and a donkey?' 'No,' said the Aide-de-camp. 'Neither do I', said the Archbishop.

[1] He was Archbishop of Dublin.

256
GEORGE GORDON, LORD BYRON
(1788–1824)

[Robert Chambers (1802–71) describes an engagement of Mrs. Siddons at the Theatre Royal, Edinburgh, in May 1784, and the night she played Isabella in Southerne's tragedy, *The Fatal Marriage*.]

PEOPLE came from distant places, even from Newcastle, to witness what all spoke of with wonder. There were one day applications for 2,557 places, while there were only 630 of that kind in the house. Porters and servants had to bivouac for a night in the streets, on mats and palliasses, in order that they might get an early chance of admission to the box-office next day. At the more thrilling parts of the performance, the audience were agitated to a degree unprecedented in this cool latitude. Many ladies fainted. This was particularly the case on the evening when *Isabella, or the Fatal Marriage*, was performed. The personator of Isabella has to exhibit the distress of a wife, on finding, after a second marriage, that her first and beloved husband, Biron, is still alive. Mrs. Siddons was left at the close in such an exhausted state, that some minutes elapsed before she could be carried off the stage. A young heiress, Miss Gordon of Gight, in Aberdeenshire, was carried out of her box in hysterics, screaming loudly the words caught from the great actress: 'Oh, my Biron! my Biron!' A strange tale was therewith connected. A gentleman, whom she had not at this time seen or heard of, the Honourable John Biron, next year met, paid his addresses, and married her. It was to her a fatal marriage in several respects, although it gave to the world the poet Lord Byron.

257

NEITHER Moore nor myself[1] had ever seen Byron when it was settled that he should dine at my house to meet Moore; nor was he known by sight to Campbell, who, happening to call upon me that morning, consented to join the party. I thought it best that I alone should be in the drawing-room when Byron entered it; and Moore and Campbell accordingly withdrew. Soon after his arrival, they returned; and I introduced them to him severally, naming them as Adam named the beasts.

When we sat down to dinner, I asked Byron if he would take soup? 'No; he never took soup.'—'Would he take some fish?'—'No; he never

[1] i.e. Thomas Moore and Samuel Rogers.

took fish.'—Presently I asked if he would eat some mutton? 'No; he never ate mutton.'—I then asked if he would take a glass of wine? 'No; he never tasted wine.'—It was now necessary to inquire what he *did* eat and drink; and the answer was, 'Nothing but hard biscuits and soda-water.' Unfortunately, neither hard biscuits nor soda-water were at hand; and he dined upon potatoes bruised down on his plate and drenched with vinegar. —My guests stayed till very late, discussing the merits of Walter Scott and Joanna Baillie. Some days after, meeting Hobhouse, I said to him, 'How long will Lord Byron persevere in his present diet?' He replied, 'Just as long as you continue to notice it.' I did not then know, what I now know to be a fact—that Byron, after leaving my house, had gone to a Club in St. James's Street, and eaten a hearty meat-supper.

258

[Thomas Moore recalls an occasion in Venice.]

HE had ordered dinner from some *tratteria*, and while waiting its arrival—as well as that of Mr. Alexander Scott, whom he had invited to join us—we stood out on the balcony, in order that, before the daylight was quite gone, I might have some glimpses of the scene which the Canal presented. Happening to remark, in looking up at the clouds, which were still bright in the west, that 'what had struck me in Italian sunsets was that peculiar rosy hue—' I had hardly pronounced the word 'rosy', when Lord Byron, clapping his hand on my mouth, said, with a laugh, 'Come, d—n it, Tom, *don't* be poetical.'

259

WHILE I[1] was in London, the melancholy death of Lord Byron was announced in the public papers, and I saw his remains borne away out of the city on its last journey to that place where fame never comes. . . . His funeral was blazed in the papers with the usual parade that accompanies the death of great men. . . . I happened to see it by chance as I was wandering up Oxford Street on my way to Mrs. Emmerson's, when my eye was suddenly arrested by straggling groups of the common people collected together and talking about a funeral. I did as the rest did, though I could not get hold of what funeral it could be; but I knew it was not a common one by the curiosity that kept watch on every countenance. By

[1] John Clare, the poet.

and by the group collected into about a hundred or more, when the train of a funeral suddenly appeared, on which a young girl that stood by me gave a deep sigh and uttered, 'Poor Lord Byron.' ... I looked up at the young girl's face. It was dark and beautiful, and I could almost feel in love with her for the sigh she had uttered for the poet.... The common people felt his merits and his power, and the common people of a country are the best feelings of a prophecy of futurity. They are the veins and arteries that feed and quicken the heart of living fame....

The young girl that stood by me had counted the carriages in her mind as they passed and she told me there were sixty-three or four in all. They were of all sorts and sizes and made up a motley show. The gilt ones that led the procession were empty. The hearse looked small and rather mean and the coach that followed carried his embers in an urn over which a pall was thrown.... I believe that his liberal principles in religion and politics did a great deal towards gaining the notice and affections of the lower orders. Be as it will, it is better to be beloved by those low and humble for undisguised honesty than flattered by the great for purchased and pensioned hypocrisies.

260

ONE day the news came to the village—the dire news which spread across the land, filling men's hearts with consternation—that Byron was dead. Tennyson was then a boy about fifteen.

'Byron was dead! I thought the whole world was at an end,' he once said, speaking of these bygone days. 'I thought everything was over and finished for everyone—that nothing else mattered. I remember I walked out alone, and carved "Byron is dead" into the sandstone.'

261

NASSAU SENIOR (1790–1864)

WE spoke of Senior.[1] He has, said Hayward, infinite *aplomb*. On one occasion when Moore was singing at Bowood, the poet was annoyed by the scratching of the pen with which Senior was writing, and stopped. 'Pray go on,' said Senior, 'you don't interrupt me.'

[1] In 1825 he became the first Professor of Political Economy at Oxford. Besides numerous publications on his subject he also wrote on literary, historical, and philosophical topics. This brief reminiscence was given to Sir Mountstuart E. Grant Duff by Abraham Hayward (1801–84).

262

PERCY BYSSHE SHELLEY (1792–1822)

ONE Sunday we[1] had been reading Plato together so diligently, that the usual hour of exercise passed away unperceived: we sallied forth hastily to take the air for half an hour before dinner. In the middle of Magdalen Bridge we met a woman with a child in her arms. Shelley was more attentive at that instant to our conduct in a life that was past, or to come, than to a decorous regulation of the present according to the established usages of society, in that fleeting moment of eternal duration styled the nineteenth century. With abrupt dexterity he caught hold of the child. The mother, who might well fear that it was about to be thrown over the parapet of the bridge into the sedgy waters below, held it fast by its long train.

'Will your baby tell us anything about pre-existence, Madam?' he asked, in a piercing voice, and with a wistful look.

The mother made no answer, but perceiving that Shelley's object was not murderous, but altogether harmless, she dismissed her apprehension, and relaxed her hold.

'Will your baby tell us anything about pre-existence, Madam?' he repeated, with unabated earnestness.

'He cannot speak, Sir,' said the mother seriously.

'Worse and worse,' cried Shelley, with an air of deep disappointment, shaking his long hair most pathetically about his young face; 'but surely the babe can speak if he will, for he is only a few weeks old. He may fancy perhaps that he cannot, but it is only a silly whim; he cannot have forgotten entirely the use of speech in so short a time; the thing is absolutely impossible.'

'It is not for me to dispute with you, Gentlemen,' the woman meekly replied, her eye glancing at our academical garb; 'but I can safely declare that I never heard him speak, nor any child, indeed, of his age.'

It was a fine placid boy; so far from being disturbed by the interruption, he looked up and smiled. Shelley pressed his fat cheeks with his fingers, we commended his healthy appearance and his equanimity, and the mother was permitted to proceed, probably to her satisfaction, for she would doubtless prefer a less speculative nurse. Shelley sighed deeply as we walked on.

'How provokingly close are those new-born babes!' he ejaculated; 'but it is not the less certain, notwithstanding the cunning attempts to conceal

[1] Thomas Jefferson Hogg and Shelley.

the truth, that all knowledge is reminiscence: the doctrine is far more ancient than the times of Plato, and as old as the venerable allegory that the Muses are the daughters of Memory . . . '

263

SHELLEY . . . was always reading; at his meals a book lay by his side, on the table, open. Tea and toast were often neglected, his author seldom; his mutton and potatoes might grow cold; his interest in a work never cooled. He invariably sallied forth, book in hand, reading to himself, if he was alone; if he had a companion reading aloud. He took a volume to bed with him, and read as long as his candle lasted; he then slept—impatiently, no doubt—until it was light, and he recommenced reading at the early dawn. . . . In consequence of this great watching, and of almost incessant reading, he would often fall asleep in the day-time—dropping off in a moment—like an infant. He often quietly transferred himself from his chair to the floor, and slept soundly on the carpet, and in the winter upon the rug, basking in the warmth like a cat; and like a cat his little round head was roasted before a blazing fire. If anyone humanely covered the poor head to shield it from the heat, the covering was impatiently put aside in his sleep. . . .

Southey was addicted to reading his terrible epics—before they were printed—to anyone who seemed to be a fit subject for the cruel experiment. He soon set his eyes on the newcomer, and one day having effected the caption of Shelley,[1] he immediately lodged him securely in a little study up-stairs, carefully locking the door upon himself and his prisoner and putting the key in his waistcoat-pocket. There was a window in the room, it is true, but it was so high above the ground that Baron Trenck himself would not have attempted it. 'Now you shall be delighted,' Southey said; 'but sit down.' Poor Bysshe sighed, and took his seat at the table. The author seated himself opposite, and placing his MS. on the table before him, began to read slowly and distinctly. The poem, if I mistake not, was 'The Curse of Kehamah'. Charmed with his own composition the admiring author read on, varying his voice occasionally, to point out the finer passages and invite applause. There was no commendation; no criticism; all was hushed. This was strange. Southey raised his eyes from the neatly written MS.: Shelley had disappeared. This was still more strange. Escape was impossible; every precaution had been taken, yet he had vanished. Shelley had glided noiselessly from his chair to the floor, and the insensible young Vandal lay buried in profound sleep underneath the table.

[1] In the winter of 1811–12 Shelley was living at Keswick.

264

ON Monday, the 8th of July, 1822, I[1] went with Shelley to his bankers, and then to a store. It was past one p.m. when we went on board our respective boats—Shelley and Williams to return to their home in the Gulf of Spezia; I in the *Bolivar*, to accompany them into the offing. When we were under weigh, the guard-boat boarded us to overhaul our papers. I had not got my port clearance, the captain of the port having refused to give it to the mate, as I had often gone out without. The officer of the Health Office consequently threatened me with forty days' quarantine. It was hopeless to think of detaining my friends. Williams had been for days fretting and fuming to be off; they had no time to spare, it was past two o'clock, and there was very little wind.

Sullenly and reluctantly I re-anchored, furled my sails, and with a ship's glass watched the progress of my friends' boat. My Genoese mate observed—'They should have sailed this morning at three or four a.m., instead of three p.m. They are standing too much in shore; the current will set them there.'

I said, 'They will soon have the land-breeze.'

'May be', continued the mate, 'she will soon have too much breeze; that gaff top-sail is foolish in a boat with no deck and no sailor on board.' Then pointing to the S.W., 'Look at those black lines and the dirty rags hanging on them out of the sky—they are a warning; look at the smoke on the water; the devil is brewing mischief.'

There was a sea-fog, in which Shelley's boat was soon after enveloped, and we saw nothing more of her.

Although the sun was obscured by mists, it was oppressively sultry. There was not a breath of air in the harbour. The heaviness of the atmosphere and an unwonted stillness benumbed my senses. I went down into the cabin and sank into a slumber. I was roused up by a noise overhead and went on deck. The men were getting up a chain cable to let go another anchor. There was a general stir among the shipping; shifting berths, getting down yards and masts, veering out cables, hauling in of hawsers, letting go anchors, hailing from the ships and quays, boats sculling rapidly to and fro. It was almost dark, although only half-past six o'clock. The sea was of the colour, and looked as solid and smooth, as a sheet of lead, and covered with an oily scum. Gusts of wind swept over without ruffling it, and big drops of rain fell on its surface, rebounding as if they could not penetrate it. There was a commotion in the air, made up of many threatening sounds, coming upon us from the sea. Fishing-craft and coasting-vessels under bare poles rushed by us in shoals, running

[1] E. J. Trelawny (1792–1881).

foul of the ships in the harbour. As yet the din and hubbub was that made by men, but their shrill pipings were suddenly silenced by the crashing voice of a thunder squall that burst right over our heads. For some time no other sounds were to be heard than the thunder, wind, and rain. When the fury of the storm, which did not last for more than twenty minutes, had abated, and the horizon was in some degree cleared, I looked to seaward anxiously, in the hope of descrying Shelley's boat, among the many small craft scattered about. I watched every speck that loomed on the horizon, thinking that they would have borne up on their return to the port, as all the other boats that had gone out in the same direction had done.

I sent our Genoese mate on board some of the returning craft to make inquiries, but they all professed not to have seen the English boat . . . I did not leave the *Bolivar* until dark. During the night it was gusty and showery, and the lightning flashed along the coast: at daylight I returned on board, and resumed my examinations of crews of the various boats which had returned to the port during the night. They either knew nothing, or would say nothing. My Genoese, with the quick eye of a sailor, pointed out, on board a fishing-boat, an English-made oar, that he thought he had seen in Shelley's boat, but the entire crew swore by all the saints in the calendar that this was not so. Another day passed in horrid suspense. On the morning of the third day I rode to Pisa. Byron had returned to the Lanfranchi Palace. I hoped to find a letter from the Villa Magni:[1] there was none. I told my fears to Hunt, and then went upstairs to Byron. When I told him, his lip quivered, and his voice faltered as he questioned me. I sent a courier to Leghorn to dispatch the *Bolivar* to cruise along the coast, while I mounted my horse and rode in the same direction. I also dispatched a courier along the coast to go as far as Nice. On my arrival at Viareggio I heard that a punt, a water-keg, and some bottles had been found on the beach. These things I recognized as having been in Shelley's boat when he left Leghorn. Nothing more was found for seven or eight days, during which time of painful suspense I patrolled the coast with the coast-guard, stimulating them to keep a good look-out by the promise of a reward. It was not until many days after this that my worst fears were confirmed. Two bodies were found on the shore,—one near Viareggio, which I went and examined. The face and hands, and parts of the body not protected by the dress, were fleshless. The tall slight figure, the jacket, the volume of Sophocles in one pocket, and Keats's poems in the other, doubled back, as if the reader, in the act of reading, had hastily thrust it away, were all too familiar to me to leave a doubt on my mind that this mutilated corpse was any other than Shelley's. The other body was washed on shore three miles distant from Shelley's, near

[1] The house which Shelley was renting on the Gulf of Spezia.

the town of Migliarino, at the Bocca Lericcio. I went there at once. This corpse was much more mutilated; it had no other covering than—the shreds of a shirt, and that partly drawn over the head, as if the wearer had been in the act of taking it off—a black silk handkerchief, tied sailor-fashion round the neck—socks—and one boot, indicating also that he had attempted to strip. The flesh, sinews, and muscles hung about in rags, like the shirt, exposing the ribs and bones. I had brought with me from Shelley's house a boot of Williams's, and this exactly matched the one the corpse had on. That, and the handkerchief, satisfied me that it was the body of Shelley's comrade. . . .

[Trelawny obtained permission, through the good offices of the British minister at Florence, to take possession of the bodies of Shelley and Williams. He then arranged for two separate cremations, that of Williams taking place first, and that of Shelley on the following day, 16 August.]

Three white wands had been stuck in the sand to mark the Poet's grave, but as they were at some distance from each other, we had to cut a trench thirty yards in length, in line of the sticks, to ascertain the exact spot, and it was nearly an hour before we came upon the grave.

In the mean time Byron and Leigh Hunt arrived in the carriage, attended by soldiers, and the Health Officer, as before. The lonely and grand scenery that surrounded us so exactly harmonized with Shelley's genius, that I could imagine his spirit soaring over us. The sea, with the islands of Gorgona, Capraia, and Elba, was before us; old battlemented watch-towers stretched along the coast, backed by the marble-crested Apennines glistening in the sun, picturesque from their diversified out-lines, and not a human dwelling was in sight. As I thought of the delight Shelley felt in such scenes of loneliness and grandeur while living, I felt we were no better than a herd of wolves or a pack of wild dogs, in tearing out his battered and naked body from the pure yellow sand that lay so lightly over it, to drag him back to the light of day: but the dead have no voice, nor had I power to check the sacrilege—the work went on silently in the deep and unresisting sand, not a word was spoken, for the Italians have a touch of sentiment, and their feelings are easily excited into sympathy. Even Byron was silent and thoughtful. We were startled and drawn together by a dull hollow sound that followed the blow of a mattock; the iron had struck a skull, and the body was soon recovered. Lime had been strewn on it; this, or decomposition, had the effect of staining it of a dark and ghastly indigo colour. Byron asked me to preserve the skull for him; but remembering that he had formerly used one as a drinking-cup, I was determined Shelley's should not be so profaned. The limbs did not separate from the trunk, as in the case of Williams's body, so that the corpse was removed entire into the furnace. I had taken the precaution of having more and larger pieces of timber, in consequence of my experience of the day before of the difficulty of consuming a corpse in the open air with our apparatus. After the fire was well kindled we repeated the ceremony of the previous day; and more wine was poured over Shelley's dead body than he had consumed during his life. This with the oil and salt made the yellow flames glisten and quiver. The heat from the sun and fire was so intense that the atmosphere was tremulous and wavy. The corpse fell open and the heart was laid bare. The frontal bone of the skull, where it had been struck with the mattock, fell off; and, as the back of the head rested on the red-hot bottom bars of the furnace, the brains literally seethed, bubbled, and boiled as in a cauldron, for a very long time.

Byron could not face this scene, he withdrew to the beach and swam off to the *Bolivar*. Leigh Hunt remained in the carriage. The fire was so fierce as to produce a white heat on the iron, and to reduce its contents to grey ashes. The only portions that were not consumed were some fragments of bones, the jaw, and the skull, but what surprised us all, was that the heart remained entire. In snatching this relic from the fiery furnace, my hand was severely burnt; and had anyone seen me do the act I should have been put in quarantine.

After cooling the iron machine in the sea, I collected the human ashes and placed them in a box, which I took on board the *Bolivar*. Byron and Hunt retraced their steps to their home, and the officers and soldiers returned to their quarters. . . .

When I arrived at Leghorn, as I could not immediately go on to Rome, I consigned Shelley's ashes to our Consul at Rome, Mr. Freeborn, requesting him to keep them in his custody until my arrival. When I reached Rome, Freeborn told me that to quiet the authorities there, he had been obliged to inter the ashes with the usual ceremonies in the Protestant burying-place. When I came to examine the ground with the man who had the custody of it, I found Shelley's grave amidst a cluster of others. The old Roman wall partly inclosed the place, and there was a niche in the wall formed by two buttresses—immediately under an ancient pyramid, said to be the tomb of Caius Cestius. There were no graves near it at that time. This suited my taste, so I purchased the recess, and sufficient space for planting a row of the Italian upright cypresses. As the souls of Heretics are foredoomed by the Roman priests, they do not affect to trouble themselves about their bodies. There was no 'faculty' to apply for, nor Bishop's licence to exhume the body. The custode or guardian who dwelt within the enclosure and had the key of the gate, seemed to have uncontrolled power within his domain, and scudi impressed with the image of Saint Peter with the two keys ruled him. Without more ado, masons were hired, and two tombs built in the recess. In one of these, when completed, I deposited the box, with Shelley's ashes, and covered it in with solid stone, inscribed with a Latin epitaph, written by Leigh Hunt. . . . To which I added [three] lines from Shelley's favourite play *The Tempest*:

> Nothing of him that doth fade,
> But doth suffer a sea change
> Into something rich and strange.

The other tomb, built merely to fill up the recess, was likewise covered in in the same way—but blank without as within. I planted eight seedling cypresses. When I last saw them in 1844, the seven which remained were about thirty-five feet in height. I added flowers as well. The ground I had purchased, I inclosed, and so ended my task.

[Shelley's heart was given by Trelawny to Mary Shelley. When, in 1881, Trelawny died, his ashes were taken to Rome and interred in the other tomb beside that of his friend Shelley.]

265

NOWADAYS all things appear in print sooner or later; but I[1] have heard from a lady who knew Mrs. Shelley a story of her which, so far as I know, has not appeared in print hitherto. Mrs. Shelley was choosing a school for her son, and asked the advice of this lady, who gave for advice—to use her own words to me—'Just the sort of banality, you know, one does come out with: Oh, send him somewhere where they will teach him to think for himself!' I have had far too long a training as a school inspector to presume to call an utterance of this kind a *banality*; however, it is not on this advice that I now wish to lay stress, but upon Mrs. Shelley's reply to it. Mrs. Shelley answered: 'Teach him to think for himself? Oh, my God, teach him rather to think like other people!'

266
HENRY HETHERINGTON (1792–1849)

AMONG the mass of penny periodicals the one that made the most stir was unquestionably the *Poor Man's Guardian*,[2] the publication of which had preceded the *Penny Magazine* by several months. In those days of intense political excitement the working-classes hungered for political news, and this was the kind of intelligence the paper chiefly gave. It boldly announced in each number that it was 'established contrary to

[1] Matthew Arnold. [2] No. 1, 9 July 1831.

law . . . and published despite the laws, or the will and pleasure of any tyrant or bodies of tyrants'. It attacked king, lords, and commons all round, protested against the new civil list and the proposed extra grant to the Duchess of Kent and her daughter, and denounced the Reform Bill as an accursed measure promoted in the interests of the middle classes.

Still, on the whole, the language of the *Guardian* was far less violent than that employed by several of its unstamped contemporaries, such as the *Republican*, which talked of 'the diabolical machinations of the villains in power', and the *Prompter*, which proclaimed 'down with kings, priests, and lords, whose system is a system of murder, plunder, and spoliation'. The most reprehensible article published in the *Poor Man's Guardian* was one which professed to be a review of a book by the aide-de-camp of the King of Naples, and gave what it called 'Defensive instructions for the people', the illustrative engravings to which showed how civilians armed with long lances might rout cavalry successfully, and parry bayonet charges.

Before, however, many numbers of the *Guardian* had appeared, Hetherington, its publisher and proprietor, was summoned on the charge of publishing a newspaper without a stamp—every copy of a newspaper was then required to be impressed with a fourpenny stamp. Instead of obeying the Bow-street mandate, Hetherington sent a note to the magistrates informing them that he could not have the pleasure of the proposed interview, as he was going out of town; and he at once set off on a provincial tour to push the sale of his publication. In a second summons that was issued Hetherington was apprised that if he failed to attend, the court would proceed *ex parte*. To this he responded by a chaffing note asking the magistrates the meaning of the phrase, and why the English language, which he could understand, was not made use of.

This was too much for the Bow-street justices, and runners were started on Hetherington's track. They soon discovered from the public meetings he had been holding that he was at Manchester, but owing to their having invoked the assistance of a couple of local constables to assist in his capture, Hetherington was forewarned, and as the officers made their entrance at the door of his lodgings, he sprang out of the window and made his way to Macclesfield. His mother being seriously ill, he returned secretly to London; but spies were on the watch, and he was seized the very moment he laid his hand on the door knocker, and lodged in the police station. By the Bow-street magistrates he was ordered to be imprisoned for six months in Clerkenwell jail; and soon after the expiration of his sentence he was again consigned to the same prison for a like term. Still the *Poor Man's Guardian* continued to be published, and every week newsagents and street hawkers were sent to jail for selling a paper which it was contended ought to bear a fourpenny stamp.

But these repressive measures were of no avail; people suffered imprisonment again and again, and yet still went on selling the *Guardian*. Nor was this remarkable pertinacity confined to the humble vendors of the publication. Cleave, a fairly well-to-do radical newsagent in Shoe-lane, whom I knew very well in after years, and from whom I gathered many of these particulars of the dangers and difficulties which beset the vendors of the unstamped press in the days I am speaking of, was more than once incarcerated. So was Guest, the largest newsagent in Birmingham, and so, I believe, was Mrs. Mann of Leeds. Abel Heywood of Manchester, a man of considerable substance, who subsequently had the honour of being chosen chief magistrate of the city, after suffering alike in person and in pocket, resolutely refused to discontinue the sale of the *Guardian*.

Many of the more humble distributors of the paper sought to argue both the law and the justice of the case with the magistrates, and on being promptly silenced, hurled defiance at the bench, although they knew that by so doing they were increasing their sentences fourfold. One sapient city alderman sent a little boy, who had sold a copy of the paper, to prison for three months, on the pretence that a severe sentence was necessary, otherwise children would be made use of wholesale to set at naught the supreme majesty of the law.

All manner of ruses were adopted to evade the vigilance of the stamp-office officials, who were ever lying in wait to seize the *Poor Man's Guardian* in the hands of the London retailers, or on its way to provincial newsagents. Dummy parcels used to be made up and sent out of the office by apparent stealth, the bearers glancing furtively around before proceeding on their way. They had received instructions to throw themselves, as if unconsciously, into the officers' arms, and then to argue and dispute with them with reference to the contents of the parcels they were carrying, so as to detain the officers as long as possible, while the genuine parcels for country customers were being smuggled out the back way. The authorities, finding themselves foiled in this fashion, took to seizing parcels of the *Guardian* at the carriers' receiving offices, and from vans and stage coaches; but in order to baulk them in these proceedings the papers were packed, by arrangement, in cases containing shoes, chests of tea ordered by country grocers, and bales destined for provincial haberdashers, and were claimed by the newsagents on reaching their destination.

Bundles of the *Poor Man's Guardian* were also conveyed privately at night time from the printing office to private houses and other 'safe places' in various quarters of the metropolis, where neighbouring retailers were enabled to obtain their supplies. These they wrapped round their bodies beneath their waistcoats, or stowed away in capacious pockets, and concealed in tall top-hats, for so vigilant had the authorities become that people were stopped in the streets, and compelled to open any parcels suspected to contain unstamped publications. Hetherington announced that he lent the paper out to read at the charge of a penny, being able, he said, by this means to evade the stamp act, which only related to papers 'published for, and exposed to sale'. After his painful prison experiences —he having had to endure all the hardships to which a common criminal was subjected—Hetherington took every possible precaution to avoid being re-arrested. He lived out of town, and entered his place of business in the Strand by a roundabout way through the Savoy, and generally in the disguise of a drab-coated quaker.

His time, however, came at last; but instead of being again dealt with by police magistrates, he was tried in a superior court before Lord Chief Baron Lyndhurst and a special jury. He made a clever and sensible defence, urged the jury not to accept a mere lawyer's definition of a newspaper, whether given by the Solicitor-General, or even by the Lord Chief Baron himself, insisting that his opinion as to what formed a newspaper was quite as good as theirs. Lyndhurst laughed heartily, and in the end left the matter entirely to the jury—the prosecution being instigated by the Whig Reform government, the Tory Chief Baron, likely enough, was not particularly anxious for it to succeed. To Hetherington's surprise the jury acquitted him, and he jubilantly announced in all future numbers of the *Poor Man's Guardian* that the paper, 'after sustaining a government prosecution of three and a half years, during which five hundred persons had been unjustly imprisoned for vending it, had at a trial in the Court of Exchequer, before Lord Chief Baron Lyndhurst and a special jury, been declared a legal publication'. Henceforth Hetherington gave no quarter to his Whig prosecutors, 'those knaves', he said, 'who use to split the ears of the groundlings with talk about the palladium of our liberties, and of a free press being like the air we breathe; which, if we have not, we die'.

267
JOHN CLARE (1793–1864)

THE first publication of my poems brought many visitors to my house, out of a mere curiosity, I expect, to know whether I was really the son of a thresher and a labouring rustic, as had been stated; and when they found it really was so, they looked at each other as a matter of satisfied surprise, asked some gossiping questions, and on finding me a vulgar fellow that mimicked at no pretensions but spoke in the rough way of a thorough-bred clown, they soon turned to the door, and dropping their heads in a good-morning attitude, they departed. I was often annoyed by such visits, and got out of the way whenever I could. . . .

I was now wearing into the sunshine, and the villagers saw carriages now and then come to the house filled with gossiping gentry that were tempted more by curiosity than anything else to seek me. From these I got invitations to correspond and was swarmed with promises of books till my mother was troubled and fancied that the house would not hold them. But her trouble was soon set aside, for the books never came.

268

CLARE remained for several days a guest at the residence of the Bishop,[1] and on the last evening of his visit was taken by Mrs. Marsh to the theatre. A select band of roving tragedians had taken possession of the Peterborough stage—converted, by a more prosaic generation, into a corn exchange—and was delighting the inhabitants of the episcopal city with Shakespeare and the latest French melodramas. On the evening when Clare went to the theatre in company with Mrs. Marsh, the *Merchant of Venice* was performed. Clare sat and listened quietly while the first three acts were being played, not even replying to the questions as to how he liked the piece, addressed to him by Mrs. Marsh. But at the commencement of the fourth act, he got restless and evidently excited, and in the scene where Portia delivered judgement, he suddenly sprang up on his seat, and began addressing the actor who performed the part of Shylock. Great was the astonishment of all the good citizens of Peterborough, when a shrill voice, coming from the box reserved to the wife of the Lord Bishop, exclaimed, 'You villain, you murderous villain!' Such an utter breach of decorum was never heard of within the walls of the episcopal city. It was in vain that those nearest to Clare tried to keep him on his seat and induce him to be quiet; he kept shouting louder than ever, and ended by making attempts to get upon the stage. At last the performance had to be suspended, and Mrs. Marsh, after some difficulty, got away with her guest. The old lady, in her innocence, even now did not apprehend the real cause of the exciting scene which she had witnessed, but, as before, attributed the behaviour of her unfortunate visitor to poetic eccentricity. But she began thinking that he was almost too eccentric.

The next morning Clare went back to Northborough . . . The poor wife soothed him as best she could, and after some efforts succeeded in calming his mind. At the end of a few days, Clare seemed again sufficiently well to leave the house, and renewed his daily walks in company with one

[1] Herbert Marsh (1757–1839), Bishop of Peterborough.

or other of his children. The inhabitants of the village, together with most of his acquaintances in the neighbourhood, were still ignorant that the poet whom they saw daily roving through the fields was a madman.

269
JOHN GIBSON LOCKHART (1794–1854)

LANDSEER says that I was a good-looking chap twenty or thirty years ago, and he therefore asked me to sit to him, whereto I replied, 'Is thy servant a dog, that he should do this thing?' The *mot* is universally given to Sydney Smith, but Edwin Landseer swears he never did, nor could have asked so ugly a fellow to sit, and thinks it unfair that I should have been robbed of my joke in favour of so wealthy a joke-smith. If it was mine, I had quite forgot the fact and adopted the general creed on the weighty point. If Landseer be correct, I fancy he must have thought of introducing me into his picture of Scott with his dogs in the Rhymer's Glen; but if so, I can't imagine why I did not accede to the flattering proposal. Here is a good illustration of the value of evidence, however. Pity the doubt was not raised before Sydney joined the majority, that we might have had his say also. What I object to is the allegation of his ugliness. I always admired his countenance as the most splendid combination of sense and sensuality.

270
WILLIAM WHEWELL (1794–1866)

[William Whewell, who was Master of Trinity College, Cambridge, wrote voluminously on scientific, philosophical, and theological subjects. His absorption in literary activities and in college and university administration resulted in a certain distancing between him and his pupils.]

HE could not give the requisite time to his pupils, and, in fact, hardly knew some of them by sight. . . . One day he gave his servant a list of names of certain of his pupils whom he wished to see at a wine-party after Hall, a form of entertainment then much in fashion. Among the names was that of an undergraduate who had died some weeks before. 'Mr. Smith, sir; why, he died last term, sir!' objected the man. 'You ought to tell me when my pupils die', replied the tutor sternly; and Whewell could be stern when he was vexed.

271

SOMEONE having said of Whewell that his *forte* was science, 'Yes,' assented Sydney Smith, 'and his foible is omniscience.'

272

JOHN KEATS (1795–1821)

THAT night he took away with him the first volume of *The Faerie Queene*, and he went through it, as I formerly told his noble biographer,[1] 'as a young horse would through a spring meadow—ramping!' Like a true poet, too, a poet 'born not manufactured', he especially singled out epithets, for that felicity and power in which Spenser is so eminent. He *hoisted* himself up, and looked burly and dominant as he said, 'What an image that is—*sea-shouldering whales*!'

273

I[2] OBSERVED that every short poem which he was tempted to compose was scrawled on the first piece of paper at hand, and that it was afterwards used as a mark to a book, or thrust anywhere aside. In the spring of 1819 a nightingale had built her nest near my house. Keats felt a tranquil and continual joy in her song; and one morning he took his chair from the breakfast-table to the grass plot under a plum-tree, where he sat for two or three hours. When he came into the house, I perceived he had some scraps of paper in his hand, and these he was quietly thrusting behind the books. On inquiry I found those scraps, four or five in number, contained his poetic feeling on the song of our nightingale. The writing was not well legible; and it was difficult to arrange the stanzas on so many scraps. With his assistance I succeeded, and this was his *Ode to a Nightingale*, a poem which has been the delight of everyone. Immediately afterwards I searched for more of his (in reality) fugitive pieces, in which task, at my request, he again assisted me. Thus I rescued that *Ode* and other valuable short poems, which might otherwise have been lost. From that day he gave me permission to copy any verses he might write, and I

[1] Lord Houghton. The narrator is Charles Cowden Clarke.
[2] This anecdote and the one that follows come from Charles Armitage Brown.

fully availed myself of it. He cared so little for them himself when once, as it appeared to me, his imagination was released from their influence, that it required a friend at hand to preserve them.

274

ONE night, at eleven o'clock, he came into the house in a state that looked like fierce intoxication. Such a state in him, I knew, was impossible; it therefore was the more fearful. I asked hurriedly, 'What is the matter?—You are fevered?' 'Yes, yes,' he answered, 'I was on the outside of the stage this bitter day till I was severely chilled—but now I don't feel it. Fevered!—of course, a little.' He mildly and instantly yielded—a property in his nature towards any friend—to my request that he should go to bed. I followed with the best immediate remedy in my power. I entered the chamber as he leapt into bed. On entering the cold sheets, before his head was on the pillow, he slightly coughed, and I heard him say, 'That is blood from my mouth.' I went towards him; he was examining a single drop of blood upon the sheet. 'Bring me the candle, Brown, and let me see this blood.' After regarding it steadfastly, he looked up in my face, with a calmness of countenance that I can never forget, and said: 'I know the colour of that blood;—it is arterial blood;—I cannot be deceived in that colour; that drop of blood is my death-warrant—I must die.'

275

AS Keats lay in his corner room in Rome next to the Spanish Steps, listening night after night to the constant play of water in the fountain outside, the words kept coming back to him from a play of Beaumont and Fletcher (*Philaster*):

> all your better deeds
> Shall be in water writ.

Finally, a week or two before he died, he told Severn he wanted no name upon his grave, no epitaph, but only the words, 'Here lies one whose name was writ in water.'

276
THOMAS CARLYLE (1795–1881)

[In June 1834 Carlyle settled with his wife at No. 5 Cheyne Row, Chelsea, and for some years was hard put to it to keep the wolf from the door. He was now at work on his *History of the French Revolution*, and had completed the first volume early in 1835. John Stuart Mill, who had helped him with advice and with a generous loan of books, now asked to see the manuscript, and Carlyle lent it to him. What followed is told below. 'How well I still remember that night,' Carlyle wrote many years later, 'when Mill came to tell us, pale as Hector's ghost, that my unfortunate first volume was burnt.' The Mrs. Taylor who was waiting below, and whose maid it was that had done the deed, was the lady whom Mill later married. The account given here was sent by Carlyle to his brother in Rome, in a letter dated 23 March 1835.]

MILL had borrowed that first volume of my poor *French Revolution* (pieces of it more than once) that he might have it all before him, and write down some observations on it, which perhaps I might print as notes. I was busy meanwhile with Volume Second; toiling along like a *Nigger*, but with the heart of a free Roman: indeed, I know not how it was, I had not felt so clear and independent, sure of myself and of my task for many long years. Well, one night about three weeks ago, we sat at tea, and Mill's short rap was heard at the door: Jane rose to welcome him; but he stood there unresponsive, pale, the very picture of despair; said, half-articulately gasping, that she must go down and speak to Mrs. Taylor. . . . After some considerable additional gasping, I learned from Mill this fact: that my poor Manuscript, all except some four tattered leaves, was *annihilated*! He had left it out (too carelessly); it had been taken for waste-paper: and so five months of as tough labour as I could remember of, were as good as vanished, gone like a whiff of smoke.—There never in my life had come upon me any other *accident* of such moment; but this I could not but feel to be a sore one. The thing was *lost*, and perhaps worse; for I had not only forgotten the structure of it, but the spirit it was written with was past; only the general impression seemed to remain, and the recollection that I was on the whole well satisfied with that, and could now hardly hope to equal it. Mill, whom I had to comfort and speak peace to, remained injudiciously enough till almost midnight, and my poor Dame and I had to sit talking of indifferent matters; and could not till then get our lament freely uttered. *She* was very good to me; and the thing did not beat us. I felt in general that I was as a little schoolboy, who had laboriously written out his *Copy* as he could, and was showing it not without satisfaction to the Master: but lo! the Master had suddenly torn it, saying: 'No, boy, thou must go and write it *better*.' What could I do but sorrowing go and try to obey? That night was a hard one; something from time to time tying me tight as it were all round the region of the heart, and strange dreams haunting me: however, I was not without good thoughts too that came like healing life into me; and I got it somewhat reasonably crushed down, not abolished, yet subjected to me with the resolution and prophecy of abolishing. Next morning accordingly I wrote to Fraser (who had advertised the Book as 'preparing for publication') that it was all gone back; that he must not *speak of it* to anyone (till it was made good again); finally that he must send me some *better paper*, and also a *Biographie Universelle*, for I was determined to risk ten pounds more upon it. Poor Fraser was very assiduous: I got Bookshelves put up (for the whole House was *flowing* with Books), where the *Biographie* (not Fraser's, however, which was countermanded, but Mill's), with much else stands all ready, much readier than before: and so, having first finished out the piece I was actually upon, I began *again* at the beginning. Early the day after tomorrow (after a hard and quite novel kind of battle) I count on having the First Chapter on paper a second time, no worse than it was, though considerably different.

[By 23 September he is able to tell his brother that he 'has done with that unutterable Manuscript', and feels like a man that has 'nearly killed himself accomplishing zero'.]

277

SPEAKING of his method of work, he said he had found the little wooden pegs, which washerwomen employ to fasten their clothes to a line, highly convenient for keeping together bits of notes and agenda on the same special point. It was his habit to paste on a screen in his workroom engraved portraits, when no better could be had, of the people he was then writing about. It kept the image of the man steadily in view, and one must have a clear image of him in the mind before it was in the least possible to make him be seen by the reader.

278

KINGSLEY, whom I[1] met for the first time, . . . talked, I recollect, much about Carlyle, and told me, on the great man's own authority, the following edifying tale. The most dyspeptic of philosophers had been terribly bored by the persistent optimism of his friend Emerson. 'I thought', he

[1] Sir Mountstuart E. Grant Duff.

said, 'that I would try to cure him, so I took him to some of the lowest parts of London and showed him all that was going on there. This done, I turned to him saying, "And noo, man, d'ye believe in the deevil noo?"—"Oh no," he replied, "all these people seem to me only parts of the great machine, and, on the whole, I think they are doing their work very satisfactorily!" '

'Then,' continued the sage, 'I took him doun to the Hoose o'Commons, where they put us under the Gallery. There I showed him ae chiel getting up after anither and leeing and leeing. Then I turned to him and said, "And noo, man, d'ye believe in the deevil noo?" He made me, however, just the same answer as before, and then I gave him up in despair!'

279

IN the course of the evening the conversation turned on the war in the United States. 'There they are,' said Carlyle, 'cutting each other's throats, because one half of them prefer hiring their servants for life, and the other by the hour.'

280

Rossetti talked . . . of Carlyle walking with William Allingham in the neighbourhood of the Kensington Museum, and announcing his intention of writing a life of Michael Angelo, and then adding, by way of remonstrance against his companion's quickening interest, 'But, mind ye, I'll no' say much about his *art*.'

281

HARTLEY COLERIDGE (1796–1849)

CARLYLE had gone to hear Coleridge when he first came to London with a certain sort of interest, and he talked an entire evening, or rather lectured, for it was not talk, on whatever came uppermost in his mind. There were a number of ingenious flashes and pleasant illustrations in his discourse, but it led nowhere, and was essentially barren. When all was said, Coleridge was a poor, greedy, sensual creature, who could not keep from his laudanum bottle though he knew it would destroy him.

One of the products of his system, he added, after a pause, was Hartley

Coleridge, whom he (Carlyle) had one day seen down in the country, and found the strangest ghost of a human creature, with eyes that gleamed like two rainbows over a ruined world. The poor fellow had fallen into worse habits than his father's, and was maintained by a few benevolent friends in a way that was altogether melancholy and humiliating. Some bookseller had got a book called *Biographia Borealis* out of him by locking him up, and only letting him out when his day's work was done. He died prematurely, as was to be expected of one who had forgotten his relation to everlasting laws, which cannot by any contrivance be ignored without worse befalling. His brother,[1] he believed, had long ceased to do anything for him. The brother was a Protestant priest: a smooth, sleek, sonorous fellow, who contrived to get on better in the world than his father or brother, for reasons that need not be inquired into. He had the management of some model High Church schools at Chelsea, and quacked away there, pouring out huge floods of rhetoric that class of persons deal in, which he tried to persuade himself he believed. These were about the entire outcome of the Coleridgian theory of human duties and responsibilities.

282
SIR ANTHONY PANIZZI (1797–1879)

YEARS after Carlyle dubbed Panizzi a fat pedant, the highest office in the Museum, the so-called Principal Librarianship, fell vacant. Two names were submitted to the Queen from which to select one for the post: those of Panizzi and the accomplished Anglo-Saxon scholar, John Mitchell Kemble. Lord Palmerston was Prime Minister, and through his correspondence with Cavour and other Italian statesmen, Panizzi had been serviceable to him and Lord Clarendon. Doubtless, it was at the instance of Lord Palmerston that the Queen appointed Panizzi to the most important literary office in the gift of the Crown, and far more important than the Laureateship. The origin and progress of controversy between Panizzi and Carlyle were the following:

While Carlyle was writing his history of the French Revolution, he contributed to the *Westminster Review* an article ('Histories of the French Revolution') on the materials accessible for the composition of a book on that great theme, with some trenchant criticisms on such of his predecessors in the attempt as Thiers and Mignet. In the course of the article he mentioned the existence in Paris of a vast collection of the pamphlets,

[1] The Revd. Derwent Coleridge.

newspapers, broad-sheets, and even street placards which were issued in the French capital day by day, as the Revolution evolved itself. Then he subjoined the following note: 'It is generally known that a similar collection, perhaps still larger and more curious, lies buried in the British Museum here, inaccessible for want of a proper catalogue. Some fifteen months ago the respectable Sub-librarian seemed to be working on such a thing. By respectful application to him you could gain access to his room, and have the satisfaction of mounting on ladders and reading the outside titles of his books, which', the satirical Carlyle adds, 'was a great help.' After 'weary months of waiting' for greater help than this, Carlyle gave up dancing attendance on Panizzi, as, he wrote, 'a game not worth the candle'.

Panizzi never forgave Carlyle this caustic comment on his procedure. It was offensive enough to find himself represented as in his official capacity as the head of the National Library obstructing the progress of a great historical work. But still more offensive, in his eyes, was in all probability the designation of 'respectable Sub-librarian', applied to the high and mighty Keeper of the Printed Books in the British Museum, a man who dined at Holland House, who was intimate with Macaulay and Brougham; with the leading Whig statesmen of the day 'and Mr. Panizzi, etc.' closing the lists, in the *Morning Post*, of guests at numbers of aristocratic receptions in London. Panizzi resented ever afterwards the sarcastic note in the *Westminster Review*, as Carlyle found to his cost. When he came to write his *Cromwell* he would fain have consulted somewhere, in the quiet interior recesses of the Museum Library, the unique collection it contains of pamphlets and so forth issued in London from day to day during the great English Civil War of the seventeenth century and the Protectorate which followed it. The 'respectable Sub-librarian' would not hear of such a concession, and Carlyle was left, with what assistance he could command, to do his best in the crowded and incommodious reading-room of those days . . . Carlyle detailed his grievance when giving evidence—very interesting and instructive, sometimes even entertaining—before the Royal Commission subsequently appointed to inquire into the affairs of the British Museum, and he mentioned as one of his reasons for wishing to escape from the reading-room into the interior of the library that he was 'thin-skinned'. Panizzi retorted in his evidence that he 'did not feel readers' skins'. Years afterwards, and deep in the composition of *Frederick*, Carlyle renewed his application, in a letter to Panizzi, which was for him not only calm but conciliatory. All the return he received was a reply from the vindictive Italian so insolent that Panizzi's biographer and panegyrist refrained from printing it. The great Lady Ashburton herself was applied to, to exert on behalf of Carlyle's application her influence with Panizzi, whom she knew, but the appearance on the scene of even this *Dea ex machina* was fruitless. . . . Clothed in a little brief authority, and having completely gained the ear of the working members of the Museum's Board of Trustees, the fat pedant and Italian language-master proved more than a match for the Scottish man of genius.

283
CATHERINE, LADY STEPNEY, novelist (d. 1845)

LADY STEPNEY told me[1] meantime that the Arctic voyagers had gone through hardships such as could never be told: but it only proved (and to this in particular she required my assent) 'that the Deity is everywhere, and more particularly in barren places'. She went on to say how very wrong she thought it to send men into such places, without any better reason than she had ever heard of. 'They say it is to discover the North Pole,' she proceeded; 'and, by the bye, it is curious that Newton should have come within thirty miles of the North Pole in his discoveries. They *say*, you know,' and here she looked exceedingly sagacious and amused; 'they *say* that they have found the magnetic pole. But you and I know what a magnet is, very well. *We* know that a little thing like that would be pulled out of its place in the middle of the sea.' When I reported this conversation to my mother, we determined to get one of this lady's novels immediately, and see what she could write that would sell for seven hundred pounds. If she was to be believed as to this, it really was a curious sign of the times. I never saw any of her books, after all. I can hardly expect to be believed about the anecdote of the magnet (which I imagine she took to be a little red horse-shoe), and I had some difficulty in believing it myself, at the moment; but I have given her very words. And they were no joke. She shook her head-dress of marabou feathers and black bugles with her excitement as she talked.

284
WILLIAM CHAMBERS (1800–83)

[William and Robert Chambers, the founders of the well-known firm of publishers, were born at Peebles, William in 1800, and his brother in 1802. Their father, who appears to have had some resemblance to Mr. Micawber, had been

[1] Harriet Martineau.

doing well in the cotton trade, but with the introduction of the power-loom his business declined. An attempt to restore his fortune by opening a drapery business in Peebles ended in his bankruptcy, and 'on a bleak day in December 1813' the family moved to Edinburgh. There, in May 1814, William was bound apprentice to a bookseller in Calton Street at a salary of four shillings a week. His duties consisted in lighting the fire in the morning, taking down and putting up the shutters in the shop, cleaning and preparing the oil-lamps, sweeping and dusting the shop, and, above all, going on all the errands. His employer ran a circulating library, and the boy was sent out daily with parcels of books, but he had also to deliver 'odious piles of lottery circulars', since his employer was also an agent for the State Lottery. It was a hard life, but there were some mitigating circumstances, one of which he describes at some length.]

IN the winter of 1815–16, when the cold and cost of candlelight would have detained me in bed, I was so fortunate as to discover an agreeable means of spending my mornings. The sale of lottery tickets, I have said, formed a branch of my employer's business. Besides distributing the lottery circulars, it fell to my lot to paste all the large show-boards with posters of glaring colours, bearing the words 'Lucky Office', 'Twenty Thousand Pounds still in the Wheel', and such-like seductive announcements. The board-carriers—shilling-a-day men—were usually a broken-down set of characters; as, for example, old waiters and footmen, with pale flabby faces and purple noses; discharged soldiers, who had returned in a shattered condition from the wars; and tattered operatives of middle age, ruined by dram-drinking.

Among the last-named class of board-carriers, there was a journeyman baker who had an eye irretrievably damaged by some rough, but possibly not unprovoked, usage in a king's birthday riot. What from the bad eye, and what from whisky, this unfortunate being had fallen out of regular employment. Now and then, when there was a push in the trade, as at the New-year, he got a day's work from his old employer, a baker in Canal Street. . . .

From this hopeful personage, whom it was my duty to look after, I one day had a proposition, which he had been charged to communicate. If I pleased, he would introduce me to his occasional employer, the baker in Canal Street, who, he said, was passionately fond of reading, but without leisure for its gratification. If I would go early—very early—say five o'clock in the morning, and read aloud to him and his two sons while they were preparing their batch, I should be regularly rewarded for my trouble with a penny roll newly drawn from the oven. Hot rolls, as I have since learned, are not to be recommended for the stomach, but I could not in these times afford to be punctilious. The proposal was too captivating to be resisted.

Behold me, then, quitting my lodgings in the West Port, before five o'clock in the winter mornings, and pursuing my way across the town to the cluster of sunk streets below the North Bridge, of which Canal Street was the principal. The scene of operations was a cellar of confined dimensions, reached by a flight of steps descending from the street, and possessing a small back window immediately beyond the baker's kneading-board. Seated on a folded-up sack in the sole of the window,[1] with a book in one hand and a penny candle stuck in a bottle near the other, I went to work for the amusement of the company. The baker was not particular as to subject. All he stipulated for was something comic and laughable. Aware of his tastes, I tried him first with the jocularities of *Roderick Random*, which was a great success, and produced shouts of laughter. I followed this up with other works of Smollett, also with the novels of Fielding, and with *Gil Blas*; the tricks and grotesque rogueries in this last-mentioned work of fiction giving the baker and his two sons unqualified satisfaction. My services as a reader for two and a half hours every morning were unfailingly recompensed by a donation of the anticipated roll, with which, after getting myself brushed of the flour, I went on my way to shop-opening, lamp-cleaning, and all the rest of it, at Calton Street. It would be vain in the present day to try to discover the baker's work-shop where these morning performances took place, for the whole of the buildings in this quarter have been removed to make way for the North British Railway station.

285
THOMAS BABINGTON MACAULAY
(1800–59)

FROM the time that he was three years old he read incessantly, for the most part lying on the rug before the fire, with his book on the ground, and a piece of bread and butter in his hand. A very clever woman who then lived in the house as a parlour-maid told how he used to sit in his nankeen frock, perched on the table by her as she was cleaning the plate, and expounding to her out of a volume as big as himself. He did not care for toys, but was very fond of taking his walk, when he would hold forth to his companion, whether nurse or mother, telling interminable stories out of his own head, or repeating what he had been reading in language far above his years. His memory retained without effort the phraseology of the book which he had been last engaged on, and he talked, as the maid said, 'quite printed words', which produced an effect that appeared formal, and often, no doubt, exceedingly droll.

[1] i.e. in the window-sill.

Mrs. Hannah More was fond of relating how she called at Mr. Macaulay's, and was met by a fair, pretty, slight child, with abundance of light hair, about four years of age, who came to the front door to receive her, and tell her that his parents were out, but that if she would be good enough to come in he would bring her a glass of old spirits: a proposition which greatly startled the good lady, who had never aspired beyond cowslip wine. When questioned as to what he knew about old spirits, he could only say that Robinson Crusoe often had some.

About this period his father took him on a visit to Lady Waldegrave at Strawberry Hill, and was much pleased to exhibit to his old friend the fair bright boy, dressed in a green coat with red collar and cuffs, a frill at the throat, and white trousers. After some time had been spent among the wonders of the Orford collection, of which he ever afterwards carried a catalogue in his head, a servant who was waiting upon the company in the great gallery spilt some hot coffee over his legs. The hostess was all kindness and compassion, and when, after a while, she asked how he was feeling, the little fellow looked up in her face and replied: 'Thank you madam, the agony is abated.'

286

As a child, during one of the numerous seasons when the social duties devolved upon Mr. Macaulay, he accompanied his father on an afternoon call, and found on a table the *Lay of the Last Minstrel* which he had never before met with. He kept himself quiet with his prize while the elders were talking, and on his return home sat down upon his mother's bed, and repeated to her as many cantos as she had the patience or the strength to listen to. At one period of his life he was known to say that, if by some miracle of vandalism all copies of *Paradise Lost* and the *Pilgrim's Progress* were destroyed off the face of the earth, he would undertake to reproduce them both from recollection whenever a revival of learning came. In 1813, while waiting in a Cambridge coffee-room for a postchaise which was to take him to his school, he picked up a country newspaper containing two such specimens of provincial poetical talent as in those days might be read in the corner of any weekly journal. One piece was headed 'Reflections of an Exile', while the other was a trumpery parody on the Welsh ballad 'Ar hyd y nos', referring to some local anecdote of an ostler whose nose had been bitten off by a filly. He looked them once through, and never gave them a thought for forty years, at the end of which time he repeated them both without missing, or, as far as he knew, changing, a single word.

287

[Macaulay is writing to his friend Thomas Flower Ellis. Since the publication of the first two volumes of *The History of England* in 1849 he had become a celebrity.]

I have seen the hippopotamus,[1] both asleep and awake; and I can assure you that, awake or asleep, he is the ugliest of the works of God. But you must hear of my triumphs. Thackeray swears that he was eye-witness and ear-witness of the proudest event of my life. Two damsels were just about to pass that doorway which we, on Monday, in vain attempted to enter, when I was pointed out to them. 'Mr. Macaulay!' cried the lovely pair. 'Is that Mr. Macaulay? Never mind the hippopotamus.' And having paid a shilling to see Behemoth, they left him in the very moment at which he was about to display himself—but spare my modesty. I can wish for nothing more on earth, now that Madame Tussaud, in whose Pantheon I hoped once for a place, is dead.

288

MACAULAY was admirable with young people. Innumerable passages in his journals and correspondence prove how closely he watched them; how completely he understood them; and how, awake or asleep, they were for ever in his thoughts. On the fragment of a letter to Mr. Ellis there is mention of a dream he had about his younger niece, 'so vivid that I must tell it. She came to me with a penitential face, and told me that she had a great sin to confess; that Pepys's Diary was all a forgery, and that she had forged it. I was in the greatest dismay. "What! I have been quoting in reviews, and in my *History*, a forgery of yours as a book of the highest authority. How shall I ever hold up my head again?" I awoke with the fright, poor Alice's supplicating voice still in my ears.'

[1] On 1 June 1850, *The Illustrated London News* announced the safe arrival of the first living hippopotamus to be seen in England; it had been imported by the Zoological Society, and was now on view in the Society's gardens. An excellent engraving of the beast with its Arab attendant showed the public what to expect. On 8 June the same periodical was able to report that 'the long lines of carriages which are daily to be seen at the entrance of the Society's Garden are conclusive evidence that the Hippopotamus has now, as we prognosticated, completely established himself as the great lion of the day.'

289

JANE WELSH CARLYLE (1801–66)

JENNY kissed me when we met,
  Jumping from the chair she sat in;
Time, you thief, who love to get
  Sweets into your list, put that in:
Say I'm weary, say I'm sad,
  Say that health and wealth have missed me,
Say I'm growing old, but add,
  Jenny kissed me.

Leigh Hunt was prospering and writing freely now, but during an influenza epidemic he was ill for some weeks. There were many deaths, and Mrs. Carlyle was anxious about him. This being told him when he suddenly recovered, he went himself to be the bearer of his good news. When Mrs. Carlyle beheld him unexpectedly enter, she jumped up and kissed him; and that was what inspired his verse in the *Monthly Chronicle*. . . . 'I never heard of Mrs. Carlyle kissing any other man,' said one of her later favourites; 'not even me,' he concluded with a sigh.

290

MRS. CARLYLE did not, like her husband, write books, but in her own way she was, to use a favourite expression of his, as 'articulate' as her husband. She was too bright and clever a talker not to enjoy practising her gift. . . . It was better, at least, if they were at home, when they talked successively rather than simultaneously, but her husband did not always allow her that alternative. She once repeated to me, with quiet glee, a remark dropped by Samuel Rogers at one of his breakfast-parties at which Carlyle and she were among the guests. When Carlyle's thunder had been followed by his wife's sparkle, their sardonic host said in a half-soliloquy which was intended to be audible: 'As soon as that man's tongue stops, that woman's begins!'

291

[On 21 November 1855, in her life-long endeavour to preserve Carlyle for higher things and to save him (and so incidentally herself) from the consequences of his own irritable temperament, Mrs. Carlyle undertook the task of interviewing the Income Tax Commissioners and appealing against their assessment of her husband's literary earnings.]

Mr. C. said 'the voice of honour seemed to call on him to go himself.' But either it did not call loud enough, or he would not listen to that charmer. I went in a cab, to save all my breath for appealing. Set down at 30 Hornton Street, I found a dirty private-like house, only with Tax Office painted on the door. A dirty woman-servant opened the door, and told me the Commissioners would not be there for half an hour, but I might walk up. There were already some half-score of men assembled in the waiting-room, among whom I saw the man who cleans our clocks, and a young apothecary of Cheyne Walk. All the others, to look at them, could not have been suspected for an instant, I should have said, of making a hundred a year. . . .

'First-come lady,' called the clerk, opening a small side-door, and I stept forward into a *grand peut-être*. There was an instant of darkness while the one door was shut behind and the other opened in front; and there I stood in a dim room where three men sat round a large table spread with papers. One held a pen ready over an open ledger; another was taking snuff, and had taken still worse in his time, to judge by his shaky, clayed appearance. The third, who was plainly the cock of that dung-heap, was sitting for Rhadamanthus—a Rhadamanthus without the justice.

'Name,' said the horned-owl-looking individual holding the pen.

'Carlyle.'

'What?'

'Carlyle.'

Seeing he still looked dubious, I spelt it for him.

'Ha!' cried Rhadamanthus, a big bloodless-faced, insolent-looking fellow, 'What is this? why is Mr. Carlyle not come himself? Didn't he get a letter ordering him to appear? Mr. Carlyle wrote some nonsense about being exempted from coming, and I desired an answer to be sent that he must come, must do as other people.'

'Then, sir,' I said, 'your desire has been neglected, it would seem, my husband having received no such letter; and I was told by one of your fellow Commissioners that Mr. Carlyle's personal appearance was not indispensable.'

'Huffgh! Huffgh! what does Mr. Carlyle mean by saying he has no income from his writings, when he himself fixed it in the beginning at a hundred and fifty?'

'It means, sir, that, in ceasing to write, one ceases to be paid for writing, and Mr. Carlyle has published nothing for several years.'

'Huffgh! Huffgh! I understand nothing about that.'

'I do,' whispered the snuff-taking Commissioner at my ear. 'I can quite understand a literary man does not always make money. I would take it off, for my share, but (sinking his voice still lower) I am only one voice here, and not the most important.'

'There,' said I, handing to Rhadamanthus Chapman and Hall's account; 'that will prove Mr. Carlyle's statement.'

'What am I to make of that? Huffgh! We should have Mr. Carlyle here to swear to this before we believe it.'

'If a gentleman's word of honour written at the bottom of that paper is not enough, you can put me on my oath: I am ready to swear to it.'

'You! you, indeed! No, no! we can do nothing with *your* oath.'

'But, sir, I understand my husband's affairs fully, better than he does himself.'

'That I can well believe; but we can make nothing of this'—flinging my document contemptuously on the table. The horned owl picked it up, glanced over it while Rhadamanthus was tossing papers about and grumbling about 'people that wouldn't conform to rules'; then handed it back to him, saying deprecatingly, 'But, sir, this is a very plain statement.'

'Then what has Mr. Carlyle to live upon? You don't mean to tell me he lives on *that*?'—pointing to the document.

'Heaven forbid, sir! but I am not here to explain what Mr. Carlyle has to live on, only to declare his income from literature during the last three years.'

'True! true!' mumbled the not-most-important voice at my elbow.

'Mr. Carlyle, I believe, has landed income?'

'Of which,' said I haughtily, for my spirit was up, 'I have fortunately no account to render in this kingdom and to this board.'

'Take off fifty pounds, say a hundred—take off a hundred pounds,' said Rhadamanthus to the horned owl. 'If we write Mr. Carlyle down a hundred and fifty he has no reason to complain, I think. There, you may go, Mr. Carlyle has no reason to complain.'

Second-come woman was already introduced, and I was motioned to the door; but I could not depart without saying that 'at all events there was no use in complaining, since they had the power to enforce their decision.' On stepping out, my first thought was, what a mercy Carlyle didn't come himself! For the rest, though it might have gone better, I was thankful it had not gone worse.

292

BROWNING said, 'I never minded what Carlyle said of things outside his own little circle (drawing a circle in the air with his forefinger)—what was it to me what he thought of Poetry or Music? One day I was talking of Keats, and Carlyle's opinion of him, to Mrs. Carlyle; she asked me to lend her something of Keats's, and I brought her *Isabella* and *The Eve of St. Agnes* (I was too knowing to try her with *Endymion*). She wrote me a letter—"Almost any young gentleman with a sweet tooth might be expected to write such things. *Isabella* might have been written by a seamstress who had eaten something too rich for supper and slept upon her back."—Do you think,' Browning said, 'I cared about this more than for the barking of a little dog?'

293
LETITIA ELIZABETH LANDON ('L.E.L.'), 1802–38

MY cottage[1] overlooked the mansion and grounds of Mr. Landon, the father of L.E.L., at Old Brompton; a narrow lane only dividing our residences. My first recollection of the future poetess is that of a plump girl, grown enough to be almost mistaken for a woman, bowling a hoop round the walks, with the hoop-stick in one hand and a book in the other, reading as she ran, and as well as she could manage both exercise and instruction at the same time. The exercise was prescribed and insisted upon; the book was her own irrepressible choice.

294

[From a letter of L.E.L. to William Jerdan.]

35 Rue-le-Grande, Lundi,
which being done into English means Monday.

Dear Sir,

I hope you will not think that I intend writing you to death; but I cannot let this opportunity pass. . . . I am quite surprised that I should have so little to tell you; but really I have nothing, as ill-luck would have it. I went to call on Madame Tastu, from whom I received a charming note, and while I was out Monsieur Sainte-Beuve and Monsieur Odilon Barrot called. . . . M. Heine called yesterday; a most pleasant person. I am afraid he did not think me a *personne bien spirituelle*, for you know it takes a long time with me to get over the shame of speaking to a stranger by way of conversation. He said, 'Mademoiselle donc a beaucoup couru les boutiques?'

Mais non.

[1] The narrator is William Jerdan (1782–1869), journalist, and editor for many years of the *Literary Gazette*.

A-t-elle été au Jardin des Plantes?
Mais non.
Avez-vous été à l'opéra, aux théâtres?
Mais non.
Peut-être Mademoiselle aime la promenade?
Mais non.
A-t-elle donc apporté beaucoup de livres, ou peut-être elle écrit?
Mais non.
At last, in seeming despair, he exclaimed, 'Mais, Mademoiselle, qu'est que ce donc, qu'elle a fait?'
Mais—mais—j'ai regardé par la fenêtre.
Was there ever anything *si bête*? but I really could think of nothing else.

295
HARRIET MARTINEAU (1802–76)

AT this time (I think it must have been in 1821) was my first appearance in print. . . .

My brother James, then my idolized companion, discovered how wretched I was when he left me for his college after the vacation; and he told me that I must not permit myself to be so miserable. He advised me to take refuge, on each occasion, in a new pursuit; and on that particular occasion, in an attempt at authorship. I said, as usual, that I would if he would: to which he answered that it would never do for him, a young student, to rush into print before the eyes of his tutors; but he desired me to write something that was in my head, and try my chance with it in the *Monthly Repository*—the poor little Unitarian periodical in which I have mentioned that Talfourd tried his young powers. What James desired, I always did, as of course; and after he had left me to my widowhood soon after six o'clock one bright September morning, I was at my desk before seven, beginning a letter to the Editor of the *Monthly Repository*—that editor being the formidable prime minister of his sect, Revd. Robert Aspland. I suppose I must tell what that first paper was, though I had much rather not; for I am so heartily ashamed of the whole business as never to have looked at the article since the first flutter of it went off. It was on Female Writers on Practical Divinity. I wrote away, in my abominable scrawl of those days, on foolscap paper, feeling mightily like a fool all the time. I told no one, and carried my expensive packet to the post-office myself, to pay the postage. I took the letter V for my signature—I cannot at all remember why. The time was very near the end of the month: I had no definite expectation that I should ever hear anything of my paper; and certainly did not suppose it could be in the forthcoming number. That number was sent in before service-time on a Sunday morning. My heart may have been beating when I laid hands on it; but it thumped prodigiously when I saw my article there, and, in the Notices to Correspondents, a request to hear more from V. of Norwich. There is certainly something entirely peculiar in the sensation of seeing oneself in print for the first time: the lines burn themselves in upon the brain in a way of which black ink is incapable, in any other mode. So I felt that day, when I went about with my secret. I have said what my eldest brother was to us—in what reverence we held him. He was just married, and he and his bride asked me to return from chapel with them to tea. After tea he said, 'Come now, we have had plenty of talk; I will read you something;' and he held out his hand for the new *Repository*. After glancing at it, he exclaimed, 'They have got a new hand here. Listen.' After a paragraph, he repeated, 'Ah! this is a new hand; they have had nothing so good as this for a long while.' (It would be impossible to convey to any who do not know the *Monthly Repository* of that day, how very small a compliment this was.) I was silent, of course. At the end of the first column, he exclaimed about the style, looking at me in some wonder at my being as still as a mouse. Next (and well I remember his tone, and thrill to it still) his words were—'What a fine sentence that is! Why, do you not think so?' I mumbled out, sillily enough, that it did not seem anything particular. 'Then', said he, 'you were not listening. I will read it again. There now!' As he still got nothing out of me, he turned round upon me as we sat side by side on the sofa, with 'Harriet, what is the matter with you? I never knew you so slow to praise anything before.' I replied, in utter confusion, 'I never could baffle anybody. The truth is, that paper is mine.' He made no reply; read on in silence, and spoke no more till I was on my feet to come away. He then laid his hand on my shoulder, and said gravely (calling me 'dear' for the first time), 'Now, dear, leave it to other women to make shirts and darn stockings; and do you devote yourself to this.' I went home in a sort of dream, so that the squares of the pavement seemed to float before my eyes. That evening made me an authoress.

296

ON landing at Liverpool[1] I found various letters from publishers awaiting me. One was from Mr. Bentley, reminding me of his having met me at Miss Berry's, and expressing his hope of having my manuscript immediately in his hands. My reply was that I had no manuscript. Another letter was

[1] She returned from a visit to the United States on 26 August 1836.

from Messrs. Saunders and Otley to my mother, saying that they desired the pleasure of publishing my travels. I was disposed to treat with them, because the negotiation for the *Two Old Men's Tales* had been an agreeable one. I therefore explained to these gentlemen the precise state of the case, and at length agreed to an interview when I should return to town. My mother and I reached home before London began to fill; and I took some pains to remain unseen for two or three weeks, while arranging my books, and my dress and my other affairs. One November morning, however, my return was announced in the *Morning Chronicle*; and such a day as that I never passed, and hoped at the time never to pass again.

First, Mr. Bentley bustled down, and obtained entrance to my study before anybody else. Mr. Colburn came next, and had to wait. He bided his time in the drawing-room. In a few minutes arrived Mr. Saunders, and was shown into my mother's parlour. These gentlemen were all notoriously on the worst terms with each other; and the fear was that they should meet and quarrel on the stairs. Some friends who happened to call at the time were beyond measure amused.

Mr. Bentley began business. Looking hard into the fire, he 'made no doubt' I remembered the promise I had made him at Miss Berry's house. I had no recollection of having promised anything to Mr. Bentley. He told me it was impossible I should forget having assured him that if anybody published for me, except Fox, it should be himself. I laughed at the idea of such an engagement. Mr. Bentley declared it might be his silliness; but he should go to his grave persuaded that I had made him such a promise. It might be his silliness, he repeated. I replied that indeed it was; as I had a perfect recollection that no book of mine was in question at all, but the Series, which he had talked of putting among his Standard Novels. He now offered the most extravagant terms for a book on America, and threw in, as a bribe, an offer of a thousand pounds for the first novel I should write. Though my refusals were as positive as I could make them, I had great difficulty in getting rid of him: and I doubt whether I was so rude to Mr. Harper himself as to the London speculator.—Mr. Colburn, meantime, sent in his letter of introduction, which was from the poet Campbell, with a message that he would shortly return. So Mr. Saunders entered next. I liked him, as before; and our conversation about the book became quite confidential. I explained to him fully my doubt as to the reception of the work, on the ground of its broad republican character. I told him plainly that I believed it would ruin me, because it would be the principle of the book to regard everything American from the American point of view: and this method, though the only fair one, was so unlike the usual practice, and must lead to a judgement so unlike what English people were prepared for, that I should not be surprised by a total condemnation of my book and myself. I told him that after this warning, he could retreat or negotiate, as he pleased: but that, being thus warned, he and not I must propose terms: and moreover, it must be understood that, our negotiation once concluded, I could listen to no remonstrance or objection, in regard to the contents of my book. Mr. Saunders replied that he had no difficulty in agreeing to these conditions, and that we might now proceed to business. When he had ascertained that the work would consist of three volumes, and what their probable size would be, the amusing part of the affair began. 'Well, Ma'am,' said he, 'what do you propose that we should give you for the copyright of the first edition?' 'Why, you know,' said I, 'I have written to you, from the beginning that I would propose no terms. I am quite resolved against it.'—'Well, Ma'am; supposing the edition to consist of three thousand copies, will you just give me an idea what you would expect for it?'—'No, Mr. Saunders: that is your business. I wait to hear your terms.'

So I sat strenuously looking into the fire, Mr. Saunders no less strenuously looking at me, till it was all I could do to keep my countenance. He waited for me to speak; but I would not; and I wondered where the matter would end, when he at last opened his lips. 'What would you think, Ma'am, of £900 for the first edition?'—'Including the twenty-five copies I stipulated for?'—'Including twenty-five copies of the work, and all proceeds of the sale in America, over and above expenses.' I thought these liberal terms; and I said so; but I suggested that each party should take a day or two for consideration, to leave no room for repentance hereafter. I inquired whether Messrs. Saunders and Otley had any objection to my naming their house as the one I was negotiating with, as I disliked the appearance of entertaining the proffers of various houses, which yet I could not get rid of without a distinct answer to give. Apparently amused at the question, Mr. Saunders replied that it would be gratifying to them to be so named.

On the stairs, Mr. Saunders met Mr. Colburn, who chose to be confident that Campbell's introduction would secure to him all he wished. The interview was remarkably disagreeable, from his refusing to be refused, and pretending to believe that what I wanted was more and more money. At last, on my giving him a broad hint to go away, he said that, having no intention of giving up his object, he should spend the day at a coffee-house in the neighbourhood, whence he should shortly send in terms for my consideration. He now only implored a promise that I would not finally pass my word that day. The moment he was gone, I slipped out into the Park to refresh my mind and body; for I was heated and wearied with the conferences of the morning. On my return, I found that Mr. Colburn had called again; and while we were at dinner, he sent in a letter, containing his fresh terms. They were so absurdly high that if I had had any confidence in the soundness of the negotiation before, it would now be overthrown. Mr. Colburn offered £2,000 for the present work, on the supposition of the sale of I forget what number, and £1,000 for the first novel I should write. The worst of it was, he left word that he should call again at ten o'clock in the evening. When we were at tea, Mr. Bentley sent in a set of amended proposals; and at ten, Mr. Colburn arrived. He set forth his whole array of 'advantages', and declared himself positive that no house in London could have offered higher terms than his. I reminded him that I had been telling him all day that my objections did not relate to the amount of money; and that I was going to accept much less: that it was impossible that my work should yield what he had offered, and leave anything over for himself; and that I therefore felt that these proposals were intended to bind me to his house—an obligation which I did not choose to incur. He pathetically complained of having raised up rivals to himself in the assistants whom he had trained, and concluded with an affected air of resignation which was highly amusing. Hanging his head on one side, and sighing, he enunciated the sentiment: 'When, in pursuing any praiseworthy object, we have done all we can, and find it in vain, we can but be resigned.' With great satisfaction I saw him lighted down stairs, and heard the house-door locked, at near midnight, on the last of the booksellers for that day. . . . I went to bed that night with a disgusted and offended feeling of having been offered bribes, all day long, with a confidence which was not a little insulting.

297
DOUGLAS JERROLD (1803-57)

JERROLD would perceive the germ of a retort before you had well begun to form your sentence, and would bring it forth in full blossom the instant you had done speaking . . . When the publisher of *Bentley's Miscellany* said to Jerrold, 'I had some doubts about the name I should give the magazine; I thought at one time of calling it "The Wits' Miscellany" '—'Well,' was the rejoinder, 'but you needn't have gone to the other extremity.'

298

BENJAMIN DISRAELI, EARL OF BEACONSFIELD (1804–81)

IT was while he was at Bournemouth that Disraeli completed the arrangement for one of the most picturesque features of his first year of office—the offer to Thomas Carlyle of the G.C.B. and a pension. He had been corresponding with Derby in the autumn as to what could be done to honour men of science. . . . 'Can we do anything for literature?' wrote Derby on November 28. He suggested that Tennyson and Carlyle were the only conspicuous names; and in pressing Carlyle's claims mentioned that he was, 'for whatever reason, most vehement against Gladstone. . . . Anything that could be done for him would be a really good political investment. What it should be you know best.' Disraeli caught at the idea; he realized the splendour of Carlyle's genius and the reproach of its total neglect by the State; and his imagination supplied the unique distinction which might not unfitly be offered to the *doyen* of English letters.

To Queen Victoria.

B—mouth, Dec. 12, 1874.—Mr. Disraeli with his humble duty to your Majesty:

As your Majesty was graciously pleased to say that your Majesty would sometimes aid him with your advice, he presumes to lay before your Majesty a subject on which he would much like to be favoured with your Majesty's judgement.

Your Majesty's Government is now in favour with the scientific world. The Arctic Expedition, and some small grants which may be made to their favourite institutions, will secure their sympathy, which is not to be despised.

Can nothing be done for Literature?

Eminent literary men are so few, that there would be no trouble as to choice, if any compliment in the way of honour was contemplated. Mr. Disraeli knows of only two authors who are especially conspicuous at this moment: Tennyson and Carlyle. . . .

Mr. Carlyle is old, and childless, and poor; but he is very popular and respected by the nation. There is no K.C.B. vacant. Would a G.C.B. be too much? It might be combined with a pension, perhaps, not less than your Majesty's royal grandfather conferred on Dr. Johnson, and which that great man cheerfully accepted, and much enjoyed.

These thoughts are humbly submitted to the consideration of your Majesty, with, Mr. Disraeli hopes, not too much freedom.

The Queen, in Disraeli's words, 'entered into the spirit of the affair', and he conveyed the offer to Carlyle in a letter conceived in the grand manner, to the composition of which, it is evident from the interlined draft found among his papers, he had devoted considerable labour. As a proffer of

State recognition by a literary man in power to a literary man in (so to speak) permanent opposition, it would be difficult to excel it either in delicacy or in dignity. Fully to appreciate its magnanimity, it must be remembered that Carlyle had always treated Disraeli as a 'conscious juggler', 'a superlative Hebrew conjurer'. 'He is the only man', Carlyle wrote to John Carlyle, 'I almost never spoke of except with contempt; and if there is anything of scurrility anywhere chargeable against me, he is the subject of it; and yet see, here he comes with a pan of hot coals for my guilty head.' . . .

Carlyle's answer was reported to Derby by Disraeli.

To Lord Derby.

B—mouth, Jan. 1, '75.—. . . Alas! the Philosopher of Chelsea, tho' evidently delighted with the proposal, and grateful in wondrous sentences, will accept of nothing—'Titles of honour, of all degrees, are out of keeping with the tenor of my poor life', and as for money—'after years of rigorous and frugal, but, thank God, never degrading poverty', it has become 'amply abundant, even super-abundant in this later time'.

Nevertheless the proposal is 'magnanimous and noble, without example in the history of governing persons with men of letters', and a great deal more in the same highly-sublimated Teutonic vein. . . .

For the moment Carlyle recognized that he had misjudged Disraeli. Lady Derby, whom Carlyle credited, perhaps rightly, with the origination of the idea, wrote to Disraeli on January 15: 'I saw old Mr. Carlyle today, and he scarcely knew how to be grateful enough for the mark of attention you had paid him. I assure you it was quite touching to see and hear his high appreciation of the offer.' But, save that he continued to prefer Disraeli to Gladstone, the feeling was transient; and when, a few years later, he dissented from Ministerial policy in the East, he reverted once again to his earlier language, and was not ashamed to talk of the Prime Minister as 'a cursed old Jew, not worth his weight in cold bacon', 'an accursed being, the worst man who ever lived'.

299

JOHN FREDERICK SMITH (1804?–90)

THE little world of purveyors of penny popular literature . . . was startled about this time with the news that Stiff, the lank, cadaverous-looking proprietor of the *London Journal*, one of the most successful cheap publications of the epoch, had sold the copyright of it to Ingram and McMurray, the papermaker, for the large sum of £24,000. . . .

Eventually Stiff worked up the weekly circulation of the *London Journal* to several hundred thousand copies, for he allowed nothing to turn him aside from his one set purpose—the increasing of the sale of this publication; not, however, by means of bogus prizes and illusory insurance tickets after the favourite practice of the present day, but by providing his factory and servant girl readers with lengthy and exciting stories, telling how rich and poor babies were wickedly changed in their perambulators by conniving nursemaids, how long-lost wills miraculously turned up in the nick of time, and penniless beauty and virtue were 'led to the hymeneal altar by the wealthy scion of a noble house', after he had gained the fair one's affections under some humble disguise.

In the early days of the *London Journal*, radical G. W. M. Reynolds furnished Stiff with his fiction, but he subsequently resigned the task, and started a miscellany of his own, when Stiff luckily came across J. F. Smith . . . So cleverly did J. F. Smith pile up the excitement towards the end of the stories which he wrote for Stiff, that the latter told me his weekly circulation used to rise as many as 50,000 when the dénouement approached. He surmised that the factory girls in the north, the great patrons of the journal, were in the habit of lending it to one another, and that when their curiosity as to how the story would end was at its greatest tension, the borrowers, being unable to wait for the journal to be lent to them, expended their pennies in buying it outright.

Eventually John Cassell enticed J. F. Smith away from the *London Journal* on to some publication of his own, and the pair kept the affair a profound secret. Smith, who always wrote his weekly instalment of 'copy' at the *London Journal* office, chanced to be in the middle of a story for Stiff at the moment he had chosen for abandoning him. In this dilemma he decided upon bringing the tale to a sudden close, and to accomplish this artistically he blew up all the principal characters on board a Mississippi steamboat, and handed the 'copy' to the boy in waiting. Then, proud at having solved a troublesome difficulty, he descended the office stairs, and directed his steps to La Belle Sauvage yard to take service under his new employer. When Stiff saw the number after it was printed off, and recognized how completely he had been tricked, he was thunderstruck, but he speedily secured a new novelist—Pierce Egan, the younger, I believe—who ingeniously brought about the resurrection of such of the characters as it was desirable to resuscitate, and continued the marvellous story in the *London Journal* for several months longer.

300
FREDERICK DENISON MAURICE (1805–72)

I[1] WENT, as usual about this time, to hear F. D. Maurice preach at Lincoln's Inn. I suppose I must have heard him, first and last, some thirty or forty times, and never carried away one clear idea, or even the impression that he had more than the faintest conception of what he himself meant.

Aubrey de Vere was quite right when he said that listening to him was like eating pea-soup with a fork, and Jowett's answer was no less to the purpose, when I asked him what a sermon which Maurice had just preached before the University was about, and he replied—'Well! all that I could make out was that today was yesterday, and this world the same as the next.'

301
RICHARD CHENEVIX TRENCH (1807–86)

[Trench became Archbishop of Dublin in 1864, and retired to London twenty years later. The visit paid to his successor must have been made not long before his death. Of his numerous writings the best known today are on philological subjects; e.g. *The Study of Words* and *English, Past and Present*.]

THE late Archbishop Trench, a man of singularly vague and dreamy habits, resigned the see of Dublin on account of advancing years, and settled in London. He once went back to pay a visit to his successor, Lord Plunket. Finding himself back again in his old palace, sitting at his old dinner-table, and gazing across it at his old wife, he lapsed in memory to the days when he was master of the house, and gently remarked to Mrs. Trench, 'I am afraid, my love, that we must put this cook down among our failures.'

[1] Sir Mounstuart E. Grant Duff.

302

ALFRED, LORD TENNYSON (1809–92)

[To 'Will Waterproof's Lyrical Monologue', first published in 1842, Tennyson added the words 'Made at the Cock', i.e. the Cock chophouse in Fleet Street. The opening lines are addressed to the head waiter:

> O plump head-waiter at the Cock,
> To which I most resort,
> How goes the time? 'Tis five o'clock.
> Go fetch a pint of port . . .

On Sunday 5 August 1849, William Allingham, who was to become a sort of Boswell to Tennyson, went to the Cock to see what biographical scraps he could pick up, and noted the results in his diary.]

Sunday, August 5 . . . Chop at 'The Cock'. Curious old mantlepiece, which I sketched on fly-leaf of Poe's Poems, bought at a book-stall. Had the waiter ever heard of a Mr. Tennyson?—'Mr. Tennyson, sir?—No, sir.' Tried the other waiter: he *had* heard of him, but had never seen him.

I.—'You're not the plump head-waiter?'—'Oh, you mean William, sir. He's here every day but Sunday.'

Thursday, August 9 . . . Chop at 'Cock' with half a pint of port to drink the Poet's health. The veritable William waited on me.

'Are you Mr. Tennyson's friend?'

William.—'He says so, sir.'

This answer puzzled me. (Does William think it was a liberty to put him in rhyme?) 'Has he been often here?'

W.—'I don't know his appearance at all, sir. A gen'elman might be coming here for twenty years without my knowing his name. Thousands have asked me the same question, and some won't believe but that I know all about it. But I don't. I should like to see him—very much. I'm told he's *breaking*, sir. I should like to see him.' William evidently felt sorrowful, and in a manner aggrieved, at never having identified the man who spoke of *him* so familiarly.

303

[Charles Babbage (1792–1871), who occupied for about ten years the Lucasian chair of mathematics at Cambridge, was the inventor of an elaborate calculating machine which was never completely constructed owing to his failure to obtain sufficient financial backing.]

TENNYSON'S

> Every minute dies a man,
> Every minute one is born

drew from Babbage the remark that the world's population was in fact constantly increasing: 'I would therefore take the liberty of suggesting that in the next edition of your excellent poem the erroneous calculation to which I refer should be corrected as follows: "Every moment dies a man/And one and a sixteenth is born." This figure, he added, was a concession to metre, since the actual ratio was 1:167. Tennyson did eventually blur his assertion to the extent of changing 'minute' to 'moment'.

304

[William Allingham records a conversation with Coventry Patmore, 18 August 1849.]

AFTER some supper Patmore . . . went on to tell me: 'I have in this room perhaps the greatest literary treasure in England—the manuscript of Tennyson's *next poem*. It is written in a thing like a butcher's account-book. He left it behind him in his lodging when he was up in London and wrote to me to go and look for it. He had no other copy, and he never remembers his verses. I found it by chance, in a drawer; if I had been a little later it would probably have been sold to a butter-shop.' Before I went away Patmore took out this MS. book from a cabinet and turned over the leaves before my longing eyes, but Tennyson had told him not to show it to anybody. Mrs. Patmore had copied it out for the press, and Tennyson gave her the original.

I was not even told the title at this time. It was *In Memoriam*.

305

WHEN Tennyson entered the Oxford Theatre to receive his honorary degree of D.C.L.,[1] his locks hanging in admired disorder on his shoulders, dishevelled and unkempt, a voice from the gallery was heard crying out to him, 'Did your mother call you early, dear?'

[1] June 1855.

306

... LONDON visits enabled Alfred to renew the acquaintance made at Pontresina with little Elspeth Thompson. She would accompany him on long tramps through the streets, trotting beside him to keep pace with his long massive stride, never wearying, though he was often silent and plunged in deep contemplation, for his very silences were companionable. He would always wear his great Spanish cloak and sombrero, which excited much interest. The real cause of this he never seemed to realize, for he would say to his little companion: 'Child, your mother should dress you less conspicuously; people are staring at us.'

307

[Tennyson talks to William Allingham, 29 July 1865.]

I WAS at an hotel in Covent Garden, and went out one morning for a walk in the Piazza. A man met me, tolerably well-dressed but battered-looking. I never saw him before that I know of. He pulled off his hat and said, 'Beg pardon, Mr. Tennyson, might I say a word to you?' I stopped. 'I've been drunk for three days and I want to make a solemn promise to you, Mr. Tennyson, that I won't do so any more.' I said that was a good resolve, and I hoped he would keep it. He said, 'I promise you I will, Mr. Tennyson,' and added, 'Might I shake your hand?' I shook hands with him, and he thanked me and went on his way.

308

I[1] WAS told a characteristic story of Tennyson.... An enthusiastic admirer of his, who was staying at Aldworth, was, to her intense delight, invited to accompany him for a walk in his old English garden.

They paced the terrace together in silence; he said nothing and she was afraid to speak for fear of losing some priceless utterance. The silence remained unbroken until they had returned to their starting-point, when he remarked abruptly, 'Coals are very dear.' She received this without comment and he remained in abstraction for another tour of the terrace, when he spoke again. 'I get all my meat from London', he said, and again

[1] F. Anstey (i.e. Thomas Anstey Guthrie, 1856–1934), author of *Vice Versa* and other successful novels and plays.

she did not see her way to following up the subject. Another long silence, and then he stopped beside a clump of carnations which were obviously drooping, and she waited hopefully for a comment that she could always treasure. But all Tennyson said was: 'It's those cursed rabbits!' which was the sum total of his conversation on that particular afternoon.

309

[Margot Tennant, later Countess of Oxford and Asquith, meets the Poet Laureate.]

LADY TENNYSON was an invalid; and we were received on our arrival by the poet. Tennyson was a magnificent creature to look at. He had everything: height, figure, carriage, feature, and expression. Added to this he had what George Meredith called 'the feminine hint to perfection'. He greeted me by saying:

'Well, are you as clever and spurty as your sister Laura?'

I had never heard the word 'spurty' before, nor indeed have I since. To answer this kind of frontal attack one has to be either saucy or servile; so I said nothing memorable . . .

Tennyson: . . . 'Have you read Jane Welsh Carlyle's letters?'

Margot: 'Yes, I have, and I think them excellent. It seems a pity', I added, with the commonplace that is apt to overcome one in a first conversation with a man of eminence, 'that they were ever married; with anyone but each other, they might have been perfectly happy.'

Tennyson: 'I totally disagree with you. By any other arrangement four people would have been unhappy instead of two.'

After this I went up to my room. The hours kept at Aldworth were peculiar: we dined early and after dinner the poet went to bed. At ten o'clock he came downstairs and, if asked, would read his poetry to the company till past midnight.

I dressed for dinner with great care that first night and, placing myself next to him when he came down, I asked him to read out loud to me.

Tennyson: 'What do you want me to read?'

Margot: '*Maud*.'

Tennyson: 'That was the poem I was cursed for writing! When it came out no word was bad enough for me! I was a blackguard, a ruffian and an atheist! You will live to have as great a contempt for literary critics and the public as I have, my child!'

While he was speaking, I found on the floor, among piles of books, a small copy of *Maud*, a shilling volume, bound in blue paper. I put it into his hands and, pulling the lamp nearer him, he began to read. . . .

He began 'Birds in the high Hall-garden' . . . When he had finished, he pulled me on to his knee and said:

'Many have written as well as that, but nothing ever sounded so well!'

I could not speak.

He then told us that he had had an unfortunate experience with a young lady to whom he was reading *Maud*.

'She was sitting on my knee,' he said, 'as you are doing now, and after reading,

> Birds in the high Hall-garden,
> When twilight was falling,
> Maud, Maud, Maud, Maud,
> They were crying and calling,

I asked her what bird she thought I meant. She said, "A nightingale." This made me so angry that I nearly flung her to the ground: "No, fool! . . . Rook!" said I.'

310

IN the summer[1] the usual wandering fit came on the poet. Emily took the boys to Grasby to see Charles and her father, and Alfred met Woolner, Spedding, and other friends in London to discuss plans—he spoke of going to the Levant, or the West Indies, or Cornwall, or Brittany. Palgrave was for the latter place. . . . In the end, however, Cornwall was decided on.

When the time came to start, Palgrave was detained by the necessity of seeing his brother Gifford off on his perilous pilgrimage to Mecca, and Woolner went with the poet through Bath, Bideford, Clovelly, Bude, and Boscastle to Tintagel and Trevenna, where Palgrave joined them; thence they went through Camelford to Penzance to meet Holman Hunt and Val Prinsep. The choice of district showed that the Arthurian saga was still very much in Tennyson's mind. At first all went delightfully. . . . After some days in the Lizard and Land's End districts, diving off steep rocks and scrambling about the thymy promontories (Alfred always with his Homer or Virgil in his pocket), the party crossed to the Scilly Isles, over the sea said to cover the legendary land of Lyonesse, returning to the Lizard about September 10th.

Here, unfortunately, signs of strain began to appear. Palgrave, who felt

[1] 1860. The friends mentioned in the opening paragraph are Thomas Woolner (1825–92), sculptor and poet; James Spedding (1808–81), the editor of Bacon's works, and F. T. Palgrave (1824–97), now remembered as compiler of the *Golden Treasury* (1861), in which he had some help from Tennyson.

himself bound by instructions, which he imagined that he had received from Emily, never to let the poet out of his view, for fear that through his short sight he might fall over a cliff or come to some similar harm, was perpetually pursuing him over the rocks and calling out, 'Tennyson! Tennyson!'—which drove poor Alfred to frenzy. One evening there was a violent upheaval between the two, after which Alfred took up his candlestick to light himself to bed, saying: 'Each must do as he thinks best, but I have no doubt what to do. There is no pleasure for any of us in this wrangling. I shall go tomorrow to Falmouth and take the train home.'

Palgrave went up soon after, and then, while the three younger men were sitting below talking over the trouble, the door was quietly opened and Tennyson appeared in his dressing-gown and slippers. Taking a chair, he spread both his hands out on the table and said: 'I've come to say to you young fellows that I'm sorry if I seem to be the cause of all the bickering that goes on between Palgrave and myself. It is, I know, calculated to spoil your holiday, and that would be a great shame. I don't mean to quarrel with anyone, but all day long I am trying to get a quiet moment for reflection. Sometimes I want to compose a stanza or two and to find a quiet nook where I can wind off my words; but before I have finished a couplet I hear Palgrave's voice like a bee in a bottle, making the neighbourhood resound with my name, and I have to give myself up to escape the consequences. I know he means well, but it worries me and I am going away tomorrow morning . . . but I hope you will all stay and enjoy yourselves.' The last scene of the comedy, as reported by Hunt, shows Tennyson moving off in the dog-cart and Palgrave jumping up beside him to his evident surprise, and driving away with him amid protests and explanations.

311

ON 8 September 1883, he and Hallam joined Gladstone at Chester, and went with him and a large party for a cruise in the *Pembroke Castle*, which Sir Donald Currie had put at their disposal for the purpose. . . . Sir William Harcourt joined the ship at Ardnamurchan Point and sailed with them to Tobermory, and it was then that he made the classic pun which has been so often quoted. Tennyson was, as he frequently did, talking about tobacco and saying that the first pipe after breakfast was the best of the day. 'Ah,' said Harcourt, 'the earliest pipe of half-awakened *bards*.' It was observed that the poet did not at all appreciate this burlesquing of one of his most treasured poems.

312

DURING the twenty-minute crossing over to Yarmouth from Lymington, on his way from Aldworth to Farringford, there came to him, almost in a flash, the most famous of all his lyrics, *Crossing the Bar*. He unfolded a used envelope and jotted the sixteen short lines roughly down on the inside of it, but showed them to no one at the time. That evening when Nurse Durham went to light the candles in his study at dusk, she found him sitting at his desk, with a paper before him.

'Will this do for you, old woman?' he asked, remembering what she had said to him about writing a hymn of thanksgiving for his recovery—and he recited the poem, almost in the form in which it is now printed. The lines came as a great shock to her, for, as she listened, it seemed to her that he had written his own death song. Without a word, she turned and ran from the room. When she came back a few minutes afterwards, he was still sitting silent in the darkness. After dinner that night he showed the lines to Hallam, who said: 'That is the crown of your life's work.' He replied: 'It came in a moment.'

313
EDWARD FITZGERALD (1809–93)

[In 1858 Edward Fitzgerald sent the manuscript of *The Rubáiyát of Omar Khayyám* to the editor of *Fraser's Magazine*, but about a year, later, since there was apparently no prospect of its being published, he asked for it to be returned to him. He then had it printed at his own expense in February 1859, and this small quarto pamphlet in a brown wrapper was published by Bernard Quaritch, the second-hand bookseller, who offered it to the public at half a crown. Little or no interest was taken in the poem, and Quaritch reduced the price to a shilling, and ultimately placed the pamphlet in 'the penny box outside his door', where some copies were picked up by passers-by. When at length Fitzgerald's poem reached the hands of Rossetti, Swinburne, and Sir Richard Burton, it began to be talked about, and the market price soon soared. In a letter to A. C. Benson, Swinburne gives his own account of what had happened.]

NEITHER Burton nor Rossetti nor I had anything to do with the discovery of Omar Fitzgerald. . . . Two friends of Rossetti's—Mr. Whitley Stokes and Mr. Ormsby—told him (he told me) of this wonderful little pamphlet for sale on a stall (in St. Martin's Lane if you know where that is) to which Mr. Quaritch, finding that the British public unanimously declined to give a shilling for it, had relegated it to be disposed of for a penny. Having read it, Rossetti and I invested upwards of sixpence apiece—or possibly threepence—I would not wish to exaggerate our extravagance—in copies at that not exorbitant price. Next day we thought we might get some more for presents among friends—but the man at the stall asked twopence! Rossetti expostulated with him in terms of such humorously indignant remonstrance as none but he could ever have commanded. We took a few, and left him. In a week or two, if I am not mistaken, the remaining copies were sold at a guinea; I have since—as I dare say you have—seen copies offered for still more absurd prices. I kept my own pennyworth (the tidiest copy of the lot) and have it still.

314

RICHARD MONCKTON MILNES, LORD HOUGHTON (1809–85)

'RICHARD MILNES,' said Carlyle one day, withdrawing his pipe from his mouth, as they were seated together in the little house in Cheyne Row, 'when are you going to get that pension for Alfred Tennyson?'

'My dear Carlyle,' responded Milnes, 'the thing is not so easy as you seem to suppose. What will my constituents say if I do get the pension for Tennyson? They know nothing about him or his poetry, and they will probably think he is some poor relation of my own and that the whole affair is a job.'

Solemn and emphatic was Carlyle's response.

'Richard Milnes, on the Day of Judgement, when the Lord asks you why you didn't get that pension for Alfred Tennyson, it will not do to lay the blame on your constituents; it is you that will be damned.'[1]

315

IN the autumn of 1845, Monckton Milnes was one of a party at the Grange[2] at the same time with Carlyle and myself.[3] He was famous for the interest he took in notorieties, and especially in notorious sinners, always finding some good reason for taking an indulgent view of their misdeeds. I

[1] In 1842, in response to the recommendations of Monckton Milnes and others, Sir Robert Peel placed Tennyson's name on the civil list for a pension of £200.

[2] The home of Lord and Lady Ashburton, near Alresford.

[3] Sir Henry Taylor (1800–86).

have heard that on the occasion of some murderer being hanged, his sister, Lady Galway, expressed her satisfaction, saying that if he had been acquitted she would have been sure to have met him next week at one of her brother's Thursday morning breakfasts. At the time of this visit, Sir Robert Peel had just formed his government, and had not found a place in it for Monckton Milnes, who appeared to be somewhat dissatisfied with Sir Robert on the occasion. Carlyle took a different view: he highly commended Sir Robert's judgement and penetration, insisting that no man knew better who would suit his purposes and who not, and ended by pronouncing his own opinion, that the only office Monckton Milnes was fit for was that of 'Perpetual President of the Heaven and Hell Amalgamation Society'.

316
MARTIN TUPPER (1810–89)

TUPPER'S vanity did not decrease with the years. . . . When he called on Martin Hope Sutton, the founder of the seed firm, at his home near Reading, he was introduced to his young daughter, bent over her hand with old-world courtesy, and said: 'Now my child, you will always be able to say that you have shaken hands with the great Martin Tupper.'

317
WILLIAM MAKEPEACE THACKERAY (1811-63)

[In the summer of 1844 one of Thackeray's friends, James Emerson Tennent, who was about to set off on a voyage to the East, invited Thackeray to join his party; and, to make the invitation more attractive, promised to secure a free berth for him from the Directors of the P. & O. Company. Three days later Thackeray was on board ship. In 1846 he published *Notes of a Journey from Cornhill to Grand Cairo*. This book was not written as a puff for the P. & O., but the atrabiliar Carlyle assumed that it was, and said so. His remarks reached Thackeray in due course, and the two men were never on really cordial terms again. Some time later Charles Gavan Duffy asked Carlyle about Thackeray, and Carlyle gave his version of what had gone wrong.]

I INQUIRED if he saw much of Thackeray. No, he said, not latterly. Thackeray was much enraged with him because, after he made a book of travels for the P. & O. Company, who had invited him to go on a voyage to

Africa in one of their steamers, he (Carlyle) had compared the transaction to the practice of a blind fiddler going to and fro on a penny ferry-boat in Scotland, and playing tunes to the passengers for halfpence. Charles Buller told Thackeray; and when he complained, it was necessary to inform him frankly that it was undoubtedly his opinion that, out of respect for himself and his profession, a man like Thackeray ought not to have gone fiddling for halfpence or otherwise, in any steamboat under the sky.

318

[Thackeray's daughter looks back on her childhood.]

I CAN remember on one occasion, through a cloud of smoke, looking across a darkening room at the noble, grave head of the Poet-Laureate. He was sitting with my father in the twilight, after some family meal, in the old house in Kensington. It is Lord Tennyson himself who has reminded me how upon this occasion, while my father was speaking to me, my little sister looked up suddenly from the book in which she had been absorbed, saying, in her soft childish voice, 'Papa, why do you not write books like *Nicholas Nickleby*?'

319

IN common with most children, the stories of our father's youth always delighted and fascinated us, and we had often heard him speak of his own early days at college and in Germany, and of his happy stay at Pumpernickel-Weimar, where he went to Court and saw the great Goethe, and was in love with the beautiful Amalia von X. And now coming to Weimar we found ourselves actually *alive* in his past somehow, almost living it alongside with him, just like Gogo in Mr. du Maurier's story. I suddenly find myself walking up the centre of an empty shady street, and my father is pointing to a row of shutters on the first floor of a large and comfortable-looking house. 'That is where Frau von X used to live,' he said. 'How kind she was to us, and what a pretty girl Amalia was.' And then a little further on we passed the house in the sunshine of a *plaz* in which he told us he himself had lodged with a friend; and then we came to the palace, with the soldiers and sentries looking like toys wound up from the Burlington Arcade, and going backwards and forwards with their spikes in front of their own striped boxes; and we saw the acacia trees with their cropped heads, and the iron gates; and we went across the courtyard into the palace and were shown the ball-room and the smaller saloons, and we stood on the shining floors and beheld the classic spot where for the first and only time in all his life, I believe, my father had invited the lovely Amalia to waltz. And then coming away all absorbed and delighted with our experiences in living backwards, my father suddenly said, 'I wonder if old Weissenborne is still alive? He used to teach me German.' And lo! as he spoke, a tall thin old man, in a broad-brimmed straw hat, with a beautiful Pomeranian poodle running before him, came stalking along with a newspaper under his arm. 'Good gracious, that looks like—yes, that *is* Dr. Weissenborne. He is hardly changed a bit,' said my father, stopping short for a moment, and then he too stepped forward quickly with an outstretched hand, and the old man in turn stopped, stared, frowned. 'I am Thackeray, my name is Thackeray,' said my father eagerly and shyly as was his way; and after another stare from the doctor, suddenly came a friendly lighting up and exclaiming and welcoming and handshaking and laughing, while the pretty white dog leapt up and down, as much interested as we were in the meeting. . . .

We came back with our friend the doctor and breakfasted with him in his small apartment, in a room full of books, at a tiny table drawn to an open window; then after breakfast we sat in the Professor's garden among the nasturtiums. My sister and I were given books to read; they were translations for the use of students, I remember; and the old friends smoked together and talked over a hundred things. Amalia was married and had several children: she was away. . . .

There was a certain simple dignity and hospitality in it all which seems to belong to all the traditions of hospitable Weimar, and my father's pleasure and happy emotion gave a value and importance to every tiny detail of that short but happy time. Even the people at the inn remembered their old guest, and came to greet him; but they also sent in such an enormous bill as we were departing on the evening of the second day, that he exclaimed in dismay to the waiter, 'So much for sentimental recollections! Tell the host I shall never be able to afford to come back to Weimar again.'

The waiter stared; I wonder if he delivered the message. The hotel-bill I have just mentioned was a real disappointment to my father, and, alas for disillusions! another more serious shock, a meeting which was no meeting, somewhat dashed the remembrance of Amalia von X.

It happened at Venice, a year or two after our visit to Weimar. We were breakfasting at a long table where a fat lady also sat a little way off, with a pale fat little boy beside her. She was stout, she was dressed in light green, she was silent, she was eating an egg. The *sala* of the great marble hotel was shaded from the blaze of sunshine, but stray gleams shot across the dim hall, falling on the palms and the orange trees beyond the lady, who gravely shifted her place as the sunlight dazzled her. Our own meal was also spread, and my sister and I were only waiting for my father to begin. He came in presently, saying he had been looking at the guest-book in the outer hall, and he had seen a name which had interested him very much. 'Frau von Z. Geboren von X. It must be Amalia! She must be *here*—in the hotel,' he said; and as he spoke he asked a waiter whether Madame von Z. was still in the hotel. 'I believe that is Madame von Z.' said the waiter, pointing to the fat lady. The lady looked up and then went on with her egg, and my poor father turned away, saying in a low, overwhelmed voice, '*That* Amalia! That cannot be Amalia.' I could not understand his silence, his discomposure. 'Aren't you going to speak to her? Oh, please do go and speak to her!' we both cried. 'Do make sure if it is Amalia.' But he shook his head. 'I can't,' he said; 'I had rather not.' Amalia meanwhile, having finished her egg, rose deliberately, put down her napkin and walked away, followed by her little boy. . . .

Things don't happen altogether at the same time; they don't quite begin or end all at once. Once more I heard of Amalia long years afterwards, when by a happy hospitable chance I met Dr. Norman Macleod at the house of my old friends, Mr. and Mrs. Cunliffe. I was looking at him, and thinking that in some indefinable way he put me in mind of the past, when he suddenly asked me if I knew that he and my father had been together as boys at Weimar, learning German from the same professor, and both in love with the same beautiful girl. 'What, Amalia? Dr. Weissenborne?" I cried. 'Dear me! do you know about Amalia?' said Dr. Macleod, 'and do you know about old Weissenborne? I thought I was the only person left to remember them. We all learnt from Weissenborne; we were all in love with Amalia, every one of us, your father too! What happy days those were!' And then he went on to tell us that years and years afterwards, when they met again on the occasion of one of the lecturing tours in Scotland, he, Dr. Macleod, and all the rest of the notabilities were all assembled to receive the lecturer on the platform, and as my father came by carrying his papers and advancing to take his place at the reading-desk, he recognized Dr. Macleod as he passed, and in the face of all the audience he bent forward and said gravely, without stopping one moment on his way, '*Ich liebe Amalia doch*', and so went on to deliver his lecture.

320

THACKERAY was no cynic, but he was a satirist, and could now and then be a satirist in conversation, hitting very hard when he did hit. When he was in America he met at dinner a literary gentleman of high character, middle-aged, and most dignified deportment. The gentleman was one whose character and acquirements stood very high—deservedly so—but who, in society, had that air of wrapping his toga around him, which adds, or is supposed to add, many cubits to a man's height. But he had a broken nose. At dinner he talked much of the tender passion, and did so in a manner which stirred up Thackeray's feeling of the ridiculous. 'What has the world come to,' said Thackeray out loud to the table, 'when two broken-nosed old fogies like you and me sit talking about love to each other!' The gentleman was astounded, and could only sit wrapping his toga in silent dismay for the rest of the evening. Thackeray then, as at other similar times, had no idea of giving pain, but when he saw a foible he put his foot upon it, and tried to stamp it out.

321

No unusual incidents marked Thackeray's lectures in St. Louis and Cincinnati,[1] though he was fond of relating an anecdote which had Barnum's Hotel in the former city as its setting. Dining there one day, he overheard one Irish waiter say to another:

'Do you know who that is?'

'No', was the answer.

'That', said the first, 'is the celebrated Thacker!'

'What's *he* done?'

'D—d if I know!'

322

When Dr. Russell, so long *The Times* correspondent, was coming in a boat to the ship which was to bear him from America to England, the sea was extremely rough: the boat with great difficulty reached the ship. Turning to a gentleman sitting beside him, an American general, Dr. Russell said, 'I fear, Sir, that we shall have a rough passage': the Officer replied, 'I am not going to Europe.' 'Then will you permit me to ask what induces you to come out in such tremendous weather in an open boat?' 'I have one motive, Sir, which I think sufficient. I shall know for the rest of my life that I have spoken to one who has conversed with Thackeray.' General Garnett was killed not long afterwards, in an action at Wheeling in Western Virginia. He served in the Southern army.

[1] In 1856, when he was making his second visit to the United States.

323
CHARLES DICKENS (1812–70)

[*Pickwick Papers* appeared in monthly parts from 31 March 1836.]

HERE was a series of sketches, without the pretence to such interest as attends a well-constructed story; put forth in a form apparently ephemeral as its purpose; having none that seemed higher than to exhibit some studies of cockney manners with help from a comic artist; and after four or five parts had appeared, without newspaper notice or puffing, and itself not subserving in the public anything false or unworthy, it sprang into a popularity that each part carried higher and higher, until people at this time talked of nothing else, tradesmen recommended their goods by using its name, and its sale, outstripping at a bound that of all the most famous books of the century, had reached to an almost fabulous number. Of part one, the binder prepared four hundred; and of part fifteen, his order was for more than forty thousand. Every class, the high equally with the low, were attracted to it. The charm of its gaiety and good humour, its inexhaustible fun, its riotous overflow of animal spirits, its brightness and keenness of observation, and, above all, the incomparable ease of its many varieties of enjoyment, fascinated everybody. Judges on the bench and boys in the street, gravity and folly, the young and the old, those who were entering life and those who were quitting it alike found it to be irresistible. 'An archdeacon,' wrote Mr. Carlyle afterwards to me, 'with his own venerable lips, repeated to me, the other night, a strange profane story: of a solemn clergyman who had been administering ghostly consolation to a sick person; having finished, satisfactorily as he thought, and got out of the room, he heard the sick person ejaculate: "Well, thank God, *Pickwick* will be out in ten days any way!"—This is dreadful.'

324

THE publishers of *Pickwick* soon found themselves involved in a net of annoyance from the ingenious spirits who managed to steal their market, while keeping just outside the reach of the law. The bookshops began to bristle with continuations of *Pickwick*, so ingeniously modelled on the original as to deceive at first sight all but the very elect. The clerks at 186 Strand had to meet perpetual inquiries as to whether *The Posthumous Notes of the Pickwickian Club* by one 'Bos' were really the work of Mr. Dickens himself; and why there should be a *Penny Pickwick* in one shop, while the authentic publishers could only offer the work at twelve times that price for a number. As for dramatic copyright, it practically did not exist at all; and one stage perversion after another caused infinite annoyance to Dickens, and proportionate loss to his publishers. Perhaps the height of impudence in this regard was achieved by one William Moncrieff, who produced a play called *Sam Weller* at the Strand Theatre, in which Mrs. Bardell was represented as the wife of Jingle, and got herself imprisoned for bigamy. When Chapman & Hall protested against this particular outrage, Moncrieff coolly asked them to state on oath whether the sales of *Pickwick* had not increased since his play appeared. The trap was ingeniously set, for this was the moment when *Pickwick* was striding along from month to month, and it was scarcely possible for the publishers to prove to legal satisfaction that *post hoc* might not be *propter hoc*, though everyone concerned knew very well that it was not. So the matter had to be dropped, Dickens consoling himself with a shrug of the shoulders, and a sarcastic reference to 'the little pot of filth' which had helped to put 'a few shillings into the vermin-eaten pockets of so miserable a creature'.

325

[The Death of Little Nell.]

FORSTER had pressed upon him the artistic necessity of this death, and Dickens agreed that it was the only possible ending, but as it began to be foreshadowed in the narrative he was 'inundated with imploring letters recommending poor little Nell to mercy'. He suffered from it so intensely as to feel 'the anguish unspeakable'. . . .

Dickens's readers were drowned in a wave of grief no less overwhelming than his own. When Macready, returning home from the theatre, saw the print of the child lying dead by the window with strips of holly on her breast, a dead chill ran through his blood. 'I have never read printed words that gave me so much pain,' he noted in his diary. 'I could not weep for some time. Sensations, sufferings have returned to me, that are terrible to awaken . . .' Daniel O'Connell, the Irish M.P., reading the book in a railway carriage, burst into tears, groaned, 'He should not have killed her', and despairingly threw the volume out of the train window. Thomas Carlyle, previously inclined to be a bit patronizing about Dickens, was utterly overcome. Waiting crowds at a New York pier shouted to an incoming vessel, 'Is Little Nell dead?' . . .

326

[*Dombey and Son* was begun at Lausanne in the summer of 1846, and finished in Paris early in 1848. When Dickens had sent off the copy for the last monthly part, he remembered that when he was tying up the loose ends he had forgotten to say anything about Florence's dog Diogenes. On 25 March 1848, he wrote to the faithful Forster, who was attending to the press in London.]

THE end came; and, at the last moment when correction was possible, this note arrived. 'I suddenly remember that I have forgotten Diogenes. Will you put him in the last little chapter? After the word "favourite" in reference to Miss Tox, you can add, "except with Diogenes, who is growing old and wilful". Or, on the last page of all, after "and with them two children: boy and girl" (I quote from memory), you might say "and an old dog is generally in their company", or to that effect. Just what you think best.'

[Forster adopted the second suggestion. The passage reads: 'Autumn days are shining, and on the sea-beach there are often a young lady, and a white-haired gentleman. With them, or near them, are two children: boy and girl. And an old dog is generally in their company.' Forster must have decided that the attribution of wilfulness to the faithful Diogenes would mar the benevolent harmony of the close.]

327

A YOUNG poet, Mr. Laman Blanchard, sent Dickens a metrical contribution for *Household Words*, entitled 'Orient Pearls at random strung'; but Dickens returned them with 'Dear Blanchard, too much string—Yours. C.D.'

328

AN illustrious and very dear friend of mine,[1] though he was a double-dyed grandfather—witness a troop of grandchildren playing round him at Gad's Hill—disliked the appellation so much that he forbade the little ones to use it.

'What do they keep calling you?' said I.

'They are obedient children,' replied Dickens. 'Their infant lives would

[1] The narrator is W. P. Frith.

not be worth five minutes' purchase if they called me grandpa. My name is *wenerables* to them.'

As the word alternated between wenbull, winible, wenapple, etc. in the infantine chorus, I was obliged to ask for an interpretation.

329

ROBERT BROWNING (1812–89)

Sordello astonished his friends, and amazed the world. . . . Douglas Jerrold, when the work first appeared, was recruiting himself at Brighton after a long illness. In the progress of his convalescence a parcel arrived from London, which contained, among other things, this new volume of *Sordello*; the medical attendant had forbidden Mr. Jerrold the luxury of reading, but, owing to the absence of conjugal 'life guards' he indulged in the illicit enjoyment.

A few lines put Jerrold in a state of alarm. Sentence after sentence brought no consecutive thought to his brain. At last the idea crossed his mind that in illness his mental faculties had been wrecked. The perspiration rolled from his forehead, and smiting his head, he sat down in his sofa, crying, 'O, God, I *am* an idiot!' When his wife and her sister came, they were amused by his pushing the volume into their hands, and demanding what they thought of it. He watched them intently while they read—at last his wife said: 'I don't understand what the man means; it is gibberish.' The delighted humorist sank in his seat again: 'Thank God I am *not* an idiot.' . . .

But more illustrious personages than Douglas Jerrold were puzzled by the poem. Lord Tennyson manfully tackled it, but is reported to have admitted in bitterness of spirit: 'There were only two lines in it that I understood, and they were both lies: "Who will may hear Sordello's story told" and "Who would has heard Sordello's story told." ' Carlyle was equally candid: 'My wife', he writes, 'has read through *Sordello* without being able to make out whether "Sordello" was a man, or a city, or a book.'

330

THE new Chinese ambassador, a man of considerable literary ability, expressed a wish, shortly after his arrival in this country, of making the acquaintance of the principal English poets, and Mr. Browning was presented to him. The conversation turned to the compositions of the ambassador, who himself was a poet. 'What kind of poetry does His Excellency write?' inquired Mr. Browning. 'Pastoral, humorous, lyric, or what?' There was a pause for a short time. At length the interpreter said that His Excellency thought his poetry would be better described as 'enigmatic'.—'Surely', replied Mr. Browning, 'there ought, then, to be the deepest sympathy between us, for that is just the criticism which is brought against my own works, and I believe it to be a just one.'

331

MR. BROWNING had honoured me[1] with his company at dinner, and an unduly fervent admirer had button-holed him throughout a long evening, plying him with questions about what he meant by this line, and whom he intended by that character. It was more than flesh and blood could stand, and at last the master extricated himself from the grasp of the disciple, exclaiming with the most airy grace, 'But, my dear fellow, this is too bad. I am monopolizing you.'

332

TENNYSON told Browning he thought 'Sludge' too long. Browning answered, 'I hope *he* thought it too long!'—that is, Sludge, when the confession was forced from him. Sludge is Home, the Medium, of whom Browning told me today a great deal that was very amusing. Having witnessed a séance of Home's, at the house of a friend of Browning's, Browning was openly called upon to give his frank opinion on what had passed, in presence of Home and the company, upon which he declared with emphasis that so impudent a piece of imposture he never saw before in all his life, and so took his leave. Next day Browning's servant came into his room with a visitor's card, and close behind him followed the visitor himself—no other than Mr. Home, who advanced with a cordial smile and right hand outstretched in amity. He bore no ill-will—not he! Browning looked sternly at him (as he is very capable of doing) and pointing to the open door, not far from which is rather a steep staircase, said, 'If you are not out of that door in half a minute I'll fling you down the stairs.' Home attempted some expostulation, but Browning moved towards him, and the Medium disappeared with as much grace as he could manage. 'And now comes the best of it all,' said Browning.—'What do you suppose he says of me?—You'd never guess. He says to everybody,

[1] George W. E. Russell.

"How Browning hates me!—and how I love him!" ' He further explains Browning's animosity as arising out of a séance at Florence, where a 'spirit-wreath' was placed on Mrs. Browning's head, and none on her husband's.

333
JOHN WILLIAM BURGON (1813–88)

IN 1845 the Newdigate Prize for an English poem at Oxford was won by J. W. Burgon, afterwards Dean of Chichester. The subject was Petra. The successful poem was, on the whole, not much better and not much worse than the general run of such compositions; but it contained one couplet which Dean Stanley regarded as an absolute gem—a volume of description condensed into two lines:

> Match me such marvel, save in Eastern clime—
> A rose-red city, half as old as time.

The couplet was universally praised and quoted, and, as a natural consequence, parodied. There resided then (and long after) at Trinity College, Oxford, an extraordinary old don called Short.[1] When I was an undergraduate he was still tottering about, and we looked at him with interest because he had been Newman's tutor. To his case the parodist of the period, in a moment of inspiration, adapted Burgon's beautiful couplet, saying or singing:

> Match me such marvel, save in college port,
> That rose-red liquor, half as old as Short.

334
ANTHONY TROLLOPE (1815–82)

TAKING it as a whole, I regard *The Last Chronicle of Barset* as the best novel I have written. . . . Mrs. Proudie at the palace is a real woman; and the poor old dean dying at the deanery is also real. The archdeacon at his rectory is very real. There is a true savour of English country life all through the book. It was with many misgivings that I killed my old friend Mrs. Proudie. I could not, I think, have done it, but for a resolution taken and declared under circumstances of great momentary pressure.

[1] The Revd. Thomas Short (1789–1879).

It was thus that it came about. I was sitting one morning at work upon the novel at the end of the long drawing-room of the Athenaeum Club, as was then my wont when I had slept the previous night in London. As I was there, two clergymen, each with a magazine in his hand, seated themselves, one on one side of the fire and one on the other, close to me. They soon began to abuse what they were reading, and each was reading some part of some novel of mine. The gravamen of their complaint lay in the fact that I reintroduced the same characters so often! 'Here', said one, 'is that archdeacon whom we have had in every novel he has ever written.' 'And here', said the other, 'is the old duke whom he has talked about till everybody is tired of him. If I could not invent new characters, I would not write novels at all.' Then one of them fell foul of Mrs. Proudie. It was impossible for me not to hear their words, and almost impossible to hear them and be quiet. I got up, and standing between them, I acknowledged myself to be the culprit. 'As to Mrs. Proudie,' I said, 'I will go home and kill her before the week is over.' And so I did. The two gentlemen were utterly confounded, and one of them begged me to forget his frivolous observations.

I have sometimes regretted the deed, so great was my delight in writing about Mrs. Proudie, so thorough was my knowledge of all the little shades of her character . . . Since her time others have grown equally dear to me —Lady Glencora and her husband, for instance; but I have never dissevered myself from Mrs. Proudie, and still live much in company with her ghost.

335

I WILL now go back to the year 1867, in which I was still living at Waltham Cross. . . . The work I did during the twelve years that I remained there, from 1859 to 1871, was certainly very great. I feel confident that in amount no other writer contributed so much during that time to English literature. . . . Few men, I think, ever lived a fuller life. And I attribute the power of doing this altogether to the virtue of early hours. It was my practice to be at my table every morning at 5.30 a.m.; and it was also my practice to allow myself no mercy. An old groom, whose business it was to call me, and to whom I paid £5 a year extra for the duty, allowed himself no mercy. During all those years at Waltham Cross he never was once late with the coffee which it was his duty to bring me. I do not know that I ought not to feel that I owe more to him than to anyone else for the success I have had. By beginning at that hour I could complete my literary work before I dressed for breakfast.

336

[In 1880 Trollope published a *Life of Cicero* in two volumes.]

APPROACHING his subject, not as a scholar or historian, Trollope treats it in a style lively and amusing throughout. The sympathy with Cicero, especially in exile, is as delightful and refreshingly genuine as if Trollope were describing the difficulties of Phineas Finn or the troubles, during his wife's absence, of Mr. Furnival in *Orley Farm*. There are the same enlightening good sense and shrewdness in the description of Roman political parties and their leaders as form the best portion of the novels describing the rivalries of Daubeny and Gresham, and analysing the personal or political situations so severely testing the wisdom and the patience of Mr. Palliser and the Duke of Omnium. Of course, *Cicero* brought criticisms from a few experts. T. A. Trollope, Anthony's elder brother, as well as severe disciplinarian in their Winchester days, had been a classical master under Jeune at King Edward's School, Birmingham. He had therefore cultivated a more exact kind of learning than Anthony. 'You ought', he said after *Cicero* came out, 'to have let me correct the Latin words in your proof. As it is, having, in your first volume, tried successively Quintillian and Quintilian, in your second you finally relapse into Quintillian. In another error you are at least consistent; for Pætus is always given for Pœtus. Indeed,' he continued, 'these diphthongs have been among your worst enemies, because œdile is your standing version for ædile, while by Œschilus I know—what others could only guess—that you mean Æschylus.'

337
CHARLOTTE BRONTË (1816–55)

IN July 1847 a parcel containing a MS. reached our office, addressed to the firm,[1] but bearing also the scored-out addresses of three or four other publishing houses; showing that the parcel had been previously submitted to other publishers. This was not calculated to prepossess us in favour of the MS. It was clear that we were offered what had been already rejected elsewhere.

The parcel contained the MS. of *The Professor*, by 'Currer Bell', a book which was published after Charlotte Brontë's death. Mr. Williams, the

[1] Smith, Elder. This story is told by George Smith.

'reader' to the firm, read the MS., and said that it evinced great literary power, but he had doubts as to its being successful as a publication. We decided that we should write to 'Currer Bell' a letter of appreciative criticism declining the work, but expressing the opinion that he could produce a book which could command success. Before, however, our letter was despatched, there came a letter from 'Currer Bell' containing a postage-stamp for our reply, it having been hinted to the writer by 'an experienced friend' that publishers often refrained from answering communications unless a postage-stamp was furnished for the purpose! Charlotte Brontë has herself described the effect our letter had on her:

As a forlorn hope, he tried one publishing house more. Ere long, in a much shorter space than that on which experience had taught him to calculate, there came a letter, which he opened in the dreary anticipation of finding two hard hopeless lines, intimating that 'Messrs. Smith, Elder, & Co. were not disposed to publish the MS.', and, instead, he took out of the envelope a letter of two pages. He read it trembling. It declined, indeed, to publish that tale for business reasons, but it discussed its merits and demerits so courteously, so considerately, in a spirit so rational, with a discrimination so enlightened, that this very refusal cheered the author better than a vulgarly expressed acceptance would have done. It was added, that a work in three volumes would meet with careful attention.

The writer of this letter was, as I have said, Mr. W. Smith Williams. . . .

In reply to Mr. Williams's letter came a brief note from 'Currer Bell', expressing grateful appreciation of the attention which had been given to the MS., and saying that the author was on the point of finishing another book, which would be sent to us as soon as completed.

The second MS. was *Jane Eyre*. Here again 'Currer Bell's' suspicion as to the excessive parsimony of London publishers in regard to postage-stamps found expression in the letter accompanying the MS. She wrote:

I find I cannot prepay the carriage of the parcel, as money for that purpose is not received at the small station where it is left. If, when you acknowledge the receipt of the MS. you would have the goodness to mention the amount charged on delivery, I will immediately transmit it in postage-stamps.

The MS. of *Jane Eyre* was read by Mr. Williams in due course. He brought it to me on a Saturday, and said that he would like me to read it. There were no Saturday half-holidays in those days, and, as was usual, I did not reach home until late. I had made an appointment with a friend for Sunday morning; I was to meet him about twelve o'clock, at a place some two or three miles from our house, and ride with him into the country.

After breakfast on Sunday morning I took the MS. of *Jane Eyre* to my little study, and began to read it. The story quickly took me captive. Before twelve o'clock my horse came to the door, but I could not put the book down. I scribbled two or three lines to my friend, saying I was very sorry that circumstances had arisen to prevent my meeting him, sent the note off by my groom, and went on reading the MS. Presently the servant came to tell me that luncheon was ready; I asked him to bring me a sandwich and a glass of wine, and still went on with *Jane Eyre*. Dinner came; for me the meal was a very hasty one, and before I went to bed that night I had finished reading the manuscript.

The next day we wrote to 'Currer Bell' accepting the book for publication. I need say nothing about the success which the book achieved, and the speculations as to whether it was written by a man or a woman. For my own part I never had much doubt on the subject of the writer's sex; but then I had the advantage over the general public of having the handwriting of the author before me. There were qualities of style, too, and turns of expression, which satisfied me that 'Currer Bell' was a woman, an opinion in which Mr. Williams concurred. We were bound, however, to respect the writer's anonymity, and our letters continued to be addressed to 'Currer Bell, Esq.' Her sisters were always referred to in the correspondence as 'Messrs. Ellis and Acton Bell'. The works of Ellis and Acton Bell had been published by a Mr. Newby, on terms which rather depleted the scanty purses of the authors. When we were about to publish *Shirley*—the work which, in the summer of 1848, succeeded *Jane Eyre*—we endeavoured to make an arrangement with an American publisher to sell him advance sheets of the book, in order to give him an advantage in regard to time over other American publishers. There was, of course, no copyright with America in those days. We were met during the negotiations with our American correspondents by the statement that Mr. Newby had informed them that he was about to publish the next book by the author of *Jane Eyre*, under her other *nom de plume* of Acton Bell—Currer, Ellis, and Acton Bell being, in fact, according to him, one person. We wrote to 'Currer Bell' to say that we should be glad to be in a position to contradict the statement, adding at the same time we were quite sure Mr. Newby's assertion was untrue. Charlotte Brontë has related how the letter affected her. She was persuaded that her honour was impugned. 'With rapid decision,' says Mrs. Gaskell in her *Life of Charlotte Brontë*, 'Charlotte and her sister Anne resolved that they should start for London that very day in order to prove their separate identity to Messrs. Smith, Elder, and Co.'

With what haste and energy the sisters plunged into what was, for them, a serious expedition, how they reached London at eight o'clock on a Saturday morning, took lodgings in the 'Chapter' coffee-house in Paternoster Row, and, after an agitated breakfast, set out on a pilgrimage to my office in Cornhill, is told at length in Mrs. Gaskell's *Life of Charlotte Brontë*.

That particular Saturday morning I was at work in my room, when a clerk reported that two ladies wished to see me. I was very busy and sent out to ask their names. The clerk returned to say that the ladies declined to give their names, but wished to see me on a private matter. After a moment's hesitation I told him to show them in. I was in the midst of my correspondence, and my thoughts were far from 'Currer Bell' and *Jane Eyre*. Two rather quaintly dressed little ladies, pale-faced and anxious-looking, walked into my room; one of them came forward and presented me with a letter addressed, in my own handwriting, to 'Currer Bell, Esq.' I noticed that the letter had been opened, and said, with some sharpness, 'Where did you get this from?' 'From the post-office,' was the reply; 'it was addressed to me. We have both come that you might have ocular proof that there are at least two of us.' This then was 'Currer Bell' in person. I need hardly say that I was at once keenly interested, not to say excited. Mr. Williams was called down and introduced, and I began to plan all sorts of attentions to our visitors. I tried to persuade them to come and stay at our house. This they positively declined to do, but they agreed that I should call with my sister and take them to the Opera in the evening. She has herself given an account of her own and her sister Anne's sensations on that occasion: how they dressed for the Opera in their plain, high-necked dresses:

Fine ladies and gentlemen glanced at us, as we stood by the box-door, which was not yet opened, with a slight graceful superciliousness, quite warranted by the circumstances. Still I felt pleasurably excited, in spite of headache, sickness, and conscious clownishness; and I saw Anne was calm and gentle, which she always is. The performance was Rossini's *Barber of Seville*—very brilliant, though I fancy there are things I should like better. We got home after one o'clock. We had never been in bed the night before; had been in constant excitement for twenty-four hours; you may imagine we were tired.

My mother called upon them the next day. The sisters, after barely three days in London, returned to Haworth. In what condition of mind and body those few days left them is graphically told by Charlotte Brontë herself:

On Tuesday morning we left London, laden with books Mr. Smith had given us, and got safely home. A more jaded wretch than I looked, it would be difficult to conceive. I was thin when I went, but I was meagre indeed when I returned, my face looking grey and very old, with strange deep lines ploughed in it—my eyes staring unnaturally. I was weak and yet restless.

This is the only occasion on which I saw Anne Brontë. She was a gentle, quiet, rather subdued person, by no means pretty, yet of a pleasing appearance. Her manner was curiously expressive of a wish for protection and encouragement, a kind of constant appeal which invited sympathy.

338

One of the most notable persons who ever came into our old bow-windowed drawing-room in Young Street[1] is a guest never to be forgotten by me, a tiny, delicate, little person, whose small hand nevertheless grasped a mighty lever which set all the literary world of that day vibrating. I can still see the scene quite plainly!—the hot summer evening, the open windows, the carriage driving to the door as we all sat silent and expectant; my father, who rarely waited, waiting with us; our governess and my sister and I all in a row, and prepared for the great event. We saw the carriage stop, and out of it sprang the active, well-knit figure of young Mr. George Smith, who was bringing Miss Brontë to see our father. My father, who had been walking up and down the room, goes out into the hall to meet his guests, and then after a moment's delay the doors open wide, and the two gentlemen come in, leading a tiny, delicate, serious, little lady, with fair straight hair, and steady eyes. She may be a little over thirty; she is dressed in a little *barège* dress with a pattern of faint green moss. She enters in mittens, in silence, in seriousness; our hearts are beating with wild excitement. This then is the authoress, the unknown power whose books have set all London talking, reading, speculating; some people even say our father wrote the books—the wonderful books. To say that we little girls had been given *Jane Eyre* to read scarcely represents the facts of the case; to say that we had taken it without leave, read bits here and bits there, been carried away by an undreamed-of and hitherto unimagined whirlwind into things, times, places, all utterly absorbing and at the same time absolutely unintelligible to us, would more accurately describe our states of mind on that summer's evening as we look at Jane Eyre—the great Jane Eyre—the tiny little lady. The moment is so breathless that dinner comes as a relief to the solemnity of the occasion, and we all smile as my father stoops to offer his arm; for, genius though she may be, Miss Brontë can barely reach his elbow. My own personal impressions are that she is somewhat grave and stern, specially to forward little girls who wish to chatter; Mr. George Smith has since told me how she afterwards remarked upon my father's wonderful forbearance and gentleness with our uncalled-for incursions into the conversation. She sat gazing at him with kindling eyes of interest; lighting up with a sort of illumination every now and then as she answered him. I can see her bending forward over the table, not eating, but listening to what he said as he carved the dish before him.

I think it must have been on this very occasion that my father invited

[1] Thackeray's home. This meeting with Charlotte Brontë is narrated by his daughter, Anne, Lady Ritchie.

some of his friends in the evening to meet Miss Brontë—for everybody was interested and anxious to see her. Mrs. Crowe, the reciter of ghost-stories, was there. Mrs. Brookfield, Mrs. Carlyle, Mr. Carlyle himself was present, so I am told, railing at the appearance of cockneys upon Scotch mountain sides; there were also too many Americans for his taste, 'but the Americans were as gods compared to the cockneys', says the philosopher. Besides the Carlyles, there were Mrs. Elliott and Miss Perry, Mrs. Procter and her daughter, most of my father's habitual friends and companions. In the recent life of Lord Houghton I was amused to see a note quoted in which Lord Houghton also was convened. Would that he had been present!—perhaps the party would have gone off better. It was a gloomy and a silent evening. Every one waited for the brilliant conversation which never began at all. Miss Brontë retired to the sofa in the study, and murmured a low word now and then to our kind governess, Miss Truelock. The room looked very dark, the lamp began to smoke a little, the conversation grew dimmer and more dim, the ladies sat round still expectant, my father was too much perturbed by the gloom and the silence to be able to cope with it at all. Mrs. Brookfield, who was in the doorway by the study, near the corner in which Miss Brontë was sitting, leant forward with a little commonplace, since brilliance was not to be the order of the evening. 'Do you like London, Miss Brontë', she said; another silence, a pause, then Miss Brontë answers, 'Yes and No', very gravely; Mrs. Brookfield has herself reported the conversation. My sister and I were much too young to be bored in those days; alarmed, oppressed we might be, but not yet bored. A party was a party, a lioness was a lioness; and—shall I confess it?—at that time an extra dish of biscuits was enough to mark the evening. We felt all the importance of the occasion; tea spread in the dining-room, ladies in the drawing-room; we roamed about inconveniently, no doubt, and excitedly, and in one of my excursions crossing the hall, after Miss Brontë had left, I was surprised to see my father opening the front door with his hat on. He put his fingers to his lips, walked out into the darkness, and shut the door quietly behind him. When I went back to the drawing-room again, the ladies asked me where he was. I vaguely answered that I thought he was coming back. I was puzzled at the time, nor was it all made clear to me till long afterwards, when one day Mrs. Procter asked me if I knew what had happened once when my father had invited a party to meet Jane Eyre at his house. It was one of the dullest evenings she had ever spent in her life, she said. And then with a good deal of humour she described the situation—the ladies who had all come expecting so much delightful conversation, and the gloom and the constraint, and how finally, overwhelmed by the situation, my father had quietly left the room, left the house, and gone off to his club.

339
BENJAMIN JOWETT (1817–93)

THE word 'research' as a university ideal had, indeed, been ominously spoken in Oxford by that extremely cantankerous person, Mark Pattison, some years ago; but the notion of this ideal, threatening as it did to discredit the whole tutorial and examinational system which was making Oxford into the highest of high schools for boys, was received there with anger and contempt. In Balliol, the birthplace and most illustrious home of this great system, it was regarded with especial scorn. If the prize fellowships and the fellowships of All Souls were to be no longer regarded as the legitimate reward of those who had won First Classes in the Schools; if the means they provided were not to be spent in helping ambitious young men on the first rungs of the ladder of worldly success, but used, as Mark Pattison's ill-mannered supporters suggested, in the maintenance of researchers, ambitious of the fame of scholars, would not the whole tutorial system be deprived of one of its important features, and the university endowments be seriously abused? This ideal of endowment for research was particularly shocking to Benjamin Jowett, the great inventor of the tutorial system which it threatened. I[1] remember once, when staying with him at Malvern, inadvertently pronouncing the ill-omened word. 'Research!' the Master exclaimed. 'Research!' he said. 'A mere excuse for idleness; it has never achieved, and will never achieve any results of the slightest value.' At this sweeping statement I protested; whereupon I was peremptorily told, if I knew of any such results of value, to name them without delay. My ideas on the subject were by no means profound, and anyhow it is difficult to give definite instances of a general proposition at a moment's notice. The only thing that came into my head was the recent discovery, of which I had read somewhere, that on striking a patient's kneecap sharply he would give an involuntary kick, and that by the vigour or lack of vigour of this 'knee jerk', as it is called, a judgement could be formed of his general state of health.

'I don't believe a word of it,' Jowett replied. 'Just give my knee a tap.'

I was extremely reluctant to perform this irreverent act upon his person, but the Master angrily insisted, and the undergraduate could do nothing but obey. The little leg reacted with a vigour which almost alarmed me, and must, I think, have considerably disconcerted that elderly and eminent opponent of research.

[1] Logan Pearsall Smith (1865–1946).

340

PROFESSOR JOWETT . . . is one of the lions of Oxford. That town is subjected to constant inroads of tourists, all of whom crave a sight of the famous professor. It so happened, while he was engaged on his translation of Plato, that a guide discovered the professor's study-window looked into the Broad Street. Coming with his menagerie under the window, the guide would begin: 'This, ladies and gentlemen, is Balliol College, one of the very holdest in the huniversity, and famous for the herudition of its scholars. The 'ead of Balliol College is called the Master. The present Master of Balliol is the celebrated Professor Benjamin Jowett, Regius Professor of Greek. Those are Professor Jowett's study-windows, and there' (here the ruffian would stoop down, take up a handful of gravel and throw it against the panes, bringing poor Jowett, livid with fury, to the window) 'ladies and gentlemen, is Professor Benjamin Jowett himself.'

341
JOHN RUSKIN (1819–1900)

[Thomas Pringle (d. 1834) was an acquaintance of the Ruskin family during Ruskin's boyhood, editor of *Friendship's Offering*, and (in Ruskin's words) 'a pious Scotch missionary, and minor—very much minor-key poet'.]

MR. PRINGLE visited us at Herne Hill, heard the traditions of my literary life, expressed some interest in its farther progress,—and sometimes took a copy of verses away in his pocket. He was the first person who intimated to my father and mother, with some decision, that there were as yet no wholly trustworthy indications of my one day occupying a higher place in English literature than either Milton or Byron; and accordingly I think none of us attached much importance to his opinions. . . . He himself found interest enough in my real love of nature and ready faculty of rhyme, to induce him to read and criticize for me some of my verses with attention; and at last, as a sacred Eleusinian initiation and Delphic pilgrimage, to take me in his hand one day when he had a visit to pay to the poet Rogers.

The old man, previously warned of my admissible claims, in Mr. Pringle's sight, to the beatitude of such introduction, was sufficiently gracious to me, though the cultivation of germinating genius was never held by Mr. Rogers to be an industry altogether delectable to genius in its zenith. Moreover, I was unfortunate in the line of observations by which, in return for his notice, I endeavoured to show myself worthy of it. I congratulated him with enthusiasm on the beauty of the engravings by which his poems were illustrated—but betrayed, I fear me, at the same time some lack of an equally vivid interest in the composition of the poems themselves. At all events, Mr. Pringle—I thought at the time, somewhat abruptly—diverted the conversation to subjects connected with Africa. These were doubtless more calculated to interest the polished minstrel of St. James's Place; but again I fell into misdemeanours by allowing my own attention, as my wandering eyes too frankly confessed, to determine itself on the pictures glowing from the crimson-silk walls; and accordingly, after we had taken leave, Mr. Pringle took occasion to advise me that, in future, when I was in the company of distinguished men, I should listen more attentively to their conversation.

342

GEORGE ELIOT (1819–80)

MY uncle William Rossetti Mr. James[1] considered to be an unbelievable bore. He once heard him recount how he had seen George Eliot proposed to by Herbert Spencer on the leads of the terrace at Somerset House. . . .

'You would think', Mr. James exclaimed with indignation, his dark eyes really flashing, 'that a man would make something out of a story like *that*. But the way he told it was like this', and heightening and thinning his tones into a sort of querulous official organ[2], Mr. James quoted: 'I have as a matter of fact frequently meditated on the motives which induced the Lady's refusal of one so distinguished; and after mature consideration I have arrived at the conclusion that although Mr. Spencer with correctness went down upon one knee and grasped the Lady's hand he completely omitted the ceremony of removing his high hat, a proceeding which her sense of the occasion might have demanded . . . '—'Is that', Mr. James concluded, 'the way to tell *that* story?'

343

THE impact of *Middlemarch*, which was even stronger than the sales indicate, came more from word of mouth than from reviews. . . . Taine, whom Morley tried in vain to persuade to review the book in the *Fort-*

[1] i.e. Henry James. The narrator of this anecdote is Ford Madox Ford. [2] W. M. Rossetti was a civil servant on the Board of Inland Revenue (1845–94) See also No. 362.

nightly, pronounced George Eliot 'the greatest of English romancers'. When Bulstrode was being described in Book VII, a West End clergyman, in a sermon on Hosea, said: 'Many of you no doubt have read the work which that great teacher George Eliot is now publishing and have shuddered as I shuddered at the awful dissection of a guilty conscience. Well, *that* is what I mean by the prophetic spirit.' Judge Fitzgerald reported that 'at the opening of the Dublin Exhibition he was struck with the attention of the Archbishop[1] to the interior of his hat, which at first he took for devout listening to the speeches, but on close examination saw he was reading something, and as this was so intent he was prompted to look also into the hat, and found the Archbishop had *Middlemarch* there laid open—what a much better way of listening to "opening speeches"!'

344

[One of Henry James's early acquaintances in England was Mrs. Richard Greville, whom he was to refer to in a letter as 'on the whole the greatest fool I have ever known'. On 19 October 1878, she made one of her frequent visits to her neighbours George Eliot and George Henry Lewes, carrying with her on this occasion the copy of *The Europeans* which James had given her. Then on 1 November, on an afternoon of incessant rain, she had paid another of her unsolicited and gushing visits, this time accompanied by James, who recalls his complicated impressions on that occasion. What he doesn't say is that Lewes was now a dying man, and by the end of the month was dead.]

I HAD driven over with Mrs. Greville from Milford Cottage, in Surrey, to the villa George Eliot and George Lewes had not long before built themselves, and which they much inhabited, at Witley—this indeed, I well remember, in no great flush of assurance that my own measure of our intended felicity would be quite that of my buoyant hostess. . . . What had come most to characterize the Leweses to my apprehension was that there couldn't be a thing in the world about which they weren't, and on the most conceded and assured grounds, almost scientifically particular; which presumption, however, only added to the relevance of one's learning how such a matter as their relation with Mrs. Greville could in accordance with noble consistencies be carried on. I could trust *her* for it perfectly, as she knew no law but that of innocent and exquisite aberration, never wanting and never less than consecrating, and I fear I but took refuge for the rest in declining all responsibility. I remember trying to say to myself that, even such as we were, our visit couldn't but scatter a little the weight of cloud on the Olympus we scaled—given the dreadful drenching afternoon we were after all an imaginable short solace there; and this indeed would have borne me through to the end save for an incident which,

[1] Richard Chenevix Trench. See No. 301.

with a quite ideal logic, left our adventure an approved ruin. I see again our bland, benign, commiserating hostess beside the fire in a chill desert of a room where the master of the house guarded the opposite hearthstone, and I catch once more the impression of no occurrence of anything at all appreciable but their liking us to have come, with our terribly trivial contribution, mainly from a prevision of how they should more devoutly like it when we departed. It is remarkable, but the occasion yields me no single echo of a remark on the part of any of us—nothing more than the sense that our great author herself peculiarly suffered from the fury of the elements, and that they had about them rather the minimum of the paraphernalia of reading and writing, not to speak of that of tea, a conceivable feature of the hour, but which was not provided for. Again I felt touched with privilege, but not, as in '69,[1] with a form of it redeemed from barrenness by a motion of my own, and the taste of barrenness was in fact in my mouth under the effect of our taking leave. We did so with considerable flourish till we had passed out to the hall again, indeed to the door of the waiting carriage, toward which G. H. Lewes himself all sociably, *then* above all conversingly, wafted us—yet staying me by a sudden remembrance before I had entered the brougham and signing me to wait while he repaired his omission. I returned to the doorstep, whence I still see him reissue from the room we had just left and hurry toward me across the hall shaking high the pair of blue-bound volumes his allusion to the uninvited, the verily importunate loan of which by Mrs. Greville had lingered on the air after his dash in quest of them; 'Ah those books—take them away, please, away, away!' I hear him unreservedly plead while he thrusts them again at me, and I scurry back into our conveyance, where, and where only, settled afresh with my companion, I venture to assure myself of the horrid truth that had squinted at me as I relieved our good friend of his superfluity. What indeed was this superfluity but the two volumes of my own precious 'last'—we were still in the blest age of volumes—presented by its author to the lady of Milford Cottage, and by her, misguided votary, dropped with the best conscience in the world into the Witley abyss, out of which it had jumped with violence, under the touch of accident, straight up again into my own exposed face?

The bruise inflicted there I remember feeling for the moment only as sharp, such a mixture of delightful small questions at once salved it over and such a charm in particular for me to my recognizing that this particular wrong—inflicted all unawares, which exactly made it sublime—was the only rightness of our visit. Our hosts hadn't so much as connected book with author, or author with visitor, or visitor with anything but the convenience of his ridding them of an unconsidered trifle; grudging as

[1] He had first met George Eliot in April 1869, and had been of some service on that occasion by dashing out to summon a doctor for one of Lewes's sons.

they so justifiedly did the impingement of such matters on their consciousness. The vivid demonstration of one's failure to penetrate there had been in the sweep of Lewes's gesture, which could scarcely have been bettered by his actually wielding a broom.

345
CHARLES KINGSLEY (1819–75)

[Charles Kingsley, who had been Professor of Modern History at Cambridge, resigned his chair in 1869 owing to ill health. He was succeeded by John Robert Seeley, author of a popular and controversial religious work, *Ecce Homo* (1865). The 'late Master of Trinity' is William Hepworth Thompson (1810–86).]

OF the late Master of Trinity—Dr. Thompson—it was said: 'He casteth forth his ice like morsels. Who is able to abide his frost?' . . . He was nothing if not critical. At Seeley's inaugural lecture as Professor of History his only remark was—'Well, well. I did not think we could so soon have had occasion to regret poor Kingsley.'

346
HERBERT SPENCER (1820–1903)

IN a discussion which took place at a reception at G. H. Lewes's, somebody asserted that everyone had written a tragedy. Lewes agreed with the statement, saying, 'Yes, everyone—even Herbert Spencer.'—'Ah,' interposed Huxley, 'I know what the catastrophe would be—an induction killed by a fact.'

347
MATTHEW ARNOLD (1822–88)

WITH his wife and his daughter Lucy, Arnold sailed from Liverpool in October 1883 on the Cunard liner, *Servia*, and was met at the New York pier by Andrew Carnegie and his secretary . . .

Everyone has heard the story of Arnold's pointing to a plate of pancakes and saying to his wife, 'Do try one, my dear, they are not nearly so nasty as they look.' But Dr. Leonard has found the story told, as at first hand, by a score of hostesses, and he concludes that it is apocryphal. . . . Still, it was increasingly whispered about that Arnold was a difficult and arrogant guest. America, proud of having culture, proud of having no culture, watched him with sharp eyes; his whiskers, his eyeglass, his clothes, his accent, his complexion, all came under scrutiny and comment. The knowledge that he had come to the country to make money gave a handle to irritation—that handle by which America can always lay hold of the foreign lecturer who comes to talk about things of the spirit; the attitude of Arnold's managers, apparently no more than business-like, added to the irritation. James Whitcomb Riley met Arnold on the train to Binghamton, N.Y., and found significant the care with which he stowed away his 2¢ change from a 3¢ newspaper; he admits that Arnold is poor but he finds the gesture distressing enough to make him say, ' 'Tis very good to be an American.'

And Arnold was cold; one wanted, said the Detroit *News*, to poke him in the ribs and say, 'Hello Matt! Won't you have suthin'?' This friendly desire was perhaps what Arnold reprobated in democracy, its fear of distinction and its loss of the discipline of respect.

348

I AM ashamed to say that in spite of encouragement from Mother, and delightful hours spent with Aunt Fanny listening to poetry, I was a very backward child and could not read at six years old . . .[1]

Mother failed to make me study, and one day she said: 'I am going to bring someone to talk to you. He is a great poet, and perhaps he could persuade you to learn to read.'

This was Matthew Arnold, a friend of Aunt Fanny, whose poems she used to read to me. I was thrilled to see him, and after all these years I can still see his tall, angular figure, as he stood with his back to the fire looking down upon me from what seemed to me an immense height. He never smiled that day. His whiskers were thicker and longer than any I had seen; and I was glad that Father wore a neatly trimmed beard. This stern-looking man then sat down and took me on his knee while he talked to me about books, seeking to fire my interest; and in this he succeeded, for I could have listened to him all day. Then he stopped talking of poetry, and said very seriously:

'Your mother tells me that you do not know how to read, and are refusing to learn. It surprises me very much that a little girl of six should

[1] The narrator is Lina Waterfield.

not know how to read, and expects to be read to. It is disgraceful, and you must promise me to learn at once; if you don't, I shall have to put your father and mother in prison.'

I was startled and frightened by his threat, and at the same time very puzzled that a poet could put people in prison. I asked Father whether he could put him in prison.

Father hesitated: 'No, I don't think he could, although he *is* a Government Inspector of Schools.'

I still felt mystified, but his threat made me start in earnest to work with my nursery governess, and, to my surprise and pleasure, I found I could read *Grimm's Fairy Tales* within a few weeks.

349

WILKIE COLLINS (1824–89)

IMMEDIATELY after the production of *The Woman in White*, when all England was admiring the arch-villainy of 'Fosco', the author received a letter from a lady who has since figured very largely in the public view. She congratulated him upon his success with somewhat icy cheer, and then said, 'But, Mr. Collins, the great failure of your book is your villain. Excuse me if I say, you really do not know a villain. Your Count Fosco is a very poor one, and when next you want a character of that description I trust you will not disdain to come to me. *I* know a villain, and have one in my eye at this moment that would far eclipse anything that I have read of in books. Don't think that I am drawing upon my imagination. The man is alive and constantly under my gaze. *In fact he is my own husband.*' The lady was the wife of Edward Bulwer Lytton.[1]

350

EVERYBODY has heard of the storm created by the publication of *Tess*[2] and *Jude*, but much earlier than this, the love scenes in *Two on a Tower* had been censured as unpleasantly suggestive, while *The Return of the Native*—*The Return of the Native* of all books—had been described in the pages of a prominent literary journal as 'betraying the influence' of

[1] In 1836 Lord Lytton's unhappy relations with his wife had led to a legal separation. In 1839 Lady Lytton published a novel called *Cheveley, or the Man of Honour*, in which her husband was the villain. She was certified insane in 1858, and spent a short time in the care of a physician, but was soon discharged. She died in 1882. [2] See No. 381.

decadent French fiction. Earlier still, and still more amazingly, Wilkie Collins had contrived to offend the innocents. . . . An editorial note which appeared in *The Graphic* of 30 January 1875 reveals the remarkable state of mind that had been created by an attitude of excessive moral vigilance.

In last week's instalment of *The Law and the Lady* the following paragraph, which occurs on page 83, column 2, was printed thus:—'He caught my hand in his and covered it with kisses. In the indignation of the moment I cried out for help.' In the author's proof the passage stood as follows:—'He caught my hand in his, and devoured it with kisses. His lips burnt me like fire. He twisted himself suddenly in the chair, and wound his arm round my waist. In the terror and indignation of the moment, vainly struggling with him, I cried out for help.' The editor of this journal suppressed a portion of the paragraph on the ground that the description as originally given was objectionable. Mr. Wilkie Collins having since informed us, through his legal advisers, that, according to the terms of his agreement with the proprietors of *The Graphic*, his proofs are to be published *verbatim* from his MS., the passage in question is here given in its original form.

One up to Wilkie! we may think, but this was not to be the last word. Our editor perfectly foresaw *his* opportunity, and sure enough, when *The Law and the Lady* had run its course as a serial and was issued in three volumes, *The Graphic*, instead of the customary review, simply printed beneath the title of the work an apology to its readers for having provided them with a tale the true nature of which had only been discovered after its first chapters were in print.

351

DANTE GABRIEL ROSSETTI (1828–82)

[In May 1860, after a long engagement, Dante Gabriel Rossetti and Elizabeth Eleanor Siddal were married. When they first met she was a dressmaker's assistant, a beautiful and talented young woman who had sat as a model for one of Rossetti's friends, and who was the Beatrice of Rossetti's own pictures. Hall Caine, who became a close friend of Rossetti in his last years, relates the tragic outcome of this marriage and its strange sequel.]

THEY were living in rooms in Chatham Place, by the old Blackfriars Bridge, and one evening, about half-past six, having been invited to dine with friends at a hotel in Leicester Square, they got into a carriage to go. It had been a bad day for the young wife, and they had hardly reached the Strand when her nervousness became distressing to Rossetti, and he wished her to return. She was unwilling to do so, and they went on to their appointment; but it may be assumed that her condition did not improve, for at eight o'clock they were back at home.

Soon after that Rossetti left his wife preparing to retire for the night, and went out again apparently to walk. When he returned at half-past eleven o'clock, he found his rooms full of a strong odour of laudanum; his wife was breathing stertorously and lying unconscious on the bed. He called a doctor, who saw at once, what was only too obvious, that the lady had taken an overdose of her accustomed sleeping draught. Other doctors were summoned, and every effort was made to save the patient's life; but after lingering several hours without recovering consciousness for a moment—therefore without offering a word of explanation—towards seven o'clock in the morning she died. . . .

This was in 1862, no more than two years after the marriage that had been waited for so long. The blow to Rossetti was a terrible one. It was some days before he seemed to realize fully the loss that had befallen him; but after that his grief knew no bounds, and it first expressed itself in a way that was full of the tragic grace and beauty of a great renunciation.

Many of his poems had been inspired by and addressed to his wife, and at her request he had copied them out, sometimes from memory, into a little book which she had given him for this purpose. With this book in his hand, on the day of her funeral, he walked into the room where her body lay, and quite unmindful of the presence of others, he spoke to his dead wife as though she could hear, saying the poems it contained had been written to her and for her and she must take them with her to the grave. With these words, or words to the same effect, he placed the little volume in the coffin by the side of his wife's face and wrapped it round with her beautiful golden hair, and it was buried with her in Highgate Cemetery. . . .

Thus seven years passed, and during that time Rossetti, who frequently immersed himself in the aims and achievements of his friends, and witnessed their rise to fame and honour, began to think with pain of the aspirations as a poet which he had himself renounced, and to cast backward glances at the book he had buried in his wife's coffin. That book contained the only perfect copy of his poems, other copies being either incomplete or unrevised; and it is hardly to be wondered at that he asked himself at length if it could not be regained. The impulse of grief or regret, or even remorse, that had prompted him to the act of renunciation had been satisfied, and for seven years he had denied himself the reward of his best poetical effort—was not his penance at an end? It was doing no good to the dead to leave hidden in the grave the most beautiful works he had been able to produce—was it not his duty to the living, to himself, and perhaps even to God, to recover and publish them?

. . . According to his own account given to me twelve years afterwards, the preparations were endless before the work could be begun. But at length the licence of the Home Secretary was obtained, the faculty of the Consistory Court was granted, and one night, seven and a half years after the burial, a fire was built by the side of the grave of Rossetti's wife in Highgate Cemetery, the grave was opened, the coffin was raised to the surface, and the buried book was removed. . . .

The volume was not much the worse for the years it had lain in the earth, but nevertheless it was found necessary to take it back to Rossetti, that illegible words might be deciphered and deficiencies filled in. This was done, with what results of fresh distress can easily be imagined; and then, with certain additions of subsequent sonnets, the manuscript was complete. Under the simple title of *Poems* it was published in 1870, fifteen years after the greater part of it was produced, and when the author was forty-two.

The success of the book was immediate and immense, six or seven considerable editions being called for in rapid succession.

352

GEORGE MEREDITH (1828–1909)

ROBERT LOUIS STEVENSON numbers *The Egoist* among the books which have most powerfully influenced him, and owns to having read it seven or eight times. 'Meredith read me some chapters', he says, 'before it was published, and at last I could stand it no longer. I interrupted him, and said, "Now, Meredith, own up—you have drawn Sir Willoughby Patterne from *me*!" Meredith laughed, and said, "No, no, my dear fellow, I've taken him from all of us, but principally from myself." '

353

[Alfred Sutro obtained permission from Meredith to make a stage adaptation of *The Egoist*, and Meredith collaborated with him.]

ONE typical instance of this collaboration is worth recording. The scene between Clara Middleton and Horace de Craye at the railway station had been, at my request, specially re-written by Meredith—the scene in which Clara is trying to escape from Sir Willoughby, and de Craye is assuring her of his devotion. Meredith read me the new dialogue; it was brilliant and splendid, but, alas, far too long! He looked inquiringly at me; I was silent, I did not know what to say. 'Remember, my dear fellow,' came from him, 'remember that we are collaborators. Tell me exactly what you think.' Thus encouraged, I said that de Craye's protestations after Clara had told him that she merely regarded him as a friend were too long—for an act that was already lengthy. He agreed, and pondered for a moment. 'I have it,' he said, 'I have it! After Clara has mentioned the word friendship, Horace shall protest: "Am I to banquet on that wafer?" ' Gloriously Meredithian—and so superbly adequate!

354

HAROLD LOWRY, the specialist in Victorian literature, . . . visiting London before the war, became acquainted with a banker who lived in the same hotel in which he was staying. The banker was in the habit of speaking about George Meredith, though never as Meredith the novelist and poet. When Lowry had got to know him sufficiently well, he asked the banker why he was so fascinated by Meredith. 'Meredith', the Londoner replied, 'after his first unsuccessful marriage wanted to wed the woman who later became my mother-in-law. Her family thought his talents were more literary than domestic and discouraged the match. But Meredith always remained her devoted friend and the friend of my wife; he wrote my wife a long letter on our wedding day. I'm sorry that we didn't talk of this before. Just three weeks ago in that very fireplace I burned some seventy-five of Meredith's letters—they took up room, you know. Anyhow, they would not have interested you very much, for they were just personal letters!'

355

WILLIAM MICHAEL ROSSETTI (1829–1919)

GOSSE was much in the self-sufficing and exclusive society of the surviving Pre-Raphaelites, sauntering in that fenced and Olympian circle, equally at ease with high priest and acolyte. He abounded in recollections of their idiosyncrasies, their passionate dedication to art, and their sectional differences of opinion. It was at a time when 'anarchist' was as much on people's lips as 'Bolshevik' in the present day; soft dark hats, cloaks and spreading neckties, were common to artist and revolutionary. Gosse entering a crowded omnibus found himself opposite W. M. Rossetti and his daughter.—'I understand you are an anarchist,' said Gosse, urged to the remark by the appearance of his friend. 'I must differentiate,' replied Rossetti in the loud tones that seemed to have been habitual with the Brotherhood. '*I* am an atheist: my daughter is an anarchist.' An answer that led to a speedy evacuation of the conveyance by the other passengers.

356

T. W. ROBERTSON (1829–71)

WHEN the great success of the Christmas numbers of Dickens's *All the Year Round* led to endless imitations of them, there was sent to the *Illustrated Times*[1] office the Christmas number of a newly-fledged publication—*Saturday Night*, I think it was, a clever weekly edited by young Tom Hood. In this number was a pathetic story immeasurably superior, as I thought, to the rest of the contents, telling, if I remember rightly, of a once popular clown dying in the direst distress at this so-called merry Christmastide. The story so impressed me that I at once addressed a letter to T.W.R., the initials appended to it and my only clue to the author, at the publishing office of the periodical in question, asking the writer to favour me with a visit.

Months went by and I heard nothing, although the letter had not been returned through the post-office, when one day a youngish-looking fellow, whose shabby attire and careworn, dejected expression conveyed the idea that he was not one of the fortunate ones of this world, called upon me. Taking my almost forgotten letter from his pocket he handed it to me, with the remark that he was T.W.R., and had only received the communication the day before. I gathered from him that his name was Robertson, and that he had been on the 'boards'. This, however, conveyed nothing whatever to my mind, he being then an utterly unknown scribe, though some years afterwards he was to become celebrated as the author of *Caste* and half-a-score of other clever social dramas, which secured him not only fame but fortune. There was an anxious, pleading look in my visitor's eyes, which had its effect upon me, and when, after a brief conversation, I gave him a commission to write a dozen or more theatrical sketches for the paper at three guineas each, I could not help observing the gleam of satisfaction that brightened up his doleful countenance.

[1] Edited (1855–65) by Henry Vizetelly, the narrator of this anecdote.

357
FREDERICK GREENWOOD (1830–1909)

FREDERICK GREENWOOD, editor of the *Pall Mall Gazette*, met in his club one day Lord Riddell, who died a few years ago, and in the course of conversation Riddell said to him, 'You know, I own a paper.' 'Oh, do you?' said Greenwood, 'what is it?' 'It's called the *News of the World*—I'll send you a copy,' replied Riddell, and in due course did so. Next time they met Riddell said, 'Well Greenwood, what do you think of my paper?' 'I looked at it,' replied Greenwood, 'and then I put it in the wastepaper basket. And then I thought, "If I leave it there the cook may read it"—so I burned it!'

358
CHARLES STUART CALVERLEY (1831–84)

[The narrator of this anecdote, James Payn (1830–98), was a prolific Victorian novelist.]

CALVERLEY was my junior by some years, so that I had not the privilege of knowing him at Cambridge, but in after-years I often met him. We were neighbours at Grasmere for a whole summer, when I saw a great deal of him. His classical attainments were of course far beyond me, but not more so than his physical gifts. He was the best runner and jumper I ever knew; but my admiration never led me to imitate him. Nevertheless, in company with W. and S., his almost equally athletic friends, and himself, I was once persuaded to climb Sca Fell from Wastwater. They went up it like mountain cats, while I (like panting Time) toiled after them in vain. 'The labour we delight in *physics* Payn,' was his appropriate quotation.

359
SIR LESLIE STEPHEN (1832–1904)

ONE day (23 March 1875) I[1] received from Stephen a mysterious note asking me to call in the evening, as late as I liked. I went, and found him alone, wandering up and down his library in slippers; his tall thin figure

[1] Thomas Hardy.

wrapt in a heath-coloured dressing-gown. After a few remarks on our magazine arrangements he said he wanted me to witness his signature to what, for a moment, I thought was his will; but it turned out to be a deed renunciatory of holy-orders under the act of 1870. He said grimly that he was really a reverend gentleman still, little as he might look it, and that he thought it was as well to cut himself adrift of a calling for which, to say the least, he had always been utterly unfit. The deed was executed with due formality. Our conversation then turned upon theologies decayed and defunct, the origin of things, the constitution of matter, the unreality of time, and kindred subjects. He told me that he had 'wasted' much time on systems of religion and metaphysics, and that the new theory of vortex rings had 'a staggering fascination' for him.

360

SIR LEWIS MORRIS (1833–1907)

THAT Oscar Wilde had the power of true spontaneous wit is shown by his happy retort on Sir Lewis Morris. Morris was complaining about what he considered the studied neglect of his claims when possible successors to the laureateship were being discussed after Tennyson's death. Said the author of *The Epic of Hades*: 'It is a complete conspiracy of silence against me—a conspiracy of silence! What ought I to do, Oscar?' 'Join it', replied Wilde with happy readiness.

361

GEORGE DU MAURIER (1834–96)

HENRY JAMES, I[1] heard from Du Maurier, came up to New Grove House after *Trilby* had become the talk of the town, and invited him to come for a walk. 'Let us', said Henry James, 'find a seat and sit down and endeavour—if it is in any way possible to arrive at a solution—to discover some reason for such a phenomenon as the success of *Trilby*.'

[1] F. Anstey.

362
WILLIAM MORRIS (1834–96)

MORRIS had sent Rossetti a copy of *Sigurd the Volsung* when it appeared. As time went by, and no letter of thanks or appreciation arrived from him, Morris grew more and more annoyed. Eventually, one morning he charged —he was a very burly man—into Rossetti's studio and at once broached the subject with a typical directness.

'Evidently', he boomed at his friend, who was painting, 'you do not like my book, or you would have written to me about it.'

'To tell you the truth, Topsy,' the other confessed with nonchalance, 'I must own that I find it difficult to take much interest in a man whose father was a dragon.'

Morris at once brought the conversation down to more human level by roaring out, 'I don't see it's any odder than having a brother who's an idiot!' and rushed out of the room.[1]

363
SAMUEL BUTLER (1835–1902)

MANY years after the novel[2] was written we were in Palermo and went to the Palazzo Reale to see the mosaics in the Cappella Palatina. Butler paid at the door and the custode gave him a bad lira among his change; he noticed it at once and they had words about it, but it was of no use. The custode was a lordly old gentleman, voluble in his speech and overwhelming in his gestures and manners; he carried too many guns and deafened us with his protestations—first, that it was a good lira; secondly, that it was not the one he had given us, and so on, and so on. We could not have felt more ashamed of ourselves if we had been foiled in an attempt to convict the Cardinal-Archbishop himself of uttering counterfeit coin. So we gave it up and passed in defeated. When we came out we had recovered a little, and the custode, who had forgotten all about so usual an occurrence, returned our umbrellas to us with an obsequiousness capable of but one interpretation.

'I shall not give him anything', said Butler severely to me. 'Oh yes, I

[1] The brother was William Michael Rossetti, 'considered by the elect to be the least gifted—to put it at its highest—of his family' (Sir Osbert Sitwell, *Noble Essences*, 1950, p. 48). [2] *The Way of All Flesh.*

will though', he added, and his eyes twinkled as he fumbled in his pocket. Then, with a very fair approach to Sicilian politeness, he handed the bad lira back to the old gentleman.

The custode's face changed and changed again like a field of corn on a breezy morning. In spite of his archiepiscopal appearance he would have been contented with a few soldi; seeing a whole lira he beamed with delight; then, detecting its badness, his countenance fell and he began to object; almost immediately he identified it as his own coin and was on the point of bursting with rage, but suddenly realizing that he could have nothing to say, he laughed heartily, shook hands with both of us, and apologized for not being able to leave his post as he would so much have liked to drink a glass of wine with us.

'There, now we have made another friend for life,' said Butler as he drove away. 'This comes of doing the right thing. We must really be more careful. It is another illustration of what I am so constantly telling you; this is the sort of thing that must have been in the Apostle's mind when he said that about all things working together for good to them that love God.'

364

THE wit of Lady Ritchie[1] was so lightly lambent that often people missed her points. Samuel Butler went to call upon her one day soon after his *Authoress of the Odyssey* (which insists that book was written by a woman) had been published. He told her he was at work on a book on Shakespeare's sonnets. He was, however, only bewildered at her saying, 'Oh, Mr. Butler, do you know my theory about the sonnets? They were written by Anne Hathaway!' It was not she who repeated this story, but the author of *Erewhon*. He never saw that she was laughing at him, and used to tell it, shaking his head sadly and saying, 'Poor lady, that was a silly thing to say.'

365

EDWARD TINSLEY (1835?–66)

[Edward Tinsley and his better-known brother William were partners in the firm of Tinsley Brothers, and were for some time highly successful publishers of fiction. Henry Vizetelly recalls a dinner party given by one of their authors, G. A. Sala, at some time in the 1860s.]

[1] Thackeray's elder daughter. See No. 373.

OUR host, I remember, returned thanks on his health being proposed during the small hours of the morning, and kept his guests laughing heartily through a long speech, full of humorous autobiographical reminiscences of his early days.

Later on, Tinsley's health was drunk, and he replied in characteristic fashion, detailing among other things his first arrival in the great metropolis on the top of a haycart, with the traditional three half-pence in his pocket. A day or two afterwards I chanced to meet Tinsley, when he anxiously inquired if he was not drunk on the occasion, and whether he had not made a great ass of himself. On my assuring him this was not so, he asked if he had said anything about his first coming to London on the top of a load of hay, with a billycock hat on his head and less than sixpenn'orth of coppers in his pocket. On my replying, 'Yes', 'Then I must have been as tight as a drum,' he exclaimed, 'for whenever I return thanks for my health being drunk, somehow or other it always comes into my head to tell of my coming up to London when a farmer's boy with only a few coppers, but I do my utmost to keep the matter dark. If I let it escape me the other night, I must have been tightly screwed indeed.'

366

SIR W. S. GILBERT (1836–1911)

SOON after the death of a well-known composer, someone who did not keep pace with the news of the day asked Mr. Gilbert what the *maestro* in question was doing.

'He is doing nothing,' was the answer.

'Surely he is composing,' persisted the questioner.

'On the contrary,' said Mr. Gilbert, 'he is decomposing.'

367

[P. G. Wodehouse ('Plum') tells Guy Bolton of his first meeting with W. S. Gilbert.]

'SOME people I knew took me over to lunch one Sunday at his house at Harrow Weald. This would have been in 1903, when I was a shy, timid lad of twenty-two. Or, rather, not quite twenty-two, because my birthday is in October, and this was June.'

'Get on, grandpa.'

'Dash it, let me establish atmosphere and build character and all that. The story's no good unless you realize how shy I was. I was just a shrinking floweret, and when I found fourteen other guests there, I felt relieved, because I saw that I could simply sit and be inconspicuous. It was about half-way through lunch when Gilbert started to tell a story.'

'What about?'

'I can't remember, but it was one of those very long stories which you make as dull as possible all through in order to stun the audience with the surprise smash at the finish. It went on and on, and then he paused, preparatory to delivering the snapperoo.'

'And was it worth the wait?'

'That we shall never know, because, as he paused, I, thinking the story was over, let out a yell of mirth. I had rather a distinctive laugh in those days, a little like an explosion of tri-nitro-toluol,[1] and it lasted for about five minutes, by which time the company had begun to talk of other things and Gilbert never got the point of it in at all. I can still remember his face as he glared at me. His eyes were like fire, and his whiskers quivered. It was a horrible experience.'

'Still, you have the consolation of knowing that you are the only man who ever stopped W. S. Gilbert telling a funny story.'

'Yes, there's that,' said Plum.

368

ALGERNON CHARLES SWINBURNE (1837–1909)

I[2] HAD sat next, at luncheon, to an old gentleman who owned to eighty-six years, and a fine impressive machine he looked, as he told me how much he had enjoyed his long life. 'If a man—or a schoolboy for that matter—', he continued, 'does not get on well, it's his own fault. I well remember, when I first went to Eton, the head-boy called us together, and pointing to a little fellow with a mass of curly red hair, said, "If ever you see that boy, kick him—and if you are too far off to kick him, throw a stone." . . . He was a fellow named Swinburne,' he added. 'He used to write poetry for a time, I believe, but I don't know what became of him.'

[1] T.N.T. [2] Sir Osbert Sitwell.

369

EMERSON had visited England soon after the publication of *Poems and Ballads*. In an interview with a journalist he was reported to have said things about the volume which gave deep offence to Swinburne. Swinburne wrote a mild protest, saying he felt sure that Emerson could not have used the words attributed to him. No reply was received. Swinburne was incensed. Some time afterwards Gosse and Swinburne were resting in the Green Park and the conversation turned on Emerson. Gosse learnt for the first time that Swinburne had again written to him. He said, 'I hope you said nothing rash.' 'Oh, no.' 'But what did you say?' 'I kept my temper, I preserved my equanimity.' 'Yes, but what did you say?' 'I called him', said Swinburne in his chanting voice, 'a wrinkled and toothless baboon, who, first hoisted into notoriety on the shoulders of Carlyle, now spits and splutters on a filthier platform of his own finding and fouling.' The letter like its predecessor received no answer.

370

WHEN Swinburne came back from the country to town he was always particularly anxious to recite or read aloud his own poems. In doing this he often became very much excited, and even, in his overwhelming sense of the movement of the metre, would jump about the room in a manner somewhat embarrassing to the listener. His method of procedure was uniform. He would arrive at a friend's house with a breast-pocket obviously bulging with manuscript, but buttoned across his chest. After floating about the room and greeting his host and hostess with many little becks of the head, and affectionate smiles, and light wavings of the fingers, he would settle at last upright on a chair, or, by preference, on a sofa, and sit there in a state of rigid immobility, the toe of one foot pressed against the heel of the other. Then he would say, in an airy, detached way, as though speaking of some absent person, 'I have brought with me my "Thalassius" or my "Wasted Garden" (or whatever it might happen to be), which I have just finished.' Then he would be folded again in silence, looking at nothing. We then were to say, 'Oh, do please read it to us! Will you?' Swinburne would promptly reply, 'I had no intention in the world of boring you with it, but since you ask me—' and out would come the MS. I do not remember that there was ever any variation in this little ceremony, which sometimes preluded many hours of recitation and reading. His delivery, especially of his own poetry, was delightful as long as he sat quietly in his seat. His voice, which was of extraordinary beauty, 'the pure Ashburnham voice', as his cousin explains to me, rose and fell monotonously, but with a flute-like note which was very agreeable, and the pulse of the rhythm was strongly yet delicately felt. I shall never forget the successive evenings on which he read *Bothwell* aloud in his lodgings, in particular one on which Edward Burne-Jones, Arthur O'Shaughnessy, P. B. Marston, and I sat with him at his round marble-topped table—lighted only by candles in two giant candlesticks of serpentine he had brought from the Lizard—and heard him read the magnificent second act of that tragedy. He surpassed himself in vigour and melody of utterance that night. But sometimes, in reading, he lost control of his emotions, the sound became a scream, and he would dance about the room, the paper fluttering from his finger-tips like a pennon in a gale of wind.

371

[W. H. Mallock, best known for *The New Republic*, was an undergraduate at Balliol College in the time of Dr. Jowett. He was not a favourite of Jowett's, but he records his kindness—'a kindness which survived many outbursts of what I thought was somewhat petulant disapproval'.]

I RECEIVED from him one day a curt invitation to dinner, and presented myself, wondering mildly to what this mark of favour could be due. But wonder turned to alarm when, on entering the Master's drawing-room, I discovered in the dim twilight no other figure than his own. His manner, however, though not effusive, was civil, and was certainly fraught with no menace of any coming judgement on my sins. We exchanged some ordinary observations on the weather and kindred topics. Then, looking over his shoulder, he uttered a half-audible word or two, which, being plainly not addressed to me, must have been addressed to somebody else. Presently out of the shadows a somebody else emerged. This was a person remarkable for the large size of his head, his longish hair, his insignificant stature, and his singularly sloping shoulders. I was introduced to him without catching his name. Dinner was announced forthwith. It was evident that, except for myself, this person was to be the sole guest. In the candle-light of the dinner-table I realized that this person was Swinburne.

The dinner passed off pleasantly. Swinburne showed himself an intelligent, though by no means a brilliant talker; and as soon as we had returned to the drawing-room, where we drank a cup of coffee standing, Jowett, who had some engagement, abruptly left us to finish the evening by ourselves. On Swinburne the effect of the Master's disappearance was magical. His manner and aspect began to exhibit a change like that of the moon when a dim cloud drifts away from it. Of what we discussed at starting I have not the least remembrance, but before very long Swinburne was on the subject of poetry. His observations at first consisted of general criticisms. Then he began to indulge in quotations from various poems—none of them, I think, from his own; but however this may have been, the music seemed to intoxicate him. The words began to thrill me with the spell of his own recitation of them. Here at last I realized the veritable genius who had made the English language a new instrument of passion. . . . Finally he strayed into quotations from Sydney Dobell, a writer now hardly remembered, with one of which, describing a girl bathing, he made the Master's academic rafters ring—

> She, with her body bright sprinkles the waters white,
> Which flee from her fair form, and flee in vain,
> Dyed with the dear unutterable sight,
> And circles out her beauties to the circling main.

He was almost shouting these words when another sound became audible —that of an opening door, followed by Jowett's voice, which said in high-pitched syllables, 'You'd both of you better go to bed now.'

My next meeting with Swinburne took place not many days later. He had managed meanwhile to make acquaintance with a few other undergraduates—all of them enthusiastic worshippers—one of whom arranged to entertain him at luncheon. As I could not, being otherwise engaged, be present at this feast myself, I was asked to join the party as soon as possible afterwards. I arrived at a fortunate moment. Most of the guests were still sitting at a table covered with dessert-dishes. Swinburne was much at his ease in an armchair near the fireplace, and was just beginning, as a number of smiling faces showed, to be not only interesting, but in some way entertaining also.

He was, as I presently gathered, about to begin an account of an historical drama by himself, which existed in his memory only—a sort of parody of what Victor Hugo might have written had he dramatized English events at the opening of the reign of Queen Victoria. The first act, he said, showed England on the verge of a revolution, which was due to the frightful orgies of the Queen at 'Buckingham's Palace'. The Queen, with unblushing effrontery, had taken to herself a lover, in the person of Lord John Russell, who had for his rival 'Sir Peel'. Sir Peel was represented as pleading his own cause in a passionate scene, which wound up as follows: 'Why do you love Lord John Russell, and why do you not love me? I know why you love Lord John Russell. He is young, he is beautiful, he is profligate. I cannot be young, I cannot be beautiful, but I will be profligate.' Then followed the stage direction, 'Exit for ze Haymarket.' In a later act it appeared that the Queen and Lord John Russell had between them given the world a daughter, who, having been left to her own devices, or, in other words, to the streets, reappears as 'Miss Kitty', and is accorded some respectable rank. Under these conditions she becomes the object of much princely devotion; but the moral hypocrisy of England has branded her as a public scandal. With regard to her so-called depravities nobody entertains a doubt, but one princely admirer, of broader mind than the rest, declares that in spite of these she is really the embodiment of everything that is divine in woman. 'She may', he says, 'have done everything which might have made a Messalina blush, but whenever she looked at the sky, she murmured "God", and whenever she looked at a flower she murmured "mother".'

The vivacity and mischievous humour with which Swinburne gave his account of this projected play exhibited a side of his character which I have never even seen mentioned, and the appreciation and surprise of his audience were obviously a great delight to him. He lay back in his chair, tossed off a glass of port, and presently his mood changed. Somehow or other he got to his own serious poems; and before we knew where we were, he was pouring out an account of *Poems and Ballads*, and explaining their relation to the secrets of his own experiences. . . .

Then, like a man waking up from a dream, Swinburne turned to our host, and said nervously, 'Can you give me another glass of port?' His glass was filled, he emptied it at a single draught, and then lay back in his chair like a child who had gone to sleep, the actual fact being, as his host soon recognized, that, in homely language, he was drunk.

372

AT dinner I talked to —— about Swinburne, whom he knew; he was a little in that Arts Club set. He told me Swinburne's quarrel with the Committee was due to the fact not only that he was too constantly drunk there, but that on the final occasion, being drunk and not able to find his hat, he tried others, and as each proved too small for his enormous head he threw it wrathfully on the ground and stamped on it—which naturally brought some complaints to the Committee next day.

He complained that Gosse (in his *Life*) had given nothing of Swinburne's humour, much of which indeed was not very printable, though essentially harmless enough—as his invention about Queen Victoria's confession, in French for some reason, presumably because A.C.S. liked talking French —to the Duchess of Kent of her unfortunate lapse from virtue. *Ce n'était pas un prince ; ce n'était pas un milord, ni même* Sir R. Peel. *C'était un misérable du peuple, en nomme* Wordsworth, *qui m'a recité des vers de son* Excursion *d'une sensualité si chaleureuse qu'ils m'ont ébranlé—et je suis tombée.*' I quote from memory, very likely not ——'s words.

373
ANNE THACKERAY, LADY RITCHIE
(1837–1919)

ONE of the things I[1] often did . . . was to go and stay with my aunt by marriage, Lady Ritchie, who was Thackeray's daughter.

I can see her at this moment, beautifully fresh in her lace cap, coming down the staircase of her London house in the morning after breakfast, with a few pages of manuscript fluttering in her hand. She would tell me to read it over aloud to her by the dining-room fire, then she would dictate a few alterations, put the charming impressionistic writing into an envelope, and rapidly address it to Messrs. Smith and Elder. After that, there were plans for the day to be made, and then came the unmaking of plans too impulsively undertaken. A letter is swiftly written to a millionairess to say that, alas! after all she had been rash in saying she could join her in a yachting cruise; she did not feel quite equal to it; and she would laugh at herself as she sat by the fire for having thought that she ever could impulsively have accepted anything so unsuitable to herself as going on a yachting cruise and undergoing all the fatigues it would involve, such as conversation in the wind on deck. Then she must give up her sitting for her portrait next day. Her order has been given to an artist whose talent is almost nil, but who must be helped. 'He hasn't allowed me to look at my picture yet, but I see him squeezing piles of vermilion on to his palette, and I quite dread it,' and she posts a cheque to the painter.

Very soon after we are whirling away in a little victoria in the morning sunshine. An old lady who has lost her husband must be visited: and all in a moment Aunt Anny has alighted in Queen's Gate, and is sitting in a heavy, early Victorian dining-room, under an East India Company member's portrait, among the massive mahogany chairs, encouraging and improving the old lady's spirits. The canary begins to sing. . . .

We drive on to Westminster, and the victoria stops in Dean's Yard. And now Aunt Anny begins to feel nervous and anxious about the 'odd little errand' upon which we are going. She has an appointment with the Dean, and he is ready for us: he leads us through his house and on into the Abbey and down into the crypt, and there we find in an alcove Mr. Onslow Ford, the sculptor, and his assistant, and the bust of William Thackeray that has been moved there by them from its niche in Poets' Corner.

The fact is for years, whenever she has been to Westminster Abbey, Aunt Anny has deplored the length of the whiskers on each side of the face of her father's bust. The Italian sculptor, Marachetti, made them too

[1] Mary MacCarthy, author of *A Nineteenth-Century Childhood.*

long. They spoil the likeness for her and she has longed to have them clipped, and so at last she has begged Mr. Ford and has implored the Dean to let her have her wish, and have them shortened. So now chip, chip, chip fly the bits under the white-bloused assistant's chisel. Mr. Ford stands by, very cross, for he does not like undoing another sculptor's work, and if the daughter of Thackeray had not happened to be such a charming old lady it is probable she would not have had her way. She laughs; admits that there is something absurd about the commission, but is firm that it shall be carried out; so she talks to him without paying any attention to his crossness, and makes him at last smile as he superintends the work. Finally the bust is flicked over with a cloth, as after a shave, and it is carried up into the nave and back into its own niche, and the silence and dignity of the Abbey receives it again.

Aunt Anny is a little emotional as she gets into the victoria, smiling at her tears, then weeping again a little at her smiles; she is triumphant, for it has been a great relief to her mind.

374

SIR JOHN MAHAFFY (1839–1919)

[Mahaffy was a versatile and original classical scholar, who became a fellow of Trinity College, Dublin, in 1864, a senior fellow in 1899, and at last in 1914, in his seventy-sixth year, Provost. His reputation as a wit and raconteur was high, but it made him many enemies.]

MAHAFFY could be sarcastic in a genial way when the spirit moved him. I recall his crushing question to a man who was claiming respect for Swift MacNeill[1]—'You know, he is descended from Dean Swift.'—'By whom? Stella or Vanessa?' Mahaffy inquired with a smile.

375

DR. YELVERTON TYRELL[2] was reading some comments that Mahaffy had sent to the daily paper about some poor old woman whom superstitious villagers had buried alive because they thought that she was a

[1] John Gordon Swift MacNeill, Irish politician and jurist, was descended (as Mahaffy would have known) not from the unmarried Dean (Jonathan) Swift, but from his cousin Deane Swift, a son of Jonathan Swift's uncle Godwin, and the father of Deane Swift his biographer.

[2] Robert Yelverton Tyrrell (1844–1914), who held in succession the chairs of Latin, Greek, and Ancient History at T.C.D., and who became in 1904 Senior Fellow.

witch. Little did I know, though I might have guessed it, that the village in question was the village in which the doctor's father had had his parish.

'After all,' he said quietly as he laid down the paper, 'it is only a question of premature burial, which is not such an obnoxious thing as delayed burial, which Mahaffy so obtrusively represents.'

376
WALTER PATER (1839–94)

WILDE used to tell a story, probably invented by himself, in which he delineated Pater's character and fondness for picturesque words. One morning, before beginning his lecture, Pater asked a young man named Sanctuary to remain behind at the end. As Pater was a proctor, Sanctuary felt uncomfortable, but when they were left alone together, it was the professor who looked nervous. After a period of embarrassment the young man said: 'You asked me to stay behind, sir, did you not?' Pater pulled himself together: 'Oh yes, Mr. Sanctuary. I . . . I wanted to say to you . . . what a very beautiful name you have got.'

Better still was another of Wilde's fancies. 'So you are going to see Pater!' he said to Richard Le Gallienne. 'That will be delightful. But I must tell you one thing about him to save you from disappointment. You must not expect him to talk about his prose. Of course no true artist ever does that. But Pater never talks about anything that interests him. He will not breathe one golden word about the Renaissance. No! he will probably say something like this: "So you wear cork soles in your shoes? Is that really true? And do you find them comfortable? . . . How extremely interesting!" '

377

ON the occasion of Pater's lecture on Prosper Mérimée, his friends gathered round the platform to congratulate him; he expressed a hope that the audience was able to hear what he said. 'We overheard you,' said Oscar Wilde. 'Ah, you have a phrase for everything,' replied the lecturer.

378
RHODA BROUGHTON (1840–1920)

OF the many remarkable women I[1] have known, Rhoda Broughton stands out as having been the most remarkable. . . . She had a fine mind, an acute type of intellect, and a most generous nature. Under a somewhat tart manner she had a sensitive heart, and possessed an exceptionally loyal nature. Such a person is naturally both a good lover and a good hater. The story went, and I feel sure it was true, that when she was a young woman, and a friend of hers was jilted by a man owing to efforts made by his mother, he received from Rhoda Broughton a mug on which was inscribed, 'For a Good Boy'.

379
THOMAS HARDY (1840–1928)

THERE was a young girl, a gamekeeper's pretty daughter, who won Hardy's boyish admiration because of her beautiful bay-red hair. But she despised him, as being two or three years her junior, and married early. He celebrated her later on as 'Lizbie Browne'. Yet another attachment, somewhat later, which went deeper, was to a farmer's daughter named Louisa. There were more, probably. They all appear, however, to have been quite fugitive, except perhaps the one for Louisa.

He believed that his attachment to this damsel was reciprocated, for on one occasion when he was walking home from Dorchester he beheld her sauntering down the lane as if to meet him. He longed to speak to her, but bashfulness overcame him, and he passed on with a murmured 'Good evening', while poor Louisa had no word to say.

Later he heard that she had gone to Weymouth to a boarding school for young ladies, and thither he went, Sunday after Sunday, until he discovered the church which the maiden of his affections attended with her fellow-scholars. But, alas, all that resulted from these efforts was a shy smile from Louisa.

That the vision remained may be gathered from a poem 'Louisa in the Lane' written not many months before his death. Louisa lies under a nameless mound in 'Mellstock' churchyard. That 'Good evening' was the only word that passed between them.

[1] Mrs. Belloc Lowndes.

380

[Hardy made this entry in his diary on 30 January 1879.]

IN Steven's bookshop, Holywell Street. A bustling vigorous young curate comes in—red-faced and full of life—the warm breath puffing from his mouth in a jet of frosty air, and religion sitting with an ill grace upon him.

'Have you *Able to Save*?'

Shopman addressed does not know, and passes on the inquiry to the master standing behind with his hat on: '*Able to Save*?'

'I don't know—hoi! (to boy at other end). Got *Able to Save*? Why the devil can't you attend?'

'What, Sir?'

'*Able to Save*!'

Boy's face a blank. Shopman to curate: 'Get it by tomorrow afternoon, Sir.'

'And please get *Words of Comfort*.'

'*Words of Comfort*. Yes, Sir.' Exit curate.

Master: 'Why the h— don't anybody here know what's in stock?' Business proceeds in a subdued manner.

381

As the year 1891 drew to a close an incident that took place during the publication of *Tess of the d'Urbervilles* as a serial in the *Graphic* might have prepared him for certain events that were to follow. The editor objected to the description of Angel Clare carrying in his arms, across a flooded lane, Tess and her three dairymaid companions. He suggested that it would be more decorous and suitable for the pages of a periodical intended for family reading if the damsels were wheeled across the lane in a wheel-barrow. This was accordingly done.

382

THOMAS HARDY asked me[1] to lunch, and I bicycled over from our cottage at Studland. There were only he and I and his wife—the first Mrs. Hardy, of course—at the meal; it was about the time when *Jude the Obscure* had been published, and I was loud in my praise of that work.

[1] Alfred Sutro (1863–1933), dramatist.

Mrs. Hardy was far from sharing my enthusiasm. It was the first novel of his, she told me, that he had published without first letting her read the manuscript: had she read it, she added firmly, it would *not* have been published, or at least, not without considerable emendations. The book had made a difference to them, she added, in the County . . .

The position was awkward for me, and very embarrassing. Hardy said nothing, and did not lift his eyes from the plate; I was hard put to it to manufacture some kind of conversation, and it was a great relief when Mrs. Hardy rose, and left us to our port. Even then Hardy's silence persisted, till I told him of a bird in our wood whose identity puzzled us; we had discovered at last that it was a corncrake. Hardy brightened at once, the cloud lighted, and we talked, talked of birds and trees, evidently a favourite subject of his, till I left.

383

ONE day—this was in Paris—I[1] asked Yeats what he did about books that were sent to him for signature. He became quite thoughtful about this, and then he became very happy. And then he told me this story.

He was dining once with Thomas Hardy, and as they were finishing their coffee he asked Hardy the very same question. 'What do you do, Hardy, about books that are sent to you for signature?'

'Yeats,' said Hardy, 'come with me, there is something upstairs I want to show you.' At the top of the house Hardy opened a door, and the two poets entered a larger room. This room was covered from floor to ceiling with books. Hardy waved his hand at the odd-thousand volumes that filled the room.—'Yeats,' said he, 'these are the books that were sent to me for signature.'

384

AT one of Ford's tea-parties I[2] remember seeing a little, quiet, grey old man wearing a red tie who turned out to be Thomas Hardy. I was standing next to Hugh Walpole at the back of the room, when he was pointed out to me. The conversation among the lion cubs in our neighbourhood was no doubt very brilliant and very 'literary', but suddenly there came the usual inexplicable hush. It was broken by Hardy, who, turning to an elderly lady by his side, remarked, 'And how is Johnny's Whooping Cough?'

[1] James Stephens (1880?–1950), Irish poet and miscellaneous writer.

[2] Douglas Goldring.

385

WE[1] found ourselves near Dorchester, so we turned in there to visit Thomas Hardy, whom we had met not long before when he came to Oxford to get his honorary doctor's degree. We found him active and gay, with none of the aphasia and wandering attention that we had noticed in him at Oxford.

I wrote out a record of the conversation we had with him. . . . He said that he regarded professional critics as parasites no less noxious than autograph-hunters, and wished the world rid of them. He also wished that he had not listened to them when he was a young man; on their advice he had cut out dialect-words from his early poems, though they had no exact synonyms to fit the context. And still the critics were plaguing him. One of them recently complained of a poem of his where he had written 'his shape *smalled* in the distance'. Now what in the world else could he have written? Hardy then laughed a little and said that once or twice recently he had looked up a word in the dictionary for fear of being again accused of coining, and had found it there right enough—only to read on and find that the sole authority quoted was himself in a half-forgotten novel! He talked of early literary influences, and said that he had none at all, for he did not come of literary stock. Then he corrected himself and said that a friend, a fellow-apprentice in the architect's office where he worked as a young man, used to lend him books. (His taste in literature was certainly most unexpected. Once when Lawrence had ventured to say something disparaging against Homer's *Iliad*, he protested: 'Oh, but I admire the *Iliad* greatly. Why, it's in the *Marmion* class!' Lawrence could not at first believe that Hardy was not making a little joke.)

386

HENRY JAMES (1843–1916)

JAMES, who was a frequent companion on our English motor-trips,[2] was firmly convinced that, because he lived in England and our chauffeur (an American) did not, it was necessary that the latter should be guided by him through the intricacies of the English country-side. Signposts were rare in England in those days, and for many years afterwards . . .

[1] Robert Graves and his wife and T. E. Lawrence.

[2] Edith Wharton on a visit to England with her husband.

It chanced however that Charles Cook, our faithful and skilful driver, was a born path-finder, while James's sense of direction was non-existent, or rather actively but always erroneously alert; and the consequences of his intervention were always bewildering and sometimes extremely fatiguing. The first time that my husband and I went to Lamb House by motor (coming from France) James, who had travelled to Folkestone by train to meet us, insisted on seating himself next to Cook on the plea that the roads across Romney Marsh formed such a tangle that only an old inhabitant could guide us to Rye. The suggestion resulted in our turning around and around in our tracks till long after dark, though Rye, conspicuous on its conical hill, was just ahead of us and Cook could easily have landed us there in time for tea.

Another year we had been motoring in the West Country, and on the way back were to spend a night at Malvern. As we approached (at the close of a dark rainy afternoon) I saw James growing restless, and was not surprised to hear him say: 'My dear, I once spent a summer at Malvern and know it very well; and as it is rather difficult to find the way to the hotel, it might be well if Edward were to change places with me and let me sit beside Cook.' My husband of course acceded (though with doubt in his heart) and, James having taken his place, we awaited the result. Malvern, if I am not mistaken, is encircled by a sort of upper boulevard, of the kind called in Italy a *strada di circonvallazione*, and for an hour we circled about above the outspread city while James vainly tried to remember which particular street led down most directly to our hotel. At each corner (literally) he stopped the motor, and we heard a muttering, first confident and then anguished. 'This—this, my dear Cook, yes . . . this certainly is the right corner. But no; stay! A moment longer, please—in this light it's so difficult . . . appearances are so misleading . . . It may be . . . yes! I think it *is* the next turn . . . a little farther lend thy guiding hand . . . that is, drive on; but slowly, please, my dear Cook; *very* slowly!' And at the next corner the same agitated monologue would be repeated; till at length Cook, the mildest of men, interrupted gently: 'I guess any turn'll get us down into the town, Mr. James, and after that I can ask'—and late, hungry and exhausted we arrived at length at our destination, James still convinced that the next turn would have been the right one if only we had been more patient.

The most absurd of these episodes occurred on another rainy evening when James and I chanced to arrive at Windsor long after dark. We must have been driven by a strange chauffeur—perhaps Cook was on holiday; at any rate, having fallen into the lazy habit of trusting him to know the way, I found myself at a loss to direct his substitute to the King's Road. While I was hesitating and peering out into the darkness James spied an ancient doddering man who had stopped in the rain to gaze at us. 'Wait a moment, my dear—I'll ask him where we are'; and leaning out he signalled to the spectator.

'My good man, if you'll be good enough to come here, please; a little nearer—so,' and as the old man came up: 'My friend, to put it to you in two words, this lady and I have just arrived here from *Slough*; that is to say, to be more strictly accurate, we have recently *passed through* Slough on our way here, having actually motored to Windsor from Rye, which was our point of departure; and the darkness having overtaken us, we should be much obliged if you would tell us where we now are in relation, say, to the High Street, which, as you of course know, leads to the Castle, after leaving on the left hand the turn down to the railway station.'

I was not surprised to have this extraordinary appeal met by silence, and a dazed expression on the old wrinkled face at the window; nor to have James go on: 'In short' (his invariable prelude to a fresh series of explanatory ramifications), 'in short, my good man, what I want to put to you in a word is this: supposing we have already (as I have reason to think we have) driven past the turn down to the railway station (which in that case, by the way, would probably not have been on our left hand, but on our right) where are we now in relation to . . . '

'Oh, please,' I interrupted, feeling myself utterly unable to sit through another parenthesis, 'do ask him where the King's Road is.'

'Ah—? The King's Road? Just so! Quite right! Can you, as a matter of fact, my good man, tell us where, in relation to our present position, the King's Road exactly *is*?'

'Ye're in it', said the aged face at the window.

387

[On 5 January 1895, H. G. Wells, who had been for three days dramatic critic of the *Pall Mall*, found himself at the St. James's Theatre waiting for the curtain to go up at the opening night of Henry James's *Guy Domville*.]

IT was an extremely weak drama. James was a strange unnatural human being, a sensitive man lost in an immensely abundant brain, which had had neither a scientific nor a philosophical training, but which was by education and natural aptitude alike, formal, formally aesthetic, conscientiously fastidious and delicate. Wrapped about in elaborations of gesture and speech, James regarded his fellow creatures with a face of distress and a remote effort at intercourse, like some victim of enchantment placed in the centre of an immense bladder. His life was unbelievably correct, and his home at Rye one of the most perfect pieces of suitably furnished Georgian architecture imaginable. He was an unspotted bachelor. He had always been well off and devoted to artistic ambitions; he had experienced no tragedy and he shunned the hoarse laughter of comedy; and yet he was consumed by a gnawing hunger for dramatic success. In this performance he had his first and last actual encounter with the theatre.

Guy Domville was one of those rare ripe exquisite Catholic Englishmen of ancient family conceivable only by an American mind, who gave up the woman he loved to an altogether coarser cousin, because his religious vocation was stronger than his passion. I forget the details of the action. There was a drinking scene in which Guy and the cousin, for some obscure purpose of discovery, pretended to drink and, instead, poured their wine furtively into a convenient bowl of flowers upon the table between them. Guy was played by George Alexander, at first in a mood of refined solemnity, and then, as the intimations of gathering disapproval from the pit and gallery increased, with stiffening desperation. Alexander at the close had an incredibly awkward exit. He had to stand at a door in the middle of the stage, say slowly, 'Be keynd to Her . . . *Be* keynd to Her,' and depart. By nature Alexander had a long face, but at that moment with audible defeat before him, he seemed the longest and dismalest face, all face, that I had ever seen. The slowly closing door reduced him to a strip, to a line, of perpendicular gloom. The uproar burst like a thunderstorm as the door closed and the stalls responded with feeble applause. Then the tumult was mysteriously allayed. There were some minutes of uneasy apprehension. 'Author,' cried voices, 'Au-thor!' The stalls, not understanding, redoubled their clapping.

Disaster was too much for Alexander that night. A spasm of hate for the writer of those fatal lines must surely have seized him. With incredible cruelty he led the doomed James, still not understanding clearly how things were with him, to the middle of the stage, and there the pit and gallery had him. James bowed; he knew it was the proper thing to bow. Perhaps he had selected a few words to say, but if so they went unsaid. I have never heard any sound more devastating than the crescendo of booing that ensued. The gentle applause of the stalls was altogether overwhelmed. For a moment or so James faced the storm, his round face white, his mouth opening and shutting, and then Alexander, I hope in a contrite mood, snatched him back into the wings.

388

H. J. WAS complaining to us[1] that Ellen Terry had asked him to write a play for her, and now that he had done so, and read it to her, had refused it. My wife, desiring to placate, asked: 'Perhaps she did not think the part

[1] The narrator is John Bailey (1864–1931).

suited to her?' H. J. turned upon us both, and with resonance and uplifting voice replied: 'Think? *Think*? How should the poor toothless, chattering hag THINK?' The sudden outpouring of improvised epithets had a most extraordinary effect. A crescendo on 'toothless' and then on 'chattering' and then on 'hag'—and 'think' delivered with the trumpet of an elephant.

389

ONE summer we[1] took a house at Rye, that wonderful inland island, crowned with a town as with a citadel, like a hill in a medieval picture. It happened that the house next to us was the old oak-panelled mansion which had attracted, one might almost say across the Atlantic, the fine aquiline eye of Henry James. For Henry James, of course, was an American who had reacted against America; and steeped his sensitive psychology in everything that seemed most antiquatedly and aristocratically English. In his search for the finest shades among the shadows of the past, one might have guessed that he would pick out that town from all towns and that house from all houses. It had been the seat of a considerable patrician family of the neighbourhood, which had long ago decayed and disappeared. It had, I believe, rows of family portraits, which Henry James treated as reverently as family ghosts. I think in a way he really regarded himself as a sort of steward or custodian of the mysteries and secrets of a great house, where ghosts might have walked with all possible propriety. The legend says (I never learned for certain if it was true) that he had actually traced that dead family-tree until he found that there was far away, in some manufacturing town, one unconscious descendant of the family, who was a cheerful and commonplace commercial clerk. And it is said that Henry James would ask this youth down to his dark ancestral house, and receive him with funereal hospitality, and I am sure with comments of a quite excruciating tact and delicacy. Henry James always spoke with an air which I can only call gracefully groping; that is, not so much groping in the dark in blindness as groping in the light in bewilderment, through seeing too many avenues and obstacles. I would not compare it, in the unkind phrase of Mr. H. G. Wells, to an elephant trying to pick up a pea. But I agree that it was like something with a very sensitive and flexible proboscis, feeling its way through a forest of facts; to us often invisible facts. It is said, I say, that these thin straws of sympathy and subtlety were duly split for the benefit of the astonished commercial gentleman, while Henry James, with his bowed dome-like head, drooped with unfathomable apologies and rendered a sort of silent account of his stewardship. It is

[1] Mr. and Mrs. G. K. Chesterton.

also said that the commercial gentleman thought the visit a great bore and the ancestral home a hell of a place; and probably fidgeted about with a longing to go out for a B and S and the *Pink 'Un*.

Whether this tale be true or not, it is certain that Henry James inhabited the house with all the gravity and loyalty of the family ghosts; not without something of the oppressive delicacy of a highly cultured family butler. He was in point of fact a very stately and courteous old gentleman; and in some social aspects especially, rather uniquely gracious. He proved in one point that there was a truth in his cult of tact. He was serious with children. I saw a little boy gravely present him with a crushed and dirty dandelion. He bowed; but he did not smile. That restraint was a better proof of the understanding of children than the writing of *What Maisie Knew*. But in all relations of life he erred, if he erred, on the side of solemnity and slowness; and it was this, I suppose, that got at last upon the too lively nerves of Mr. Wells; who used, even in those days, to make irreverent darts and dashes through the sombre house and the sacred garden and drop notes to me over the garden wall. I shall have more to say of Mr. H. G. Wells and his notes later; here we are halted at the moment when Mr. Henry James heard of our arrival in Rye and proceeded (after exactly the correct interval) to pay his call in state.

Needless to say, it was a very stately call of state; and James seemed to fill worthily the formal frock-coat of those far-off days. As no man is so dreadfully well-dressed as a well-dressed American, so no man is so terribly well-mannered as a well-mannered American. He brought his brother William with him, the famous American philosopher; and though William James was breezier than his brother when you knew him, there was something finally ceremonial about this idea of the whole family on the march. We talked about the best literature of the day; James a little tactfully, myself a little nervously. I found he was more strict than I had imagined about the rules of artistic arrangement; he deplored rather than depreciated Bernard Shaw, because plays like *Getting Married* were practically formless. He said something complimentary about something of mine; but represented himself as respectfully wondering how I wrote all I did. I suspected him of meaning why rather than how. We then proceeded to consider gravely the work of Hugh Walpole, with many delicate degrees of appreciation and doubt; when I heard from the front-garden a loud bellowing noise resembling that of an impatient fog-horn. I knew, however, that it was not a fog-horn; because it was roaring out, 'Gilbert! Gilbert!' and was like only one voice in the world; as rousing as that recalled in one of its former phrases, of those who

> Heard Ney shouting to the guns to unlimber
> And hold the Beresina Bridge at night.

I knew it was Belloc, probably shouting for bacon and beer; but even I had no notion of the form or guise under which he would present himself.

I had every reason to believe that he was a hundred miles away in France. And so, apparently, he had been; walking with a friend of his in the Foreign Office, a co-religionist of one of the old Catholic families; and by some miscalculation they had found themselves in the middle of their travels entirely without money. Belloc is legitimately proud of having on occasion lived, and being able to live, the life of the poor. One of the ballades of the *Eye-Witness*, which was never published, described tramping abroad in this fashion:

> To sleep and smell the incense of the tar,
> To wake and watch Italians dawns aglow
> And underneath the branch a single star,
> Good Lord, how little wealthy people know.

In this spirit they started to get home practically without money. Their clothes collapsed and they managed to get into some workmen's slops. They had no razors and could not afford a shave. They must have saved their last penny to re-cross the sea; and then they started walking from Dover to Rye; where they knew their nearest friend for the moment resided. They arrived, roaring for food and drink and derisively accusing each other of having secretly washed, in violation of an implied contract between tramps. In this fashion they burst in upon the balanced tea-cup and tentative sentence of Mr. Henry James.

Henry James had a name for being subtle; but I think that situation was too subtle for him. I doubt to this day whether he, of all men, did not miss the irony of the best comedy in which he ever played a part. He left America because he loved Europe, and all that was meant by England or France; the gentry, the gallantry, the traditions of lineage and locality, the life that had been lived beneath old portraits in oak-panelled rooms. And there, on the other side of the tea-table, was Europe, was the old thing that made France and England, the posterity of the English squires and the French soldiers; ragged, unshaven, shouting for beer, shameless above all shades of poverty and wealth; sprawling, indifferent, secure. And what looked across at it was still the Puritan refinement of Boston; and the space it looked across was wider than the Atlantic.

390

I[1] REMEMBER once walking with him in the fields beyond Rye, and two very small and grubby children opened the gate for us. James smiled beneficently, felt in his deep pocket for coppers, found some and then

[1] Sir Hugh Walpole (1884–1941).

began an elaborate explanation of what the children were to buy. They were to go to a certain sweet shop because there the sweets were better than any other; they were to see that they were not deceived and offered an inferior brand, for those particular sweets had a peculiar taste of nuts and honey, with, he fancied, an especial flavour that was *almost* the molasses of his own country. If the children took care to visit the right shop and insisted that they should have only that particular sweet called, he fancied, 'Honey-nut'—or was it something with 'delight' in it? 'Rye's Delight' or 'Honey Delights' or—But at that moment the children, who had been listening open-mouthed, their eyes fixed on the pennies, of a sudden took fright and turned, running and roaring with terror across the fields.

He stood bewildered, the pennies in his hand. What had he done? What had he said? He had meant nothing but kindness. Why had they run from him crying and screaming? He was greatly distressed, going over every possible corner of it in his mind. He alluded to it for days afterwards.

391
WILLIAM ARCHIBALD SPOONER (1844–1930)

SPOONER, who was Warden of New College at the beginning of the century—a man known to fame, but unjustly, for I believe he never in his life perpetrated a Spoonerism—was once asked whether there was much Christian Socialism in Oxford. His reply was, 'No, I shouldn't say there was much; in fact, I think there are only two Christian Socialists in Oxford, Dr. Rashdall and myself.' (Dr. Rashdall, afterwards Dean of Carlisle, was a clerical Fellow of New College.) 'Only Dr. Rashdall and myself; and I'm not very much of a Socialist, and Dr. Rashdall isn't very much of a Christian.'[1]

392
HENRY BRADLEY (1845–1923)

THE earliest record of Henry is singularly characteristic. It was before he was four years old, on the occasion of his being taken for the first time to church—the meeting-house, no doubt, of the Congregational community to which his parents belonged—where he obstinately persisted in

[1] Hastings Rashdall (1858–1924) was 'a leader of the liberal school of Anglicanism', and 'had little sympathy with the mystical element in religion' (*D.N.B.*).

holding his book upside-down. This eccentricity gave them some anxiety, until it was discovered that the child really could read, but only with the book in that position. Unknown to them he had taught himself during family prayers: while his father, sitting with a great Bible open on his knees, was reading the lesson aloud, the boy, standing in front of him closely poring over the page, had followed word by word and thus worked out the whole puzzle—and so completely, that long after he had accustomed himself to the normal position he could read equally well either way. His mature faculty seems to have been perfect in his infancy, and in this first picture of him Philology and Piety are seen hand in hand.

393

BRADLEY'S knowledge and advice were widely sought as a final resource, and many books owe their reputation to his guidance and correction: thus once when required to make some formal statement of his published work, he appended the remark that much of his best work was in other men's books. The following anecdote will illustrate his attitude towards such debtors. He was generously defending a certain scholar's philological reputation against a detractor, who, willing to concede what he might, said at last, 'Well, after all, the man can't be quite a fool who gave us that brilliant reading in * * *.' Bradley was silent, moving uncomfortably in his chair, while his honesty, his charity, and his modesty, contended within him. At length honesty prevailed and he said, 'To tell you the truth, I sent him that.'

394

SIR EDMUND GOSSE (1849–1928)

GOSSE contributed to the English Men of Letters Series a *Life of Gray* which was published in 1882. The biography has many errors of fact and unwarrantable assumptions. Unhappily, it has been accepted as reliable.

Two years later there appeared: *The Works of Thomas Gray in Prose and Verse*, edited by Edmund Gosse, 4 vols., 8vo., London, 1884.

The second and third volumes contained the letters written by Gray . . . In printing the letters Gosse 'followed Mitford's latest collations, except as regards the very numerous letters addressed to Wharton'. These, he stated, 'I have scrupulously printed, as though they had never been published before, direct from the originals, which exist, in a thick volume, among the Egerton MSS., in the Manuscript department of the British Museum. The Wharton letters are so numerous and so important, and have hitherto been so carelessly transcribed, that I regard this portion of my labour, mechanical as it is, with great satisfaction.' The statement seems to indicate, without any loop-hole of ambiguity, that whereas the Wharton letters had been carelessly transcribed before (i.e. by Mitford, for no one else had transcribed them) Gosse was scrupulously printing them 'direct from the originals', and had himself undertaken the mechanical labour of transcription. Gosse's statement was put to the proof by Tovey, who, in an Appendix to the first volume of his edition of *Gray's Letters* (published in 1900), pointed out, with a polite irony, the many coincidences of error in the texts of Mitford and Gosse. These could not be explained on any assumption except that Gosse was reproducing (with occasional corrections) Mitford's text and not that of the original letters. Gosse ignored the exposure, and when two years later he issued a 'revised edition' of his book, he left the statement that the letters had been printed 'direct from the originals' as he had written it eighteen years before.

The question remained open until in 1931 the Honourable Sir Evan Charteris, in *The Life and Letters of Sir Edmund Gosse*, offered the following explanation:

> Unfortunately Gosse had employed someone else to copy the letters in the Egerton MSS., and the copyist, wearying of the script, and finding that the letters had been published by Mitford, soon began to copy from the printed word in preference to the MSS. Mitford's edition of the letters differed from the originals, and those differences reappeared in the work of the copyist.

Thus Gosse's reiterated assertion that the Wharton letters had been 'scrupulously printed direct from the originals' and by his own labours of transcription is proved devoid of truth. In the words of his biographer he had 'been deluded into putting forward a claim that turned out not to be justified'.

395

AMONG Gosse's friends and at one time most frequent guests at Delamere Terrace was John Churton Collins (1848–1908), who, like Gosse, was a friend of Browning and Swinburne. At certain points the two men were rivals, and if an element of jealousy was present it did not proceed from Gosse. Both were experts in the same field of literature, and while the writings of Collins were not comparable in charm or brilliance to those of Gosse, yet in accuracy of scholarship and width of knowledge Collins was at that time greatly his superior. Educated at Balliol, he had been in 1885 disappointed by his failure to secure the Merton Professorship of English at the University of Oxford. On the other hand Gosse, unconnected with the Universities, had . . . been appointed Clark Lecturer at Cambridge.[1] There was nothing in the situation to suggest that the friendly feelings of Collins towards Gosse had changed. The criticisms of *From Shakespeare to Pope* had ceased, the volume itself had slipped into oblivion, when without warning in the October *Quarterly* there appeared an article by Churton Collins, written with the ferocity of a scholar's contempt for off-hand inaccuracies, intensified by jealousy of a successful man of letters. Never were 'conscientious criticism' and 'a painful duty' so obviously combined with enjoyment. It was Gosse's first reverse, and it was serious. He was struck in his pride and prestige, the foundations of his learning were challenged, his reputation derided, and his right to instruct the youth of Cambridge denied. And the blow had been delivered by a friend. . . .

Collins began by assailing the condition of current literature, the practice of hurrying into the world books which owe their existence to 'the paltry vanity which thrives on the sort of homage of which society of a certain kind is not grudging and which knows no distinction between notoriety and fame'. . . 'As the general public', he continued, 'are the willing dupes of puffers, it is no more difficult to palm off on them the spurious wares of literary charlatans, than it is to beguile them into purchasing the wares of any other sort of charlatan.'—'It is shocking, it is disgusting, to contemplate the devices to which many men of letters will stoop for the sake of exalting themselves into a factitious reputation.' After more of the same sort he turns to the book itself, *From Shakespeare to Pope*, 'not the least mischievous characteristic of which is the skill with which its worthlessness is disguised'. . . .

Gosse was in no sense crushed, but he was humbled. His letters give only a faint impression of the extent to which he suffered. His self-confidence was undermined, his personality reduced. Firm ground had turned into quicksand. At the rival University it became a stock saying for anyone who had made a 'howler', that 'he had made a Gosse of himself'.

His own account of his sensation was that he went about feeling that he had been flayed alive. He had accepted beforehand an invitation to stay with Tennyson at Aldworth, and he felt a strong desire to get out of it; but he pulled himself together and went. He arrived in the afternoon and was sent out into the garden, where he found a large party; tea spread out at a trestle table, Tennyson at one end of it, and an empty chair near the other. To this he crept, hoping to escape notice, but in vain. Tennyson boomed out at him, 'Well, Gosse, would you like to know what I think of Churton Collins?' This was worse than anything he had anticipated. He

[1] Gosse's Clark lectures, *From Shakespeare to Pope*, were published in 1885.

managed to mumble that he would. 'I think', Tennyson went on, 'he's a Louse on the Locks of Literature.' The phrase from such a source was infinitely restoring.

396

I[1] remember Ker's friend, W. P. James, telling me how, on a holiday, when he and Ker were walking across Exmoor towards Minehead, a fog suddenly descended. As they plodded on through it, they saw ahead of them another figure magnified into something inhuman. On catching up with it, it turned out to be Edmund Gosse.

'I couldn't think what you could be,' said Ker, 'whether the Spectre of the Brocken or an Oxford don returning to nature.'

Later in the evening, when they were alone, Ker said to James: 'Did you notice how pleased Gosse was to be taken for an Oxford don—even in a fog?'

397

NOT long after the death of Swinburne, Gosse was engaged on the Bonchurch edition of the poet's works, in collaboration with that extraordinary character T. J. Wise (whose achievements as a 'bibliophile' deceived many book collectors, apparently including Gosse. These achievements are impressively recorded in that rather startling volume *Forging Ahead*, by Wilfred Partington) . . . On one of the crowded Sunday afternoons at 17 Hanover Terrace, a telephone message was misunderstood by the parlour-maid who took it. Knowing nothing of the death of the great poet, she stood in the doorway, and to my[2] amazement announced, 'Mr. Swinburne to speak to you on the telephone, sir!' Greatly as he appreciated Swinburne, it was an opportunity not to be missed by Gosse. In the breathless hush which had naturally followed the rather appalling announcement, all eyes were fixed on his glittering spectacles as he exclaimed, 'Mr. Swinburne to speak to me on the telephone? I shall certainly not speak to Mr. Swinburne. I don't know *where* he may be speaking from.'

Possibly the message came from T. J. Wise. If so it was among the more successful demonstrations of his virtuosity.

[1] E. V. Lucas (1868–1938).
[2] The narrator is Alfred Noyes (1880–1958).

398

GEORGE MOORE (1852–1933)

WITH *Esther Waters*, the epic of a housemaid and a stable boy, Moore sprang into sudden fame. An Irish landowner with a country seat, he knew nothing of the backstairs, though by birth and upbringing horses and racing were part of his life. The painful details of *Esther Waters*—most tragic of stories, with far more humanity and tenderness in it than a wilderness of French Realists could produce—had to be laboriously gathered from the person who 'did for him' in Dane's Inn, hired by the hour, it was said, to reveal the psychology of the toiling classes. Such situations should be immortalized, yet no one was ever present during these momentous interviews between George Moore and his cook, which resulted in *Esther Waters* and fame.

399

[Yeats recalls some unneighbourly bickering in Dublin.]

SOMETIMES Moore, instead of asking us to accept for true some monstrous invention, would press a spontaneous act into a deliberate comedy; starting in bad blood or blind passion, he would all in a moment see himself as others saw him. When he arrived in Dublin, all the doors in Upper Ely Place had been painted white by an agreement between the landlord and the tenants. Moore had his door painted green, and three Miss Beams—no, I have not got the name quite right—who lived next door protested to the landlord. Then began a correspondence between Moore and the landlord wherein Moore insisted on his position as an art critic, that the whole decoration of his house required a green door—I imagine that he had but wrapped the green flag around him—then the indignant young women bought a copy of *Esther Waters*, tore it up, put the fragments into a large envelope, wrote thereon: 'Too filthy to keep in the house,' dropped it into his letter-box. I was staying with Moore. I let myself in with a latch-key some night after twelve, and found a note on the hall-table asking me to put the door on the chain. As I was undressing, I heard Moore trying to get in; when I had opened the door and pointed to the note he said: 'Oh, I forgot. Every night I go out at eleven, at twelve, at one, and rattle my stick on the railings to make the Miss Beams' dogs bark.' Then I saw in the newspaper that the Miss Beams had hired organ-grinders to play under Moore's window when he was writing, that he had prosecuted the organ-grinders.

Moore had a large garden on the other side of the street, a blackbird sang there; he received his friends upon Saturday evening and made a moving speech upon the bird. 'I enjoy its song. If I were the bad man people say I am, could I enjoy its song?' He wrote every morning at an open window on the ground floor, and one morning saw the Miss Beams' cat cross the street, and thought, 'That cat will get my bird.' He went out and filled his pocket with stones, and whenever he saw the cat, threw a stone. Somebody, perhaps the typist, must have laughed, for the rest of the tale fills me with doubt. I was passing through Dublin just on my way to Coole; he came to my hotel.—'I remembered how early that cat got up. I thought it might get the blackbird if I was not there to protect it, so I set a trap. The Miss Beams wrote to the Society for the Prevention of Cruelty to Animals, and I am carrying on a correspondence with its secretary, cat versus bird.' (Perhaps, after all, the archives of the Society do contain that correspondence. The tale is not yet incredible.) I passed through Dublin again, perhaps on my way back. Moore came to see me in seeming great depression. 'Remember that trap?'—'Yes.'—'Remember that bird?'—'Yes.'—'I have caught the bird.'

400

A RELATIVE of the Somervilles told me[1] that his aunt had the unpleasant duty of announcing to George Moore that his friend Violet Martin, the 'Martin Ross' of 'Somerville and Ross' fame, was dead. As she entered Moore's study to break the sad news to him, Moore looked up from his writing. 'I have sad news for you, Mr. Moore,' she said. 'I regret to inform you that your friend Martin Ross is dead.' Moore clasped his head. 'How sad,' he said, 'how very sad.' He arose and paced his study agitatedly. 'How sad,' he repeated. 'Here am I in the midst of this,' and he waved his hand dramatically at the books around him, 'alive—and my friend, my dear friend, Edmund Gosse, dead.' The lady interrupted gently: 'I beg your pardon, Mr. Moore,' she said, 'it is Martin Ross who is dead, not Edmund Gosse.' Moore drew himself up and looked at her in an indignant fashion: 'My dear woman,' he said, 'surely you don't expect me to go through all that again?'

[1] Roger McHugh.

401

[Moore is remembered by two of his fellow countrymen.]

Oliver St. John Gogarty: Moore had sloping shoulders and pegtop trousers—he always dressed in dark blue. He had a heavy moustache, the top of which looked as if it had been stained with strong tea. He had an underlip that stuck out and a large white forehead, and the whole complexion was like porcelain—he had the most wonderful skin. He had white podgy hands—like a gourd or some vegetable divided in two. Yeats described the countenance of Moore as if it were carved out of a turnip, but it was only because Moore had described Yeats, who was addicted to wearing silk ties of the Latin Quarter and dressing in black with poetical inclinations, as an umbrella that somebody had forgotten at a picnic. . . .
Frank O'Connor: AE told the story of Philip Francis Little to Moore and Yeats, and he said he noticed the eyes of the pair of them beginning to expand and Moore said in a hushed voice, 'What a wonderful subject for a religious novel.' And Yeats said, 'What a wonder subject for a poetic tragedy.' Then they proceeded to quarrel about that. First of all they agreed to a collaboration; finally there was a legal action.

[The breach was never healed. Years later Gogarty, in London, used to go to see Moore.]

Gogarty: He'd beat about the bush for a good while and he'd say, 'Did you meet anyone of interest, any common friend?' I said, 'Oh, yes, in fact I met Yeats.' So he pointed to a book, Eckermann's *Life of Goethe*. 'Gogarty,' he said, 'that book contains any erudition that Yeats possesses, nothing else; he's never read anything else.' So when I went back to Dublin, Yeats said, 'I suppose you met nobody that I know in London, while you were over there?' I waited awhile and said, 'Oh yes, I met Moore.'—'Oh, you met Moore. You met that fellow. Well, what is he doing?' I said, 'He's going to write a book called *Perfect Poetry*.'—'But he knows nothing whatsoever about poetry. I don't want to tax your memory, but can you tell me what are the perfect poems he's including?' Yeats was waiting in vain for one of his own. 'Well,' I said, 'he put his thumb into his waistcoat; he leaned against his black marble mantlepiece, and he recited "Goldilocks, Goldilocks, over all the wheaten shocks". And that was one of his perfect poems.' 'Now I'll tell you something,' said Yeats. 'When I was down with William Morris at Kelmscott, in came the printer's devil and said, "Excuse me, Mr. Morris, but there are two blank pages at the end of your book of poems which we'd like filled in." And Morris said, "Excuse me, Yeats!" and with his left hand he scratched in that nonsense about Goldilocks, and that's what Moore gave you as perfect poetry.'

402
HALL CAINE (1853–1931)

[In 1910 Compton Mackenzie was given a part in a Hall Caine play called *The Bishop's Son*, and crossed to the Isle of Man in a paddle steamer to meet Hall Caine, and discuss the part.]

HALL CAINE met me at the quay with his car; although I could not help finding him a little ridiculous, I could not help liking him more and more as we drove to Greeba Castle. The Castle, which I supposed would have some signs of Gothic grandeur, turned out to be a medium-sized red brick villa. In the small dining-room, which opened on a small conservatory full of brown and yellow calceolarias, was an engraving of *The Blessed Damozel* in the frame of which was stuck a card, 'From D. G. Rossetti to Hall Caine 1881', a souvenir of the days when Hall Caine had attended the poet during his last days at Birchington-on-Sea.

The garden at the back ran up in a fairly steep slope to level ground on which Hall Caine had built himself a granite study, furnished inside with massive and severe furniture which included a bare table as large as a four-post bed.

'It's all so simple,' Hall Caine commented, in a dreamy, slightly sepulchral voice. 'So simple, so utterly in keeping with the simple life of this little island, and if I may say so with the books I write here in complete seclusion.'

Remembering the music-halls and dancing places of Douglas, I did not fancy that life was quite so simple in the Isle of Man as Hall Caine suggested, but I felt I ought to play up to his mood.

'Yes, indeed,' I said. 'One can imagine Æschylus writing his plays in surroundings like this.'

'Thank you,' Hall Caine almost intoned, 'thank you, Mr. Compton, that is one of the nicest things ever said to me.' (I had dropped 'Mackenzie' for the family stage name.) 'I shall cherish that observation of yours. Yes, that is one of the nicest things ever said to me. And so true!'

When Hall Caine came down to breakfast next morning he inquired how I had slept.

'Splendidly. I hope you had as good a night as I had, Mr. Caine.'

'I hardly ever sleep,' he replied in his most sepulchral voice. 'Go on with your breakfast, Mr. Compton. Pay no attention to me. I hardly ever eat breakfast.' . . .

Later that morning Hall Caine took me in his car to see the Tynwald.

'In one sense we shall be profaning that sacred spot by arriving in a motor-car,' he assured me solemnly, 'and I must confess there are moments when I reprove myself for having surrendered to such a blatant method of transport. But . . . ' he opened his arms and shrugged his shoulders in a gesture intended to convey the corroding advance of progress against which not even he could hold out.

When we arrived at the Tynwald, which was a green glen between grey hills, Hall Caine took off his hat and, as the gentle breeze of early summer played through the hair above that domed forehead, he delivered a kind of elegy upon the 'rude forefathers' of Mona, who in that glen had made the first laws of the island.

'And yet,' said Hall Caine when his elegy was finished, 'there are some people incapable of responding to the poetic and spiritual influence of this sacred spot. When his late Majesty King Edward visited the Island I was privileged to show him the original site of the Tynwald Court. He seemed completely unimpressed. Indeed, his only concern after I had tried to tell him about the Tynwald was to know what time lunch was.'

Hall Caine put on his hat with a sigh for King Edward's lack of imaginative response.

'And yet,' he went on, 'he was not incapable of responding to romance. His wife—Her Majesty Queen Alexandra—told me that what must have been the last book he read before his fatal illness was my novel *The Eternal City* . . . and graciously assured me that King Edward had much enjoyed it.'

403
W. P. KER (1855–1923)

No one that I[1] ever knew used so few words as W. P. [Ker] or did more with them. His 'Good' was worth pages of elaborate praise . . . But his condemnations were as emphatic as his praises. I shall always remember his comment when I told him that William Sharp had confided to a friend of mine that whenever he was preparing to write as Fiona Macleod he dressed himself entirely in woman's clothes. 'Did he?' said W.P.—'the bitch!'

[1] E. V. Lucas.

404

OSCAR WILDE (1856–1900)

IN his *viva voce* examination for 'Divvers' at Oxford, Oscar Wilde was required to translate from the Greek version of the New Testament, which was one of the set books. The passage chosen was from the story of the Passion. Wilde began to translate, easily and accurately. The examiners were satisfied, and told him that this was enough. Wilde ignored them and continued to translate. After another attempt the examiners at last succeeded in stopping him, and told him that they were satisfied with his translation. 'Oh, do let me go on,' said Wilde, 'I want to see how it ends.'

405

[On 2 January 1882, Wilde arrived at New York to undertake a lecture tour.]

THE reporters who mobbed him on the boat were a little downcast by his appearance, which was more like that of an athlete than an aesthete. True, he had long hair, and he wore a bottle-green fur-lined overcoat, with a round sealskin cap on his head, but he was a giant in stature and his fists looked formidable. He naturally expected them to question him concerning his mission; instead they asked him how he liked his eggs fried, what he slept in, how he trimmed his finger-nails, and what temperature he liked his bath to be. His answers displayed a lack of interest in the questions, and they button-holed the passengers for something of a livelier nature. The passengers rose to the occasion: they had heard him complain that the trip was tame, 'deucedly stupid' in fact, that the roaring ocean did not roar, and that nothing less than a storm which swept the bridge from the ship would give him any pleasure. That was enough for the reporters, who told their readers that Wilde was 'disappointed with the Atlantic Ocean', a phrase which got him far more publicity than his views on aestheticism would have done, or even a sparkling riposte on the theme of fried eggs. Wilde realized that he had not done himself justice on the boat, so made up for it the moment he stepped ashore. 'Have you anything to declare?' asked the customs official. 'No. I have nothing to declare'; he paused: 'except my genius.' Few remarks in history have travelled as widely and quickly as that one.

406

BEGGARS did not appeal to Wilde in vain, though the advice which once accompanied his help might, if followed, have seriously reduced the recipient's takings. A beggar accosted him in the Haymarket, and backed his appeal for alms with the assurance that he had no work to do and no bread to eat. 'Work!' exclaimed Wilde. 'Why should you want to work? And bread! Why should you eat bread?' He paused, put his hand on the man's shoulder, and continued in a friendly manner: 'Now if you had come to me and said that you had work to do, but you couldn't dream of working, and that you had bread to eat, but couldn't think of eating bread, I would have given you two shillings and sixpence.' A pause. 'As it is, I give you half-a-crown.'

407

[W. B. Yeats meets Wilde at a party given by W. E. Henley.]

MY first meeting with Oscar Wilde was an astonishment. I never before heard a man talking with perfect sentences, as if he had written them all overnight with labour and yet all spontaneous. There was present that night at Henley's, by right of propinquity or of accident, a man full of the secret spite of dullness, who interrupted from time to time, and always to check or disorder thought; and I noticed with what mastery he was foiled and thrown. I noticed, too, that the impression of artificiality that I think all Wilde's listeners have recorded came from the perfect rounding of the sentences and from the deliberation that made it possible. That very impression helped him, as the effect of metre, or of the antithetical prose of the seventeenth century, which is itself a true metre, helped its writers, for he could pass without incongruity from some unforeseen, swift stroke of wit to elaborate reverie. I heard him say a few nights later: 'Give me *The Winter's Tale*, "Daffodils that come before the swallow dares", but not *King Lear*. What is *King Lear* but poor life staggering in the fog?' and the slow, carefully modulated cadence sounded natural to my ears. The first night he praised Walter Pater's *Studies in the History of the Renaissance*: 'It is my golden book; I never travel anywhere without it; but it is the very flower of decadence: the last trump should have sounded the moment it was written.' 'But', said the dull man, 'would you not have given us time to read it?' 'Oh, no,' was the retort, 'there would have been plenty of time afterwards—in either world.'

408

ONCE at a garden party at the Bishop of London's, I[1] heard a lady ask Wilde if he were going to the dinner of the O.P. Club that evening. The O.P. Club had some grievance against Wilde. It was a dramatic society or something of the sort. Dramatic organizations are excitable and minatory when they dislike anybody. It was a dramatic society that booed and hissed Henry James when he took his curtain call after *Guy Domville*. But really they were venting their wrath against Sir George Alexander, the actor manager who had that evening for the first time made a charge for programmes. So Wilde would have had a rough house at the dinner of the O.P. Club. He therefore replied to the lady at the Bishop's party: '*I* go to the dinner of the O.P. Club? I should be like a poor lion in a den of savage Daniels.'

409

[After Wilde was released from prison in 1897 Sir William Rothenstein went to see him at Dieppe.]

LATER he spoke of his prison experiences, of the horrors of the first few months, and how by degrees he became reconciled to his situation. He seemed to have lost none of his old wit and gaiety. He told how, although talking was strictly forbidden, one of his warders would exchange a remark with him now and then. He had a great respect for Oscar as a literary man, and he did not intend to miss such a chance of improving himself. He could only get in a few words at a time.

'Excuse me, sir; but Charles Dickens, Sir, would he be considered a great writer now, Sir?' To which Oscar replied: 'Oh yes; a great writer, indeed; you see he is no longer alive.' 'Yes, I understand, Sir. Being dead he would be a great writer, Sir.'

Another time he asked about John Strange Winter.[2] 'Would you tell me what you think of him, Sir?' 'A charming person,' says Oscar, 'but a lady you know, not a man. Not a great stylist, perhaps, but a good, simple storyteller.' 'Thank you, Sir, I did not know he was a lady, Sir.'

And a third time: 'Excuse me, Sir, but Marie Corelli, would she be considered a great writer, Sir?'

'This was more than I could bear,' continued Oscar, 'and putting my hand on his shoulder I said: "Now don't think I have anything against her

[1] Ford Madox Ford.

[2] Mrs. Henrietta Stannard (1856–1911), who wrote under the pseudonym of 'John Strange Winter'.

moral character, but from the way she writes *she ought to be here.*" ' 'You say so, Sir, you say so,' said the warder, surprised, but respectful. Was ever so grim a jest made in so strange a situation?

410

GEORGE BERNARD SHAW (1856–1950)

THAT I can write as I do without having to think about my style is due to my having been as a child steeped in the Bible, *The Pilgrim's Progress*, and *Cassell's Illustrated Shakespeare*. I was taught to hold the Bible in such reverence that when one day, as I was buying a pennyworth of sweets in a little shop in Dublin, the shopkeeper tore a leaf out of a dismembered Bible to wrap them in, I was horrified, and half expected to see him struck by lightning. All the same I took the sweets and ate them; for to my Protestant mind the shopkeeper, as a Roman Catholic, would go to hell as such, Bible or no Bible, and was no gentleman anyhow. Besides, I liked eating sweets.

411

I WELL remember Mr. Shaw relating a sad anecdote whose date must have fallen among the eighties. As Mr. Shaw put it, like every poor young man when he first comes to London he possessed no presentable garments at all save a suit of dress clothes. In this state he received an invitation to a soirée from some gentleman high in the political world—I think it was Mr. Haldane. This gentleman was careful to add a postscript in the kindness of his heart, begging Mr. Shaw not to dress, since everyone would be in their morning clothes. Mr. Shaw was accordingly put into an extraordinary state of perturbation. He pawned or sold all the articles of clothing in his possession, including his evening suit, and with the proceeds purchased a decent suit of black, resembling, as he put it, that of a Wesleyan minister. Upon his going up the staircase of the house to which he was invited, the first person he perceived was Mr. Balfour, in evening dress; the second was Mr. Wyndham in evening dress; and immediately he was introduced into a dazzling hall that was one sea of white shirt fronts relieved by black swallow-tails. He was the only undressed person in the room. Then his kind host presented himself, his face beaming with philanthropy and with the thought of kindly encouragement that he had given to struggling genius! I think Mr. Shaw does not 'dress' at all nowadays, and, in the dress affected, at all events by his disciples, the grey homespuns, the soft hats, the comfortable bagginess about the knees, and the air that the pockets have of always being full of apples, the last faint trickle of Pre-Raphaelite influence is to be perceived.

412

[Sir Bernard Partridge recalls an occasion when Wilde and Bernard Shaw met each other.]

I WAS present at their meeting in the rooms of the late Fitzgerald Molloy in Red Lion Square. There were only the four of us. Shaw was on the threshold of his career; Oscar had already 'arrived'. But for once he was content to listen, and Shaw, delighted to meet such a listener, let himself go. His subject was a magazine, the founding of which he had in mind, and he held forth at great length on its scope and outlook. When he came to a halt, Oscar said 'That has all been most interesting, Mr. Shaw; but there's one point you haven't mentioned, and an all-important one—you haven't told us the *title* of your magazine.' 'Oh, as for that,' said Shaw, 'what I'd want to do would be to impress my own personality on the public—I'd call it *Shaw's Magazine*: Shaw—Shaw—Shaw!'; and he banged his fist on the table. 'Yes,' said Oscar, '*and how would you spell it?*' Shaw joined heartily in our laughter against him.

413

PARTLY to facilitate the labours of Mr. George Bernard Shaw's biographers, and partly by way of relieving my own conscience, I think I ought to give a short history of the genesis of *Widowers' Houses*.[1] Far away back in the olden days, while as yet the Independent Theatre slumbered in the womb of Time, together with the New Drama, the New Criticism, the New Humour, and all the other glories of our renovated world, I used to be a daily frequenter of the British Museum Reading Room. Even more assiduous in his attendance was a young man of tawny complexion and attire, beside whom I used frequently to find myself seated. My curiosity was piqued by the odd conjunction of his subjects of research. Day after day for weeks he had before him two books, which he studied alternately, if not simultaneously—Karl Marx's *Das Kapital* (in French), and an orchestral score of *Tristan und Isolde*. I did not know then how exactly

[1] The narrator is William Archer (1856–1924), critic and journalist.

this quaint juxtaposition symbolized the main interests of his life. Presently I met him at the house of a common acquaintance, and we conversed for the first time. I learned from himself that he was the author of several unpublished masterpieces of fiction. Construction, he owned with engaging modesty, was not his strong point, but his dialogue was incomparable. Now, in those days, I had still a certain hankering after the rewards, if not the glories, of the playwright. With a modesty in no way inferior to Mr. Shaw's, I had realized that I could not write dialogue a bit; but I still considered myself a born constructor. So I proposed, and Mr. Shaw agreed to, a collaboration. I was to provide him with one of the numerous plots I kept in stock, and he was to write the dialogue.

So said, so done. I drew out, scene by scene, the scheme of a twaddling cup-and-saucer comedy vaguely suggested by Augier's *Ceinture Dorée*. The details I forget, but I know it was to be called *Rhinegold*, was to open, as *Widowers' Houses* actually does, in a hotel-garden on the Rhine, and was to have two heroines, a sentimental and a comic one, according to the accepted Robertson–Byron–Carton formula. I fancy the hero was to propose to the sentimental heroine, believing her to be the poor niece instead of the rich daughter of the sweater, or slum-landlord, or whatever he may have been; and I know he was to carry on in the most heroic fashion, and was ultimately to succeed in throwing the tainted treasure of his father-in-law, metaphorically speaking, into the Rhine. All this I gravely propounded to Mr. Shaw, who listened with no less admirable gravity.

Then I thought the matter had dropped, for I heard no more of it for many weeks. I used to see Mr. Shaw at the Museum, laboriously writing page after page of the most exquisitely neat shorthand at the rate of about three words a minute; but it did not occur to me that this was our play. After about six weeks he said to me, 'Look here, I've written half the first act of that comedy, and I've used up all your plot. Now I want some more to go on with.' I told him that my plot was a rounded and perfect organic whole, and that I could no more eke it out in this fashion than I could provide him or myself with a set of supplementary arms and legs. I begged him to extend his shorthand and let me see what he had done; but this would have taken him far too long. He tried to decipher some of it orally, but the process was too lingering and painful for endurance. So he simply gave me an outline in narrative of what he had done; and I saw that, so far from having used up my plot, he had not even touched it.

There the matter rested for months and years. Mr. Shaw would now and then hold out vague threats of finishing 'our play', but I felt no serious alarm. I thought (judging from my own experience in other cases) that when he came to read over in cold blood what he had written, he would see what impossible stuff it was. Perhaps my free utterance of this view piqued him; perhaps he felt impelled to remove from the Independent Theatre the reproach of dealing solely in foreign products. The fire of his genius, at all events was not to be quenched by my persistent applications of the wet-blanket. He finished his play; Mr. Grein, as in duty bound, accepted it; and the result was the performance of Friday last[1] at the Independent Theatre.

414

[In February 1890 Shaw paid a visit to the Alhambra and greatly enjoyed the dancing of Vincenti, 'an intelligent and cultivated artist and an admirable pantomimist'. He remarked especially on 'the perfection of his *pirouettes* and *entrechats*' and on 'his amazing revolution about the centre of the stage combined with rotation on his own longitudinal axis'. On returning home in the small hours Shaw tried to reproduce those felicities in Fitzroy Square.]

WHEN I arrived at my door after these dissipations I found Fitzroy Square, in which I live, deserted. It was a clear, dry cold night; and the carriage-way round the circular railing presented such a magnificent hippodrome that I could not resist trying to go just once round in Vincenti's fashion. It proved frightfully difficult. After my fourteenth fall I was picked up by a policeman. 'What are you doing here?' he said, keeping fast hold of me. 'I'bin watching you for the last five minutes.' I explained, eloquently and enthusiastically. He hesitated a moment, and then said, 'Would you mind holding my helmet while I have a try? It don't look so hard.' Next moment his nose was buried in the macadam and his right knee was out through its torn garment. He got up bruised and bleeding, but resolute. 'I never was beaten yet,' he said, 'and I won't be beaten now. It was my coat that tripped me.' We both hung our coats on the railings, and went at it again. If each round in the square had been a round in a prize fight, we should have been less damaged and disfigured; but we persevered, and by four o'clock the policeman had just succeeded in getting round twice without a rest or a fall, when an inspector arrived and asked him bitterly whether that was his notion of fixed point duty. 'I allow it ain't fixed point,' said the constable, emboldened by his new accomplishment; 'but I'll lay a half-sovereign *you* can't do it.' The inspector could not resist the temptation to try (I was whirling round before his eyes in the most fascinating manner); and he made rapid progress after half an hour or so. We were subsequently joined by an early postman and by a milkman, who unfortunately broke his leg and had to be

[1] 9 December 1892.

carried to hospital by the other three. By that time I was quite exhausted, and could barely crawl into bed. It was perhaps a foolish scene; but nobody who has witnessed Vincenti's performance will feel surprised at it.

415

[On 21 April 1894, the first performance of Shaw's *Arms and the Man* took place at the Avenue Theatre, and the play ran till 7 July. 'It passed for a success,' Shaw reported, 'the applause on the first night being as promising as could be wished . . . To witness it the public paid £1777-5-6, an average of £23-2-5 per representation . . .']

THE first performance was boisterous. The author took a curtain call, and was received with cheers. When they had subsided, and before G.B.S. could utter a syllable, a solitary hiss was heard in the gallery. It was made by R. Goulding Bright, who was afterwards a very successful literary agent, and it was made, as he told me, under a misapprehension. He thought that G.B.S., in his satire on florid Balkan soldiers, was reflecting on the British Army. G.B.S. bowed to him, and remarked, 'I quite agree with you, sir, but what can two do against so many?'

416

BASIL DEAN told a good rehearsal story. He said that they rehearsed Shaw's *Pygmalion* for nine weeks at 'His Majesty's' and that in the middle Mrs. Pat Campbell went away for two weeks on her honeymoon. When she returned she merely said by way of explanation: 'George [her new husband] is a golden man.' There was some trouble about her rendering. When she had altered it she said to Shaw, 'Is that better?' Shaw said: 'No, it isn't. I don't want any of your flamboyant creatures, I want a simple ordinary human creation such as I have drawn.' He was getting shirty. Mrs. P.C. was taken aback. She replied, however: 'You are a terrible man, Mr. Shaw. One day you'll eat a beefsteak and then God help all women.' It is said that Shaw blushed.

417

[Shaw recalls a case of editorial interference.]

I REMEMBER a critic who was interfered with, not on artistic, but on purely political grounds. Austin Harrison was critic of the *Daily Mail*, and when I began to make trouble in the theatre Austin Harrison was interested and wrote long notices of my plays. They were either not put in or they were cut extremely short. When Harrison, not understanding why this happened, asked Lord Northcliffe the reason, Northcliffe said, 'I am not running my paper to advertise a damned Socialist.'

418
FRANK HARRIS (1856-1931)

[Frank (i.e. James Thomas) Harris was at the height of his reputation while he was editing *The Saturday Review*, from 1894 to 1899. Sir William Rothenstein recalls a dinner at the Café Royal.]

THESE were Harris's days of prosperity, when he entertained lavishly, usually at the Café Royal. I remember especially a dinner he gave there at which Oscar Wilde, Max Beerbohm, Aubrey Beardsley, Robbie Ross and myself were present. Harris on this occasion monopolized the conversation; even Wilde found it difficult to get a word in. He told us an endless story, obviously inspired by the *Étui de Nacre*,[1] while Oscar grew more and more restive. When at last it came to an end, Max said, 'Now, Frank, Anatole France would have spoiled that story.' But Harris wasn't thin-skinned; he proceeded to tell us of all the great houses he frequented. This was more than Oscar could bear.—'Yes, dear Frank,' he exclaimed, 'we believe you; you have dined in every house in London, *once*'—the only time I heard him say an unkind thing.

419
BEATRICE WEBB (1858–1943)

[From *The Journals of Arnold Bennett*.]

Yacht Club, London, Wednesday, May 9th.
I came to London Tuesday. Lunched at Webbs. Apropos of Squire's poem in current issue of *Statesman*, the Webbs were both funny. Mrs. Webb especially. She said, 'Poetry means nothing to me. It confuses me. I always want to translate it back into prose.'

[1] By Anatole France, 1892.

420
SIDNEY WEBB (1859–1947)

NOBODY is all of a piece, not even the Webbs. I[1] once remarked to Shaw that Webb seemed to me somewhat deficient in kindly feeling. 'No,' Shaw replied, 'you are quite mistaken. Webb and I were once in a tram car in Holland eating biscuits out of a bag. A handcuffed criminal was brought into the tram by policemen. All the other passengers shrank away in horror, but Webb went up to the prisoner and offered him biscuits.' I remember this story whenever I find myself becoming unduly critical of either Webb or Shaw.

421
A. E. HOUSMAN (1859–1936)

As everyone knows,[2] the poet was also a professor, and one of the first authorities on the old Pagan literature. I cherish a story about him which happens to concern this double character of the classical and the poetical. It may be a familiar story; it may be a false story. It describes the start of an after-dinner speech he made at Trinity, Cambridge; and whoever made it or invented it had a superb sense of style. 'This great College, of this ancient University, has seen some strange sights. It has seen Wordsworth drunk and Porson sober. And here am I, a better poet than Porson, and a better scholar than Wordsworth, [somewhere] betwixt and between.'

422
SIR ARTHUR CONAN DOYLE (1859–1930)

[Conan Doyle, who was married in 1885 and had been practising medicine at Southsea, decided in 1890 to set up as a specialist in London. His first book, *A Study in Scarlet* (1887), had already introduced Sherlock Holmes to the reading public.]

WE took two rooms in Montague Place, and I went forth to search for some place where I could put up my plate as an oculist. I was aware that

[1] Bertrand Russell.
[2] This well-known anecdote is told here by G. K. Chesterton.

many of the big men do not find time to work out refractions, which in some cases of astigmatism take a long time to adjust when done by retinoscopy. I was capable in this work and liked it, so I hoped that some of it might drift my way. But to get it, it was clearly necessary that I should live among the big men so that the patient could be easily referred to me. I searched the doctors' quarters and at last found suitable accommodation at 2 Devonshire Place, which is at the top of Wimpole Street and close to the classical Harley Street. There for £120 a year I got the use of a front room with part use of a waiting-room. I was soon to find that they were both waiting-rooms, and now I know that it was better so.

Every morning I walked from the lodgings, at Montague Place, reached my consulting-room at ten and sat there until three or four, with never a ring to disturb my serenity. Could better conditions for reflection be found? It was ideal, and so long as I was thoroughly unsuccessful in my professional venture there was every chance of improvement in my literary prospects. Therefore when I returned to the lodgings at tea-time I bore my little sheaves with me, the first-fruits of a considerable harvest....

Looking round for my central character I felt that Sherlock Holmes, whom I had already handled in two little books, would easily lend himself to a succession of short stories. These I began in the long hours of waiting in my consulting room.... My literary affairs had been taken up by that king of agents, A. P. Watt, who relieved me of all the hateful bargaining, and handled things so well that any immediate anxiety for money soon disappeared. It was as well, for not one single patient had ever crossed the threshold of my room.

I was now once more at the cross-roads of my life, and Providence, which I recognize at every step, made me realize it in a very energetic and unpleasant way. I was starting off for my usual trudge one morning from our lodgings when icy shivers passed over me, and I only got back in time to avoid a total collapse. It was a virulent attack of influenza, at a time when influenza was in its deadly prime.... It was then, as I surveyed my own life, that I saw how foolish I was to waste my literary earnings in keeping up an oculist's room in Wimpole Street, and I determined with a wild rush of joy to cut the painter, and to trust for ever to my power of writing.

423

THAT Sherlock Holmes was anything but mythical to many was shown by the fact that I have had many letters addressed to him with requests that I forward them. Watson has also had a number of letters in which he has been asked for the address or for the autograph of his more brilliant confrère. A press-cutting agency wrote to Watson asking whether Holmes would not wish to subscribe. When Holmes retired several elderly ladies were ready to keep house for him, and one sought to ingratiate herself by assuring me that she knew all about bee-keeping and could 'segregate the queen'. I had considerable offers also for Holmes if he would examine and solve various family mysteries. Once the offer—from Poland—was that I should myself go, and my reward was practically left to my own judgement. I had judgement enough, however, to avoid it altogether.

424
SIR JAMES BARRIE (1860–1937)

IT was one of the Llewelyn-Davies children who in very early days unconsciously provided Barrie with the 'copy' for the lines afterwards spoken in *Peter Pan* by the little boy in his night-shirt.

'You'll be sick tomorrow, Jack, if you eat any more chocolates,' Sylvia remarked severely to her small son during a picnic at which the dramatist was one of the guests.

'I shall be sick tonight,' replied the child laconically, helping himself to another sweetmeat.

So delighted was Barrie at this epigram that he offered the child a royalty of a halfpenny a performance for the copyright. The offer was promptly accepted, and must have proved a good financial investment for the youngster.

425
WALTER SICKERT (1860–1942)

[Sir Osbert Sitwell recalls a dinner party in the early 1920s.]

I RECALL later evenings, too, and one night at dinner in my present house in Chelsea, after we had left Swan Walk, comes back to me particularly. . . . Those present were Sickert, Arnold Bennett, Frank Swinnerton, Massingham, the editor of the *Nation*, Percy Wyndham Lewis, William Walton, my brother, and myself. . . . Sickert was in a peculiarly brilliant mood, led the evening and was audacious as a matador. I do not think that

Lewis enjoyed this scintillation. (It did not seem to him to come from the right quarter.) Even Arnold, an old friend of Sickert's, seemed a trifle dazed. Towards the end of dinner a controversy arose, and Sickert just danced round the rest of us. . . . Sickert then lit a cigar and, nipping round the corner of the table, pressed one upon Lewis, with the words, 'I give you this cigar because I so greatly admire your writings.' Lewis switched upon him as dazzling a smile as he had had time to prepare, but before it was really quite ready, and he had succeeded in substituting this genial grin for his more usual expression, Sickert planted the goad by adding, 'If I liked your paintings, I'd give you a bigger one!'

426
DEAN INGE (1860–1954)

DEAN INGE was delighted by an angry letter he had received from a lady who disagreed with one of his articles.

'I am praying nightly for your death,' she wrote. 'It may interest you to know that in two other cases I have had great success.'

After his retirement from the Deanery he became a regular contributor to a London journal, and told us, with a chuckle, of the critical comment that he had ceased to be a pillar of the Church, and was now two columns of the *Evening Standard.*

427
ADA LEVERSON (1862–1933)

HOW well I[1] recall that talk in the low voice which one was always compelled to ask her to raise. . . . Naturally low, the expression of a diffident and gentle disposition, it was the true vehicle of her personality. And she told me, some years after I first met her—and it proves, I think, that she had always been inclined to speak in this manner—that on the first occasion she had sat next Henry James at dinner, she had not been able to resist putting to him certain questions about his books, for she had been a lifelong admirer of them, and that, at last, after he had answered some of these murmured inquiries, he had turned his melancholy gaze upon her, and had said to her, 'Can it be—it must be—that you are that embodiment

[1] Sir Osbert Sitwell.

of the incorporeal, that elusive and ineluctable being to whom through the generations novelists have so unavailingly made invocation; in short, the *Gentle Reader*? I have often wondered in what guise you would appear or, as it were, what incarnation you would assume.'

428
F. S. BOAS (1862–1957)

MY father[1] lived till the age of ninety-five and was still working. He looked so old when I was young, and so young when I was old that he never seemed to change. . . . In 1896, the year I was born, he published *Shakspere and his Predecessors*—'Such a good book,' said an old lady, 'it saves reading Shakespeare.' So unworldly was my father that he thought that £40 which he received on publication was all he would get. He was amazed when royalties in due course followed which brought him a pleasant annual sum for over fifty years. In 1952, when he was over ninety, he signed an agreement to write a book on Sir Philip Sidney, which appeared when he was ninety-three, and he contributed his last review to the *Times Literary Supplement* within a fortnight of his death. When the *Supplement* celebrated its half-century with a sherry party the editor introduced my father to a startled American as 'Dr. Boas, our oldest contributor. He is an Elizabethan.' 'It's not quite as bad as that,' I explained, for the American seemed looking for the doublet and hose.

My father was a man of great dignity, wisdom, charm, and friendliness. His literary industry was prodigious, yet he wore his scholarship lightly. . . . 'I never knew such a reader,' said my mother. 'When the conductor gives him his ticket in the tram, he turns it over and reads the back.'

429
W. B. YEATS (1865–1939)

SOMETIMES I told myself very adventurous love-stories with myself for hero, and at other times I planned out a life of lonely austerity, and at other times mixed the ideals and planned a life of lonely austerity mitigated by periodical lapses. I had still the ambition, formed in Sligo in my teens, of living in imitation of Thoreau on Innisfree, a little island in Lough

[1] The author of these reminiscences is Guy Boas.

Gill, and when walking through Fleet Street very homesick I heard a little tinkle of water and saw a fountain in a shop-window which balanced a little ball upon its jet, and began to remember lake water. From the sudden remembrance came my poem *Innisfree*, my first lyric with anything in its rhythm of my own music.

430

YEATS never had the remotest idea of taking care of himself. He would go all day without food unless someone remembered it for him, and in the same way would go on eating unless someone checked him. That first winter, a hard one, he would come to see me,[1] five miles from Dublin, striding along over the snow-bound roads, a gaunt young figure, mouthing poetry, swinging his arms and gesticulating as he went. George Russell complained to me the other day that Willie Yeats had said somewhere of him, and printed it, that he used to walk about the streets of Dublin swinging his arms like a flail, unconscious of the alarm and bewilderment of the passers-by. It was Willie's own case. I remember how the big Dublin policemen used to eye him in those days, as though uncertain whether to 'run him in' or not. But, by and by, they used to say, 'Shure, 'tisn't mad he is, nor yet drink taken. 'Tis the poethry that's disturbin' his head,' and leave him alone.

431

[Max Beerbohm recalls his second meeting with Yeats.]

A NEW publication, entitled *The Savoy*, was afoot, with Arthur Symons for literary editor and Beardsley for art-editor. The publisher was a strange and rather depressing person, a north-countryman, known to have been engaged in the sale of disreputable books. To celebrate the first number of the magazine, he invited the contributors to supper in a room at the New Lyric Club. Besides Symons and Beardsley, there were present Yeats, Mr. Rudolf Dircks, myself, and one or two other writers whom I forget. Also there was one lady: the publisher's wife. She had not previously been heard of by anyone. She was a surprise. She was touching—dreadfully touching. It was so evident that she had been brought out from some far suburb for this occasion only. One knew that

[1] Katharine Tynan (1861–1931), Irish poet and novelist.

the dress she wore had been ordered specially; and one felt that it might never be worn again. She was small, buxom, and self-possessed. She did the honours. She dropped little remarks. It did not seem that she was nervous; one only knew that she *was* nervous. She knew that she did not matter; but she would not give in; she was brave and good. Perhaps, if I had not been so preoccupied by the pity of her, I would have been more susceptible to Yeats's magic. I wished that I, not he, had been placed next to her at the table. I could have helped her more than he. The walls of the little room in which we supped were lined with bamboo instead of wallpaper. 'Quite original, is it not?' she said to Yeats. But Yeats had no reply ready for that; only a courteous, lugubrious murmur. He had been staying in Paris, and was much engrossed in the cult of Diabolism, or Devil-worship, which appeared to have a vogue there. He had made a profound study of it; and he evidently guessed that Beardsley, whom he met now for the first time, was a confirmed worshipper in that line. So to Beardsley he talked, in deep, vibrant tones across the table, of the lore and rites of Diabolism—'Dyahbolism' he called it, thereby making it sound the more fearful. I dare say that Beardsley, who always seemed to know by instinctive erudition all about everything, knew all about Dyahbolism. Anyhow, I could see that he with that stony commonsense which always came upmost when anyone canvassed the fantastic in him, thought Dyahbolism rather silly. He was too polite not to go on saying at intervals, in his hard, quick voice, 'Oh really? How perfectly entrancing!' and 'Oh really? How perfectly sweet!' But, had I been Yeats, I would have dropped the subject sooner than he did.

At the other end of the table, Arthur Symons was talking of some foreign city, carrying in his waistcoat-pocket, as it were, the *genius loci*, anon to be embalmed in Pateresque prose. I forget whether this time it was Rome or Seville or Moscow or what; but I remember that the hostess said she had never been there. I liked Symons feigning some surprise at this, and for saying that she really ought to go. Presently I heard him saying he thought the nomadic life was the best of all lives for an artist. Yeats, in a pause of his own music, heard this too, and seemed a little pained by it. Shaking back the lock from his brow, he turned to Symons and declared that an artist worked best among his own folk and in the land of his fathers. Symons seemed rather daunted, but he stuck to his point. He argued that new sights and sounds and odours braced the whole intelligence of a man and quickened his powers of creation. Yeats, gently but firmly, would have none of this. His own arguments may not have been better than Symons's; but, in voice and manner and countenance, Symons was no match for him at all. And it was with an humane impulse that the hostess interposed.

'Mr. Symons', she said, 'is like myself. He likes a little change.'

This bathos was so sharp that it was like an actual and visible chasm: one could have sworn to a glimpse of Symons's heels, a faint cry, a thud. Yeats stood for an instant on the brink, stroking his chin enigmatically, and then turned to resume the dropped thread of Dyahbolism. I could not help wishing that he, not poor Symons, had been the victim. He would somehow have fallen on his feet; and his voice, issuing uninterruptedly from the depth of the chasm, would have been as impressive as ever.

432

I NEVER believed that WB knew anything much about philosophy, though he talked a great deal about it, but he invented a philosophy of his own, which was rather amusing.[1] One very interesting and amusing thing occurred when he was expounding this highly esoteric theory of his one night up in the Arts Club. And among those present was a little man called Cruise O'Brien, a very brilliant journalist, and one of the very few people who could be rude with impunity to WB. WB gave him, as he very often gave me, a fool's pardon. This night, at any rate, he was expounding this philosophy of his which was connected in some queer way with the phases of the moon; he was telling us all about the twenty phases of the moon and he had equated every phase against some historical figure. He said, 'Number one—the highest phase—is perfect beauty.' With a respectful silence for a few seconds we all listened, and then he said, 'Number two was Helen of Troy—the nearest approximation to perfect beauty.' And he went right round the twenty-eight, or rather twenty-seven, phases and finally he came to the last and then he said that the lowest form of all is Thomas Carlyle and all Scotsmen. This shook us all a little bit and Cruise O'Brien spoke up at once. 'WB,' he said—he'd a very mincing voice, Cruise—'have you ever read a word of Carlyle? You say Carlyle is the lowest form. Oh come! Have you ever read a word of Carlyle?'—'Carlyle, Cruise, was a dolt,' said WB.—'But I insist, WB, did you ever read one single word of Carlyle?'—'Carlyle, I tell you, was a dolt.'—'Yes, but you haven't read him.'—'No, I have not read him; my wife, George, has read him and she tells me he's a dolt.' That was the end of the philosophical treatise for the night.

[1] These reminiscences were recorded by Bertie Smyllie in a broadcast talk.

433

I[1] ENCOURAGED Yeats to speak about Mrs. Pat Campbell, who had played in his *Deirdre*. He described her as having 'an ego like a raging tooth', and spoke of her habit of 'throwing tantrums' at rehearsals. On one occasion after a particularly wild 'tantrum' she walked to the footlights and peered out at Yeats, who was pacing up and down the stalls of the Abbey Theatre. 'I'd give anything to know what you're thinking,' shouted Mrs. Pat. 'I'm thinking', replied Yeats, 'of the master of a wayside Indian railway-station who sent a message to his Company's headquarters saying: "Tigress on the line: wire instructions." '

434

ALFRED HARMSWORTH, VISCOUNT NORTHCLIFFE (1865–1922)

[In 1889 H. G. Wells became science master at Henley House private school in Kilburn, kept by J. V. Milne, the father of A. A. Milne. Among the school's former pupils was Alfred Harmsworth, later Lord Northcliffe.]

ALFRED was born in 1865, a little more than a year before me, and he seems to have entered Henley House School when he was nine or ten years old. He made a very poor impression on his teachers and became one of those unsatisfactory, rather heavy, good-tempered boys who in the usual course of things drift ineffectively through school to some second-rate employment. It was J.V.'s ability that saved him from that. Somewhere about the age of twelve, Master Harmsworth became possessed of a jelly-graph for the reproduction of MS. in violet ink, and with this he set himself to produce a mock newspaper. J.V., with the soundest pedagogic instinct, seized upon the educational possibilities of this display of interest and encouraged young Harmsworth, violet with copying ink and not quite sure whether he had done well or ill, to persist with the *Henley House Magazine* even at the cost of his school work. The first number appeared in 1878; the first printed number in 1881 'edited by Alfred C. Harmsworth' . . . During my stay at Henley House, I contributed largely, and among others who had a hand in the magazine was A. J. Montefiore, who was later to edit the *Educational Review*, and A. A.

[1] Gabriel Fallon.

Milne ('aged six'—at his first appearance in print), the novelist, essayist and playwright.

Now neither Milne nor anyone in the Harmsworth family, as they scanned the early issues of this little publication, had the faintest suspicion of the preposterous thrust of opportunity that it was destined to give its youthful editor. But in the eighties the first school generation educated under the Education Act of 1871 was demanding cheap reading matter and wanting something a little easier than *Chambers's Journal* and a little less simply feminine than the *Family Herald.* A shrewd pharmaceutical chemist named Newnes tried to make a modest profit out of a periodical, originally of cuttings and quotations, *Tit Bits*, and made a great fortune. Almost simultaneously our Harmsworth, pursuing print as if by instinct, tried to turn a modest hundred or so by creating *Answers to Correspondents* (1888). . . . *Answers* hung fire for a time until it dropped its initial idea and set out to imitate and beat *Tit Bits* at its own game, with the aid of prize competitions.

Neither Newnes nor Harmsworth, when they launched these ventures, had the slightest idea of the scale of the new forces they were tapping. They thought they were going to sell to a public of at most a few score thousands and they found they were publishing for the million. They did not so much climb to success; they were rather caught by success and blown sky high. I will not even summarize the headlong uprush of Alfred C. Harmsworth and his brother Harold; how presently they had acquired the *Evening News*, started the *Daily Mail*, and gone from strength to strength until at last Alfred sat on the highest throne in British journalism, *The Times*, and Harold was one of the richest men in the world.

Only one item in this rocket flight is really significant here. The second success of the Harmsworth brothers was a publication called *Comic Cuts.* Some rare spasm of decency seems to have prevented them calling this enormously profitable, nasty, taste-destroying appeal for the ha'pence of small boys, *Komic Kuts.* They sailed into this business of producing saleable letterpress for the coppers of the new public, with an entire disregard of good taste, good value, educational influence, social consequences or political responsibility. They were as blind as young kittens to all those aspects of life. That is the most remarkable fact about them from my present point of view, and I think posterity will find it even more astonishing.

435
RUDYARD KIPLING (1865–1936)

[Among Kipling's minor distinctions was the fact that he was one of the earliest English motorists. When, in 1902, he settled with his wife in Sussex, he bought a car and drove more or less successfully about the countryside. To the conservative Henry James this form of transport was still highly suspect, and a mechanical breakdown was something that only served to confirm his suspicions. When Ford Madox Ford visited him one day at Lamb House, Rye, James launched into the following monologue, obviously finding some malicious satisfaction in the fact that it was his much more popular and wealthy contemporary who was having trouble with his expensive new toy.]

WHEN I was admitted into his presence by the astonishingly ornate manservant he said:

'A writer who unites—if I may use the phrase—in his own person an enviable popularity to—as I am told—considerable literary gifts and whom I may say I like because he treats me'—and here Mr. James laid his hand over his heart, made the slightest of bows and, rather cruelly rolling his dark and liquid eyes and moving his lower jaw as if he were rolling in his mouth a piquant tit-bit, Mr. James continued, 'because he treats me—if again I may say any such thing—with proper respect'—and there would be an immense humorous gasp before the word 'respect'—'I refer of course to Mr. Kipling . . . has just been to see me. And—such are the rewards of an enviable popularity!—a popularity such as I—or indeed you my young friend if you have any ambitions which I sometimes doubt—could dream of far less imagine to ourselves—such are the rewards of an enviable popularity that Mr. Kipling is in the possession of a magnificent one thousand two hundred guineas motor car. And, in the course of conversation as to characteristics of motor cars in general and those of the particular one thousand two hundred guinea motor car in the possession of our friend. . . . But what do I say? . . . Of our cynosure! Mr. Kipling uttered words which have for himself no doubt a particular significance but which to me at least convey almost literally nothing beyond their immediate sound . . . Mr. Kipling said that the motor car was calculated to make the Englishman . . . ' and again came the humorous gasp and the roll of the eyes—'was calculated to make the Englishman . . . think.' And Mr. James abandoned himself for part of a second to low chuckling. 'And,' he continued, 'the conversation dissolved itself, after digressions on the advantages attendant on the possession of such a vehicle, into what I believe are styled golden dreams—such as how the magnificent one thousand two hundred guinea motor car after having this evening conveyed its master and mistress to Batemans Burwash of which the proper pronunciation is Burridge would tomorrow devotedly return here and reaching here at twelve would convey me and my nephew Billiam to Burridge in time to lunch and having partaken of that repast to return here in time to give tea to my friend Lady Maud Warrender who is honouring that humble meal with her presence tomorrow under my roof. . . . And we were all indulging in—what is it?—delightful anticipations and dilating on the agreeableness of rapid—but not for fear of the police and consideration for one's personal safety *too* rapid—speed over country roads and all, if I may use the expression, was gas and gingerbread when . . . There is a loud knocking at the door and—*avec des yeux éffarés* . . .' and here Mr. James really did make his prominent and noticeable eye almost stick out of his head . . . 'in rushes the chauffeur. . . . And in short the chauffeur has omitted to lubricate the wheels of the one thousand two hundred guinea motor car with the result that its axles have become one piece of molten metal. . . . The consequence is that its master and mistress will return to Burwash which should be pronounced Burridge by train, and the magnificent one thousand two hundred guinea motor car will *not* devotedly return here at noon and will *not* in time for lunch convey me and my nephew Billiam to Burwash and will *not* return here in time for me to give tea to my friend Lady Maud Warrender who is honouring that humble meal with her presence tomorrow beneath my roof or if the weather is fine in the garden. . . . '

'Which,' concluded the Master after subdued 'ho, ho, ho's' of merriment, 'is calculated to make Mr. Kipling think.'

436

H. G. WELLS (1866–1946)

I BEGAN the New Year with my first and only regular job on a London daily. Cust had promised that I should have the next vacancy, whatever it was, on the *Pall Mall*,[1] and the lot fell upon the dramatic criticism. I was summoned by telegram. 'Here,' said Cust and thrust two small pieces of coloured paper into my hand.

'What are these?' I asked.

'Theatres. Go and do 'em.'

'Yes,' I said and reflected. 'I'm willing to have a shot at it, but I ought to warn you that so far, not counting the Crystal Palace Pantomime and Gilbert and Sullivan, I've been only twice to a theatre.'

[1] *The Pall Mall Gazette*, edited by H. J. C. Cust from 1892 to 1896.

'Exactly what I want,' said Cust. 'You won't be in the gang. You'll make a break.'

'One wears evening dress?'

It was not in Cust's code of manners to betray astonishment. 'Oh yes. Tomorrow night especially. The Haymarket.'

We regarded each other thoughtfully for a moment. 'Right oh,' said I and hurried round to a tailor named Millar in Charles Street who knew me to be solvent. 'Can you make me evening clothes by tomorrow night?' I asked, 'or must I hire them?'

The clothes were made in time, but in the foyer I met Cust and George Steevens ready to supply a criticism if I failed them and nothing came to hand from me. But I did the job in a fashion and posted my copy fairly written out in its bright red envelope before two o'clock in the morning in the Mornington Road pillar box. The play was '*An Ideal Husband*, a new and original play of modern life by Oscar Wilde'. That was on the third of January 1895, and all went well. On the fifth I had to do *Guy Domville*, a play by Henry James at the St. James's Theatre.[1]

437
ARNOLD BENNETT (1867–1931)

[Sir William Rothenstein recalls Bennett making a gaffe.]

I DELIGHTED in Bennett. He was so human in his enjoyment of life, of his own success. He was generous both as host and guest, and was, moreover, something of a patron of the arts. On his walls were paintings by Bonnard, Sickert and Conder; there was a portrait of André Gide by Fry, and there were all sorts of amusing oddities and Victorian bric-à-brac about the rooms. He rather fancied himself as a man of taste, and gave much thought to his dress. Dining with us one night he attacked the placing of the pictures in the National Gallery, not realizing that W. G. Constable, who was dining too, was Assistant Director there. Constable challenged him to name any picture that was badly hung, and Bennett, in a difficulty, admitted he had not been at the Gallery for three years. He tried, however, to describe a particular painting, finally saying he thought there was a good deal of red in it! After dinner he confided to my son John that he had made a fool of himself. '*Made* a fool of himself!' was Max's comment on the incident.

[1] See No. 387.

438

[P. G. Wodehouse reflects upon the vanity of authors.]

DISRAELI once said that the author who talks about his books is as bad as the mother who talks about her children, but Walpole and Bennett had either not come across this dictum or had mutually agreed to ignore it. 'It would be affectation to say that the Clayhanger trilogy is not good,' said Bennett, among a great number of other things. 'Either I'm a good writer or I have been deceiving myself as well as trying to deceive the public. I place it upon record frankly—the Clayhanger trilogy is *good*.' Hugh Walpole was starting to say something about the Herries series, of which his previous conversation had shown that he approved, but Bennett rolled over him like a placid steam-roller. 'The scene, for instance, where Darius Clayhanger dies that lingering death could scarcely be bettered . . . And why?' said Bennett. 'Because I took infinite pains over it. All the time my father was dying, I was at the bedside making copious notes. You can't just slap these things down. You have to take trouble.'

439

THE BODLEIAN LIBRARY (in 1868)

THREE folio volumes of treatises in Canon and Civil Law, printed between 1502 and 1511, were given to the Bodleian by the Revd. David Royce, M.A., Vicar of Nether Swell, Gloucestershire, to which a very curious history attaches, of a kind which would have seemed almost impossible to have become a history in the latter half of this century. On the death of the owner of a certain old estate, it was thought wise by heirs or executors to destroy *en masse* certain old writings, books, and papers, which they could not read or understand, and which they were unwilling should pass into other hands, as they themselves did not know what the contents might be. So these wise men of Gotham made a fire, and condemned the books to be burned. But the soul of the village cobbler was moved, for he saw that vellum might be more useful as material for cutting out patterns of shapely shoes and as padding than as fuel; and so he hurried to the place of execution and prayed that he might have a cartful from the heap; and his prayer was granted. Some time after, Mr. Royce heard of what had occurred, and by his means the cobbler was 'interviewed', and all that was left of the precious load was obtained from him. And among vellum fragments were the three above-mentioned books on paper, perfect copies, books which the Bodleian did not possess. And by the gift of my old friend who was the means of their rescue, I have some fragments of a fine 13th-century MS. of one of St. Augustine's treatises, cut and marked for the measure of some rustic foot. That a remnant of an old monastic library perished on this occasion, there is only too much reason to fear.

440
MRS. CECIL CHESTERTON (1869–1962)

IT marked a sort of sublimation of the Fleet Street spirit in my sister-in-law that, within healthy limits, she not only could do everything, but she would do anything.[1] Her work was patchwork of the wildest and most bizarre description; and she was almost continuously in a state of hilarious irony in contemplation of its contrast. She would turn easily from a direct and demagogic, though quite tragically sincere, appeal in a Sunday paper against official oppression of poor mothers, to an almost cynical modern criticism of the most sophisticated modern plays. She would finish a hard controversial comment on the Marconi case, full of facts and figures, for the *Eye-Witness*, and lightly turn to the next chapter in a shamelessly melodramatic and Victorian serial, full of innocent heroines and infamous villains, for *Fireside Romances* or *Wedding Bells*. It was of her that the story was told that, having driven whole teams of plotters and counterplotters through a serious Scotch newspaper, she was pursuing one of the side-plots for a few chapters, when she received a telegram from the editor, 'You have left your hero and heroine tied up in a cavern under the Thames for a week, and they are not married.'

441
ROBERT ROSS (1869–1918)

[Ross was one of the most loyal friends Oscar Wilde ever had, and became his literary executor.]

LORD ALFRED DOUGLAS, Robbie's most virulent enemy, though unfortunate in all else, was fortunate in living long enough to be the last

[1] These reminiscences are by G. K. Chesterton.

surviving member of Oscar Wilde's circle, and thus able to leave for others, who had not known Ross, a distorted presentation of his character, and to show him as an unprincipled and injurious friend to the fallen writer, whereas in reality he was a martyr to this friendship, which, by the sorrows, worries and troubles it brought him, shortened and ruined his life. He had no foes, however, among the young. His wit, for which he was justly celebrated, was apt to die with the day that gave it birth, being of the type that, most exquisite of ephemerids, is so true and pointed as to depend for its value on the currents, trends and feelings almost of a particular week. A few *mots* survive, to hibernate in the mind, and come out again on an early summer day: and these, no matter if you disagree with the opinion they express, are brilliant. Such a one was the epitaph he designed for his tomb. . . . When asked one evening by a friend what he would choose to be written on his own gravestone, he replied that, at the end of so stormy a career, the appropriate inscription would be, 'Here lies one whose name is writ in hot water.'

442
HILAIRE BELLOC (1870–1953)

THREE of his books were published in the same season. I[1] ventured to suggest to him that he was overdoing it. People would not buy three books of the same author at the same time. . . .

'You should, at the beginning, have taken half a dozen pen-names,' I said. 'You have written sixty or seventy books and you have shown a specialist's knowledge of military science, of topography, of finance, and you have written poetry which will endure as long as the language endures. But people like to stick a label on authors. You could easily have made six distinct reputations, whereas skill in many things is considered in our day to be a deadly sin.'

'That may be so,' he admitted. 'I have sometimes thought of it. My advice to a young writer—who is merely thinking of fame—is to concentrate on one subject. Let him, when he is twenty, write about the earthworm. Let him continue for forty years to write of nothing but the earthworm. When he is sixty, pilgrims will make a hollow path with their feet to the door of the world's great authority on the earthworm. They will knock at his door and humbly beg to be allowed to see the Master of the Earthworm.'

[1] Sisley Huddleston.

443
W. H. DAVIES (1871–1940)

DAVIES'S grandmother, a Baptist by denomination, was of a more austere and religious turn of mind than her husband . . . Davies once told me[1] that he remembered his grandmother smacking him severely after some manifestation of childish sin, and saying between blows,

'If—you—go—on—like—this,—you'll—be—no—better—than—that —young—Brodribb—cousin—of—yours,—who's—brought—disgrace— upon—the—family!'

'That—young—Brodribb—cousin' was, in fact, known to the theatre-going audiences all over the English-speaking world as Henry Irving: but the old woman always referred to the stage as 'The Devil's Playground', and that her relative was the idol of the whole country, acclaimed everywhere, to her signified nothing; indeed worse than nothing. The wages of sin were death, and not even a knighthood—the first ever conferred upon a member of his profession—could modify that well-known decree, or moderate the sentence of doom that it pronounced.

444
JOHN MILLINGTON SYNGE (1871–1909)

YEATS prided himself on his subtlety, though as theatre manager he was very unhappy. If the current of opinion was in favour of European masterpieces—which bored him—he would have European masterpieces, but he would not have any damn English director tinkering with the sort of plays that had been written by himself, Synge and Lady Gregory, and producing them in a theatrical idiom he did not like. Though he was responsible for Mrs. Pat Campbell, his whole attitude to English directors and players could be summed up in Synge's comment on Mrs. Pat as Deirdre of the Sorrows: 'She'll turn it into The Second Mrs. Conchobar.'

[1] Sir Osbert Sitwell.

445

SIR MAX BEERBOHM (1872–1956)

[Max and his wife spent several months in Sir William Rothenstein's cottage at Oakridge.]

HERE in the little sitting-room Max spread a green cloth on the table, laying his paint brushes out neatly beside the few tubes of paint that he used, strips of blotting paper and a pot of crystal-clear water. . . . Here, too, at this table he began *Rossetti and his Circle*, his series of Pre-Raphaelite drawings, wrote the story of *Maltby and Braxton* and the play *Savonarola Brown*, published in *Seven Men*. And the children laughed at the recollection of his emerging from the cottage, dressed with scrupulous care, with stick and gloves, to walk the 100 yards to the Nelson Inn to buy cigarettes; further than this he never ventured. During the winter he was content to stay indoors with all the windows carefully shut, and we remembered how, when with us, if he noticed an open window, he would stroll round the room, talking and smoking while he gradually approached the window and, as though absent-mindedly, carefully close it. Florence would go for walks with us but never far: Max must not be left alone in the cottage. One early spring day, walking with my wife, she heard a bird singing high up in the air. 'What bird is that?' asked Florence, and when told it was a lark, 'A lark! Max has never heard a lark!' and she hurried back. When she returned later with Max, in heavy overcoat, gloved and attentive, alas, the lark had finished his song!

446

WHEN Max Beerbohm gave the world its first account of that unfortunate poet of the eighteen-nineties, Enoch Soames, he remarked very truly that there is no mention of Soames in Holbrook Jackson's well-known book on the period. That alone would scarcely account for Max's seeming reluctance to take Enoch Soames quite seriously, but there were other disquieting circumstances that seemed to throw doubt on his very existence. It will be recalled that poor Soames was consumed by a longing for recognition, and that in his desperate eagerness to know what posterity would think of him he determined to sell his soul to the Devil in return for the chance of being projected into the Reading Room of the British Museum as it would be a hundred years hence. The bargain was struck, and Soames duly found himself in the Reading Room of the year 1997.

There, as he had expected, he found his name in the Catalogue, but only on the slips recording the titles of the three slim volumes he had published in the eighteen-nineties. There was no mention of him in the *Dictionary of National Biography*, nor in any of the encyclopedias he consulted; but he was directed by an assistant to a work dated 1992, written in the phonetic spelling then apparently in use: 'Inglish Littracher 1890–1900, bi T. K. Nupton'. There at last he found his name:

Fr egzarmpl, a riter ov th time, naimed Max Beerbohm, hoo wuz stil alive in th Twentieth senchri, rote a stauri in wich e pautraid an immajanari karrakter kauld 'Enoch Soames'—a thurd-rait poit hoo beleevz imself a grate jeneus an maix a bargin with th Devvl in auder ter no wot posterriti thinx ov him! It iz a sumwot labud sattire . . .

Faced with this sceptical pronouncement of T. K. Nupton (which Soames had copied out and brought back with him) Max was driven to wonder whether Soames were not really 'an immajanari karrakter' after all— 'a figment of my brain'. He need not have wondered. If his reading had lain more in the field of scholarship he might have found evidence that must have dispelled his doubts. In that standard work of reference published for the Modern Humanities Research Association, the annual *Bibliography of English Language and Literature*, the name of Soames is among the authors listed for the year 1922, as the following entry will show:

2883. SOAMES, ENOCH. Edward Shanks, 'The Last Garland: To the Memory of Enoch Soames'. (*London Mercury* (Oct. 1922), vi. 602–6.)

True, it is only a single entry—far less than would have satisfied Soames himself—but it does at least supply the necessary confirmation of his existence.

447

FORD MADOX FORD (1873–1939)

I THINK that only one contributor to my first two numbers did not tell me that the *English Review* was ruined by the inclusion of all the other contributors. James said: 'Poor old Meredith, he writes these mysterious nonsenses and heaven alone knows what they all mean.'—Meredith had contributed merely a very short account of his dislike for Rossetti's breakfast manners. It was as comprehensible as a seedsman's catalogue.

Meredith said, on looking at James's *Jolly Corner*, which led off the prose of the *Review*: 'Poor old James, he sets down on paper these mysterious rumblings in his bowels—but who could be expected to understand them?'

448

[Douglas Goldring recalls the early days of the *English Review*.]

DURING the day time, Ford's office was perpetually inundated with visitors, so that it was chiefly at night that the actual job of editing the *English Review* could be carried on. But even at night callers dropped in casually to see how the work was going forward. In order to avoid them, at least for an hour or two, it was Ford's singular practice to attend the 'second house' at the local music-hall. At least once a week my first task, on arriving at Holland Park Avenue, was to secure a box or two stalls at the Shepherd's Bush Empire. After dinner I went out and stopped a hansom, and editor and 'sub' drove down to Shepherd's Bush with the MSS. which had accumulated during the day. During the performance, or rather during the duller turns, Ford made his decisions and I duly recorded them. But when someone really worth listening to—the late Victoria Monks for example, or 'Little Tich' or Vesta Victoria—appeared on the stage, the cares of editorship were for the moment laid aside. After the show, we went back to the flat and worked on, sometimes until two in the morning. There may have been a good deal to be said for the Shepherd's Bush Empire, from Ford's standpoint. The atmosphere was conducive, there was no one to worry him and he could think undisturbed. When he stayed at home, on the other hand, there was always the prospect of some illuminated friend arriving to drink his whisky and proffer advice, suggestions, or complaints. By contrast, the music-hall must have seemed a haven of peace.

449

WALTER DE LA MARE (1873–1956)

3 April 1928, Diary of John Bailey:
Bruce Richmond[1] has just told me a lovely story about Walter de la Mare. He is at last getting well fast after his long illness, but he was for three weeks at the very gates of death. On one of these days his younger daughter

[1] Editor of the *Times Literary Supplement*.

said to him as she left him, 'Is there nothing I could get for you, fruit or flowers?' On which in a weak voice he could just—so characteristically—answer: 'No, no, my dear; too late for fruit, too soon for flowers!'

450

G. K. CHESTERTON (1874–1936)

I AM just old enough to remember what were called Penny Readings; at which the working-classes were supposed to have good literature read to them, because they were not then sufficiently educated to read bad journalism for themselves. As a boy, or even a child, I passed one evening in something curiously called the Progressive Hall; as if the very building could not stand still, but must move onwards like an omnibus along the path of progress. There was a little chairman with eyeglasses, who was nervous; and a big stout staring schoolmaster called Ash, who was not at all nervous; and a programme of performers if not eminent no doubt excellent. Mr. Ash read 'The Charge of the Light Brigade' in resounding tones; and the audience awaited eagerly the change to a violin solo. The chairman explained hastily that Signor Robinsoni was unfortunately unable to perform that evening, but Mr. Ash had kindly consented to read 'The May Queen'. The next item on the programme was a song, probably called 'Sea Whispers', to be sung by Miss Smith accompanied by Miss Brown. But it was not sung by Miss Smith or accompanied by Miss Brown; because, as the chairman somewhat feverishly explained, they were unable to attend; but we were solaced by the announcement that Mr. Ash had kindly consented to read 'The Lord of Burleigh'. At about this point a truly extraordinary thing occurred; extraordinary at any time, to any one who knows the patience and politeness of the English poor; still more astonishing in the less sophisticated poor of those distant days. There arose slowly in the middle of the room, like some vast leviathan arising from the ocean, a huge healthy simple-faced man, of the plastering profession, who said in tones as resounding as Mr. Ash's, and far more hearty and human, 'Well, I've just 'ad about enough of this. *Good* evening, Mr. Ash; *good* evening, ladies and gentlemen.' And with a wave of universal benediction, he shouldered his way out of the Progressive Hall with an unaffected air of complete amiability and profound relief.

451
SIR WINSTON CHURCHILL (1874–1965)

I THINK it was during that second season I spent in London while living in Munich that I met Lady Randolph Churchill[1] . . . The first time I lunched at her house she was standing near the head of the stairs when I arrived, with a rather short round-faced good-looking youth—as I assumed him to be—beside her. 'My son,' she said. 'Which one?' I asked. 'Why! *Winston*—of course!' He was a Member of Parliament and the most discussed young man in England, but he did not look a day over twenty.

I sat beside him at table, and found conversation with him increasingly difficult. He seemed to me to grow sulkier and sulkier. . . . When we went up to the drawing-room young Churchill was obliged to leave at once for the House. 'Good-bye,' he said to me sulkily. Then, as he was making his exit, he turned and scowled. 'I've read your books and admired them, but that is more than you can say of mine.' And he went out and slammed the door behind him.

So that was it!

I went from Mrs. West's to the house of Mrs. John Hall. . . . I told her of my rencontre with young Winston. 'I had no idea he had written anything,' I said. 'Of course he was put out because I didn't mention his books. Authors!'

'Oh, but you should read them,' she exclaimed, '*The River War*, *London to Ladysmith*, *Ian Hamilton's March*. They are really distinguished works.'

And so they were, as I soon found to my enjoyment.

452
EDGAR WALLACE (1875–1932)

I HAD written one or two short stories while I was in Cape Town, but they were not of any account. My best practice was my 'Smithy' articles in the *Daily Mail*. . . . Collecting the 'Smithys' I sought for a publisher, but nobody seemed anxious to put his imprint upon my work, and in a moment of magnificent optimism I founded a little publishing business, which was called 'The Tallis Press'. It occupied one room in Temple Chambers, and from here I issued *Smithy* at 1*s*. and sold about 30,000 copies.

[1] Lady Randolph became Mrs. Cornwallis West in July 1900. The narrator of this anecdote was Gertrude Atherton, the American novelist.

Emboldened by this success, I sat down to turn a short story I had written, and which had been rejected by every magazine in London, into a longer one. The story was called *The Four Just Men*, in which a Minister was mysteriously killed and a prize was offered for the best explanation of his death. It was published at 3*s*. 6*d*.

I was determined, believing the story to be good, to make some sort of reputation as a story-writer, even if it broke me to do so. It broke me all right. I advertised in newspapers, on hoardings, on tubes and 'buses, the superlative merits of *The Four Just Men*. The result was that, although I sold 38,000 copies, I lost £1,400. There was, I discovered, such a thing as over-advertising.

Lord Northcliffe came to my rescue and pulled me out of the mess I'd got myself into. In disgust, I sold the remaining book rights for £72 to George Newnes. I don't know how many hundreds of thousands of copies George Newnes have sold, but they have always been good people to work for, and I hope they made big money out of my over-boomed romance—which is really a very good story.

453

OLIVER ST. JOHN GOGARTY (1878–1957)

A GOOD novelist should always be reminded of something artistic. George Moore, when he and I were crossing the railway viaduct at Donabate, was reminded by the sunset of Nathaniel Hone, the landscape painter who lived near by. He said, 'I would give ten pounds to see how that sunset will imitate Hone.' I tried to save him five by pulling the communication cord, because the fine is only five pounds if you pull it wantonly. I knew that you could never explain to a railway guard that art is more important than an accident. He must have had artistic sympathies, though, because he 'forgot' the incident for ten shillings! Instead of being grateful to me . . . Moore expostulated and told me that I was impossible. I bore that in silence. I could have retorted that he was a plagiarist, for years ago Oscar Wilde had said that Nature was always trying to imitate Art. Do not look for gratitude in novelists.

454

OLIVER GOGARTY was captured by his enemies,[1] imprisoned in a deserted house on the edge of the Liffey with every prospect of death. Pleading a natural necessity he got into the garden, plunged under a

[1] In his house, at gun point, 20 January 1923. The story is told here by Yeats.

shower of revolver bullets and as he swam the ice-cold December stream promised it, should it land him in safety, two swans. I was present when he fulfilled that vow.

455

[Shortly after the outbreak of the war in 1939 Gogarty went to live in the United States. He spent most of the rest of his life there, until his death in 1957. Two of his old friends remember him in a broadcast conversation.]

Denis Johnston: I doubt very much if he greatly enjoyed the last years of his life in America. America is not really a country for conversation.
Brian Aherne: On one occasion in New York, in a bar on Third Avenue, there were five or six of us sitting in a booth, and Gogarty was telling many of his wonderful stories. We were about to move off but he said, 'Now I want to tell you this.' So he proceeded to tell another story, and when he was about to come to the point, a young man sitting by the bar went over and placed a coin in a jukebox. All hell broke loose. The expression on Gogarty's face changed; he became very sad, a combination of sadness and anger, and he said, 'Oh dear God in Heaven, that I should find myself thousands of miles from home, an old man at the mercy of every retarded son of a bitch who has a nickel to drop in that bloody illuminated coal-scuttle.'

456

ALFRED NOYES (1880–1958)

Punch discovered a misprint in one of my peace poems in the *Irish Times.* My verses had depicted a family dreaming of the homecoming of their soldier from the wars, while

> All night he lies beneath the stars,
> And dreams no more out there.

The *Irish Times* printed it as

> All night he lies beneath the stairs,

and made matters worse by adding, 'Only a true artist could achieve this effect of quietly hopeless tragedy.' *Punch* seized upon this, and said that if I could express a wish for the New Year, it would probably be to meet the editor of the *Irish Times*. Oddly enough, a week or two later I found myself sitting next to him at a public dinner and, as an opening gambit in our conversation, remarked that we had recently met in *Punch*. To my surprise he blushed violently, and said something about having dismissed two printers, for it was the fourth time during the last month or two he had found himself in *Punch*.

457

LYTTON STRACHEY (1880–1932)

LYTTON STRACHEY was unfit, but instead of allowing himself to be rejected by the doctors he preferred to appear before a military tribunal as a conscientious objector. He told us of the extraordinary impression that was caused by an air-cushion which he inflated during the proceedings as a protest against the hardness of the benches. Asked by the chairman the usual question: 'I understand, Mr. Strachey, that you have a conscientious objection to war?' he replied (in his curious falsetto voice), 'Oh no, not at all, only to *this* war.' Better than this was his reply to the chairman's other stock question, which had previously never failed to embarrass the claimant: 'Tell me, Mr. Strachey, what would you do if you saw a German soldier trying to violate your sister?' With an air of noble virtue: 'I would try to get between them.'

458

[In the winter of 1918–19 Osbert Sitwell was lying in a military hospital recovering from a bad attack of 'Spanish influenza'.]

INTO this artificial paradise . . . visitors were admitted on certain afternoons—it may have been on every afternoon—and the silent elongated forms of Aldous Huxley and Lytton Strachey could occasionally be seen drooping round the end of my bed like the allegorical statues of Melancholy and of a rather satyr-like Father Time that mourn sometimes over departed noblemen on an eighteenth-century tombstone.

Lytton's debility prevented him from saying much, but what he did say he uttered in high, personal accents that floated to considerable distances, and the queer reasonableness, the unusual logic of what he said carried conviction. As an instance of his brevity, so off the point and on it, there is a remark of his that comes to my mind. When he was in Rome, Princess

San Faustino entertained him to luncheon, and treated him and her other guests to a long explanation of a scheme she had recently thought of to aid the unemployed. It was all dependent on growing the soya bean. Factories, and synthetic chocolates and motor-cars and building-material and bath-salts, all were to be made of this magical substance. She worked the whole idea up to an enthusiastic but boring climax, when she turned to the guest of honour, and appealed to him.

'Mr. Strachey, what do you think of my scheme?' He replied in his highest, most discouraging key,

'I'm afraid I don't *like beans*!'

459

P. G. WODEHOUSE (1881–1975)

[P. G. Wodehouse writes to a friend.]

FEBRUARY 25th, 1931.

. . . I have been away for a week at Hearst's ranch. He owns 440,000 acres, more than the whole of Long Island! We took Winks,[1] who was a great hit.

The ranch is about half-way between Hollywood and San Francisco. It is on the top of a high hill, and just inside the entrance gates is a great pile of stones, which, if you ever put them together, would form an old abbey which Hearst bought in France and shipped over and didn't know what to do with so left lying by the wayside. The next thing you see, having driven past this, is a yak or a buffalo or something in the middle of the road. Hearst collects animals and has a zoo on the premises, and the ones considered reasonably harmless are allowed to roam at large. You're apt to meet a bear or two before you get to the house.

The house is enormous, and there are always at least fifty guests staying there. All the furniture is period, and you probably sleep on a bed originally occupied by Napoleon or somebody. Ethel and I shared the Venetian suite with Sidney Blackmer, who had blown in from one of the studios.

The train that takes guests away leaves after midnight, and the one that brings new guests arrives early in the morning, so you have dinner with one lot of people and come down to breakfast next morning to find an entirely fresh crowd.

Meals are in an enormous room, and are served at a long table, with

[1] His dog.

Hearst sitting in the middle on one side and Marion Davies in the middle on the other. The longer you are there, the further you get from the middle. I sat on Marion's right the first night, then found myself being edged further and further away till I got to the extreme end, when I thought it time to leave. Another day, and I should have been feeding on the floor.

460

A NICE old lady who sat next to Wodehouse at dinner one night . . . raved about his work. She said that her sons had great masses of his books piled on their tables, and never missed reading each new one as it came out. 'And when I tell them', she concluded, 'that I have actually been sitting at dinner with Edgar Wallace, I don't know what they will say.'

461

VIRGINIA WOOLF (1882–1941)

To the Lighthouse . . . had been published on 5 May 1927. Vita Sackville-West, returning from Persia, found a copy awaiting her. Virginia had promised she would have a new book ready for her. It was inscribed: *Vita from Virginia* (*In my opinion the best novel I have ever written*). Vita was a little surprised at such shameless immodesty, but that night when she opened the book to read it in bed, she found that the inscribed copy was a dummy. . . .

Clive Bell, back in London, wrote to Vanessa in May that the town seemed particularly dull and sad. 'Only Virginia is sublimely happy, as well she may be—her book is a masterpiece.' The view was pretty generally held by the critics, and a great many people wrote enthusiastically, although one complained that her descriptions of the fauna and flora of the Hebrides were totally inaccurate. The book sold better than its predecessors—3,873 copies (two of which were purchased by the Seafarers' Educational Society) in the first year.

462

JAMES JOYCE (1882–1941)

[Gogarty recalls James Joyce as a young man.]

We both lived on the north side of the city, and we were going up Rutland Square, I think it was a horse-drawn tram in those days. I happened to mention that thing that the newspapers were full of—that it was Yeats's fortieth birthday and that Lady Gregory had collected from his friends forty pounds with which she bought a Kelmscott edition of Chaucer by William Morris. Everybody knew it was Yeats's birthday. But when I made an epiphany, so to speak, and told Joyce this, at the first tram stop he got out. Yeats was lodging in the Cavendish Hotel, in Rutland Square, and he solemnly walked in and knocked at Yeats's door. When Yeats opened the door of the sitting-room he said, 'What age are you, sir?' and Yeats said, 'I'm forty.'—'You are too old for me to help. I bid you good-bye.' And Yeats was greatly impressed at the impertinence of the thing.

463

JAMES JOYCE had come to Paris from Zürich. In the summer of 1920 I[1] went there with Thomas Stearns Eliot. We went there on our way to the Bay of Quiberon for a summer holiday, which his wife said would do him good. We descended at a small hotel, upon the left bank of the River Seine. It was there I met, in his company, James Joyce for the first time.

It has been agreed before we left London that we should contrive to see Joyce in Paris. And Eliot had been entrusted with a parcel by Ezra Pound (as a more responsible person than myself), which he had to hand to Joyce when he got there. We did not know at all what it contained. It was rather a heavy parcel and Eliot had carried it under his arm, upon his lap, as it was too big to go in a suitcase. . . .

The hotel was nearer to the quays of the Seine than to the central artery of the St. Germain quarter. It was the rue des Saints-Pères, or it may have been the rue Bonaparte: no matter, they are all the same. Our rooms were the sort of lofty, dirtily parquetted, frowsily-curtained, faded apartments that the swarms of small hotels in Paris provide, upon their floors of honour. These small hotels still abound.

T. S. Eliot, ringing for the chasseur, dispatched a *petit bleu* to James

[1] Percy Wyndham Lewis.

Joyce. He suggested that Joyce should come to the hotel, because he had a parcel entrusted to him by Ezra Pound, and which that gentleman had particularly enjoined upon him to deliver personally to the addressee; but that it would likewise be a great pleasure to meet him. This was accompanied by an invitation to dinner.

An invitation to dinner! I laugh as I write this. But at the time I did not know the empty nature of this hospitable message, seeing to whom it was directed!

The parcel was then placed in the middle of a large Second Empire marble table, standing upon gilt eagles' claws in the centre of the apartment. About six in the evening James Joyce arrived, and the Punch and Judy show began.

Joyce was accompanied by a tallish youth, whom he introduced to Eliot as his son. Eliot then introduced me to Joyce. We stood collected about the shoddily-ornamented French table, in the décor of the cheap dignity of the red-curtained apartment, as if we had been people out of a scene in an 1870 gazette, resuscitated by Max Ernst, to amuse the tired intelligentsia—bowing in a cosmopolitan manner to each other across Ezra's prize packet, which was the proximate cause of this solemn occasion.

When Joyce heard my name he started in a very flattering fashion. Politely he was galvanized by this historic scene, and then collapsed. It was as if he had been gently pricked with the ghost of a hat-pin of a corsetted demirep out of the *Police Gazette*, and had given a highly well-bred exhibition of *stimulus-response*. Suppose this exhibition to have been undertaken for a lecture (with demonstrations) on 'Behaviour', and you have the whole picture. He raised his eyebrows to denote surprise and satisfaction at the auspicious occasion; he said *Ah! Wyndham Lewis* civilly under his breath, and I bowed again in acknowledgement, at the repetition of my name. He then with a courteous haste looked around for his son, who was heavily scowling in the background, and effected an introduction. His son stiffened, and, still scowling, bowed towards me with ceremony. Bringing my heels together, unintentionally, with a noticeable report, I returned the salute. We all then sat down. But only for a moment.

Joyce lay back in the stiff chair he had taken from behind him, crossed his leg, the lifted leg laid out horizontally upon the one in support like an artificial limb, an arm flung back over the summit of the sumptuous chair. He dangled negligently his straw hat, a regulation 'boater'. We were on either side of the table, the visitors and ourselves, upon which stood the enigmatical parcel.

Eliot now rose to his feet. He approached the table, and with one eyebrow drawn up, and a finger pointing, announced to James Joyce that *this* was that parcel to which he had referred in his wire, and which had been given into his care, and he formally delivered it, thus acquitting himself of his commission.

'Ah! Is this the parcel you mentioned in your note?' inquired Joyce, overcoming the elegant reluctance of a certain undisguised fatigue in his person. And Eliot admitted that it was, and resumed his seat.

I stood up: and, turning my back upon the others, arranged my tie in the cracked Paris mirror—whose irrelevant imperfections, happening to bisect my image, bestowed upon me the mask of a syphilitic Creole. I was a little startled; but I stared out of countenance this unmannerly distortion, and then turned about, remaining standing.

James Joyce was by now attempting to untie the crafty housewifely knots of the cunning old Ezra. After a little he asked his son crossly in Italian for a penknife. Still more crossly his son informed him that he had no penknife. But Eliot got up, saying 'You want a knife? I have not got a knife, I think!' We were able, ultimately, to provide a pair of nail scissors.

At last the strings were cut. A little gingerly Joyce unrolled the slovenly swaddlings of damp British brown paper in which the good-hearted American had packed up what he had put inside. Thereupon, along with some nondescript garments for the trunk—there were no trousers, I believe—a fairly presentable pair of *old brown shoes* stood revealed, in the centre of the bourgeois French table. . . .

James Joyce exclaiming very faintly 'Oh' looked up, and we all gazed at the old shoes for a moment. 'Oh!' I echoed and laughed, and Joyce left the shoes where they were, disclosed as the matrix of the disturbed leaves of the parcel. He turned away and sat down again, placing his left ankle upon his right knee, and squeezing, and then releasing, the horizontal limb.

With a smile even slower in materializing than his still-trailing Bostonian voice (a handsome young United States President, to give you an idea—adding a Gioconda smile to the other charms of this office) Eliot asked our visitor if he would have dinner with us. Joyce turned to his son, and speaking very rapidly in Italian, the language always employed by him, so it seemed, in his family circle, he told him to go home: he would inform his mother that his father would not be home to dinner after all. . . .

James Joyce, having disposed of his foreign-bred offspring, Ezra's embarrassing present, and his family arrangements for the evening, turned to us with the air of a man who has divested himself of a few minor handicaps, and asked us where we would like to dine and did we know Paris well, or would we commit ourselves to him and allow him to conduct us to a restaurant where he dined, from time to time, not far from where we were just then, and at which it was possible to get a good meal enough, though he had not been there lately.

We replied that we would gladly go with him to the restaurant he mentioned; and so he led the way in a very business-like fashion: he bustled on ahead of us—if the word bustled can be used of a very spare and light-footed cosmopolitan gentleman: he selected a table, took up the menu before we had sat down, asked us what we liked, inspecting the violet scrawl to ascertain what was available in the matter of *plats du jour*. And before we could say Jack Robinson he had ordered a large and cleverly arranged dinner as far as possible for all palates, and with a great display of inside knowledge of the insides of civilized men and the resources of the cuisine of France, discovering what wines we were by way of liking if any. And he had asked for a bottle to start with to introduce the soup. And so on, through a first-class French repast until we had finished, he pushed on, our indefatigable host: then at a moment when we were not paying particular attention, he called for the bill: and before either of us could forestall him, he had whisked out of his breast pocket a handful of hundred-franc notes, and paid for this banquet: the wine, the liqueurs, the coffee, and added to it, it was evident, a lordly pourboire. Nor was it ever possible for T. S. Eliot or myself to pay for the smallest thing from that time onwards. . . .

We had to pay his 'Irish pride' for the affair of the old shoes. That was it! He would not let us off. He was entirely unrelenting and we found it impossible to outmanoeuvre him.

464

THOUGH he liked having Samuel Beckett with him, Joyce at the same time kept him at a distance. Once he said directly, 'I don't love anyone except my family' in a tone which suggested, 'I don't like anyone except my family either.' But Beckett's mind had a subtlety and strangeness that attracted Joyce as it attracted, in another way, his daughter. So he would ask the young man to read to him passages from Mauthner's *Beiträge zu Einer Kritik der Sprache*, in which the nominalistic view of language seemed something Joyce was looking for. Once or twice he dictated a bit of *Finnegans Wake* to Beckett, though dictation did not work very well for him; in the middle of one such session there was a knock at the door which Beckett didn't hear. Joyce said, 'Come in,' and Beckett wrote it down. Afterwards he read back what he had written and Joyce said, 'What's that "Come in"?' 'Yes, you said that,' said Beckett. Joyce thought for a moment, then said, 'Let it stand.' He was quite willing to accept coincidence as his collaborator.

465

WHEN a young man came up to him in Zurich and said, 'May I kiss the hand that wrote *Ulysses?*' Joyce replied, somewhat like King Lear, 'No, it did lots of other things too.'

466

SIR HUGH WALPOLE (1884–1941)

[Towards the end of the 1914–18 war Walpole was working for the Ministry of Information. then under the control of Lord Beaverbrook. Arnold Bennett had been appointed to direct propaganda in France.]

ONE day at the beginning of October 1918 Walpole arrived at the office 'to find that Bennett wants me to do the report on the work of the Ministry for the War Cabinet. A particularly hair-raising job and one for which I feel quite unfitted.' But he did it, and a week later dispatched it to Bennett with a letter:

This has been a beastly job—the worst I've ever attempted. When I began I hoped to make it an individual personal affair as you had suggested. But when I looked at the other chapters in the Blue Book I saw that such a method would be at once ruled out by the War Cabinet. . . . Were one writing a complete Blue Book, all by its little self, about the Ministry, one could, I think, make it both poetic and entertaining. Such an account however in this case would look like Titania sleeping with numberless Bottoms.

467

I CAN'T remember if I ever told you about meeting Hugh Walpole when I was at Oxford getting my D.Litt.[1] I was staying with the Vice-Chancellor at Magdalen and he blew in and spent the day. It was just after Hilaire Belloc had said that I was the best living English writer. It was just a gag, of course, but it worried Hugh terribly. He said to me, 'Did you see what Belloc said about you?' I said I had.—'I wonder why he said that.' 'I wonder,' I said. Long silence. 'I can't imagine why he said that,' said Hugh. I said I couldn't, either. Another long silence. 'It seems

[1] P. G. Wodehouse, who tells this story, became an Hon.D.Litt. of Oxford in 1939.

such an extraordinary thing to say!'—'Most extraordinary.' Long silence again. 'Ah, well,' said Hugh, having apparently found the solution, 'the old man's getting very old.'

468

D. H. LAWRENCE (1885–1930)

THE very first copy of *The White Peacock* that was ever sent out, I put into my mother's hands when she was dying. She looked at the outside, and then at the title-page, and then at me, with darkening eyes. And though she loved me so much, I think she doubted whether it could be much of a book, since no one more important than I had written it. Somewhere, in the helpless privacies of her being, she had wistful respect for me. But for me in the face of the world, not much. This David would never get a stone across at Goliath. And why try? Let Goliath alone! Anyway, she was beyond reading my first immortal work. It was put aside, and I never wanted to see it again. She never saw it again.

After the funeral, my father struggled through half a page, and it might as well have been Hottentot.

'And what dun they gie thee for that, lad?'

'Fifty pounds, father.'

'Fifty pounds!' He was dumbfounded, and looked at me with shrewd eyes, as if I were a swindler. 'Fifty pounds! An' tha's niver done a day's hard work in thy life.'

469

[In the summer of 1914 John Middleton Murry and Katherine Mansfield were in constant touch with D. H. Lawrence and his wife Frieda, who at that time were staying in London. Middleton Murry describes a social occasion at which all four were present.]

ON the rare occasions when we received an invitation which we could not evade, as to a party in Church Row at the house of H. G. Wells whom we genuinely admired, or to a literary at-home at the house of some editor who had power over us, we endured it in misery. What Katherine wrote of one such occasion might serve for them all. 'A silly, unreal evening. Pretty rooms and pretty people, pretty coffee, and cigarettes out of a silver tankard. A sort of sham Meredith atmosphere lurking. . . . I was wretched. I have nothing to say to "charming" women. I feel like a cat among tigers.' . . .

The party I have mentioned at the Wells's was a tremendous undertaking. Lawrence had a new dress-suit, his first one, and he insisted on wearing it. He had curious rigid ideas about polite behaviour. I was rebellious about this, and wanted to go in grey flannels; I was quite sure, I said, that not all the guests would be in evening dress, and even if they were I didn't care. Again Lawrence was annoyed with me: I was letting him down again. So I agreed to wear a dinner-jacket. That called for a good deal of improvisation, for though I had a clean boiled shirt, I had neither studs nor links: but with Katherine's help, a few pearl buttons and a piece of wire, I managed to make myself presentable. Then I had to go round and tie Lawrence's tie for him.

Now Lawrence, who looked his lithe and limber self in many kinds of attire, did not resemble himself at all when locked in a dress-suit. Though there was a slight improvement in this matter with the years, it was only slight; and to the end Lawrence in a dress-suit was hardly more than a caricature of Lawrence in his habit as he lived. While I tied his tie, I was acutely conscious of this, and was on the point of imploring him not to wear it, on the pretext that it looked too new. But something warned me that he would take such advice in bad part, and that this initiation into the dress-suit world was for him a serious and ritual affair, my attitude towards which would be construed as another example of my fundamental flippancy. So I held my peace, and tried to make his bow-tie a little more dashing—in vain, for Lawrence had bought the kind of bow-tie which I associated with nonconformist parsons—excellent in its place, but very incongruous on Lawrence at that moment. I struggled with it; but no matter what bold innovations I endeavoured, it relapsed into decorous nonconformity, demanding to be completed by an upturned eye and a Bible. And I, in my turn, began to be annoyed with Lawrence, for allowing himself to be turned into this unnatural exhibition. The author of *Sons and Lovers* had a perfect right to go to a party in his pyjamas, I thought to myself, rather than appear as a callow acolyte of the Reverend Mr. Stiggins. And when I remembered that it was to abet this travesty that I was sporting links of pearl buttons and ginger-beer wire, I felt exasperated; and particularly exasperated with Frieda, for being totally unaware that her husband looked silly. She had the blissful habit of being completely preoccupied with her own appearance; yet, oddly enough, she would submit herself entirely to be dressed by him, and he did it well.

So, once more, we had 'to pretend a bit'; but that evening we got no jolly time for our pains. We were a forlorn and somewhat irritable procession by the time we reached Hampstead. The only thing to do was to make a thorough joke of it all, which Katherine was inclined to do; but in his panoply something of the stiffness of his shirt and collar seemed to have entered into Lawrence's moral being. He became the puritan he looked, and he frowned upon Katherine's ill-timed gaiety. Inevitably, the party was a miserable affair for us all, and, as we returned, Lawrence was apocalyptic in his denunciation of H. G. Wells, who had nevertheless been very decent, and genuinely pleased to meet him. But when Katherine pointed out that one or two of the effusive ladies had had, on that evening, not much of their effusiveness to spare for him, but had lavished it on H. G. Wells, his anger fairly boiled over. The discreet insinuation that he had been letting himself down touched Lawrence on the raw. And on that journey home H. G. Wells had to suffer for it.

470

RONALD FIRBANK (1886–1926)

THE first impression of him in conversation must always have been surprise that so frail, vague and extraordinary a creature could ever have arranged—let alone have created—a book. . . . It was obvious as well, even at first sight, that Firbank's health was far from strong. But this delicacy at least was possessed of one advantage; it prevented him from being forced to waste time in the Army. The constant callings-up and medical examinations had, though, further shattered his health, just as he in his turn must have somewhat shattered the health of the various military authorities with whom he came in contact. He told us, for example, that when, after a dozen or so examinations, the War Office finally rejected him as totally unfit for service (which anyone else could have told at a single glance), and then, in its usual muddled way, immediately called him up again, he replied through his lawyer with the threat of a suit for libel. The War Office, at a time when it governed the world, was so startled by this simple piece of individual initiative that it at once sent back to him a humble apology.

471

OSBERT SITWELL was often in Oxford to visit his brother, and this led to my oddest experience there. One afternoon in February they took me[1] to see Ronald Firbank, who was living in a house opposite All Souls. None of us had met him before, but his impressionist novels had led us to expect a somewhat peculiar person, so we weren't surprised when he

[1] Siegfried Sassoon.

received us in a closely-curtained room lighted by numerous candles and filled with a profusion of exotic flowers. A large table was elaborately set out with a banquet of rich confectionery and hothouse fruits. Firbank, whose appearance was as orchidaceous as his fictional fantasies, behaved so strangely that all attempts at ordinary conversation became almost farcical. His murmured remarks were almost inaudible, and he was too nervous to sit still for more than half a minute at a time. The only coherent information he gave me was when I heavily inquired where his wonderful fruit came from. 'Blenheim,' he exclaimed with an hysterical giggle, and then darted away to put a picture-frame straight, leaving me wondering how peaches were grown at Blenheim in mid-winter. The Sitwells were more successful in mitigating his helpless discomposure, but even Osbert's suavely reassuring manner failed to elicit anything except the disconnected utterances which were his method of evading direct explanations. For instance, when Sacheverell spoke appreciatively of his latest novel, *Caprice*, he turned his head away and remarked, in a choking voice, 'I can't bear calceolarias! Can you? . . .'

A few days later I invited him to tea, for I was curious to observe how he shaped by daylight and away from his 'highly stylized' surroundings. Rather to my surprise he accepted. Anxious to entertain him appropriately, I bought a monumental bunch of grapes, and a glutinous chocolate cake. Powdered, ninetyish, and insuperably shy, he sat with eyes averted from me and my well-meaning repast. His most rational response to my attempts at drawing him out about literature and art was 'I adore italics, don't you?' His cup of tea remained untasted, and he quailed when I drew his attention to my large and cosy pile of crumpets. As a gesture of politeness he slowly absorbed a single grape.

472

T. S. ELIOT (1888–1965)

[From 1917 to 1920 Eliot was an employee of Lloyds Bank, dealing with 'documentary bills, acceptances, and foreign exchange'. I. A. Richards became acquainted with him at this time.]

IT was not long before I was with him in his bank. All very surprising. I was not a bit sure how you called on a junior member of a banking staff in Queen Henrietta Street, I think it was. But TSE was reassuring: 'Just ask for me and they will show you.' What they showed me was a figure stooping, very like a dark bird in a feeder, over a big table covered with all sorts and sizes of foreign correspondence. The big table almost entirely filled a little room under the street. Within a foot of our heads when we stood were the thick, green glass squares of the pavement on which hammered all but incessantly the heels of the passers-by. . . .

By accident shortly afterwards I got the bank's view (or at least one of the bank's views) on 'our young Mr. Eliot'. I came across a shrewd, kindly and charming man (up at Arolla in the Swiss Alps, it was) who turned out to be a high senior official in that very Queen Henrietta Street focus of the great bank's far-flung activities. When he learned that I knew TSE, I could see that he was getting ready at once to shape a question. Something in his hesitant approach made me a little wary in my turn.

Mr. W.: You know him, I suppose, as a literary man, as a writer and . . . er . . . and . . . er . . . as a poet?

I.A.R.: Yes, he's very well known, you know, as a critic and as a poet.

Mr. W.: Tell me, if you will—you won't mind my asking, will you? Tell me, is he, in your judgement, would you say, would you call him a good poet?

I.A.R.: Well, in my judgement—not everyone would agree, of course, far from it—he *is* a good poet.

Mr. W.: You know, I myself am really very glad indeed to hear you say that. Many of my colleagues wouldn't agree at all. They think a Banker has no business whatever to be a poet. They don't think the two things can combine. But I believe that anything a man does, whatever his *hobby* may be, it's all the better if he is really keen on it and does it well. I think it helps him with his work. If you see our young friend, you might tell him that we think he's doing quite well at the Bank. In fact, if he goes on as he has been doing, I don't see why—in time, of course, in time—he mightn't even become a Branch Manager.

I relayed the conversation, of course, to TSE without delay. 'Most gratifying' he found it.

473

ELIOT and Vivienne[1] had lived for a number of years in a small house at 57 Chester Terrace, in that part of London that hesitates between Belgravia and Chelsea. After the *Criterion* dinners, which generally lasted too long for me to catch my last train home, I would sometimes spend the night at Chester Terrace. I remember how on one such

[1] His first wife. The narrator is Herbert Read.

occasion I woke early and presently became conscious that the door of my room, which was on the ground floor, was slowly and silently being opened. I lay still and saw first a hand and then an arm reach round the door and lift from a hook the bowler hat that was hanging there. It was a little before seven o'clock and Mr. Eliot was on his way to an early communion service. It was the first intimation I had had of his conversion to the Christian faith.

474

I FIRST met T. S. Eliot in 1946, when I was an editor at Harcourt, Brace, under Frank Morley.[1] I was just past thirty, and Eliot was in his late fifties. . . .

We went across the street to the old Ritz-Carlton. It was a lovely spring day and the courtyard restaurant—I think it was called the Japanese Garden—had just been opened for the season. For some reason I was astonished at the sight of newly hatched ducklings swimming in the centre pond, perhaps because they seemed to embody the odd and improbable quality the occasion had for me.

Eliot could not have found a kinder, or more effective, way of putting me at my ease. As we sat down, he said, 'Tell me, as one editor to another, do you have much author trouble?' I could not help laughing, he laughed in return—he had a *booming* laugh—and that was the beginning of our friendship. His most memorable remark of the day occurred when I asked him if he agreed with the definition that most editors are failed writers, and he replied: 'Perhaps, but so are most writers.'

475

[Relations between Eliot and Yeats were marked, in the words of Richard Ellmann, 'by their long, languid incompatibility'.]

AMONG their various mild collisions none was more defined than the dinner at Wellesley College when Yeats, seated next to Eliot but oblivious of him, conversed with the guest on the other side until late in the meal. He then turned and said, 'My friend here and I have been discussing the defects of T. S. Eliot's poetry. What do you think of that poetry?'

Eliot held up his place card to excuse himself from the jury.

[1] This account of his first meeting with Eliot is by Robert Giroux.

476

DYLAN THOMAS had failed his medical test for the army, and he and Caitlin were broke. My three pounds a week[1] did not carry far: so one day Dylan and I decided to go on a borrowing raid. 'But you must stay outside, Roy,' he said. 'We'll never raise a penny if they see you with me, except in the case of so-and-so and so-and-so.' Dylan proposed to make a vast tour (on a day when I was off duty) of all the newly-rich poets in their new offices in the Central Office of Information and the Ministry of Information. The only two of these new plutocrats to whose presence Dylan admitted me were fairly crackling with Bradburies as they rose from their seats: you could hear the new bank notes crinkling and crankling against their ribs as they moved! But we raised no cash. Dylan said it had been the same in every office where he had been without me. We stood outside the M.O.I. scratching our heads. 'What about His Grace?' I asked; 'he lives just around there.' 'You mean the Archbishop?' gasped Dylan; 'I wouldn't dare.'—'Come on, you'll see. He's not only a saint in his poems, he's a bloody saint in his life too.' We went to see Eliot, and the great man helped us so lavishly that it lasted till by some curious coincidence we both got our first considerable radio jobs, almost simultaneously, and were able to pay Eliot back. (Dylan never forgot his kindness. Neither do I.)

477
RONALD KNOX (1888–1957)

IT is alleged by a friend of my family that I used to suffer from insomnia at the age of four; and that when she asked me how I managed to occupy my time at night I answered, 'I lie awake and think about the past.'

[1] Roy Campbell, who tells this story, was at this time 'chief air-raid warden of Post 33 in St. Pancras district'. The Ministry of Information was then housed in the Senate House of the University of London, and in the immediate neighbourhood were the offices of Faber and Faber, where T. S. Eliot worked.

478
SIR JOHN NEALE (1890–)

As late as 1930, when I was writing my biography of Queen Elizabeth, I was conscious that the title of professor was calculated to frighten people off a book; and it was this lack of interest in academic writing that led me to suppress all my footnotes—an act of self-denial which, in the climate of today, I would neither need, nor wish, to repeat. . . . Shortly after the publication of my *Queen Elizabeth*, Eileen Power—a historian who wrote with style and charm—was dining at one of the women's colleges at Oxford. My book came under discussion, particularly the lack of footnotes, and a history don remarked: 'Neale has sold the pass.' 'I don't know about selling the pass,' retorted Eileen Power, 'but he has sold twenty thousand copies.'

479
FRANK O'CONNOR (1903–66)

[When he was a young man, Michael O'Donovan (who took the pen name of Frank O'Connor) worked as a librarian. An important part of his duties was setting up local libraries in country districts of Ireland.]

During my time in Wicklow, I could see the consequences of this restrictiveness all round me. There was the problem of getting local sanction to establish our libraries. . . . Some of the priests would allow no libraries at all. In Rathdrum, a town up the country from us, the parish priest initially resisted all our efforts to start a branch library. At last I decided that the time had come to visit him. Phibbs and I called first on the curate, a splendid young fellow who was in despair with the parish priest and with Ireland. A couple of nights a week he went off to the local technical school and took off his coat to practise carpentry so as to encourage the unemployed lads of the town to learn a trade, all to no purpose.

'You'll go up to that parochial house,' he said, 'and see the old man at the table with his dinner gone cold and a volume of Thomas Aquinas propped up in front of him. And between you and me and the wall,' he added, 'Thomas Aquinas was a bloody old cod.'

We found the parish priest exactly as the curate had predicted, Aquinas and all, but there seemed to be nothing of the obscurantist about the delightful old man we met. On the contrary, when we introduced ourselves, he beamed and regretted that we hadn't come to lunch. He took a particular fancy to me because I spoke Irish, and he was devoted to Irish and Irish literature. In fact, one of his dearest friends had been George Moore. Poor George. Of course he had been greatly wronged in Ireland, where people did not understand his work, but George had been a really dear and good man.

I didn't, of course, believe for an instant that he had been friendly with George Moore, but if the illusion made him more tolerant of our business it was all right with me. But when I introduced the subject I saw at once what the curate had meant. Oh, libraries. Libraries, hm! Well, libraries, of course, were wonderful things in their own place, but town libraries were a great responsibility. It was all very well for sophisticated people like ourselves to read the works of dear George, but could we really thrust them into the hands of simple Irish townspeople?

I damn near told him that from the little I knew of simple Irish townspeople they could give us all odds, but I knew this would get us nowhere. Charm was the thing, and charm won us permission at last, but only if the curate took full responsibility and satisfied himself of the innocuousness of the books we sent out. Swift wondered how it was that every virtuous English bishop translated to Ireland was murdered on Hounslow Heath and his place taken by a highwayman, but I wondered what happened to those nice, broadminded young curates one met after they became parish priests.

Nevertheless I was beginning to suspect that as an authority on Irish ways I was a wash-out. And now I had another shock coming to me, because, as we left, the parish priest said to me, 'I know you'll be interested in this,' and handed me a presentation copy of *The Untilled Field*, in Irish, with an affectionate inscription by George Moore.

480
DYLAN THOMAS (1914–53)

[Dylan Thomas and Daniel Jones first met when, as boys, they had a fight on the school playground in Swansea, and they immediately became close friends. For the next ten years or so they were in each other's company almost daily, either at the Thomas home in Cwmdonkin Drive or at the Jones home, 'Warmley'. Daniel Jones recalls what used to take place on those occasions.]

FIVE, Cwmdonkin Drive, and Warmley, the two houses, were very different in atmosphere. At Dylan's we had a gas fire that spluttered, an asthmatic sheep that coughed in the field opposite, and always a few owls hooting in the woods. I remember one terrifying night when we stared at one another in the gathering darkness until our heads became griffin and wyvern heads.

Warmley was not so mysterious, but it was more popular for several reasons; there were, for example, the Broadcasting Station and the Cricket Pitch. The Cricket Pitch in the back garden was about twelve feet long; every fine evening we played there without subtlety, hurling or driving the ball with the utmost force at one another, while old Harding, the neighbour, leaned on the wall smoking his pipe, sometimes calling out with perfect solemnity 'Well played, sir!' and finally asking, with a certain wistfulness, 'Will you be playing again tomorrow evening?'

Through the W.B.S. system, which consisted of two loud-speakers connected to the pick-up of a radiogram, we were able to broadcast from the upstairs to the downstairs rooms. I still have some of the programmes: 'The Revd. Percy will play three piano pieces, Buzzards at Dinner, Salute to Admiral Beattie, and Badgers Beneath My Vest'; 'Rebecca Mn will give a recital on the Rebmetpes'; 'Locomotive Bowen, the one-eyed cowhand, will give a talk on the Rocking Horse and Varnishing Industry'; 'Zoilredb Pogoho will read his poem Fiffokorp'. These broadcasters became real people to us, and we collaborated in a biography of the greatest of them, Percy. Here is a description of one of the trying experiences we inflicted on Percy's old mother: 'Near the outskirts of Panama the crippled Negress was bitten severely and time upon time, invariably upon the nape, by a white hat-shaped bird.'

481

DYLAN and Caitlin . . . were at a guest house called the Lobster Pot in Mousehole. Off Mousehole lay a small island, once, it was said, occupied by a hermit. After an evening's drinking in Lamorna, we[1] came down over the hill when a huge, brilliant moon lay over this island, its light reflected with only the faintest tremor in the still waters of the bay. The splendour of the spectacle infuriated Dylan, who made savage remarks about picture-postcards and visual *clichés*. I also recall a morning occasion in a sunny field above Newlyn. Dylan was carrying around with him and intermittently sipping from a flagon of 'champagne wine tonic', a Penzance herbalist's highly intoxicating brew sold very cheaply and without licence. Dylan talked copiously, then stopped.

'Somebody's boring me,' he said. 'I think it's me.'

[1] The writer is Rayner Heppenstall.

482

DESMOND MACCARTHY had got me[1] a fine full-time job on the B.B.C. . . . I had four years with an immense salary and the chance to find work for Dylan. It was about then that the famous Third Programme was started with Barnes[2] at the head, myself in charge of the Literature, and Commander Ian Cox, also a disabled ex-service man, in charge of Science. Ian and Dylan and I became very thick from then on. . . . Dylan had only one weakness—he could not read correct poets like Pope or Dryden. He was at his best at the 'wild and woolly' poets. I used to keep him on beer all day till he had done his night's work and then take him down to the duty room where the charming Miss Backhouse or Miss Tofield would pour us both a treble whisky as a reward for our labours. It was with Blake and Manley Hopkins that Dylan became almost Superman; but we had bad luck with Dryden. Dylan had got at the whisky first and he started behaving like a prima donna. He insisted on having an announcer instead of beginning the programme right away as we used to on the Third Programme. There were only two minutes to go and I rushed back to the studio and found Dylan snoring in front of the mike with only twenty seconds left. He was slumped back in his chair, with an almost seraphic expression of blissful peace. I shook him awake, and, to his horror and consternation, began announcing him, not in my South African accent, but trying to talk like an English announcer, with my tonsils, in an 'Oxford accent'. Dylan nearly jumped out of his skin with fright and horror, and was almost sober when he got the green light, though he did bungle the title as 'Ode on Shaint Sheshilia's Day'; but after that his voice cleared up and I began to breathe again.

When he had finished reading the 'Ode' I got another fright: he began to beckon me wildly with his arms and point to the page before him. I got the engineer to switch off the mike and slipped into the studio again. Dylan had forgotten how to pronounce 'Religio Laici'. I told him and slipped out. He had about three shots at it, bungled it, gave it up; and then went on reading. The next day I was hauled up in front of George Barnes, but he was a good boss and had a sense of humour. I promised to keep an eye on Dylan: Dylan promised me to keep an eye on himself—and he kept his word.

[1] Roy Campbell.
[2] Sir George Barnes (1904–60).

483

ONCE in New York, not long before he died, he was talking about writing. 'When I experience anything,' he said, 'I experience it as a thing and a word at the same time, both equally amazing.' He told me once that writing the 'Ballad of the Long Legged Bait' had been like carrying a huge armful of words to a table he thought was upstairs, and wondering if he could reach it in time, or if it would still be there.

484
ENVOY

PRINTERS' errors form a thriving sub-genre of the literary anecdote. I will end this book with two examples.

In his autobiographical volume *Memories*, Charles Kegan Paul tells of a writer who had occasion to describe a tract of land between the base of a volcanic mountain and the sea, and who did so to his own satisfaction by relating that 'the whole plain was strewn with erratic blocks'. But the printer must have been thinking of something else; for when in due course the book was published, the author was dismayed to find that he had been made responsible for stating that 'the whole plain was strewn with erotic blacks'.

Many years ago the late Dr. R. B. McKerrow told me an astonishing story about an edition of the letters of Madame de Sévigné. When the galley proofs began to reach the editor, he found that the proof-reader had his own idea of how to spell Madame de Sévigné's name, for he kept querying the accent on the first syllable. The editor meticulously wrote 'stet' beside each query; but with the next batch of proofs the process of query and 'stet' began all over again. When finally the page proofs arrived and the persistent proof-reader was still querying the accent, the editor lost his patience. Addressing himself to the proof-reader on the margin of the proof, he demanded that this futile exercise should stop. But now it was the printer's turn. When the editor at last received an advance copy of his book, he was horrified to find in the middle of one of Madame de Sévigné's letters the very words that he had written in anger on the final proof: '*For God's sake, stop popping up between Madame de Sévigné and me!*'

ACKNOWLEDGEMENTS

THIS book began as a dream-child of the late Kenneth Sisam, and for some years he had hopes that Sir Humphrey Milford would compile it. Shortly after Milford's death in 1952, he invited me to try my hand, and in a light-hearted moment I consented. I was then a good deal busier than I am now; but Mr. Sisam asked me to go ahead in my spare time, gave me some preliminary suggestions, and never failed to inquire about my progress whenever he had occasion to write to me. This amiable prodding has been continued by Mr. D. M. Davin, and more recently by Mr. Jon Stallworthy, who have both encouraged me by their interest and their practical advice.

In the early stages I was helped for some years by a succession of research assistants at University College, London, who kindly read various memoirs and biographies for me—I hope without prejudice to their severer studies. This book has been so long a-growing that I may well have forgotten some of those who gave me suggestions; but for assistance of various kinds I am indebted to Professor Nelson Adkins, Mrs. Gloria Cigman, Professor Richard Ellmann (for several anecdotes), Dr. Macdonald Emslie, Miss Joyce Hawkins (for several anecdotes), Professor Park Honan, Professor William Matthews, Sir John Neale, Mr. Simon Nowell-Smith, Miss Helen M. Palmer, Mr. Eric Partridge, Dr. Tulsi Ram, Dr. Gordon N. Ray, Professor Ian Ross, Professor Terence Spencer, Professor Robert E. Spiller, Miss Margaret Weedon, Sir Edgar Williams, Professor F. P. Wilson, and Mrs. Joanna Wilson.

NOTES AND REFERENCES

ABBREVIATED TITLES

Allingham, *Diary*: *William Allingham. A Diary*, ed. H. Allingham and D. Radford (1907).

Aubrey, *Brief Lives*: '*Brief Lives*', *Chiefly of Contemporaries, set down by John Aubrey* . . ., ed. Andrew Clark (2 vols., 1898).

Bailey, *Letters and Diaries*: *John Bailey, 1864–1931: Letters and Diaries, Edited by his Wife* (1935).

Beste, *Memorials*: Henry Digby Beste, *Personal and Literary Memorials* (1829).

Boswell, *Life of Johnson*: *Boswell's Life of Johnson, Together with Boswell's Journal of a Tour to the Hebrides*, ed. G. Birkbeck Hill, revised and enlarged by L. F. Powell (6 vols., 1934–64).

Charteris, *Life of Gosse*: The Hon. Evan Charteris, *The Life and Letters of Sir Edmund Gosse* (1931).

Cibber, *Lives*: Theophilus Cibber [i.e. Robert Shiels], *The Lives of the Poets of Great Britain and Ireland* . . . (5 vols., 1753).

Duffy, *Conversations*: Sir Charles Grant Duffy, *Conversations with Carlyle* (1892).

Grant Duff, *Notes*: Sir Mountstuart Elphinstone Grant Duff, *Notes from a Diary* (2 vols., 1897).

Hall Caine: *My Story*: Sir Thomas Henry Hall Caine, *My Story*, (1908).

Harriet Martineau, *Autobiography*: *Harriet Martineau's Autobiography, With Memorials by Maria Weston Chapman* (3 vols., 1877).

Haydon, *Autobiography*: *The Autobiography and Memoirs of Benjamin Robert Haydon*, ed. Tom Taylor (2 vols., 1926).

Hogg, *Shelley*: Thomas Jefferson Hogg, *The Life of Percy Bysshe Shelley* (2 vols., 1858).

Irish Literary Portraits: *Irish Literary Portraits . . . W. R. Rodgers's broadcast conversations with those that knew them* (1972).

Jerdan, *Autobiography*: *The Autobiography of William Jerdan* (4 vols., 1852–3).

Johnson, *Lives*: Samuel Johnson, *Lives of the English Poets*, ed. G. Birkbeck Hill (3 vols., 1905).

Johnsonian Miscellanies: *Johnsonian Miscellanies*, arranged and edited by G. Birkbeck Hill (2 vols., 1897).

Lady Ritchie, *Chapters*: Anne Thackeray, Lady Ritchie, *Chapters from some Memoirs* (1894).

Lady Ritchie, *Records*: Anne Thackeray, Lady Ritchie, *Records of Tennyson, Ruskin, and Robert and Elizabeth Browning* (1892).

Lockhart, *Scott*: John Gibson Lockhart, *Memoirs of the Life of Sir Walter Scott, Bart.* (7 vols., 1837–8).

Moore, *Journals*: *Memoirs, Journals, and Correspondence of Thomas Moore*, ed. Lord John Russell (8 vols., 1853–6).

Nichols, *Anecdotes*: John Nichols, *Literary Anecdotes of the Eighteenth Century* (9 vols., 1812–15).

Nichols, *Illustrations*: John Nichols, *Illustrations of the Literary History of the Eighteenth Century* (8 vols., 1817–58).

Prior, *Malone*: Sir James Prior, *Life of Edmond Malone, . . . with Selections from his MSS. Anecdotes* (1860).

Rogers, *Table Talk*: *Reminiscences and Table Talk of Samuel Rogers. . . . Collected by G. H. Powell* (1903).

Russell, *Collections*: George W. E. Russell, *Collections and Recollections* (1903).

Sitwell, *Noble Essences*: Sir Osbert Sitwell, *Noble Essences and Courteous Revelations* (1950).

Spence, *Anecdotes*: Joseph Spence, *Observations, Anecdotes, and Characters of Books and Men*, ed. James M. Osborn (2 vols., 1966).

Taylor, *Autobiography*: *The Autobiography of Henry Taylor* (2 vols., 1885).

Thraliana: *Thraliana*, ed. Katherine C. Balderston (2 vols., 1942).

Trevelyan, *Macaulay*: Sir George Otto Trevelyan, *The Life and Letters of Lord Macaulay* (2 vols., 1876).

Vizetelly, *Glancing Back*: Henry Vizetelly, *Glancing back through Seventy Years* (2 vols., 1893).

Walsh, *Handy-book*: W. S. Walsh, *A Handy-book of Literary Curiosities* (Philadelphia, Pa., 1893).

Walton, *Lives*: Izaak Walton, *The Lives of John Donne, . . . Robert Sanderson* (World's Classics edn., 1956).

Young, *Memoir*: Julian Charles Young, *A Memoir of Charles Mayne Young . . . With Extracts from his Son's Journal* (2 vols., 1871).

NOTES

1. *Bede's Ecclesiastical History of the English People*, ed. Bertram Colgrave and R. A. B. Mynors (1969), pp. 415–19 (the translation by Bertram Colgrave). © 1969 Oxford University Press. Reprinted by permission of the Clarendon Press.

2. *Bedae Opera Historica*, ed. Charles Plummer (1896), i, clx–clxiv. The translation was made by Professor William Matthews. Reprinted by permission of the Clarendon Press.

3. *Asser's Life of King Alfred*, trs. Albert S. Cook (1906), pp. 14–15. Reprinted by permission of the Clarendon Press.

4. Giraldus Cambrensis, *The Historical Works*, trs. Sir Richard Colt Hoare, Bart. (1863), pp. 374–5 (from *The Itinerary of Wales*).

5. Edward Hall, *Henry VIII*, ed. Charles Whibley (1904), ii. 160 ff.

6. Isaac D'Israeli, *Calamities of Authors* (1812), pp. 60–3.

7. William Camden, *Annales* (1625), iii. 14–16.

8. Cibber, *Lives*, i. 95.

9. William Camden, *Annales*; repr. in *A Complete History of England with the Lives of all the Kings and Queens thereof* (2nd edn., 1719), ii. 612, col. 2.

10. *Aubrey's Brief Lives*, ed. Oliver Lawson Dick (Ann Arbor Paperbacks, Michigan, 1962), pp. 255–6.

11. Walton, *Lives*, pp. 176, 177–80. The case for questioning the reliability of this anecdote was put by C. J. Sisson in *The Judicious Marriage of Mr. Hooker* (1940).

12. Aubrey, *Brief Lives*, i. 75–6.

13. E. K. Chambers, *William Shakespeare. A Study of Facts and Problems* (1930), ii. 212 (from John Manningham's *Diary*, Harl. MS. 5353, f. 29^{v}, ed. J. Bruce (1868)). Reprinted by permission of the Clarendon Press.

14. Ibid. ii. 243 (from 'Merry Passages and Jeasts', Harl. MS. 6395, f. 2).

15. Spence, *Anecdotes*, i. 185. Pope gave Thomas Betterton as his authority, but the anecdote had appeared, without specific application to Shakespeare and Davenant, in John Taylor's *Wit and Mirth* (1629) (James M. Osborn, ed. cit.).

16. *Gentleman's Magazine*, xliv (1774), 17 (from Dr. Ferdinando Warner, *Remarks on the History of Fingal* (1762), p. 26, 'on the authority of Judge Burnet', i.e. Sir Thomas Burnet (1694–1753), the son of Bishop Burnet).

17. Samuel Schoenbaum, *Shakespeare's Lives* (1970), pp. 154, 155, 156–7. Reprinted by permission of the Clarendon Press.

18. Vizetelly, *Glances Back*, ii. 105–7, 109–10. The earlier account to which Vizetelly refers appeared in *The Illustrated Times*, 12 December 1863 (Gordon N. Ray, *Thackeray: The Age of Wisdom, 1847–1863* (1958), p. 407).

19. Samuel Schoenbaum, op. cit., pp. 82–3.

20. Walton, *Lives*, pp. 120–1.

21. Logan Pearsall Smith, *Unforgotten Years* (1938), pp. 218–23. Reprinted by permission of Constable Publishers and the Hon. Robert Gathorne-Hardy.

22. Prior, *Malone*, p. 396.

23. Walton, *Lives*, pp. 77–8. In a forthcoming article Dame Helen Gardner gives strong reasons for questioning the reliability of Walton's long-accepted account of how Donne's picture was drawn.

24. *Notes of Ben Jonson's Conversations with William Drummond of Hawthornden*, ed. David Laing (1842), pp. 19–20.

25. Ibid., p. 20.

26. Ibid., p. 21.

27. White Kennet, *A Register and Chronicle Ecclesiastical and Civil* (1728), pp. 320–1.

28. Aubrey, *Brief Lives*, i. 185.
29. Aubrey, *Brief Lives*, ii. 220, 221.
30. *The Life and Times of Anthony Wood* . . . , ed. Andrew Clark (1891–1900), i. 282.
31. Aubrey, *Brief Lives*, i. 332, 333.
32. Ibid. i. 340.
33. Ibid. i. 347–8, 349, 351, 352.
34. Anthony Wood, *Athenae Oxonienses*, ed. Philip Bliss (1813–20), iii. 762.
35. Aubrey, *Brief Lives*, ii. 174–5.
36. *Biographia Britannica* (1760), v. 3375.
37. See *The Works of Edmund Waller*, ed. Elijah Fenton (1729), p. lxvii.
38. Cibber, *Lives*, ii. 243–4.
39. *The Early Lives of Milton*, ed. Helen Darbishire (1932), pp. 77–8 (from Edward Phillips, 'The Life of John Milton'(1694)).
40. Mark Pattison, *Milton* (1879), pp. 159–61. Pattison takes the traditional view of 'the waste-paper price' that Milton obtained from the publisher of *Paradise Lost*. William Riley Parker (*Milton: A Biography* (1968), i. 601) suggests that the transaction should be viewed in its contemporary perspective: 'The agreement was normal enough—perhaps even generous on Simmons's part, for he was taking a big chance in publishing 1,500 copies of a poem on an unstylish subject, in an unstylish literary form, by an author who was still anathema to a multitude of people.'
41. William Riley Parker, *Milton: A Biography* (1968), i. 634–5. For the sources on which Professor Parker drew for this anecdote, see vol. ii, p. 1148. © 1968 Oxford University Press. Reprinted by permission of the Clarendon Press.
42. *Notes & Queries*, 7th Ser. ix (10 May 1890), 361 ff.
43. Jonathan Swift, *Prose Works*, ed. Herbert Davis *et al.* (1939–68), ix. 65–6 (from *A Letter to a young Gentleman lately entered into Holy Orders* (1721)).
44. Samuel Pepys, *Diary* (30 July 1667), ed. Lord Braybrooke (1924), iii. 185–6.
45. Abraham Cowley, *Essays, Plays and Sundry Verses*, ed. A. R. Waller (1906), pp. 457–8.
46. *Essays of John Dryden*, ed. W. P. Ker (1900), ii. 229–30.
47. *The Works of Andrew Marvell, Esq. . . . With a new life of the Author, by Capt. Edward Thompson* (1776), iii. 460–3. As Pierre Legouis notes (*Andrew Marvell: Poet, Puritan, Patriot* (1965), p. 120), 'the oldest form of the anecdote, and the least untrustworthy' appears in *The Works of Andrew Marvell*, ed. Thomas Cooke (1726). I have preferred the better-known and more circumstantial version: if Captain Thompson embroiders, his embroidery is harmless.
48. Aubrey, *Brief Lives*, ii. 143.
49. *The Critical Works of John Dennis*, ed. Edward Niles Hooker (1939–43), ii. 405–6 (in a letter dated 23 June 1719).
50. F. A. Mumby, *Publishing and Bookselling* (1930), pp. 122–3. Reprinted by permission of Jonathan Cape Ltd. on behalf of the Estate of Frank Mumby, and R. R. Bowker Co. See also C. H. Timperley, *Encyclopaedia of Literary and Typographical Anecdote* (1842), p. 484.
51. Prior, *Malone*, pp. 436–7.
52. Spence, *Anecdotes*, i. 319.
53. George Colman, *The Circle of Anecdote* (4th edn., 1823), p. 294.
54. Ibid., pp. 17–18.
55. Jonathan Richardson, *Richardsoniana* (1776), pp. 89–90. As Defender of the Faith, Charles II had to listen to a good many sermons, and he disliked having them *read* to him. Stillingfleet, one of the most learned divines of the day and a prolific champion of the Church of England, was also one of the most popular preachers of the Restoration period.
56. Anthony Wood, *Athenae Oxonienses*, ed. cit. iv. 246.

57. Cibber, *Lives*, iii. 97–8.
58. *The Critical Works of John Dennis*, ed. cit. ii. 409–10 (from a letter of Dennis, 1 September 1720).
59. Spence, *Anecdotes*, i. 321–2.
60. John Pinkerton, *Walpoliana* (2nd edn., n.d.), i. 133.
61. Lord Macaulay, *The History of England from the Accession of James the Second* (1899 edn.), ii. 410–13.
62. *The Dramatic Works of Roger Boyle, Earl of Orrery*, ed. William Smith Clark (Harvard, 1937), ii. 951–2 (from a MS. note by John Boyle, fifth Earl of Orrery).
63. George Colman, the Younger, *Random Records* (1830), i. 172–3.
64. See William Congreve, *Amendments of Mr. Collier's False and Imperfect Citations* (1699), p. 39; Jeremy Collier, *A Defence of the Short View* (1699), p. 42.
65. Cibber, *Lives*, ii. 230. Lee's mind gave way in 1684, and for some years he was confined intermittently in Bedlam Hospital. For other odd sayings of his, see R. G. Ham, *Otway and Lee* (1931), pp. 209–10.
66. Cibber, *Lives*, iv. 234. 'Whether Mr. Dennis was the inventor of that improvement [of making stage thunder "by troughs of wood with stops in them"] I know not; but it is certain that being once at the tragedy of a new author with a friend of his, he fell into a great passion at hearing some, and cry'd, " 'Sdeath! that is *my* Thunder!" ' (Alexander Pope, *The Dunciad* (1729), Bk. ii, l. 218 n.) The accepted modern version is 'Damn them! They will not let my play run, but they steal my thunder.' (Walsh, *Handy-book*.)
67. Cibber, *Lives*, iv. 221–2.
68. Richard Polwhele, *Traditions and Recollections* (1826), ii. 718–20.
69. *The Percy Anecdotes, Collected and Edited by Reuben and Sholto Percy* [i.e. J. Byerley and J. C. Robertson] (1868 edn.), i. 544.
70. *Political and Literary Anecdotes of his own Times. By Dr. William King, Principal of St. Mary's Hall, Oxon.* (1819), pp. 7–9.
71. Thomas Sheridan, *The Life of the Rev. Dr. Jonathan Swift* (1785), pp. 37–9.
72. Ibid., pp. 40–1.
73. Johnson, *Lives*, iii. 31–3.
74. Thomas Sheridan, op. cit., pp. 215–16.
75. Ibid., p. 237.
76. *The Correspondence of Jonathan Swift*, ed. Harold Williams (1963), iii. 189 (Swift to Pope, 27 (?) November 1726).
77. *The Circle of Anecdote and Wit. By George Coleman, Esq.* (4th edn., 1823), p. 257. (Apparently *not* by George Colman, the Younger.)
78. *The Correspondence of Jonathan Swift*, ed. cit. iii. 329 (Swift to Bolingbroke, 5 April 1729).
79. T. Whincop, *A Compleat List of all the English Dramatic Poets* (1747), p. 191.
80. Voltaire, *Letters Concerning the English Nation. By Mr. de Voltaire* (1733), pp. 188–9.
81. Thomas Davies, *Dramatic Miscellanies* (1784), iii. 417–18.
82. George Colman, the Younger, *Random Records* (1830), i. 220.
83. *The Correspondence of Alexander Pope*, ed. George Sherburn (1956), i. 174–5 (Pope to John Caryll, 30 April 1713).
84. *Addisoniana* (1803), ii. 10–11. See also Spence, *Anecdotes*, i. 77; ii. 626.
85. Edward Young, *Conjectures on Original Composition* (1759); reprinted in *English Critical Essays* (*Sixteenth, Seventeenth and Eighteenth Centuries*), ed. Edmund D. Jones (1922), pp. 358–9.
86. Johnson, *Lives*, ii. 331–2.
87. Ibid. ii. 332–3.
88. George Lockhart (1673–1731), *The Lockhart Papers* (1817), i. 372. Pope's charitable explanation (Spence, *Anecdotes*, i. 96) was that 'Lord Oxford was huddled in

his thoughts, and obscure in his manner of delivering them'; but he had also been drinking heavily in the later years of Queen Anne's reign, and quite possibly had no idea what Rowe was talking about.

89. Johnson, *Lives*, ii. 65, 69. I have substituted '1704' (the year in which *The Biter* was disastrously produced) for Johnson's '1706'.

90. *Thraliana*, i. 142. The authority for this anecdote was 'Harry Fox, who was present at the scene'; i.e. Henry Fox (1705–74), first Baron Holland, one of Walpole's most faithful supporters.

91. W. W. Greg, 'The Bakings of Betsy', *Library*, 3rd Ser. ii (1911), 225–6, 258–9. Reprinted by permission of Oxford University Press, London.

92. Cibber, *Lives*, v. 13.

93. Spence, *Anecdotes*, i. 87–8.

94. *The Correspondence of Alexander Pope*, ed. cit. i. 371–5.

95. Prior, *Malone*, p. 369.

96. A. D. McKillop, *Samuel Richardson: Printer and Novelist* (Chapel Hill, N.C., 1936), pp. 6–7 (Richardson to Johannes Strinstra, 2 June 1753). Reprinted by permission of the University of North Carolina Press.

97. *Thraliana*, i. 145. For other versions of this anecdote, see A. D. McKillop, 'Wedding Bells for Pamela', *Philological Quarterly*, xxviii (1949), 323–5.

98. Rogers, *Table Talk*, p. 141. The incident is related by Mrs. Barbauld in her edition of *The Correspondence of Samuel Richardson* (1804), i. cix.

99. Boswell, *Life of Johnson*, iv. 28 n. Reprinted by permission of the Clarendon Press.

100. *Byron, A Self Portrait*, ed. Peter Quennell (1950), ii. 551.

101. *The Letters of the Earl of Chesterfield to his Son*, ed. Charles Strachey and Annette Calthorp (1901), i. 192.

102. Prior, *Malone*, p. 345.

103. Cibber, *Lives*, v. 209–10.

104. Johnson, *Lives*, iii. 344–5.

105. Ibid. ii. 409–10, 410–11, 413–15, 416–19, 429, 433.

106. John Taylor, *Records of my Life* (1832), i. 211.

107. Owen Ruffhead, *The Life of Alexander Pope* (1769), p. 532. Ruffhead must have got this anecdote from Warburton himself, who is known to have helped him in his *Life of Pope*.

108. Cibber, *Lives*, v. 168–9. Similar accounts will be found in John Nichols, *A Select Collection of Poems* (1780–2), ii. 163, and *Gentleman's Magazine*, xlix (1779), 32.

109. (a) *Biographia Britannica* (1789), iv (Corrigenda and Addenda to vol. iii); (b) See Boswell, *Life of Johnson*, i. 417–18.

110. Boswell, *Life of Johnson*, iv. 99. Reprinted by permission of the Clarendon Press.

111. E. H. Barker, *Literary Anecdotes and Contemporary Reminiscences* (1852), ii. 35.

112. Nichols, *Anecdotes*, iii. 384.

113. Boswell, *Life of Johnson*, i. 40. Reprinted by permission of the Clarendon Press.

114. *Johnsonian Miscellanies*, i. 378–9 (from Arthur Murphy, *An Essay on the Life and Genius of Samuel Johnson, LL.D.* (1792)).

115. Ibid. i. 380–1 (from Arthur Murphy, op. cit.). Questioned by Boswell, Johnson gave a rather different account of how he chastised Osborne: 'Sir, he was impertinent to me, and I beat him. But it was not in his shop: it was in my own chamber' (Boswell, *Life of Johnson*, i. 154).

116. Nichols, *Anecdotes*, v. 32–3 n. Boswell also had this story from Edmond Malone (*Life of Johnson*, i. 163 n.).

117. Walsh, *Handy-book*, p. 234.

118. Boswell, *Life of Johnson*, i. 256, 257–8, 259–60, 261–3. Reprinted by permission of the Clarendon Press.

119. Beste, *Memorials*, pp. 11–12.

120. Boswell, *Life of Johnson*, iii. 64–9, 76–7, 79. Reprinted by permission of the Clarendon Press.
121. Nichols, *Illustrations*, vi. 153–4.
122. Beste, *Memorials*, pp. 64–5.
123. *Johnsonian Miscellanies*, ii. 68–9 (from Joseph Cradock, 'Anecdotes of Dr. Sam. Johnson', *Gentleman's Magazine*, xcviii (January 1828), 24.
124. *Johnsonian Miscellanies*, ii. 426–7 (from Richard Warner, *A Tour through the Northern Counties* (1802), i. 105).
125. Prior, *Malone*, p. 350.
126. Joseph Cradock, *Literary and Miscellaneous Memoirs* (1828), i. 208.
127. Robert Kerr, *Memoirs of the Life, Writings and Correspondence of William Smellie* (1811), i. 357–8.
128. William Smellie, *Literary and Characteristical Lives* (1800), pp. 166–9.
129. John Macdonald, *Travels in Various Parts of Europe, Asia, and Africa* (1790) (reprinted as *Memoirs of an Eighteenth-Century Footman*, ed. John Beresford (1927), pp. 91–2).
130. Treadway Russell Nash, *Collections for the History and Antiquities of Worcestershire* (1781–2), i. 529.
131. E. L. Cloyd, *James Burnett, Lord Monboddo* (1972), pp. 106–7. © 1972 Oxford University Press. Reprinted by permission of the Clarendon Press.
132. John Ramsay of Ochtertyre, *Scotland and Scotsmen in the Eighteenth Century* (1888), pp. 355–6 n.
133. Nichols, *Illustrations*, vi. 805 (from a letter of Revd. John Sharp, 12 March 1756).
134. *Thraliana*, i. 151. The Hon. Charles Howard published *Thoughts, Essays, and Maxims, Chiefly Religious and Political* (1768). In 1777 he succeeded a second cousin as tenth Duke of Norfolk.
135. *Memoirs of the Life and Writings of Percival Stockdale, Written by Himself* (1809), i. 318.
136. Sir Walter Scott, *Lives of the Novelists* (World's Classics edn., 1906), pp. 47–8.
137. Boswell, *Life of Johnson*, ii. 453–4. Reprinted by permission of the Clarendon Press.
138. James C. Dibdin, *Annals of the Edinburgh Stage* (1888), p. 87. For earlier or alternative versions of this celebrated anecdote, see Macdonald Emslie, 'Home's *Douglas* and Wully Shakespeare', *Studies in Scottish Literature* (October 1964), ii. 128–9.
139. Boswell, *Life of Johnson*, i. 397. Reprinted by permission of the Clarendon Press.
140. Prior, *Malone*, pp. 405–6.
141. Ibid., pp. 427–8.
142. *The Life of Samuel Johnson, LL.D.*, ed. John Wilson Croker, v (1844), 114–15 n. This was one of Scott's contributions to Croker's edition of Boswell's *Life*. Croker added, however, that he disbelieved the story, and that it was 'reported here for the sake of contradiction'.
143. *Memoirs of the Life and Correspondence of Hannah More* (1834), i. 200–1.
144. *Thraliana*, i. 153. The *Rambler* used by Murphy was No. 190.
145. *Thraliana*, i. 27.
146. Henry, Lord Cockburn, *Memorials of his Time* (1856), pp. 50–1. Black, who published a few important scientific papers, and whose *Lectures on Chemistry* were collected and published after his death, has perhaps little right to appear in a volume of literary anecdotes. I hope the manner of his death will atone.
147. Boswell, *Life of Johnson*, i. 415–16. Reprinted by permission of the Clarendon Press.
148. *Memoirs of Richard Cumberland Written by Himself* (1806–7), pp. 268–70.
149. Boswell, *Life of Johnson*, ii. 231. Reprinted by permission of the Clarendon Press.
150. John Pinkerton, *Walpoliana* (2nd edn., n.d.), ii. 2–3.

151. Thomas Wright, *The Life of William Cowper* (1892), pp. 457–8.

152. *Sheridaniana, or Anecdotes of the Life of Richard Brinsley Sheridan* (1826), pp. 86–7.

153. E. K. Chambers, *William Shakespeare* (1930), ii. 378–9. Reprinted by permission of the Clarendon Press.

154. Isaac D'Israeli, *Curiosities of Literature* (14th edn., 1849), pp. 327–31.

155. Sir Sidney Lee, in *Dictionary of National Biography*, art. 'George Steevens', xviii. 1034, col. 1.

156. Boswell, *Life of Johnson*, iv. 178. Reprinted by permission of the Clarendon Press.

157. Jerdan, *Autobiography*, iii. 296–7.

158. *Autobiography of Edward Gibbon* (World's Classics edn., 1907), pp. 155–9, 160, 205.

159. Beste, *Memorials*, p. 68. This devastating remark has been attributed elsewhere to the Duke of Cumberland. Cf. *The Memoirs of the Life of Edward Gibbon*, ed. G. B. Hill (1900), p. 127 n.

160. Rogers, *Table Talk*, p. 81.

161. Moore, *Journals* (21 December, 1844), vii. 374. Writing to his stepmother in 1782, Gibbon described Lady Elizabeth Foster as 'a bewitching animal' (*The Letters of Edmund Gibbon*, ed. J. E. Norton (1956), ii. 294).

162. Charles Knight, *Passages of a Working Life during Half a Century* (1864), i. 37–8.

163. Cyrus Redding, *Fifty Years Recollections, Literary and Personal* (1858), i. 257–8.

164. Boswell, *Life of Johnson*, i. 383–4, 390–3, 395. Reprinted by permission of the Clarendon Press.

165. *Boswell on the Grand Tour*, ed. Frederick A. Pottle (1953), pp. 272–3, 285–6.

166. Boswell, *Life of Johnson*, v. 132–3 (from *The Journal of a Tour to the Hebrides*). Reprinted by permission of the Clarendon Press.

167. *Memoirs of the late Thomas Holcroft Written by Himself*, ed. William Hazlitt (1816; World's Classics edn., 1926), pp. 254–5.

168. *Memoirs of the Forty-Five First Years of the Life of James Lackington, Bookseller* (1830), pp. 129–30.

169. Jerdan, *Autobiography*, ii. 168–9.

170. Haydon, *Autobiography*, i. 171–2.

171. *The Life and Times of Frederic Reynolds Written by Himself* (2nd edn., 1827), ii. 227–8.

172. Ibid. ii. 228.

173. *Reminiscences of Michael Kelly* (1826), ii. 308–9.

174. Ibid. ii. 226.

175. Rogers, *Table Talk*, pp. 37–8. Gibbon was present in Westminster Hall when Sheridan was speaking. According to the *Morning Chronicle*, 14 June 1788, the words used by Sheridan were 'the luminous page of Gibbon'.

176. Thomas Moore, *Memoirs of the Life of the Right Honourable Richard Brinsley Sheridan* (1825), ii. 368.

177. Bertrand H. Bronson, *Joseph Ritson, Scholar-at-arms* (Berkeley, Calif., 1938), i. 266–7. Originally published by the University of California Press; reprinted by permission of the Regents of the University of California.

178. *The Anecdotes and Egotisms of Henry Mackenzie*, ed. H. W. Thompson (1927), pp. 172–3.

179. Abstracted from *The Life of George Crabbe, By his Son* (i.e. Revd. George Crabbe) (1834), by a reviewer in the *Gentleman's Magazine*, New Ser. i. (1834), 257–8.

180. *The Life of George Crabbe, By his Son* (1834; Cresset Press edn., 1947), pp. 116, 143–4.

181. Ibid., p. 153.

182. Ibid., pp. 228–9.

183. *Quarterly Review* (July 1878), pp. 27–8, 29–30.
184. Alexander Gilchrist, *The Life of William Blake*, ed. Ruthven Todd (1942), pp. 96–7 (*Blake Records*, ed. G. E. Bentley, Jr. (1969), p. 54).
185. Gilchrist, *Blake*, pp. 312–13 (*Blake Records*, ed. cit., pp. 307–8).
186. Allan Cunningham, *The Cabinet Gallery of Pictures* (1833), i. 11–13 (*Blake Records*, pp. 182–3).
187. Allan Cunningham, *The Lives of the most Eminent British Painters* . . . (2nd edn., 1830), ii (*Blake Records*, pp. 497–8).
188. Frederick Tatham, MS. Life of Blake, *Blake Records*, pp. 527–8.
189. J. G. Lockhart, *The Life of Robert Burns* (1828; Everyman edn., 1959), p. 111.
190. Charles Mackay, *Forty Years' Recollections of Life, Literature and Public Affairs* (1877), i. 258–61.
191. Rogers, *Table Talk*, p. 270.
192. E. H. Barker, *Literary Recollections and Contemporary Reminiscences* (1852), ii. 2.
193. Rogers, *Table Talk*, p. 283.
194 W. P. Frith, *My Autobiography and Reminiscences* (1887), ii. 132–7. Frith closes this account by adding an assurance: 'I am in a position to assure my reader that this story of Fonthill Abbey is absolutely true.'
195. *Cobbett's Weekly Political Register*, 19 February 1820 (*The Life and Adventures of Peter Porcupine . . . By William Cobbett*, ed. G. D. H. Cole (1927), pp. 139–41).
196. Maria Edgeworth, *Letters from England, 1813–1844*, ed. Christina Colvin (1971), p. 96.
197. Rogers, *Table Talk*, pp. 5–6.
198. C. R. Leslie, *Autobiographical Recollections* (1860), i. 254.
199. Taylor, *Autobiography*, i. 321.
200. Harriet Martineau, *Biographical Sketches* (1869), p. 371.
201. Lady Ritchie, *Chapters*, p. 69.
202. Trevelyan, *Macaulay*, ii. 265–6.
203. Wordsworth, *The Prelude* (1805–6 version), ed. E. De Selincourt (1926), Bk. iii, ll. 294–328.
204. Joseph Cottle, *Early Recollections, Chiefly relating to the late Samuel Taylor Coleridge* (1837), ii. 25–7.
205. Haydon, *Autobiography*, i. 351.
206. Charles Cowden Clarke, *Recollections of Writers* (1878), pp. 149–50.
207. *Reminiscences by Thomas Carlyle*, ed. J. A. Froude (1881), ii. 338–41.
208. Duffy, *Conversations* (1892), pp. 53–5.
209. Thomas Powell, *The Living Authors of England* (1849), p. 29.
210. Edward Heneage Dering, *Memoirs of Georgiana, Lady Chatterton* (1878), pp. 83–4.
211. Lockhart, *Scott*, i. 329, 407, 408–9.
212. Ibid. iii. 109–11.
213. Ibid. iii. 128–9.
214. Ibid. iv. 195–6.
215. Ibid. iv. 256.
216. Ibid. v. 195.
217. N. P. Willis, *Pencillings by the Way* (1835), iii. 97–9.
218. Harriet Martineau, *Autobiography* (1877), i. 325–6.
219. Rogers, *Table Talk*, p. 228 (slightly re-worded).
220. *A Memoir of the Reverend Sydney Smith. By his Daughter* (2nd edn., 1855), p. 366.
221. Ibid., pp. 244–5.
222. *Collected Letters of Samuel Taylor Coleridge*, ed. Earl Leslie Griggs (1956–71), i. 347–8.
223. S. T. Coleridge, *Biographia Literaria*, ed. J. Shawcross (1907), i. 4–5.

224. Joseph Cottle, *Early Recollections . . .* (1837), ii. 54, 56–9, 62–3, 64.
225. Ibid. i. 38–42.
226. Note by Coleridge prefixed to 'Kubla Khan', first published in *Christabel; Kubla Khan, a Vision; The Pains of Sleep* (1816).
227. A. J. Eagleston, 'Wordsworth, Coleridge and the Spy', *Coleridge Studies*, ed. E. Blunden and E. L. Griggs (1934), pp. 80–3: S. T. Coleridge, *Biographia Literaria*, ed. cit. i. 126–9. Reprinted by permission of Constable Publishers.
228. John Payne Collier, *An Old Man's Diary, Forty Years Ago* (1872), pp. 81–2. Some doubt must cling to this anecdote (which obviously refers to Coleridge's early married life) owing to the fact that the Hugh James Rose to whom Coleridge went 'in great trouble' was born in 1795—the same year as Coleridge married Sara Fricker—and so could not have been more than a boy when the poet and his wife finally agreed to live apart. It is reasonable to suppose, however, that Rose merely passed on the story to Collier as something he had been told, and that Collier, then in his eighties, erred only in making Rose a participant in the incident. As Sir Edmund Chambers put it (*Coleridge* (1938), p. 144), 'This narrative reads to me more like an old man's muddle than a deliberate fabrication.'
229. Jerdan, *Autobiography*, iv. 231–3. A slightly different account of this hilarious occasion was given by J. G. Lockhart in the *Quarterly Review*, lxii (1843), 65–6. As Lockhart recalled the scene, the demolition of the wine-glasses began when Hook pitched his through a window, to be followed in this act by Coleridge and the rest of the guests. *In vino veritas?*
230. C. R. Leslie, *Autobiographical Recollections* (1860), i. 50–1.
231. Moore, *Journals* (4 August 1833), vi. 331.
232. Rogers, *Table Talk*, p. 158.
233. Graham Wallas, *The Life of Francis Place* (rev. edn., New York, 1951), pp. 90–1. The version I first heard some fifty years ago, viz. 'I can see what poor Kant would be at', may have been slightly sophisticated.
234. Young, *Memoir*, ii. 111.
235. Hogg, *Shelley*, ii. 27–8.
236. Rogers, *Table Talk*, p. 281.
237. *Reminiscences by Thomas Carlyle*, ed. J. A. Froude (1881), ii. 323–6.
238. *Leigh Hunt's London Journal*, 17 October 1835 (Edmund Blunden, *Charles Lamb: His Life Recorded by his Contemporaries* (1934), p. 246).
239. Haydon, *Autobiography*, i. 269–71.
240. P. G. Patmore, *My Friends and Acquaintances* (1854), i. 29–40.
241. Thomas Hood, *Hood's Own* (1827) (Blunden, op. cit., p. 164).
242. Mary Balmanno, *Pen and Pencil* (1858) (Blunden, op. cit., pp. 158–9).
243. *Byron: A Self Portrait*, ed. Peter Quennell (1950), ii. 614.
244. *Jane Austen's Letters . . .* Collected and edited by R. W. Chapman (2nd edn., 1952), pp. 451–3.
245. Trevelyan, *Macaulay*, ii. 247. The bookseller (i.e. publisher) who was shot was Johann Philipp Palm of Nuremberg (F. A. Mumby, *Publishing and Bookselling* (1930), p. 265 n.).
246. William Beattie, *The Life and Letters of Thomas Campbell* (1849), iii. 397–9.
247. Moore, *Journals* (9 September 1820), iii. 146.
248. W. H. Mallock, *Memoirs of Life and Literature* (1920), p. 24. As an author, Bishop Phillpotts was well known in his own day as a determinedly anti-Catholic and high Tory pamphleteer.
249. Moore, *Journals*, i. 199–200, 201–2, 203–5.
250. *The Treasury of Modern Anecdote*, ed. W. Davenport Adams (1881), p. 123.
251. George Smith, *Cornhill Magazine*, New Ser. ix (1900), 584–5.
252. Augustus J. C. Hare, *The Story of my Life* (1896–1900), v. 384.

253. Grant Duff, *Notes*, i. 60.
254. *Harriette Wilson's Memoirs of Herself and Others. With a Preface by James Laver* (1929), pp. xi–xii (from Mr. Laver's Preface).
255. Taylor, *Autobiography*, i. 322–3. Whately wrote mainly on religious subjects, but also on Logic, Rhetoric, and Political Economy.
256. William Chambers, *Memoir of Robert Chambers. With Autobiographic Reminiscences of William Chambers* (5th edn., 1872), p. 300.
257. Rogers, *Table Talk*, pp. 176–7.
258. Ernest J. Lovell, ed., *His Very Self and Voice* (New York, 1954), p. 235. Copyright, 1954, by The Macmillan Company. Reprinted by permission of Macmillan Publishing Co. Inc.
259. J. W. and Anne Tibble, *John Clare: A Life* (1932), pp. 226–7. Reprinted by permission of Michael Joseph Ltd.
260. Lady Ritchie, *Records*, p. 12.
261. Grant Duff, *Notes*, i. 187.
262. Hogg, *Shelley*, i. 239–41.
263. Ibid. ii. 28–30.
264. E. J. Trelawny, *Recollections of the Last Days of Shelley and Byron* (1858), pp. 115–39. Leslie A. Marchand supplies some additional details in the *Keats–Shelley Memorial Bulletin* (Richmond, Surrey, 1955), vi. 1–3.
265. Matthew Arnold, *Essays in Criticism* (1888), pp. 205–6. The lady 'who knew Mrs. Shelley' was Fanny Kemble (Anne Thackeray, Lady Ritchie, *Chapters from some Memoirs* (1894), pp. 205–6).
266. Vizetelly, *Glances Back*, i. 90–4.
267. J. W. and Anne Tibble, *John Clare: A Life* (1932), p. 115. Reprinted by permission of Michael Joseph Ltd.
268. Frederick Martin, *The Life of John Clare* (1865), pp. 265–7.
269. J. G. Lockhart, in a letter to Patrick Robertson, Lord Robertson, Scottish judge, *c.* 1850; Andrew Lang, *The Life and Letters of John Gibson Lockhart* (1897), ii. 329–30.
270. John Willis Clark, *Old Friends at Cambridge and Elsewhere* (1900), pp. 42–3. Reprinted by permission of Macmillan, London and Basingstoke.
271. Walter Jerrold, *A Book of Famous Wits* (1912), p. 263. Reprinted by permission of Methuen & Co Ltd.
272. Charles Cowden Clarke, *Recollections of Writers* (1878), p. 126.
273. Charles Armitage Brown, 'Life of John Keats', *The Keats Circle: Letters and Papers 1816–78*, ed. Hyder E. Rollins (Harvard, 2nd edn., 1965), ii. 656.
274. Ibid. ii. 73–4.
275. Walter Jackson Bate, *John Keats* (Harvard, 1964), p. 694. Reprinted by permission of the Belknap Press of Harvard University Press.
276. *Letters of Thomas Carlyle (1826–1836)*, ed. C. E. Norton (2 vols., 1888), ii. 286–9.
277. Duffy, *Conversations*, p. 92.
278. Grant Duff, *Notes*, i. 51–2.
279. Ibid. i. 204.
280. Hall Caine, *My Story* (1908), p. 179.
281. Duffy, *Conversations*, pp. 59–61.
282. Francis Espinasse, *Literary Recollections and Sketches* (1893), pp. 190–2.
283. Harriet Martineau, *Autobiography* (1877), i. 372–3.
284. William Chambers, *Memoirs of Robert Chambers . . .*, ed. cit., pp. 102–4.
285. Trevelyan, *Macaulay*, i. 27–8.
286. Ibid. i. 51–2.
287. Ibid. ii. 254–5.
288. Ibid. ii. 418.

289. D. A. Wilson, *Carlyle on Cromwell and Others* (1925), p. 30. Reprinted by permission of Routledge & Kegan Paul Ltd.

290. Francis Espinasse, *Literary Recollections and Sketches* (1893), pp. 205–6.

291. *Letters and Memorials of Jane Welsh Carlyle*, ed. J. A. Froude (1883), ii. 263–7.

292. Allingham, *Diary*, p. 310.

293. Jerdan, *Autobiography*, ii. 174.

294. Ibid. iii. 195.

295. Harriet Martineau, *Autobiography*, i. 177–200.

296. Ibid. ii. 95–100.

297. Charles Cowden Clarke, *Recollections of Writers* (1878), p. 281.

298. W. F. Monypenny and G. E. Buckle, *The Life of Benjamin D'Israeli, Lord Beaconsfield* (rev. edn., 1929), ii. 695–8. Reprinted by permission of John Murray (Publishers) Ltd.

299. Vizetelly, *Glances Back*, ii. 12–13.

300. Grant Duff, *Notes*, i. 78.

301. Russell, *Collections* p. 289. Reprinted by permission of John Murray (Publishers) Ltd.

302. Allingham, *Diary*, pp. 52–3.

303. Hugh Kenner, *The Counterfeiters* (Bloomington, Ind., 1968), p. 106. Reprinted by permission of Indiana University Press.

304. Allingham, *Diary*, pp. 54–5.

305. Young, *Memoir*, p. 283.

306. Sir Charles Tennyson, *Alfred Tennyson* (1949), p. 425. Reprinted by permission of Macmillan, London and Basingstoke.

307. Allingham, *Diary*, p. 119. This anecdote is also recorded by Lady Ritchie, *Records of Tennyson, Ruskin and . . . Browning* (1896), p. 64.

308. F. Anstey, *A Long Retrospect* (1936), p. 134. Reprinted by permission of Oxford University Press, London.

309. *The Autobiography of Margot Asquith* (Penguin edn., 1936), pp. 166–8. Reprinted by permission of Eyre & Spottiswoode (Publishers) Ltd.

310. Sir Charles Tennyson, *Alfred Tennyson* (1949), pp. 327–8. Reprinted by permission of Macmillan, London and Basingstoke.

311. Ibid., p. 469.

312. Ibid., p. 515.

313. *The Swinburne Letters*, ed. Cecil Y. Lang (Yale, 1959–62), vi. 187–8.

314. T. Wemyss Reid, *The Life, Letters and Friendships of Richard Monckton Milnes, First Lord Houghton* (1890), i. 295–6.

315. Taylor, *Autobiography*, i. 330–1.

316. Derek Hudson, *Martin Tupper: His Rise and Fall* (1949), p. 274.

317. Duffy, *Conversations*, pp. 76–7.

318. Lady Ritchie, *Records*, pp. 49–50.

319. Lady Ritchie, *Chapters*, pp. 109–20. 'Amalia' was probably Melanie von Spiegel, 'a Junoesque beauty', but may have been Jenny von Pappenheim. See Gordon N. Ray, *Thackeray: The Uses of Adversity* (New York, 1955), pp. 142–3.

320. Anthony Trollope, *Thackeray* (1879), pp. 60–1.

321. Bayard Taylor, *Critical Essays and Literary Notes* (New York, 1880), pp. 149–50; quoted in Gordon N. Ray, *Thackeray: The Age of Wisdom, 1847–1863* (New York, 1958), pp. 262–3.

322. Sir William Fraser, *Hic et Ubique* (1893), p. 170.

323. John Forster, *The Life of Charles Dickens* (1872–4), ed. J. W. T. Ley (1928), pp. 90–1.

324. Arthur Waugh, *A Hundred Years of Publishing, being the Story of Chapman and Hall, Ltd.* (1930), pp. 38–9. Reprinted by permission of Chapman & Hall, Ltd.

325. Edgar Johnson, *Charles Dickens: His Tragedy and Triumph* (New York, 1952), i. 303–4. Reprinted by permission of George Weidenfeld & Nicolson, Ltd.

326. John Forster, op. cit., p. 484.

327. Frederick Locker-Lampson, *My Confidences* (1896), pp. 326–7.

328. W. P. Frith, *My Autobiography and Reminiscences* (1887), iii. 276–7.

329. Thomas Powell, *The Living Authors of England* (1849), p. 73; William Sharp, *The Life of Robert Browning* (1890), p. 110.

330. 'A Bibliography of Robert Browning from 1833 to 1881, compiled by Frederick J. Furnivall', *Browning Society Papers 1881–4*, pp. 112–13. This anecdote is said to be taken from a London correspondent's letter in a provincial newspaper.

331. Russell, *Collections*, pp. 134–5. Reprinted by permission of John Murray (Publishers) Ltd.

332. Allingham, *Diary*, pp. 101–2.

333. Russell, *Collections*, p. 254. Reprinted by permission of John Murray (Publishers) Ltd.

334. *An Autobiography by Anthony Trollope* (World's Classics edn., 1924), pp. 251–2.

335. Ibid., pp. 247–8.

336. T. H. S. Escott, *Anthony Trollope: his Work, Associates and Literary Originals* (1913), pp. 290–1.

337. George Smith, *Cornhill Magazine*, New Ser. ix (1900), 782 ff.

338. Lady Ritchie, *Chapters*, pp. 60–5.

339. Logan Pearsall Smith, *Unforgotten Years* (1938), pp. 168–70. Reprinted by permission of Constable Publishers and the Hon. Robert Gathorne-Hardy.

340. Walsh, *Handy-book*, pp. 640–1.

341. John Ruskin, *Praeterita* (1886); *The Works of John Ruskin*, ed. Sir. E. T. Cook and A. D. O. Wedderburn (1902–12), xxxv. 92–3.

342. Ford Madox Ford, *Return to Yesterday* (1931), p. 412. Reprinted by permission of David Higham and Mrs. Theodora Zavin. Ford's stories were not always reliable but at least the setting of this one is right: William Rossetti was Secretary to the Inland Revenue, which was based on Somerset House. In the Spring of 1852 Mary Anne Evans and Herbert Spencer 'would walk on the terrace of Somerset House, to which [John] Chapman had a key', and there 'they would pace backwards and forwards for hours, "discussing many things"' (Gordon S. Haight, *George Eliot: A Biography* (1968), p. 112).

343. Haight, op. cit., pp. 444–5. © 1968 Oxford University Press. Reprinted by permission of the Clarendon Press.

344. Henry James, *The Middle Years* (1917), pp. 72, 79–83. Henry James's 'assumption that the Leweses did not connect [*The Europeans*] with him and had not read it was wrong. They had' (Haight, op. cit., p. 514).

345. Russell, *Collections*, p. 172. Reprinted by permission of John Murray (Publishers) Ltd.

346. Walter Jerrold, *A Book of Famous Wits* (1912), p. 320. Reprinted by permission of Methuen & Co. Ltd.

347. Lionel Trilling, *Matthew Arnold* (9th impression, 1963), pp. 394, 395–6. Reprinted by permission of George Allen & Unwin Ltd. and Columbia U.P.

348. Lina Waterfield, *Castle in Italy. An Autobiography* (1961), pp. 11–12. Reprinted by permission of John Murray (Publishers) Ltd.

349. Hall Caine, *My Story* (1908), pp. 334–5. Reprinted by permission of the author's executors.

350. Forrest Reid, 'Minor Fiction in the Eighties', *The Eighteen-Eighties: Essays*, ed. Walter de la Mare (1930), pp. 111–12. Reprinted by permission of Cambridge University Press.

351. Hall Caine, *My Story* (1908), pp. 84–91. Reprinted by permission of the author's executors.

352. William Archer, *The Critic* (New York), 5 November 1887; reprinted in J. A. Hammerton, *Stevensoniana* (1903), p. 79.

353. Alfred Sutro, *Celebrities and Simple Souls* (1933), p. 55. Reprinted by permission of Gerald Duckworth. Sutro goes on to say that a well-known manager accepted the adaptation, 'and then suddenly, in the odd way that things happen in the theatre, everything was broken off'.

354. Richard D. Altick. *The Scholar Adventurers* (New York, 1950), pp. 237–8. Copyright, 1950, by Richard D. Altick. Reprinted by permission of Macmillan Publishing Co. Inc.

355. Charteris, *Life of Gosse*, p. 200.

356. Vizetelly, *Glances Back*, ii. 120–1. I have been unable to trace *Saturday Night*, 'the clever weekly edited by young Tom Hood', i.e. Tom Hood the Younger (1835–74), who from 1865 was editor of the comic weekly *Fun*.

357. J. W. Robertson Scott, *The Story of the Pall Mall Gazette* (1950), p. 417. Reprinted by permission of Mr. John Cripps.

358. James Payn, *Some Literary Recollections* (1884), pp. 180–1.

359. Florence Emily Hardy, *The Early Life of Thomas Hardy* (1928), p. 139 (from Hardy's diary). Reprinted by permission of the Trustees of the Hardy Estate and Macmillan, London and Basingstoke, and Canada.

360. Walter Jerrold, *A Book of Famous Wits* (1912), p. 318. Reprinted by permission of Methuen & Co. Ltd.

361. F. Anstey, *A Long Retrospect* (1938), p. 170. Reprinted by permission of Oxford University Press, London.

362. Sitwell, *Noble Essences*, p. 47. Reprinted by permission of David Higham Assoc. and William Morris Agency. Copyright © 1950, Little, Brown & Co.

363. H. Festing Jones, *Samuel Butler: A Memoir* (1920), ii. 15–16. Reprinted by permission of the Estate of Henry Festing Jones and Jonathan Cape Ltd.

364. Mary MacCarthy, *A Nineteenth-Century Childhood* (1924), pp. 88–9. Reprinted by permission of Wm. Heinemann Ltd.

365. Vizetelly, *Glances Back*, ii. 114–15.

366. H. Sutherland Evans, *Personal Recollections* (1900), pp. 185–6.

367. P. G. Wodehouse and Guy Bolton, *Bring on the Girls* (1954), p. 209. Copyright, 1953, by P. G. Wodehouse and Guy Bolton. Reprinted by permission of the authors, Barrie & Jenkins and Scott Meredith Literary Agency, Inc., New York.

368. Sitwell, *Noble Essences*, pp. 112–13. Reprinted by permission of David Higham Assoc. and William Morris Agency.

369. Charteris, *Life of Gosse*, p. 132.

370. Sir Edmund Gosse, *Portraits and Sketches* (1912), pp. 48–9. Reprinted by permission of Wm. Heinemann Ltd.

371. W. H. Mallock, *Memoirs of Life and Literature* (1920), pp. 53–5, 55–7, 58.

372. Bailey, *Letters and Diaries*, p. 175. Reprinted by permission of John Murray (Publishers) Ltd.

373. Mary MacCarthy, op. cit., pp. 85–8.

374. Oliver St. John Gogarty, *It Isn't This Time of Year at All* (1954), p. 163. Copyright, 1954, by Oliver St. John Gogarty. Reprinted by permission of MacGibbon & Kee and Doubleday & Co. Inc.

375. Ibid., p. 165.

376. Hesketh Pearson, *The Life of Oscar Wilde* (1946), pp. 30–1. Reprinted by permission of A. P. Watt & Son on behalf of Mrs. Hesketh Pearson.

377. Robert Ross, *Masques and Phases* (1909), p. 131.

378. Mrs. Belloc Lowndes, *The Merry Wives of Westminster* (1946), pp. 188–9. Reprinted by permission of Macmillan, London and Basingstoke.

379. Florence Emily Hardy, *The Early Life of Thomas Hardy* (1928), pp. 33–4.

Reprinted by permission of the Trustees of the Hardy Estate and Macmillan, London and Basingstoke, and Canada.

380. Ibid., p. 139.

381. Ibid., p. 315.

382. Alfred Sutro, *Celebrities and Simple Souls* (1933), pp. 58–9. Reprinted by permission of Gerald Duckworth.

383. James Stephens, *James, Seumas and Jacques*, ed. Lloyd Frankenberg (1964), pp. 70–1. Copyright © 1964 by Iris Clare Wise. Copyright © 1964 by Macmillan Publishing Co., Inc. Reprinted by permission of Macmillan, London and Basingstoke, Macmillan Publishing Co. Inc., and the Macmillan Company of Canada.

384. Douglas Goldring, *Odd Man Out* (1935), p. 99. Reprinted by permission of Chapman & Hall Ltd.

385. Robert Graves, *Good-bye to All That* (1929), pp. 374, 378. Reprinted by permission of A. P. Watt & Son on behalf of Mr. Robert Graves.

386. Edith Wharton, *A Backward Glance* (1934), pp. 240–3. Published in U.K. by Constable and in U.S. by Scribner's Sons. Reprinted by permission of A. Watkins, Inc.

387. H. G. Wells, *Experiment in Autobiography* (1934), ii. 535–6. Reprinted by permission of A. P. Watt & Son on behalf of the Estate of H. G. Wells.

388. Bailey, *Letters and Diaries*, p. 175 (in a letter from Gosse to Bailey, 14 April 1920). Reprinted by permission of John Murray (Publishers) Ltd.

389. G. K. Chesteron, *Autobiography* (1936), pp. 218–22. Reprinted by permission of A. P. Watt & Son on behalf of Miss D. E. Collins and Hutchinson & Co. Ltd.

390. Hugh Walpole, *The Apple Trees* (1932), p. 59.

391. Ronald Knox, *Literary Distractions* (1958), p. 59. Reprinted by permission of A. P. Watt & Son on behalf of the Estate of Ronald Knox, Sheed & Ward Ltd. and Sheed and Ward, Inc.

392. Robert Bridges, *Three Friends* (1932), p. 152. Reprinted by permission of Oxford University Press, London.

393. Ibid., pp. 225–6.

394. *The Correspondence of Thomas Gray*, ed. Paget Toynbee and Leonard Whibley (1935), i. xx–xxii. Reprinted by permission of the Clarendon Press.

395. Charteris, *Life of Gosse*, p. 132.

396. E. V. Lucas, *Reading, Writing and Remembering* (1932), p. 103. Reprinted by permission of Methuen & Co. Ltd.

397. Alfred Noyes, *Two Worlds for Memory* (1953), pp. 55–6. Reprinted by permission of Hugh Noyes, Esq.

398. Ella Hepworth Dixon, *As I knew Them* (1930), p. 55. Reprinted by permission of Hutchinson Publishing Group.

399. W. B. Yeats, *Dramatis Personae, 1896–1902* (1936), pp. 66–8. Reprinted by permission of A. P. Watt & Son on behalf of M. B. Yeats, Miss Anne Yeats, Macmillan, London and Basingstoke, and Macmillan Company of Canada and Macmillan Publishing Co. Inc. Copyright 1916, 1935 by Macmillan Publishing Co. Inc., renewed 1944, 1963 by Bertha Georgie Yeats.

400. *Irish Literary Portraits*, pp. 89–90. Reprinted by permission of Roger McHugh.

401. Ibid., pp. 78, 87–8. Reprinted by permission of Mr. Oliver D. Gogarty.

402. Sir Compton Mackenzie, *My Life and Times, Octave Four, 1907–1915* (1965), pp. 95–6. Reprinted by permission of Chatto & Windus Ltd. and the Society of Authors on behalf of the Estate of the late Sir Compton Mackenzie.

403. E. V. Lucas, *Reading, Writing, and Remembering* (1932), p. 82. Reprinted by permission of Methuen & Co.

404. I am indebted to Miss Joyce Hawkins for this anecdote, but I am unable to supply a printed source.

405. Hesketh Pearson, *The Life of Oscar Wilde* (1946), pp. 58–9. Reprinted by per-

mission of A. P. Watt & Son on behalf of Mrs Hesketh Pearson.

406. Ibid., p. 177.

407. W. B. Yeats, *Autobiographies* (1955), p. 130 ('The Trembling of the Veil'). Reprinted by permission of A. P. Watt & Son on behalf of M. B. Yeats, Miss Anne Yeats, Macmillan, London and Basingstoke, and Macmillan Company of Canada and Macmillan Publishing Co. Inc. Copyright 1916, 1935 by Macmillan Publishing Co. Inc., renewed 1944, 1963 by Bertha Georgie Yeats.

408. Ford Madox Ford, *Return to Yesterday* (1931), p. 41. Reprinted by permission of David Higham and Mrs. Theodora Zavin.

409. Sir William Rothenstein, *Men and Memories* (1931), i. 311. Reprinted by permission of the Author's executors, Sir John and Mr. Michael Rothenstein.

410. George Bernard Shaw, *Everybody's Political What's What* (1944), p. 181. Reprinted by permission of the Society of Authors on behalf of the Bernard Shaw Estate.

411. Ford Madox Ford, *Ancient Lights* (1911), pp. 127–8. Reprinted by permission of David Higham and Mrs. Theodora Zavin.

412. Hesketh Pearson, op. cit., p. 158.

413. William Archer, *The World*, 14 December 1892.

414. George Bernard Shaw, *The Star*, 21 February 1890; reprinted in *London Music in 1888–89* (*The Works*, xxxiii (1938), 299–300). Reprinted by permission of the Society of Authors on behalf of the Bernard Shaw Estate.

415. St. John Ervine, *Bernard Shaw: His Life, Work and Friends* (1956), p. 265. Reprinted by permission of Constable Publishers and the Society of Authors for the Estate of St. John Ervine

416. *The Journals of Arnold Bennett, 1911–1921* (1932), p. 252. Reprinted by permission of A. P. Watt & Son on behalf of Mrs. Dorothy Cheston Bennett.

417. *Shaw on Theatre*, ed. E. J. West (1960), p. 243. Reprinted by permission of the Society of Authors on behalf of the Bernard Shaw Estate.

418. Sir William Rothenstein, op. cit. i. 213.

419. *The Journals of Arnold Bennett, 1911–1921* (1932), p. 196. Reprinted by permission of A. P. Watt & Son on behalf of Mrs. Dorothy Cheston Bennett.

420. Bertrand Russell, *Portraits from Memory . . .* (1956), p. 100. Reprinted by permission of George Allen & Unwin Ltd.

421. G. K. Chesterton, *Autobiography* (1936), p. 283. Reprinted by permission of A. P. Watt & Son on behalf of Miss D. E. Collins and Hutchinson & Co. Ltd.

422. Sir Arthur Conan Doyle, *Memories and Adventures* (1930), pp. 112–14. Reprinted by permission of Jonathan Clowes Ltd.

423. Ibid., pp. 118–19.

424. *Mrs. J. Comyns Carr's Reminiscences*, ed. Eve Adams (1926), p. 93. Reprinted by permission of Hutchinson & Co. Ltd.

425. Sitwell, *Noble Essences*, p. 196. Reprinted by permission of David Higham and William Morris Agency.

426. Alfred Noyes, *Two Worlds for Memory* (1953), p. 244. Reprinted by permission of Hugh Noyes, Esq.

427. Sitwell, *Noble Essences*, pp. 130–1. Reprinted by permission of David Higham and William Morris Agency.

428. Guy Boas, *A Teacher's Story* (1963), pp. 3–4. Reprinted by permission of Mr Robert Boas.

429. W. B. Yeats, *Autobiographies* (1970), p. 153. Reprinted by permission of A. P. Watt & Son on behalf of M. B. Yeats, Miss Anne Yeats, Macmillan, London and Basingstoke, and Macmillan Company of Canada, and Macmillan Publishing Co. Inc. Copyright 1916, 1935 by Macmillan Publishing Co. Inc., renewed 1944, 1963 by Bertha Georgie Yeats.

430. Katharine Tynan, *Twenty-five Years: Reminiscences* (1913), p. 191. Reprinted by permission of John Murray (Publishers) Ltd.

431. Sir Max Beerbohm, 'First Meetings with W. B. Yeats', *The Listener*, 6 January 1955; reprinted in *Mainly on the Air* (1957 edn.), pp. 98–100. Reprinted by permission of William Heinemann Ltd. on behalf of the author's Estate.

432. *Irish Literary Portraits*, p. 17 (related by Bertie Smyllie). Reprinted by permission of the author.

433. Gabriel Fallon, *Sean O'Casey: The Man I Knew* (1965), p. 86. Reprinted by permission of Routledge & Kegan Paul Ltd., and Little, Brown & Co.

434. H. G. Wells, *Experiment in Autobiography* (1934), i. 326–8. Reprinted by permission of A. P. Watt & Son on behalf of the Estate of H. G. Wells.

435. Ford Madox Ford, *Return to Yesterday* (1931), pp. 6–7. Reprinted by permission of David Higham and Mrs. Theodora Zavin.

436. H. G. Wells, op. cit. ii. 534–5.

437. Sir William Rothenstein, *Since Fifty* (1939), pp. 157–8. Reprinted by permission of the author's executors Sir John and Mr. Michael Rothenstein.

438. P. G. Wodehouse and Guy Bolton, *Bring on the Girls*, pp. 207–8. Reprinted by permission of the authors, Barrie & Jenkins, and Scott Meredith Literary Agency, Inc.

439. W. D. Macray, *Annals of the Bodleian* (2nd edn., 1890), p. 384.

440. G. K. Chesterton, *Autobiography* (1936), p. 189. Reprinted by permission of A. P. Watt & Son on behalf of Miss D. E. Collins and Hutchinson & Co. Ltd. At the time of her death, on 20 January 1962, *The Times* reported that Mrs. Chesterton was 'in her nineties'. Writing in the *Tablet*, 10 February 1962, P. C. Heseltine was slightly more specific: 'Not only does nobody, now that she is gone, know her age, but there is abundant evidence that she did not know it herself. Reasonable estimates put it between ninety-two and ninety-eight.' Miss Helen M. Palmer, however, has kindly supplied me with a copy of the death certificate, in which it appears that Mrs. (Ada Elizabeth Chesterton died at the age of 93. This may possibly have been someone's guess, but I have given the date of her birth as 1869. G. K. Chesterton's anecdote about his sisters-in-law does justice to only one small side of her literary activity: she was a prolific journalist, and her book *In Darkest London* not only gave memorable expression to her social conscience, but led to the foundation of Cecil Houses (Incorporated)—Women's Public Lodging Houses and Residential Clubs.

441. Sitwell, *Noble Essences*, pp. 99–100. Reprinted by permission of David Higham and William Morris Agency.

442. Sisley Huddleston, *Paris Salons, Cafes, Studios* (Philadelphia, Pa., 1928), pp. 111–12. Reprinted by permission of George G. Harrap & Co. Ltd.

443. Sitwell, *Noble Essences*, pp. 210–11. Reprinted by permission of David Higham and William Morris Agency.

444. Frank O'Connor, *My Father's Son* (1968), p. 153. Copyright 1964, 1965, 1966, 1967, 1968, by Harriet O'Donovan. Reprinted by permission of A. D. Peters & Co., and Alfred A. Knopf, Inc.

445. Sir William Rothenstein, *Since Fifty* (1939), pp. 2–3. Reprinted by permission of Sir John and Mr. Michael Rothenstein.

446. See Modern Humanities Research Association, *Annual Bibliography of English Language and Literature* (1922). I am indebted to Professor Terence Spencer for drawing my attention to this bibliographical curiosity.

447. Ford Madox Ford, *Return to Yesterday* (1931), p. 16. Reprinted by permission of David Higham and Mrs. Theodora Zavin.

448. Douglas Goldring, *South Lodge* (1943), p. 32.

449. Bailey, *Letters and Diaries*, p. 294. Reprinted by permission of John Murray (Publishers) Ltd.

450. G. K. Chesterton, *Autobiography* (1936), pp. 275–6. Reprinted by permission of

A. P. Watt & Son on behalf of Miss D. E. Collins and Hutchinson & Co. Ltd.

451. Gertrude Atherton, *Adventures of a Novelist* (1932), pp. 381–2. Reprinted by permission of Curtis Brown Ltd. and Liveright, Inc.

452. Edgar Wallace, *People. A Short Autobiography* (1926), pp. 196–7. Reprinted by permission of A. P. Watt & Son on behalf of the Estate of Edgar Wallace.

453. Oliver St. John Gogarty, *It Isn't This Time of Year at All*, p. 151. Reprinted by permission of MacGibbon & Kee and Doubleday & Co.

454. W. B. Yeats, *The Oxford Book of Modern Verse* (1936), Introduction, p. xv. Reprinted by permission of the Clarendon Press.

455. *Irish Literary Portraits*, p. 164.

456. Alfred Noyes, *Two Worlds for Memory* (1953), pp. 182–3. Reprinted by permission of Hugh Noyes, Esq.

457. Robert Graves, *Good-bye to All That* (1929), p. 308. Reprinted by pemission of A. P. Watt & Son on behalf of Mr. Robert Graves.

458. Sir Osbert Sitwell, *Laughter in the Next Room* (1949), pp. 38–9. Reprinted by permission of David Higham and William Morris Agency Inc.

459. P. G. Wodehouse, *Performing Flea. A Self-Portrait in Letters*, ed. W. Townend (Copyright 1953), pp. 56–7. Reprinted by permission of the author, Barrie & Jenkins, and Scott Meredith Literary Agency, Inc.

460. Ibid., p. 163 n. (note by W. Townend to a letter of 30 October 1950).

461. Quentin Bell, *Virginia Woolf. A Biography*, ii (1972), 127, 129. Reprinted by permission of the Hogarth Press and Harcourt Brace Jovanovich Inc.

462. *Irish Literary Portraits*, p. 24. Reprinted by permission of Mr. Oliver D. Gogarty.

463. Percy Wyndham Lewis, *Blasting and Bombardiering* (1937; 1967 edn.), pp. 265, 267–9, 270, 270–1. Reprinted by permission of Calder & Boyars Ltd.

464. Richard Ellmann, *James Joyce* (New York, 1959), pp. 661–2. Copyright © Richard Ellmann 1959. Reprinted by permission of Oxford University Press, London and New York.

465. Ibid., p. 114.

466. Rupert Hart-Davis, *Hugh Walpole: A Biography* (1952), p. 176. Reprinted by permission of Sir Rupert Hart-Davis.

467. P. G. Wodehouse, op. cit., p. 128 (letter of 1 August 1945).

468. D. H. Lawrence, *Phoenix: The Posthumous Papers*, ed. Edward D. McDonald (1936), p. 232; reprinted in Edward Nehls, *D. H. Lawrence: A Composite Biography* (Madison, Wis., 1957), i. 137. Copyright 1936, Copyright © renewed 1964 by the Estate of the late Frieda Lawrence. Reprinted by permission of Laurence Pollinger Ltd., the Estate of the late Mrs. Frieda Lawrence and the Viking Press, Inc.

469. John Middleton Murry, *Between Two Worlds* (1935), pp. 290–3. Reprinted by permission of the Society of Authors for the Estate of John Middleton Murry.

470. Sitwell, *Noble Essences*, pp. 78–9. Reprinted by permission of David Higham and William Morris Agency.

471. Siegfried Sassoon, *Siegfried's Journey, 1916–1920* (1945), pp. 135–6. Reprinted by permission of G. T. Sassoon, Esq.

472. *T. S. Eliot: The Man and his Work* (1967), pp. 3, 4–5 (I. A. Richards, 'On T.S.E.'). Reprinted by permission of Professor I. A. Richards.

473. Ibid., p. 22 (Sir Herbert Read, 'T.S.E.—A Memoir'; reprinted from *Sewanee Review*, vol. 74 (1966)). Reprinted by permission of the editor of the *Sewanee Review*.

474. Ibid., pp. 338–9 (Robert Giroux, 'A Personal Memoir'; reprinted from *Sewanee Review*, vol. 74 (1966)). Reprinted by permission of the editor of the *Sewanee Review*

475. Richard Ellmann, *Eminent Domain* (New York, 1967), p. 89. Copyright © 1967 by Oxford University Press Inc. Reprinted by permission.

476. Roy Campbell, in *Dylan Thomas: The Legend and the Poet* (Mercury Books,

1963), pp. 41–2. Reprinted by permission of the editor of *Poetry* and Curtis Brown Ltd. on behalf of the author's Estate.

477. Ronald Knox, *Literary Distractions* (1941), p. 208. Reprinted by permission of A. P. Watt & Son on behalf of the Estate of Ronald Knox, Sheed & Ward Ltd. and Sheed & Ward Inc.

478. Sir John Neale, 'History in a Scientific Age', *Nature*, vol. ccxcix, no. 4895, 24 August 1963. Reprinted by permission of the author and the editor of *Nature*.

479. Frank O'Connor, *My Father's Son* (1968), pp. 36–8. Copyright © 1964, 1965, 1966, 1967, 1968 by Harriet O'Donovan. Reprinted by permission of A. D. Peters & Co. and Alfred A. Knopf, Inc.

480. Daniel Jones, in *Dylan Thomas: The Legend and the Poet*, ed. cit., pp. 15–16; reprinted from *Encounter* (1954). Reprinted by permission of the editor of *Encounter*.

481. Rayner Heppenstall, *Four Absentees* (1960), p. 139. Reprinted by permission of Barrie & Jenkins and David Higham Assoc. Ltd.

482. Roy Campbell, in *Dylan Thomas: The Legend and the Poet*, ed. cit., pp. 42–4. Reprinted by permission of the editor of *Poetry* and Curtis Brown Ltd. on behalf of the author's Estate.

483. Alastair Reid, in *Dylan Thomas: The Legend and the Poet*, ed. cit., p. 54; reprinted from the *Yale Literary Magazine* (1954). Reprinted by permission of *The Yale LIT*, copyright 1954.

484. Envoy.

INDEX

1. Names

References are to pages. Main entries are in heavier type.

2. Topics